Studies in Christianity and Judaism / Études sur le christianisme et le judaïsme : 7

Studies in Christianity and Judaism /
Études sur le christianisme et le judaïsme

Studies in Christianity and Judaism / Études sur le christianisme et le judaïsme publishes monographs on Christianity
and Judaism in the last two centuries before the common era
and the first six centuries of the common era, with a special
interest in studies of their interrelationship or the cultural
and social context in which they developed.

STUDIES IN CHRISTIANITY
AND JUDAISM

Number 7

WHOSE HISTORICAL JESUS?

Edited by
William E. Arnal and Michel Desjardins

Published for the Canadian Corporation for Studies in
Religion / Corporation Canadienne des Sciences Religieuses
by Wilfrid Laurier University Press

1997

Canadian Cataloguing in Publication Data

Main entry under title:

Whose historical Jesus?

(Studies in Christianity and Judaism = Études sur le
christianisme et le judaisme ESCJ ; v. 7)
Edited papers presented at the annual meetings of the
Canadian Society of Biblical Studies on June 8-9, 1993
and June 6, 1994.
Includes bibliographical references and index.
ISBN 0-88920-295-8

1. Jesus Christ – Historicity.   I. Arnal, William E.
(William Edward), 1967-   .   II. Desjardins, Michel Robert,
1951-   .   III. Canadian Corporation for Studies in
Religion.   IV. Series.

BT303.2.W46 1997   232.9′08   C97-930748-1

Cover design by Leslie Macredie

Whose Historical Jesus? has been produced from a manuscript sup-
plied in camera-ready form by the author.

Order from:

Wilfrid Laurier University Press
Wilfrid Laurier University
Waterloo, Ontario, Canada   N2L 3C5

Printed in Canada

CONTENTS

PART TWO: ENDURING CONCERNS

CONCLUSION

CONTRIBUTORS

INDICES

PREFACE
Michel Desjardins

The 1980s and 1990s have witnessed a breath-taking revival of historical-Jesus studies. Recovering the first-century Jesus matters more to Christian Origins scholars now than it has for over a century. Particularly in North America, the "Jesus Seminar" has reflected and enhanced this modern quest;[1] so too have several major studies, most notably E. P. Sanders' *Jesus and Judaism*[2] and John Dominic Crossan's *The Historical Jesus*.[3] The approach of the millenium—the year 2000, after all, elicits connections with Jesus' birth and return—ensures that this revival has not yet run its course.

Anniversaries also form the matrix of this book, which emerges from two successive years of discussions held at the annual meetings of the Canadian Society of Biblical Studies on June 8-9, 1993 and June 6, 1994. The year 1993 marked the fiftieth anniversary of the Canadian Learneds, the regular venue for members of the CSBS. It also marked, as some of us whimsically observed after our 1992 meeting, a more likely two-thousandth anniversary of Jesus' birth, a fitting occasion to address the burgeoning field of historical-Jesus studies.

This synchronicity led to plans for a special CSBS seminar on the historical Jesus at the 1993 Carleton University Learneds in Ottawa, highlighting some of the major theorists in the field, and for a second round of assessments and analyses at the University of Calgary Learneds the following year. Peter Richardson and I assumed organizational responsibility for these meetings. We were delighted to gain the participation of some of the most exciting historical-Jesus scholars from outside the country, as well as an exceptionally wide range of gifted Canadian academics. The 1993 session revolved around presentations by John Dominic Crossan (Chicago), Burton Mack (Claremont), Jane Schaberg (Detroit), Seán Freyne (Dublin) and Halvor Moxnes (Oslo)—with closing

---

1   The Jesus Seminar was established by Robert Funk in March 1985 to examine the parables and aphorisms attributed to Jesus, in order to separate what Jesus might have really said from what the early Christian communities ascribed to him. The Seminar's voting practice (scholars dropping red, pink, grey and black beads into boxes to reflect their assessment of the historical reliability of each saying) and frequent engagements with the media have given it a measure of notoriety. Some important publications to emerge from the context of this seminar include: Robert W. Funk, ed., *New Gospel Parallels*, 2 vols. (Philadelphia: Fortress, 1985); John Dominic Crossan, ed., *Sayings Parallels: A Workbook for the Jesus Tradition* (Philadelphia: Fortress, 1986); John S. Kloppenborg, *Q Parallels: Synopsis, Critical Notes, and Concordance* (Sonoma: Polebridge, 1988); Robert W. Funk, Bernard Brandon Scott and James R. Butts, *The Parables of Jesus: Red Letter Edition* (Sonoma: Polebridge, 1988); and Robert W. Funk, *The Five Gospels: The Search for the Authentic Words of Jesus* (New York: Macmillan, 1993).

2   E. P. Sanders, *Jesus and Judaism* (Philadelphia: Fortress, 1985). This book appeared when Sanders was still associated with the Department of Religious Studies at McMaster University, having recently left his position there to take up another at Oxford University.

3   John Dominic Crossan, *The Historical Jesus: The Life of a Mediterranean Jewish Peasant* (San Francisco: HarperSanFrancisco, 1991).

remarks by Paula Fredriksen (Boston).[4] Other participants (some joining a round-table discussion, some also responding formally to the papers) included Sandra Walker-Ramisch (Montréal), Willi Braun (Toronto), William Arnal (Toronto), Edith Humphrey (Montréal), Gregory Bloomquist (Ottawa), Margaret MacDonald (Ottawa), Lloyd Gaston (Vancouver), Leif Vaage (Toronto) and Stephen Wilson (Ottawa). The 1994 session highlighted papers by Wendy Cotter (Chicago), Gregory Bloomquist (Ottawa), Robert Cousland (Calgary), John Marshall (Princeton), Wayne McCready (Calgary), Grant LeMarquand (Toronto), Edith Humphrey (Montréal), Larry Hurtado (Winnipeg) and Barry Henaut (Ottawa). Responding were Daniel Fraikin (Kingston), Willi Braun (Toronto), Dietmar Neufeld (Vancouver), Terence Donaldson (Saskatoon), William Klassen (Waterloo), Stephen Westerholm (Hamilton) and Robert Webb (Regina). Both sessions attracted broad audiences (scholars in the field and in related fields, graduate students, non-academics). They were distinguished by their serious conversations and collegial tone.

This book captures the remarkable spirit of these meetings. It includes the major papers,[5] edited to reflect their new setting, fresh introductions by original respondents and section conclusions by Leif Vaage and Peter Richardson.[6] Readers will find here a representative sample of current academic perspectives on Jesus—with the occasional surprise (e.g., Schaberg, LeMarquand) and plea for change (e.g., Cotter, Bloomquist). Readers will also hear more Canadian voices on this issue than ever before collected in a single volume. The combination is as noteworthy as the revival of historical-Jesus studies in our own time; it brings to mind the 1993 program's closing words: *gaudeamus igitur.*

Bill and I are deeply thankful for the help we have received in preparing this book. Most notable have been the grants from Wilfrid Laurier University's Office of Research and from the Canadian Corporation for Studies in Religion, as well as the support of Sandra Woolfrey, Director of Wilfrid Laurier University Press. Most importantly, without Peter Richardson's initiative and expert guidance, this book would never have seen the light of day.

---

4   The presence of these individuals was made possible by generous financial support from the Social Sciences and Humanities Research Council of Canada, the Religion Department of Carleton University through its Davidson Fund, the Faculty of Theology of St. Paul University/Université St. Paul and the Craigie Fund of the Canadian Society of Biblical Studies.

5   The one exception is Robert Cousland's paper, "Jesus and the Historical Crowds" (delivered June 5, 1994), which the author chose not to submit for publication.

6   The book format has regretfully not allowed all who contributed to the success of the meetings to contribute directly to the book. Missing here (but not forgotten) are Robert Cousland (see previous note), Daniel Fraikin, Lloyd Gaston, Margaret MacDonald, Stephen Wilson and Paula Fredriksen. Another omission is John Kloppenborg (he chaired one of the 1993 sessions), whose academic pursuits—note the many references to him throughout this book—have been highly influential in recent historical-Jesus studies, but whose travel and publishing commitments removed him from direct involvement in this project.

PART ONE: RECENT CONCERNS

Research on the historical Jesus has recently exploded, becoming a publishing cottage industry and a revivified academic sub-field. This veritable blizzard of productivity has involved more than a rethinking of old problems; it has witnessed the introduction of several controversial themes into the scholarly imagination of who Jesus might have been. There has been a broad reassessment of Jesus' relationship to his environment, perhaps most obviously in the comparison of Jesus to contemporary Cynic philosophers, but also including the religiosity and everyday life of Galilean Jews, economic matters, and the persuasive strategies and normative world-views adopted by Jesus' Hellenistic contemporaries. In addition, recent decades have seen scholars of Christian origins slowly begin to take notice of the epistemic challenge of marginalized perspectives: the way in which women, the poor, blacks and colonized peoples are systematically written out of the historical record by, and because of, supposedly neutral and "scientific" historiography.

These new developments have all had an impact on the complexion of the historical-Jesus project. The following selection of papers is representative of these new developments in research. They indicate the basic issues and the evidence adduced for them, offering clues as to whether these concerns will prove to be ephemeral, or will eventually become part of the enduring fabric of the discipline.

1. The Mediterranean Jesus: Context

William Klassen

The following papers make an important contribution to the discussion about the relation of Jesus or the Jesus movement to first-century Cynicism. All three engage the issues forthrightly and contribute to the most lively segment of New Testament research at present.

John Dominic Crossan accepts Theissen's thesis as "completely correct in emphasizing the Cynic-like life-style of Jesus and those first missionaries." The paper deals then with an analysis of the categories of charisma and itinerancy. On charisma Crossan rejects Theissen's view as being psychological; it should be sociological. What marks the Jesus group is co-dependency, not independence. On itinerancy Crossan provides a fascinating treatment of how the itinerants and the householders interact; in this regard, his use of the *Didache* is both timely and pertinent to the discussion. This is especially the case since Crossan now views the *Didache* as "totally independent of synoptic influence." The keynote in the Jesus community is ethical radicalism and what matters most is not accurate recall of what Jesus taught but "how similar their lives were to what he did." The ethical is placed here against the esoteric, ascetic or gnostic—even against the apocalyptic. There is something distinctly un-Jewish about this opposition. Jewish apocalyptic was ethical to the core, and this dichotomy remains therefore Crossan's most vulnerable point.

Crossan has been and continues to be criticized for engaging as he does in the pursuit of the historical Jesus. That criticism has been levelled at the work of the Jesus Seminar, co-directed by him and Robert Funk,[1] but also includes his major study on Jesus as a "Mediterranean Jewish Peasant."[2] He invites such criticism because he is not afraid to state his conclusions. There is no doubt that the quest for the historical Jesus is essential and necessary, legitimate and important, and that Crossan has carried it further in a brilliant way.

John Marshall's primary focus is to ascertain whether the *Gospel of Thomas* can provide new material for redactional analysis of the gospel materials. Does *Thomas* support the theory of a Cynic Jesus? He concludes that "the reason Jesus is not described outright as a Cynic in the first century seems to be that he was not seen as a Cynic in the first century," so the results of his study are

---

1   Luke Timothy Johnson, "The Jesus Seminar's Misguided Quest for the Historical Jesus," *Christian Century* 113 (January, 1996): 16-22 (excerpted from his book, *The Real Jesus* [San Francisco: HarperCollins, 1995]).

2   John Dominic Crossan, *The Historical Jesus: The Life of a Mediterranean Jewish Peasant* (San Francisco: HarperSanFrancisco, 1991). For Crossan's response to Johnson, see his article, "Why Christians Must Search for the Historical Jesus," *Bible Review* 13 (April, 1996): 34-38, 42-45.

that "Cynicism has only a limited (though genuine) usefulness in understanding the historical Jesus." It may be an arguable conclusion, but it is based on a careful reading of texts, which will be an indispensable tool for further research.

Burton Mack's study of Q and the Cynic strains in the portrait of Jesus is described as part of his "stepping off the high ridge," seen in his book, *A Myth of Innocence*. His thesis is provocative and arresting. Parts of it strike me as indubitably accurate, as for example his agreement with Crossan on the communal nature of the Jesus people. Christian thinkers have slyly interred this notion or at least minimized it, but the sources leave us no alternative but to see this as the centre of the activity of Jesus. Apparently we have been seduced by the metaphor of the kingdom, which, at least in Western thought, muddies the central metaphors of peoplehood and "unity" so central to Qumran and to the early followers of Jesus. Perhaps we reject the communal nature of the Jesus people because it makes us uncomfortable; nothing is more individualistic than biblical criticism—unless perhaps the Church, which has for centuries almost totally disowned the communal nature of the kingdom of God.

Mack argues that due to a tendency to treat the narrative gospels as history we have lost sight of early Christian mythmaking. Maybe. He assures us that "the Cynic-like data from Q and Mark are as close as we shall ever get to the real Jesus of history. Punkt." He does note some deviations between the Cynics and the Jesus people. I wonder, however, whether these may not be more extensive and deserve greater emphasis. It is often more intriguing to see similarities or analogies in unexpected places, which may lead to theories of genealogy or generation of one from the other. But it may be in the differences that genius, individuality and uniqueness can be discerned. In all of this discussion I miss the sensitivity to Judaism which characterizes Mack's brilliant study of the Wisdom of Ben Sira.[3]

The first three centuries of our era can be viewed as a womb in which the Cynics were struggling to be reborn and the Christians were struggling to be born. Modern studies of the Cynics have illuminated the strength of the movement and its wide dissemination throughout the Roman Empire. Mack shows how strong the view of community is among the Jesus people. We need to bear in mind, however, that it is here that they also most strongly departed from Cynic individualism. The Cynics were not noted for their ability to build relationships or community. No one ever said of them, "Behold how they love one another." Instead of teaching that they should love their enemies, Dio cites the example of Heracles who "could look with scorn" upon others and thus find freedom. Is it by chance that the very word Dio uses as a virtue, "regard

---

3   Burton L. Mack, *Wisdom and the Hebrew Epic: Ben Sira's Hymn in Praise of the Fathers* (Chicago: University of Chicago Press, 1985).

slightly, contemptuously" (καταφρονέω), is considered a serious sin by the Jesus people (Matt 18:10)?[4]

What needs further work is the description and definition of Cynic "verve" and its relation to early Christian "boldness" (παρρησία). It was, after all, seen as a central datum, a defining virtue for Cynics,[5] and possibly for Christians as well. At least I am confident that this was a term shared by both groups. But to think of the Christian application of this term to *both* the Christian's approach to God and to one's fellow humans is immediately to note how different were the worlds in which the Cynics and Christians lived.[6]

Moreover, work needs to be done on the modern notion of social critique. We need someone to analyze what is meant by that term and whether it can even be applied to anything we have learned about Jesus and the activities of Christians.[7] There is no question that Cynics and Christians had much in common. As John Marshall reminds us, however, Jesus and the Cynics had much less in common than is often assumed. Jesus' view of love was different, his hopes were much more informed by Jewish apocalypticism, and his faith deeply-formed and driven by a view of God both personal and beyond the personal.

All three of these papers invite us to reflect upon the similarities and the differences between a motley group of people called Cynics, about whom we know much more now than we did fifty years ago, and the followers of Jesus and Jesus himself. I consider it much more likely that Christians, in trying to explain Jesus to their contemporaries, depicted Jesus in Cynic terms than that Jesus was deeply influenced by them. First and foremost, Jesus was a Jew and the evidence that Judaism was deeply influenced by Cynicism during the first century is still quite slim. Crossan, Marshall and Mack, each in their own way, make a substantial contribution to this important discussion.[8] They pursue their research and state their conclusions courageously and clearly. Only when that is done and such positions are evaluated can the discussion move forward.

---

4   Dio 66.24. See, e.g., the Loeb edition: *Dio Chrysostom*, trans. H. Lamar Crosby (Cambridge: Harvard University Press, 1964), vol. 5, 110-11.

5   Lucian, *Demonax* 50.

6   See the collection of essays on this topic in John Fitzgerald, ed., *Friendship, Flattery and Frankness of Speech: Studies in Friendship in the New Testament World* (Leiden: Brill, 1966).

7   See my review of Leif Vaage's excellent book, *Galilean Upstarts: Jesus' First Followers According to Q* (Valley Forge: Trinity Press International, 1994) in *Revue Biblique* 102 (1995): 425-28.

8   For other important discussions of this theme see Hans Dieter Betz, "Jesus and the Cynics: Survey and Analysis of a Hypothesis," *Journal of Religion* 74 (1994): 453-75; and for a critique of both Mack and Vaage, see Martin Ebner, "Kynische Jesusinterpretation—'Disciplined Exaggeration?'" *Biblische Zeitschrift* 40 (1996): 93-100.

2. Itinerants and Householders in the Earliest Jesus Movement

John Dominic Crossan

[There are] evil rumours and reports concerning shameless men, who, under pretext of the fear of God, have their dwelling with maidens, and so expose themselves to danger, and walk with them along the road and in solitary places alone. . . . Now we, if God helps us, conduct ourselves thus: with maidens we do not dwell, nor have anything in common with them; with maidens we do not eat, nor drink; and, where a maiden sleeps, we do not sleep; neither do women wash our feet, nor anoint us; and on no account do we sleep where a maiden sleeps who is unmarried or has taken the vow [of celibacy]: even though she be in some other place if she be alone, we do not pass the night there. Moreover, if it chance that the time for rest overtake us in a place, whether in the country, or in a village, or in a town, or in a hamlet, or wheresoever we happen to be, and there are found brethren in that place, we turn in to [them . . . and] they set before us bread and water and that which God provides, and we . . . stay through the night with them. . . . But the women and the maidens will wrap their hands in their garments; and we also, with circumspection and with all purity, our eyes looking upwards, shall wrap our right hand in our garments and then they will come and give us the salutation on our right hand wrapped in our garments.

Pseudo-Clement of Rome, *Two Epistles Concerning Virginity*.[1] The text is dated to the first half of the third century and contains a detailed account of where and with whom celibate itinerants should travel and stay.

1. Charismatics and Sympathizers

About twenty years ago, in a series of extremely provocative studies, Gerd Theissen discussed earliest Christianity using words translated as "itinerant radicalism," "ethical radicalism," "wandering charismatics" and "charismatic begging." He also drew attention to the similarities between those itinerant preachers and the Cynic missionaries of the first two centuries.[2] I have two

---

1 In Alexander Roberts and James Donaldson, eds., *The Ante-Nicene Fathers*, rev. by A. Cleveland Coxe (New York: Charles Scribner's Sons, 1916 [1886]), vol. 8, 55-66.

2 Basic readings for Gerd Theissen are: (1) "Wanderradikalismus: Literatursoziologische Aspekte der Überlieferung von Worten Jesu im Urchristentum," *Zeitschrift für Theologie und Kirche* 70 (1973): 245-71 [Lecture at the University of Bonn, November 25, 1972]. Translated, with abbreviated footnotes, as: "Itinerant Radicalism: The Tradition of Jesus Sayings from the Perspective of the Sociology of Literature," *Radical Religion* 2 (1975): 84-93. Retranslated in full as: "The Wandering Radicals: Light Shed by the Sociology of

major criticisms of Theissen's pioneering work, both of them made possible, however, by his own most insightful initiatives.[3] The first criticism is of lesser importance but it is also symptomatic or even symbolic of the second and much more significant one.

First, his understanding of charisma is problematic. It is used incorrectly or at least inadequately as a psychological or psycho-theological term rather than as a sociological or socio-theological one. He describes it as "grounded in a call over which he had no control."[4] A far better definition is that of Bryan Wilson:

> *Charisma* as a term expresses less a quality of person than of relationship; it contains the acceptability of a leader by a following, the endorsement of his personality, and the social endowment of power. . . . *Charisma* is a sociological, and not a psychological concept. . . . [It] expresses the balance of claim and acceptance—it is not a dynamic, causally explanatory, concept; it relates to an established state of affairs, when the leader is already accepted, not to the power of one man to cause events to move in a particular direction.[5]

Charisma, in other words, is an interactive sociological term describing how a person is seen as incarnating and symbolizing the hopes and fears, desires and plans of a group. It is not just a matter of private revelation or transcendental call; it is a matter of public acceptance of an individual as the embodiment of some group's projected future.

Literature on the Early Transmission of Jesus Sayings," in his *Social Reality and the Early Christians: Theology, Ethics, and the World of the New Testament*, trans. Margaret Kohl (Minneapolis: Fortress, 1992), 33-59. (2) "Legitimation und Lebensunterhalt: Ein Beitrag zur Soziologie urchristlicher Missionare," *New Testament Studies* 21 (1974-75): 192-221. Translated as: "Legitimation and Subsistence: An Essay on the Sociology of Early Christian Missionaries," in his *The Social Setting of Pauline Christianity: Essays on Corinth*, trans. John H. Schütz (Philadelphia: Fortress, 1982), 27-67. (3) "'Wir haben alles verlassen' (MC. X 28): Nachfolge und soziale Entwurzelung in der jüdisch-palästinischen Gesellschaft des I. Jahrhunderts n. Ch," *Novum Testamentum* 19 (1977): 161-96. Translated as: "'We Have Left Everything ...' (Mark 10:28): Discipleship and Social Uprooting in the Jewish-Palestinian Society of the First Century," in his *Social Reality and the Early Christians*, 60-93. (4) *Soziologie der Jesusbewegung: Ein Beitrag zur Entstehungsgeschichte des Urchristentums* (Munich: Kaiser, 1977). Translated as: *The First Followers of Jesus* (London: SCM, 1978) and *Sociology of Early Palestinian Christianity*, trans. John Bowden (Philadelphia: Fortress, 1978).

3   Note the trenchant criticisms of Richard A. Horsley, *Sociology and the Jesus Movement* (New York: Crossroad, 1989). See also his studies: "The Q People: Renovation, not Radicalism," *Continuum* 1/3 (1991): 49-63; and "Q and Jesus: Assumptions, Approaches, and Analyses," *Semeia* 55 (1991): 175-209. I agree with Horsley that Jesus' program was one of renovation, but it was, against his disjunction, one of *radical* renovation.

4   Theissen, *Early Palestinian Christianity*, 8.

5   Bryan Wilson, *Magic and the Millennium: A Sociological Study of Religious Movements of Protest among Tribal and Third-World Peoples* (New York: Harper & Row, 1973), 499.

That leads into my second, more significant, criticism of Theissen. In 1973 he wrote primarily of "wandering" or "itinerant" charismatics and noted almost in passing "that there would always be people who would freely provide the necessary support." In other words, they "had some sympathizers in the various towns and villages."[6] In 1975 he distinguished between "two types of primitive Christian itinerant preachers: . . . itinerant charismatics on the one hand and community organizers on the other." The former were more rural and Palestinian, the latter more urban and Diaspora-based. But, once again, those Palestinian charismatic itinerants "could depend on small groups of sympathizers."[7] Finally, in his more fully developed 1977 book, he proposed

a complementary relationship between the wandering charismatics and the local communities: wandering charismatics were the decisive spiritual authorities in the local communities and local communities were the indispensable social and material basis for the wandering charismatics. . . . It is impossible to understand the Jesus movement and the synoptic tradition exclusively in terms of the wandering charismatics. In addition to them there were "local communities", settled groups of sympathizers.[8]

In that same book he gave a first chapter to the "wandering charismatics" and a second one to "the sympathizers in the local communities." What is striking in those formulations is that both charisma and itinerancy seem almost ends in themselves so that the function of "sympathizers" is only secondary and supportive. Even their later phrasing as "sympathizers in the local communities" or "local communities, settled groups of sympathizers" is not enough to redress that inaugural imbalance. As I read Theissen I keep imagining athletes accepting applause from admiring spectators, or runners in a marathon receiving cups of water from support stations along their route.

2. Itinerants and Householders

My own understanding of that earliest Jesus movement is absolutely different and I ask your indulgence in summarizing results from *The Historical Jesus: The Life of a Mediterranean Jewish Peasant* to make that difference as clear as possible.[9] First, the historical Jesus had both a personal or individual vision and a corporate or social program for the kingdom of God there and then in Lower Galilee during that early first century CE. Second, negatively, that program

---

6   Theissen, "Wandering Radicals," 43, 48, 50.
7   Theissen, *Pauline Christianity*, 28.
8   Theissen, *Early Palestinian Christianity*, 7, 17.
9   John Dominic Crossan, *The Historical Jesus: The Life of a Mediterranean Jewish Peasant* (San Francisco: HarperSanFrancisco, 1991), 303-53; also *Jesus: A Revolutionary Biography* (San Francisco: HarperSanFrancisco,1994).

opposed the systemic injustice and structural violence (as distinct from but also including personal or individual evil) of colonial oppression by Roman imperialism. Third, positively, that program's implementation involved a network of missionaries (not just the twelve apostles, of course, since that was a much later institution connected primarily with Peter), of individuals willing to live like Jesus and empowered to announce the kingdom's presence in and by their life-style. That, and that alone, is what I mean by the term missionaries here and hereafter. It entails not just words but deeds, not just proclamation but performance. Those missionaries were not just supposed to tell people about Jesus nor to bring people to Jesus. They were to assert that the Kingdom of God was present anywhere and with anyone living, as they did, just as he did. Fourth, that mission involved an absolute reciprocity of healing and eating, not just an imbalance of charismatic begging and sympathetic almsgiving. The missionaries brought with them healing and they received not just a handout at the door but a shared meal inside the house. I emphasize the mutuality and reciprocity of this program. They not only gave healing and got eating in exchange. By healing others they continued to heal themselves; and by eating with them, those with very little to offer received some dignity from that association itself. And that, Jesus said, was the kingdom of God already present. That conclusion derives from the presence of the healing/eating dyad for the Jesus missionaries in three independent sources: Q (*Q Gospel* is more descriptive), the *Gospel of Thomas* and Mark.[10]

---

10 The three texts are:

(1) "After this the Lord appointed seventy [or: seventy-two?] others, and sent them on ahead of him in pairs to every town and place where he himself intended to go. He said to them, 'The harvest is plentiful, but the laborers are few; therefore ask the Lord of the harvest to send out laborers into his harvest. . . . Carry no purse, no bag, no sandals; and greet no one on the road. Whatever house you enter, first say, "Peace to this house!" And if anyone is there who shares in peace, your peace will rest on that person; but if not, it will return to you. Remain in the same house, eating and drinking whatever they provide, for the laborer deserves to be paid. Do not move from house to house. Whenever you enter a town and its people welcome you, eat what is set before you; cure the sick who are there and say to them, "The kingdom of God has come near to you." But whenever you enter a town and they do not welcome you, go out into its streets and say, "Even the dust of your town that clings to our feet, we wipe off in protest against you: Yet know this: the kingdom of God has come near"'" (Q in Luke 10:[1], 2-11 = Matt 9:37-38; 10:7, 10b, 12-14, 16);

(2) "When you go into any land and walk about in the districts, if they receive you, eat what they will set before you, and heal the sick among them" (*Gos. Thom.* 14:2);

(3) "He called the twelve, and began to send them out two by two, and gave them authority over the unclean spirits. He ordered them to take nothing for their journey except a staff; no bread, no bag, no money in their belts; but to wear sandals and not to put on two tunics. He said to them, 'Wherever you enter a house, stay there until you leave the place. If any place will not welcome you and they refuse to hear you, as you leave, shake off the dust that is on your feet as a testimony against them.' So they went out and proclaimed that all should repent. They cast out many demons, and anointed with oil many who were sick and cured

Fifth, Theissen is completely correct in emphasizing the Cynic-like life-style of Jesus and those first missionaries; however, just as the knapsack, in the Cynics' symbolic catechesis, proclaimed self-sufficiency, so did its programmatic absence, in the symbolic catechesis of the Jesus-missionaries, announce co-dependency with whatever followers the missionaries found. This program was a strategy for building or rebuilding peasant community on radically different principles from the accepted Mediterranean ones of honour and shame, patronage and clientage. It was based on an egalitarian sharing of spiritual power or healing, and material power or eating, at the most grassroots level. Sixth, most of those first missionaries were probably from the rural poor, and many of them may have been forced off the land so that the Jesus mission represented an alternative to beggary or banditry. Seventh, I accept the term "ethical radicalism" from Theissen as a very good description of this program. But I mean it in a very specific sense and I distinguish it from, say, ascetic or apocalyptic or esoteric or gnostic radicalism. In a systemically evil situation of injustice and oppression only the destitute are structurally innocent. Ethical radicalism is, above all else, a political statement of dissociation from a systemically unjust situation. What made the Jesus itinerants charismatic was not a psychological call but a sociological interaction in which destitution, as that which the householders most feared, was enacted and performed as the kingdom's presence by the itinerants. If Gandhi, for example, wore only hand-woven Indian cotton clothing and advised other Indians to do so against the British Raj, it was not just ascetic radicalism but ethical radicalism that drove him to do so. If a minister today started to live on the streets with the homeless, that would be ethical and not just ascetic radicalism. And, above all, if one of the homeless had the vision to assert, "Blessed are the homeless," or, in better translation, "Only the homeless are innocent," and strove to implement a program of social restoration based on that vision, we would have today something akin to the earliest Jesus-movement under discussion.

That brings me to the eighth, final and most important point. On the one hand, that mission by immediate life-style obviated any need for a theoretical schooling process before those first followers could themselves perform the kingdom just as well as Jesus. On the other, there was necessarily a paradoxical relationship between itinerants and householders. Were all supposed to become itinerants? Was that the point of the mission so that, as Theissen proposed, the householders were but sympathizers, supporters and admirers at best? Was there a tendency for the itinerants to see itinerancy as an end in itself rather than as

---

them" (Mark 6:7-13 = Matt 10:1, 8-10a, 11 = Luke 9:1-6).
Unless otherwise noted, Bible quotations are taken from the New Revised Standard Version. *Gospel of Thomas* quotations are from Thomas O. Lambdin's translation in James M. Robinson, ed., *The Nag Hammadi Library in English,* 3rd ed. (Leiden: Brill, 1988 [1977]).

a symbolic catechesis of mission? How did itinerants and householders interact in practice and not just in theory?

In his inaugural study of ethical radicalism Theissen noted that, "in the charge with which the disciples are sent out in the Synoptics and in the *Didache* too, direct statements about the early Christian itinerant charismatics have been preserved for us. In the Synoptics we are told the rules given to the first Christian missionaries. The *Didache* gives the rules for dealing with these people."[11] Within the earliest rural Jesus movement in Galilee and southern Syria, I focus, therefore, more precisely on Q to hear the voice of the itinerant missionaries and their reproaches against the householders who accepted them, and on the *Didache* to hear the response of the householders who accepted the itinerants' mission but also defended themselves against its too-radical implications.

2.1 The Itinerants Speak Out

Q refers to that other source besides Mark used by both Matthew and Luke. It is a document, but one hypothesized and then reconstructed by scholars to explain the non-Markan agreement in sequence and content between Matthew and Luke.[12] In considering Q I presume some major recent studies on its stratification. First, in a 1987 book John Kloppenborg proposed three successive layers in that document: a first sapiential layer advocating a radical counter-cultural life-style, a second apocalyptic layer threatening those who had refused to accept that former vision and a third exegetical layer moving the Q tradition back into closer continuity with Torah-observant Judaism.[13] Second, both Kloppenborg and Burton Mack have independently studied the correlation between redactional stratification and social formation across those three layers, from what is now termed Q^1 to Q^2 to Q^3.[14] Finally, both Kloppenborg, in a 1990

---

11 Theissen, "Wandering Radicals," 40-41. This is discussed in much greater detail in Stephen J. Patterson, *The Gospel of Thomas and Jesus* (Sonoma: Polebridge, 1993), 171-78.

12 Harvey K. McArthur, "The Origin of the 'Q' Symbol," *Expository Times* 88 (1977): 119-20; Frans Neirynck, "The Symbol Q (=Quelle)," *Ephemerides Theologicae Lovanienses* 54 (1978): 119-25; and "Once More: The Symbol Q," *Ephemerides Theologicae Lovanienses* 55 (1979): 372-89.

13 John S. Kloppenborg, *The Formation of Q: Trajectories in Ancient Wisdom Collections* (Philadelphia: Fortress, 1987). See also Ronald A. Piper, *Wisdom in the Q-Tradition: The Aphoristic Teaching of Jesus* (New York: Cambridge University Press, 1989). Piper focused on those smaller units within that first layer (but without using Kloppenborg's stratification; see 208-209, n. 61) and argued that several of them supported a fourfold compositional structure involving aphorism, support, illustration and application.

14 Burton L. Mack, "The Kingdom that Didn't Come: A Social History of the Q Tradents," in David J. Lull, ed., *Society of Biblical Literature 1988 Seminar Papers* (Atlanta: Scholars Press, 1988), 608-35; John S. Kloppenborg, "Literary Convention, Self-Evidence and the Social History of the Q People," *Semeia* 55 (1991): 77-102. Both papers were given at the

article, and Mack, in a 1993 book, have compellingly raised the question of successive stages of redactional stratification and social formation even within that first layer itself, within Q^1. That first layer, Q^1, which alone concerns me here, is a collection of six similarly-composed complexes of Jesus sayings. Its model is, as Kloppenborg summarized it in that 1990 article, that of "the instruction, a well-defined Near Eastern genre of didactic literature . . . characterized by admonitions with motive clauses gathered into thematically coherent clusters, often prefaced with a programmatic wisdom pronouncement and concluded aphoristically."[15] Since I have cited Mack and learned tremendously from his work, it is only fair to note that his book disagrees emphatically with my idea that Jesus had a social program rather than just a personal Cynic-like life-style. His position is that, on the one hand, "there is no indication that the purpose of this behavior was to change society at large. It is especially important to see that the purpose of the change was not a social reform"; on the other, a "movement based on such a personal challenge was nevertheless capable of generating a social vision. . . . [A]n association of like-minded persons began to form."[16] That is certainly not an impossible position, since a person's individual option could always be made by others into a founder's social movement. But I find it less likely than its alternative, namely, that Jesus himself inaugurated a social movement. And I find that indicated not by this or that saying on the level of thought and the mind but by the conjunction of free healing and common eating on the level of action and the body.

2.1.1 Both Hearing and Doing

I focus here on the first of those six mini-collections in that stratum of sapiential radicalism termed Q^1, the Inaugural Speech of Jesus in Q 6:20-23, 27-45, which precedes the Mission Speech in Q 9:57-62; 10:2-11, 16. What is most striking about that complex is how it breaks in the very middle from the radical idealism of the first half to the almost petty bickering of the second half. The first half in 6:20-23, 27-36 opens with a fourfold anti-beatitude as programmatic introduction: for destitution, hunger, sorrow, rejection. Next come two more

---

same 1988 meeting of the SBL's Q Seminar. A response to their papers was given by Richard A. Horsley, "Questions about Redactional Strata and the Social Relations Reflected in Q," in David J. Lull, ed., *Society of Biblical Literature 1989 Seminar Papers* (Atlanta: Scholars Press, 1989), 186-203. A counter-response in the same volume was given by Kloppenborg, "The Formation of Q Revisited: A Response to Richard Horsley," 204-15. See also Horsley, *Sociology and the Jesus Movement*; "Q People"; and "Q and Jesus."

15 John S. Kloppenborg, "'Easter Faith' and the Sayings Gospel Q," *Semeia* 49 (1990): 71-99 (see 85 for quote); Burton L. Mack, *The Lost Gospel: The Book of Q and Christian Origins* (San Francisco: HarperSanFrancisco, 1993), esp. 121.

16 Mack, *Lost Gospel*, 120.

fourfold clauses: the first is love, do good, bless, pray for enemies, with plural "you"; the second is cheek/other, shin/cloak, mile/another, give/unreturned, with singular "you." Finally, after some motivation clauses, this section concludes with "Be merciful, even as your Father is merciful." The second half in 6:37-49 has, I think, a very different tone. It warns against judging, against the blind leading the blind, against students thinking themselves better than their teachers and against missing the stick in your own eye while removing the splinter in another's. Then it compares trees, fruits and people: good with good, evil with evil. So far, however, specific applications are not exactly obvious. But then this half concludes with these two units:

> [1] Why do you call me "Lord, Lord," and do not do what I tell you?
> [2] I will show you what someone is like who comes to me, hears my words,
> and acts on them. That one is like a man building a house, who dug deeply,
> and laid the foundation on rock; when a flood arose, the river burst against
> that house but could not shake it, because it had been well built. But the one
> who hears and does not act is like a man who built a house on the ground
> without a foundation. When the river burst against it, immediately it fell, and
> great was the ruin of that house.

On the one hand, as Kloppenborg noted in his 1987 book, "many sapiential instructions end (or begin) with descriptions of the rewards which await those who attend to the instructions, and the consequences for those who do not."[17] On the other, none of his examples makes such a specific distinction between hearing and doing, and hearing but not doing. The usual distinction is simply between accepting or rejecting. He gives the following warning from "*Cebes' Tablet*, a well-known piece of popular philosophy":

> [1] If you pay attention and understand what is said, you will be wise and
> happy. If, on the other hand, you do not, you will become foolish, unhappy,
> sullen and stupid and you will fare badly in life. . . .
> [2] [I]f anyone does not understand these things, he is destroyed. . . . [B]ut if
> one does understand . . . he himself is saved and is blessed and happy in his
> whole life.

Does the *specific form* of that traditional conclusion to this first mini-collection in Q^1 on hearing, with or without doing, as well as the even more precise preceding one concerning invocation without obedience, cast light backwards on all those other warnings which make up the second half of the complex? Moreover, what light does that second half cast back on the first half?

The complex is revealing in terms of itinerants and householders. Most of the first half is simply an accurate description of the itinerants (including Jesus), who assert the kingdom's presence in their life-style. But what of the

---

17 Kloppenborg, *Formation of Q*, 186-87.

householders? They certainly could not accept the message in exactly the same sense as did the itinerants or else they would no longer be householders but itinerants. And the Jesus movement would be primarily, as I think it is for Theissen, a caste of itinerants, with sympathizers providing no more than support system. Could householders follow any of those admonitions at all or did they simply admire and ignore them?

We have there a divergence, first, between *invoking* and *not doing* and, second, between *hearing* and *doing or not doing*.[18] But that distinction is surely subsequent to the one between *acceptance* or *rejection*. In Q's Mission Speech of Jesus the missionaries were clearly warned to be ready for either acceptance or rejection, according to Luke 10:2-11. But, in the Inaugural Speech of Q, we have this warning against hearing and not doing as its conclusion. First comes acceptance or rejection. Next comes, within acceptance, either *acceptance with practice* or *acceptance without practice*. In Mack's terms, the stage of social formation in hearing and not doing is later than that in accepting or rejecting. We hear in that specific warning the reproach of itinerant to householder, the reproach of one who has given up everything against the one who has not given up enough. And it will require much more study to see what, between everything and nothing, *enough* might mean. How, in other words, did the radical and absolute counter-culturalism of the itinerant translate into the relative and pragmatic counter-culturalism of the householder? If the householder did not drop everything and join in itinerancy, how was *acceptable acceptance* to be calculated for such a person? Would some itinerants ever be satisfied with householders? I propose that the crucible for the earliest tradition about the words of Jesus was the necessarily paradoxical tension between itinerant and householder with the former justifying their life-style with "Jesus said" and the latter replying, in effect, "Yes, but."

2.1.2 Mimetics not Mnemonics

The important passages here are those short lists of Jesus-sayings in Q's first or radical sapiential layer and especially of those similarly constructed smaller units within them. There would have been very little point in citing them to

---

18 A similar distinction appears in Luke 11:27-28 which, lacking any Matthean parallel, is not securely from Q: "A woman in the crowd raised her voice and said to him, 'Blessed is the womb that bore you, and the breasts that nursed you!' But he said, 'Blessed rather are those who hear the word of God and keep it!'" But that same distinction is also present in *Thomas* 79: "A woman in the crowd said to him, 'Fortunate are the womb that bore you and the breasts that fed you.' He said to [her], 'Fortunate are those who have heard the word of the Father and have truly kept it.'" In both those places, it is a question of hearing and keeping the word of God. About one third of Q and the *Gospel of Thomas* is common material: Q has 37 out of 102 units in the *Gospel of Thomas* (36.2%); the *Gospel of Thomas* has 37 out of 132 units in Q (28%). It seems most likely that Luke 11:27-28 was in Q.

those first hearers, challenged either to accept or reject the missionaries. To say that one's counter-cultural life-style is based on that of Jesus only impresses those who have already somehow accepted Jesus. No, their first challenge was that the kingdom of God was here and now present in their own words and deeds, their own performances and practices, their own healings and exorcisms. Thereafter, with some minimal acceptance already obtained, it might be possible to speak of Jesus. It might be possible, for example, to cite sayings in justification both of his and their own life-styles and of what he and they were asking people to do. For "Jesus said" was clearly important to both Q and *Thomas*. The itinerants were not ready, even though they had been themselves empowered to proclaim the kingdom's presence, to speak only on their own individual authority.

My argument is not that they had memorized all or even any of Jesus' sayings. The continuity is not in mnemonics but in mimetics, not in remembrance but in imitation, not in word but in deed. They were living, dressing and preaching as physically similar to Jesus as was possible. More simply, most of them were originally as poor or destitute as he was. When they quoted him, we cannot be sure whether they had memorized an aphorism or summarized an attitude. But it is the continuity of life-style between Jesus and itinerants that gives the oral tradition its validity even if one were ready to accept every single aphorism or parable we now have as reconstructed summary or redacted expansion.

2.2 The Householders Talk Back

The *Didache*, unlike Q, is an actual document discovered in 1873 by the Greek Orthodox Metropolitan, Philotheos Bryennios, in the library of the Most Holy Sepulchre Monastery in Constantinople's Fener Quarter.[19] Stratification is certainly evident in the present text but I am, in general, reading those layers as preceding developments pre-laminated into its constitutive formulation rather than succeeding redactions post-laminated upon its basic literary composition.

---

19 It was part of a vellum codex dated to the 11th of June in 1056 and was published by its discoverer, Philotheos Bryennios, in 1883. Tiny fragments, dated to the late fourth century, have also been found among the Oxyrhynchus papyri. See Bernard Pyne Grenfell and Arthur Surridge Hunt, *The Oxyrhynchus Papyri*, part XV, nos. 1782-1828 (London: Oxford University Press, 1922), 12-15 (i.e., no. 1782, *Didache* 1-3). These tiny scraps, about 2 by 2 inches apiece, contain verses 1:3c-4a and 2:7-3:2. Quotations in this paper are taken (with the gender-exclusive language changed and the archaic "thou" and "thy" forms modernized) from the Loeb edition of *The Apostolic Fathers*, trans. Kirsopp Lake (Cambridge: Harvard University Press, 1912), vol. 1, 303-33.

Two sets of scholars with differing interests have studied this text and have arrived at, in general, quite different conclusions. One set of researchers was primarily interested in whether *Didache* sayings with parallels in the synoptic gospels were or were not dependent on them, and their studies have led to an almost total impasse. The *Didache*, with regard to the synoptic gospels, is totally independent,[20] is totally dependent,[21] is totally independent save for *Didache* 1:3b-2:1 which is a later insertion into the completed text,[22] or is in some even more complicated combination of independence and dependence.[23] Another set of scholars is primarily interested in the *Didache* itself, so that relations with the synoptic gospels arise only within that wider and more complete framework. In general, many of those scholars have concluded that the *Didache* is totally independent of synoptic tradition and should be studied in its

---

20 Richard Glover, "The Didache's Quotations and the Synoptic Gospels," *New Testament Studies* 5 (1958-59): 12-29. He concluded that "the *Didache* does not bear witness to our gospels, but quotes directly from sources used by Luke and Matthew" (12), that is to say, "from their common source" (25) in Q (29).

21 Christopher M. Tuckett, "Synoptic Tradition in the Didache," in Jean-Marie Sevrin, ed., *The New Testament in Early Christianity: La réception des écrits néotestamentaires dans le christianisme primitif* (Louvain: Louvain University Press, 1989), 197-230. He concluded that "these parallels can be best explained if the Didache presupposes the finished gospels of Matthew and Luke [and] is primarily a witness to the post-redactional history of the synoptic tradition. It is not a witness to any pre-redactional developments" (230).

22 Helmut Köster, *Synoptische Überlieferung bei den Apostolischen Vätern* (Berlin: Akademie, 1957), 159-241, 260; Bentley Layton, "The Sources, Date and Transmission of Didache 1.3b-2.1," *Harvard Theological Review* 61 (1968): 343-83.

23 Clayton N. Jefford, *The Sayings of Jesus in the Teaching of the Twelve Apostles* (Leiden: Brill, 1989). This 1988 doctoral dissertation at the Claremont Graduate School under James M. Robinson concluded that there are four main sources in the *Didache*: "1) a tradition of sayings materials that were similar in nature to those materials which were collected in the Sayings Gospel Q and in the Marcan Gospel, 2) the OT, 3) the Synoptic Gospels in some final literary form (or some harmony of those Gospels) and 4) a corpus of apocalyptic sayings, whose origin is unknown" (142). Such divergent results are not just derived from disagreements over methodology. Tuckett states the basic principle most clearly: "if material which owes it origin to the redactional activity of a synoptic evangelist reappears in another work, then the latter presupposes the finished work of that evangelist" ("Synoptic Tradition," 199). That principle works best when we have Matthew and Luke using Mark as a source. We can then determine, by comparison with Mark, what exactly is redactional in their texts. It works worst when we have Matthew and Luke using Q as a source. We know Q itself for sure only when Matthew and Luke agree exactly in their separate presentations of it; when, in other words, they fail to redact it at all. If either redacts it or even if both redact it differently, we lose any secure base text for comparison and cannot really tell what was there in Q and what was done to it by either evangelist or both. In such a situation as *Didache* 1:3-5, for example, the parallels from Q in Matthew 5:39b-42, 44b-48 and Luke 6:27-30, 32-36 are so different that it is already notoriously difficult to decide for sure the sequence and content of that Q section. It may, therefore, judging by two such careful analyses as Koester's and Tuckett's, be almost a lost cause to approach the *Didache* along that narrow focus.

own right and in its own entirety and integrity.[24] In *The Historical Jesus* I accepted Layton's argumentation that *Didache* 1:3b-2:1 was dependent on our canonical gospels, but the recent studies by Aaron Milavec in 1989 and Ian Henderson in 1992 have changed my mind. My present working hypothesis is that the *Didache* knows no canonical gospel, but what it means by "gospel" is something akin to the radical itinerant life-style itself, *possibly* as summarized in complexes akin to those mini-collections in Q's first stratum.

The *Didache* speaks with a certain serene authority but it is that of lateral consensus rather than vertical hierarchy. It bespeaks a rural situation (note the list of first-fruits in *Did.* 13), and it speaks to rural *householders* (note *Did.* 4:9-11):

> You shall not withhold discipline [literally: your hand] from your son or from your daughter, but you shall teach them the fear of God from their youth up. You shall not command in bitterness your slave or your handmaid, who hope in the same God, lest they cease to fear the God who is over you both; for he comes not to call with respect of persons, but those whom the Spirit has prepared. But do you who are slaves be subject to your masters, as to God's representative, in reverence and fear.

The *Didache*'s constitutive moment was in response to a pressing social crisis within the network of rural households for whom and to whom it spoke. Some members, called "hypocrites" in *Didache* 8, have broken away from the *Didache*'s groups because, apparently, Gentile converts were not observing Torah in both its ethical and ritual obligations as they considered they should. In response, the *Didache* proposes an initiation program for all future, but especially Gentile, converts which would both precede baptism and serve as a

---

24   (1) Jean-Paul Audet, *La Didachè: Instructions des apôtres* (Paris: Gabalda, 1958); (2) Willy Rordorf and André Tuilier, *La doctrine des douze apôtres (Didachè)* (Paris: Cerf, 1978); (3) Willy Rordorf, "Le problème de la transmission textuelle de Didachè 1,3b-2,1," in Franz Paschke, ed., *Überlieferungsgeschichtliche Untersuchungen* (Berlin: Akademie, 1981), 499-513; (4) Jonathan Draper, "The Jesus Tradition in the Didache," in David Wenham, ed., *Gospel Perspectives*; Volume 5: *The Jesus Tradition Outside the Gospels* (Sheffield: JSOT, 1985), derived from "A Commentary on the Didache in the Light of the Dead Sea Scrolls and Related Documents" (Ph.D. diss., Cambridge University, 1983), 269-87; (5) Aaron Milavec, "The Pastoral Genius of the Didache: An Analytical Translation and Commentary," in Jacob Neusner, Ernest S. Frerichs and Amy-Jill Levine, eds., *Religious Writings and Religious Systems: Systemic Analysis of Holy Books in Christianity, Islam, Buddhism, Greco-Roman Religions, Ancient Israel, and Judaism*; Volume 2: *Christianity* (Atlanta: Scholars Press, 1989), 89-125; (6) Kurt Niederwimmer, *Die Didache: Kommentar zu den Apostolischen Vätern* (Göttingen: Vandenhoeck & Ruprecht, 1989); (7) Ian H. Henderson, "Didache and Orality in Synoptic Comparison," *Journal of Biblical Literature* 111 (1992): 283-306; (8) Willy Rordorf, "Does the Didache Contain Jesus Tradition Independently of the Synoptic Gospels?" in Henry Wansbrough, ed., *Jesus and the Oral Gospel Tradition* (Sheffield: JSOT, 1992), 394-423.

weekly confession of faults before the community eucharist.[25] But how does this internal organization, this official and agreed-upon teaching, stand with regard to itinerant authority?

2.2.1 Radical Itinerants and Pragmatic Householders

The *Didache* has twin titles in its only full codex, Hierosolymitanus 54. A shorter title, with four dots in cruciform pattern before and after, is placed above the text and reads: *Teaching of the Twelve Apostles*. A longer title begins the text itself and reads: *Teaching of the Lord through the Twelve Apostles to the Nations*. Neither title, however, appears to be original—e.g., there is no mention of the Twelve within the document itself.[26] *Didache* 15:1-2 says: "Appoint therefore for yourselves bishops and deacons worthy of the Lord, meek men, and not lovers of money, and truthful and approved, for they also minister to you the ministry of the prophets and teachers. Therefore do not despise them, for they are your honourable ones together with the prophets and teachers." That formulation is redolent of transitional social formation. It bespeaks the moment when itinerant authorities (prophets and teachers) are being combined with but not yet confronted—let alone replaced—by resident ones (bishops and deacons). Finally, then, it is on those itinerant authorities that I focus here, although seen not from their own point of view, as in Q, but from that of the householders.

Itinerant authorities come, for the *Didache*, in three types: apostles, prophets and teachers. One could almost describe the *Didache* as the slow and careful ascendancy of teacher or, better, "teaching" (διδαχή), over prophet and apostle. But the transition proceeds very slowly and very carefully. Notice how these figures represent a different problem from "travellers" who, in *Didache* 12:2-5, are to be helped as much as possible but must stay at most two or three days. If they settle down, they must work, or else they become, in a bitingly accurate epithet, a "christ-peddler" or "christ-hustler" (χριστέμπορος). Never does the *Didache* use that epithet for even a false prophet.

Itinerant teachers and apostles are easily contained. Teachers, according to *Didache* 11:1-2, must conform to the moral and liturgical teaching laid down in *Didache* 1-10: "Whosoever then comes and teaches you all these things aforesaid, receive them. But if the teachers themselves be perverted and teach another doctrine to destroy these things, do not listen to them, but if their teaching be for the increase of righteousness and knowledge of the Lord, receive them as the Lord." Apostles are, by definition, prophets on their way

---

25 See Milavec, "Pastoral Genius."
26 See, for example, Rordorf and Tuilier, *La doctrine*, 13-17; and Niederwimmer, *Didache*, 81-82.

to founding new Christian households or communities elsewhere and are supported by already-established ones. They can, according to *Didache* 11:4-6, stay only one or two days and take only bread until the next night's lodging:

> Let every Apostle who comes to you be received as the Lord,
> but let them not stay more than one day, or if need be a second as well;
> but if they stay three days, they are false prophets.
> And when an Apostle goes forth
> let them accept nothing but bread till they reach their night's lodging;
> but if they ask for money, they are false prophets.

Prophets, however, are much more difficult and the text returns to focus on them repeatedly: 10:7; 11:7-12; and 13:1, 3-7. I look only at 11:7-12, a marvellously delicate and intricate dance of containment. The basic principle concerning itinerant prophets is very clear; of particular note is the passage's emphasis on behaviour (literally: "ways"), a term which should be taken not just as ethically good behaviour but as continuity with Jesus' own ethically radical behaviour. Here is the core principle, in *Didache* 11:7-8:

> Do not test or examine any prophet who is speaking in a spirit,
> "for every sin shall be forgiven, but this sin shall not be forgiven."
> But not everyone who speaks in a spirit is a prophet,
> except those who have the behaviour [plural, τρόπους: ways] of the Lord.
> From their behaviour [plural, τρόπων: ways], then,
> the false prophet and the true prophet shall be known.

Next are four examples (*Did.* 11:9-12). The first two are straightforward and give criteria by which one can judge a prophet to be false:

> And no prophet who orders a meal in a spirit shall eat of it:
> otherwise they are false prophets.
> And every prophet who teaches the truth, if they do not do what they teach,
> are false prophets.

The third one (11:11) is difficult to understand but it helps us see the difference between prophet and teacher. With a prophet we are looking primarily at performance, at life-style, at symbolic catechesis, and not just at a teaching, a word, a saying—even one backed by divine revelation.

> But no prophet who has been tried and is genuine, though they enact a worldly mystery of the Church, if they teach not others to do what they do themselves, shall be judged by you:
> for they have their judgment with God,
> for so also did the prophets of old.

What does it mean "to enact a worldly mystery of the Church"? Theissen suggests that this is "probably an allusion to women who accompanied the wandering prophets, and whose relations with them were not unequivocal. Sexual abstinence was no doubt an official requirement. However, the passage is still a μυστήριον for us too."[27] That is possible but should be articulated more carefully. The only way the earliest Jesus movement could have had women as itinerant prophets in that cultural situation was if they travelled with a male as his "wife." As long as she was with a male, nobody really cared about the relationship or would even bother to ask about it. It did not threaten patriarchal domination in any way and a woman accompanying a man could be servant or slave, sister, mistress or wife without others caring enough even to ask for definition. That is how I would also understand Paul's mention of a "sister wife" in 1 Corinthians 9:5, the "two by two" behind Mark 6:7 and Luke 10:1, and Cleopas's unnamed companion on the road to Emmaus in Luke 24:13, 18. But, of course, "the worldly mystery of the church" could also mean the entire itinerant life-style itself, including such companionship but not necessarily pointing only to it.

It is fascinating, in any case, to watch the *Didache* handle the problem: do not dare to judge them but do not learn to imitate them either. Does that parallel, by the way, the "do not judge" seen in Q 6:37? Gently, delicately, carefully, lines are being drawn between itinerant and householder, between the symbolic catechesis of the former and the settled *didachē* of the latter. The fourth example (11:12) is also relatively straightforward:

> But whosoever shall say in a spirit "Give me money, or something else," you shall not listen to them;
> but if they tell you to give on behalf of others in want,
> let none judge them.

Note again that delicacy: Do not give it for the prophet's own benefit; but, for others, do not judge. Does that mean to give or not to give? The *Didache* leaves it open and would probably answer, if directly asked: do what you can, as in 6:1 on teaching, 6:2 on food and 12:2 on hospitality.

These householders, networked together by the consensual documentation of their *Didache*, can both accept and contain the radical message of itinerant apostles, prophets or teachers, whose words and ways must agree. Their words must agree with the *Didache* and their ways must be admired rather than imitated.

---

27 Theissen, "Wandering Radicals," 41.

2.2.2 Moderating Radical Jesus Sayings

Imagine now those itinerant missionaries, like the ones still visible in Q, insisting that Jesus said this and Jesus said that as they preached to resident householders, such as those of the *Didache*. We have just seen how to contain the spiritual pyrotechnics of an itinerant prophet, of one programmatically imitating the life-style of Jesus himself, but how does one contain the sayings they quoted? How does one live *with* if one cannot totally live *by* those most radical Jesus sayings themselves?

The first six chapters of the *Didache* contain a very traditional instruction known as the Two Ways which has both pre-Christian Jewish models and other Christian parallels. It also has two fascinating elements unusual to such an instruction, absent from Jewish or Christian parallels, and therefore indicative of the redactional activity of the *Didache*'s constitutive moment.[28] They occur, respectively, at the start and at the end of the instruction. The one at the end

---

28 *Didache* 1:1-6:1 is, apart from the inserted unit of 1:3b-2:1 and the appended conclusion of 6:2, taken bodily from a Jewish teaching known as the Two Ways. Its general format is: (a) dualistic introduction; (b) lists of virtues and vices; (c) eschatological conclusion. See, for example: M. Jack Suggs, "The Christian Two Ways Tradition: Its Antiquity, Form, and Function," in David Edward Aune, ed., *Studies in New Testament and Early Christian Literature: Essays in Honor of Allen P. Wikgren* (Leiden: Brill, 1972), 60-74; Margaret Mary McKenna, "'The Two Ways' in Jewish and Christian Writings of the Greco-Roman Period: A Study of the Form of Repentance Parenesis" (Ph.D. diss., University of Pennsylvania, 1981). It is known, for example, from the Qumran *Community Rule (Manual of Discipline)*, 1QS 3:13-4:26, which begins as follows (Geza Vermes, *The Dead Sea Scrolls in English* [Baltimore: Penguin, 1968], 75-76): "[God] has created man to govern the world, and has appointed for him two spirits in which to walk until the time of His visitation: the spirits of truth and falsehood. Those born of truth spring from a fountain of light, but those born of falsehood spring from a source of darkness. All the children of righteousness are ruled by the Prince of Light and walk in the ways of light, but all the children of falsehood are ruled by the Angel of Darkness and walk in the ways of darkness." Versions of that pre-Christian Two Ways teaching pattern were taken over bodily and unchanged into Christian documents. One version with no overt Christianization concludes (as an addition?) the *Epistle of Barnabas* 18-21, which begins like this: "There are two Ways of teaching and power, one of Light and one of Darkness. And there is a great difference between the two Ways. For over the one are set light-bringing angels of God, but over the other angels of Satan. And the one is Lord from eternity to eternity, and the other is the ruler of the present time of iniquity." Another version, Christianized only by its concluding doxology, appears in a Latin translation of a now-lost Greek original called *[De] Doctrina Apostolorum*. It is instructive to compare its beginning and ending with that in the *Didache* because, although it is certainly not the direct source for that document's own Two Ways, it shows what such a source would have looked like and, even more clearly, it shows that the units in *Didache* 1:3b-2:1 and 6:2 are deliberate insertions into such a source. See Rordorf and Tuilier, *La doctrine*, 22-34, 116-118, 207-10. For the Latin text see J. B. Lightfoot, *The Apostolic Fathers* (London: Macmillan, 1895), 225; for an English translation, see Robert A. Kraft, *The Apostolic Fathers*; Volume 3: *Barnabas and the Didache* (Toronto: Thomas Nelson, 1965).

(6:1-2) is this marvellously gentle and benign conclusion: "See 'that no one makes you err' from this Way of the teaching, for such a one teaches you without God. For if you can bear the whole yoke of the Lord, you will be perfect, but if you cannot, do what you can." That former sentence (6:1) is from the Two Ways source and is typical of the either/or tenor of that pattern. The second one (6:2) breathes another world and invites us to wonder what exactly from the preceding Two Ways might be omitted with loss of perfection but not of God. Surely, "do what you can" does not apply, for example, to murder, adultery or sodomy.

That question about the redacted *ending* in 6:1-2 forces us back to review the redacted *beginning* in 1:3b-2:1. Does 6:2 refer precisely to 1:3b-2:1? That insertion has two parts. In them we hear, respectively, the voice of the itinerants and the response of the householders. The first part, in 1:3b-4, is composed of twin fourfold injunctions: (1) bless, fast for, pray for, love enemies—with plural "you"; (2) turn the other cheek, go another mile, give both garments, give your possessions—with singular "you." That is precisely the same syntactically disparate (singular/plural "you") combination seen in the first cluster of Q's radical sapiential layer in the preceding major section of this paper. And that is, I think, too much coincidence for oral memories simply recalling isolated sayings of Jesus. Somewhere within the delicate interface of orality and literacy, lists of radical Jesus sayings are being assembled from disparate units or even multiplied from a single unit. They are still very close to lists, but they are also already evincing a common theme and even a common form. If one agrees, as I now do, with recent work on the *Didache* as a holistic document totally independent of synoptic influence, then those coincidences between the twinned foursomes in 1:3b-4 and the first complex of Q's earliest stratum will require much more explanation. My present tentative hypothesis is that the itinerants started at a fairly early stage to organize short lists of Jesus sayings justifying their life-style and presented as such to their householder converts.

If we hear their voices in 1:3b-4, we hear that of the householders in 1:5-6. Those two verses immediately follow and comment on the preceding final unit of that second foursome, "If anyone will take what is yours, do not refuse it, for you cannot," as follows:

> Give to everyone that asks you, and do not refuse, for the Father's will is that
> we give to all from the gifts we have received.
> Blessed is the one who gives according to the mandate (ἐντολήν);
> for that one is innocent.
> Woe to the one who receives;
> for if anyone receive alms under pressure of need they are innocent;
> but the one who receives it without need shall be tried as to why they took
> and for what, and being in prison they shall be examined as to their deeds,
> and "that one shall not come out thence until the last farthing is paid."

But concerning this it was also said, "Let your alms sweat into your palms until you know to whom you are giving."

What is happening here? Those preceding twin foursomes are never designated as stemming from Jesus. They are, even granted their pride of place, simply part of the Two Ways teaching. Thus the syntactical inclusion of 1:3b-2:1 within *Didache* 1-6 mirrors the jurisdictional subordination of itinerant prophet (even, or especially, armed with Jesus sayings) to the resident teacher. But it is all done so very delicately, gently, firmly and even serenely. Hence the radical dispossession advocated in 1:4e ("do not refuse one who takes what is yours for you cannot do so") is contained somewhat by this absorption within the Two Ways teaching. But it is also deradicalized in a more telling fashion by the subsequent long interpretative gloss in 1:5-6.

There is no way to think that the speaker of 1:3b-4 is not the same as that of 1:5-6. Hence that interpretation is as authoritative as what it glosses. And that glossed interpretation is known also to the *Shepherd of Hermas* in *Mandate* 2:4b-7. Clearly, early Christians found people who were abusing the mandated generosity, and 1:5-6 tries for an even balance between commanding alms-giving to those who can give and warning those who take that they must be in need to do so. Jesus' injunction demanding readiness for radical dispossession, on the lips of those itinerant prophets who possessed nothing, in any case is here carefully and quietly deradicalized by householders into ready almsgiving despite the possibility, and probably past experience, of abuse. And it is, I propose, precisely to that inserted beginning that the inserted ending, "do what you can," applies. Here, say those householders, is where "perfection" lies, and here also is where your best is enough.

3. Conclusion

During his life Jesus was the centre of a network of missionaries, itinerants empowered to announce the kingdom's presence by the ethical (rather than apocalyptic, esoteric, ascetic or gnostic) radicalism of their lives, and by the reciprocity and mutuality of their interactions with householders to whom they brought healing and with whom they shared an open commensality. That interaction, with all its necessary tensions and inevitable paradoxes, was the kingdom in practice and performance, here and now. The continuity between his sayings and their remembrances was guaranteed not by how good their memories were about what he said but by how similar their lives were to what he did. Based on mimetic rather than mnemonic continuities, they recalled, multiplied and created his sayings to justify and explain his and their common life-style. The primary crucible for the tradition of Jesus sayings was the delicate interaction between itinerant and householder. Herein has also been the crux of my paper.

3. Q and a Cynic-Like Jesus

Burton L. Mack

1. Introduction

There is loose shale on the eastern slope of the Mission Mountains in Montana. A single step off the high ridge can start a slide that cannot be stopped for a thousand feet to the glacier lakes below. You need good boots and a bit of balance if you want to enjoy the ride. It is dangerous otherwise.

I think I inadvertently stepped off the high ridge when I wrote the chapter on "The Followers of Jesus" for *A Myth of Innocence.*[1] I was crossing a saddle headed for the peaks beyond where we could all see that Mark was myth, and early Christian fantasy would appear as obvious and exhilarating as a breathtaking panorama. But I knew that Christian mentality would resist viewing Mark as a mythmaker, so I needed a foil for a contrast to his story to make the point that Mark's portrait of Jesus was not a photograph, but a painting, fiction instead of historical account. To gain that leverage I mentioned the correspondence I saw between early Jesus traditions and what we imagine the Cynics were like. That was as far as most readers got and it started the slide that took me with them tumbling back to the camps below where the only question that anyone asked was about the historical Jesus. Now here I am still discussing Jesus instead of myth. It is myth that makes the world go 'round, not the lacklustre Jesus I find myself defending.

Still, I must admit that the topic has grown on me. Especially when the contributions of others begin to stack up in interesting ways. I am thinking of Ron Cameron's essay on John the Baptist and Jesus,[2] Gerald Downing's recent article on Cynics and Christians,[3] Leif Vaage's work on the Cynic flavour of the early Q traditions,[4] and a rumour I have heard about John Dominic Crossan making reference to some early Christian iconography that has Jesus dressed in Cynic garb.[5] Heady stuff, really.

---

1   Burton L. Mack, *A Myth of Innocence: Mark and Christian Origins* (Philadelphia: Fortress, 1988).
2   Ron Cameron, "'What Have You Come Out to See?': Characterizations of John and Jesus in the Gospels," in his (edited) *Semeia 49: The Apocryphal Jesus and Christian Origins* (Atlanta: Scholars Press, 1990), 35-69.
3   F. Gerald Downing, "Cynics and Christians, Oedipus and Thyestes," *Journal of Ecclesiastical History* 44 (1993): 1-10. Downing argues that charges of incest and cannibalism against early Christians were labels that intended to classify and castigate them as Cynics.
4   Leif Vaage, *Galilean Upstarts: Jesus' First Followers According to Q* (Valley Forge: Trinity Press International, 1994). See also his "The Woes in Q (and Matthew and Luke): Deciphering the Rhetoric of Criticism," in David J. Lull, ed., *Society of Biblical Literature 1988 Seminar Papers* (Atlanta: Scholars Press, 1988), 582-607.
5   See John Dominic Crossan, *The Essential Jesus: Original Sayings and Earliest Images* (San Francisco: HarperSanFrancisco, 1994), esp. 96, 180. [Eds.]

I should have known, of course, that the notion of a Cynic Jesus would not appeal to everyone. Consternation reigns in certain quarters, and the first move from the other side of the table has already been made. Cynics? What do we know about Cynics? In Galilee? In the first century? Prophets perhaps, but Cynics?[6] Cynics just do not fit the picture of Galilee and Christian origins that we have all had in mind. So caution is called for. And it is true that we will not find it any easier to trace the connection between the Jesus movement and Cynicism than the links that have occasionally been suspected for Ben Sira's wisdom, Qohelet's advice and the early *chreiai* about Hillel that Henry Fischel explored.[7] But the possibility of being more sure (as well as precise) about such connections has been increasing with recent studies on Cynicism by classicists,[8] research on the shape of Hellenistic influence in Galilee,[9] and continuing explorations of the rhetorics of Jesus[10] and Paul.[11] It is also the case that, according to recent readings, *Thomas*, Mark, Matthew, the *Didache* and Luke no longer stand in the way of a Cynic hypothesis for the historical Jesus.[12] So the topic is worth pursuing for a while and, as I hope to make clear, strikes me as serious business that calls for a major revision of the traditional picture of Christian origins.

---

6   For a forthright, critical engagement of the Cynic question, see Christopher M. Tuckett, "A Cynic Q?" *Biblica* 70 (1989): 349-76.

7   Henry A. Fischel, "Studies in Cynicism and the Ancient Near East: The Transformation of a *chria*," in J. Neusner, ed., *Religions in Antiquity: Essays in Memory of Erwin Ramsdell Goodenough* (Leiden: Brill, 1968), 372-411.

8   Bracht Branham and Marie-Odile Goulet-Cazé, "The Cynics: The Cynic Movement in Antiquity and its Legacy for Europe" (Unpublished paper from a conference in Paris, July 1992).

9   A shift in the scholarly imagination of cultural and demographic conditions in Galilee is currently underway. The shift is away from thinking of Galilee as inhabited only by conservative Jews, loyal to the Second Temple state, toward consideration of the increasing evidence for a pervasive Hellenistic environment. It now seems likely that Galilee supported a complex ethos with an ethnic and cultural mix of peoples.

10 On the rhetoric of anecdotes on the Jesus traditions see Burton L. Mack and Vernon K. Robbins, *Patterns of Persuasion in the Gospels* (Sonoma: Polebridge, 1989).

11 For examples of studies on popular philosophical discourse in Paul, including Cynic and Stoic reason and rhetoric, see Ronald F. Hock, *The Social Context of Paul's Ministry* (Philadelphia: Fortress, 1980); Abraham J. Malherbe, *Paul and the Popular Philosophers* (Minneapolis: Fortress, 1989); Stanley Stowers, "Paul on the Use and Abuse of Reason," in David L. Balch, Everett Ferguson and Wayne A. Meeks, eds., *Greeks, Romans, and Christians: Essays in Honor of Abraham J. Malherbe* (Minneapolis: Fortress, 1990), 253-86.

12 I refer to a softly-focused consensus emerging to the effect that the narrative gospels in the Jesus traditions cannot bear the weight of a kerygmatic (Pauline) interpretation of the death and resurrection of Jesus. The gap between a Cynic Jesus and the Jesus traditions is not as great as that between Jesus and the Pauline Christ.

To make the case for a Cynic style with regard to the historical Jesus, there are two bits of textual data that must bear the weight of the demonstration: the rhetoric of the *chreiai* at the core of the pronouncement stories of Jesus, and the recurrent themes guiding the social critique and behavioural recommendations in the oldest stratum of Q. Each set of texts is complicated by the fact that, to isolate them as the Cynic core of larger literary contexts, rather complex compositional histories have to be imagined. For the purposes of this paper I would like to assume those histories (as well as my discussions of them in other contexts[13]) and concentrate on the core sayings. Once the Cynic analogy has been seen, however, and the compositional histories are granted, the twists and turns of logic encountered in the elaboration of these basic sayings do count as a third argument for the hypothesis.

2. The *Chreiai*

Mark evinces more than two dozen stories about Jesus that we call pronouncement stories. Jesus is depicted in a certain situation, someone questions what he is saying or doing, and Jesus gives a sharp response. In most cases, these stories are embellished in order to describe the situation in just a certain way, explain why the questions are raised, characterize those who question or object to Jesus and perhaps give Jesus the chance for some repartee with his objectors before making the final pronouncement. Jesus always has the last word, of course, a pronouncement upon the situation from which the stories have taken their modern designation. It is frequently the case, however, that the longer story can be reduced to a single exchange of challenge and response, and this produces the *chreia* at the core. Consider the following core *chreiai* for comparison with Cynic anecdotes:[14]

> 1. When asked why he ate with tax collectors and sinners, Jesus replied, "Those who are well have no need of a physician." (Mark 2:17)
> 2. When asked why his disciples did not fast, Jesus replied, "Can wedding guests fast while the bridegroom is with them?" (Mark 2:19)

---

13 For detailed discussion of the pronouncement stories as elaborated *chreiai*, see Burton L. Mack, *Anecdotes and Arguments: The Chreia in Antiquity and Early Christianity* (Claremont: Institute for Antiquity and Christianity, 1987); "The Pronouncement Stories," Chapter 7 in *Myth of Innocence*; and Mack and Robbins, *Patterns of Persuasion*. For a more detailed discussion of the compositional history of the oldest layer in Q, see Mack, "Dancing to the Pipes," Chapter 6 in *The Lost Gospel: The Book of Q and Christian Origins* (San Francisco: HarperCollins, 1993).

14 In the following list of *chreiai*, as well as the ensuing lists of aphorisms and imperatives, Mack is deliberately paraphrasing the original text—not following a literal translation—in order to accentuate more forcefully the basic gist of the material and facilitate a comparison with the Cynic materials. He adopts the same procedure in *Lost Gospel*, esp. 110-13. [Eds.]

3. When asked why his disciples plucked grain on the sabbath, Jesus replied, "The sabbath was made for people, not people for the sabbath." (Mark 2:27)
4. When asked why they ate with unclean hands, Jesus replied, "It is not what goes into a person, but what comes out that makes unclean." (Mark 7:15)
5. When asked who was the greatest, Jesus replied, "Whoever wants to be first must be last." (Mark 9:35)
6. When someone addressed him as "Good teacher," Jesus replied, "Why do you call me good?" (Mark 10:18)
7. When asked if the rich could enter the kingdom, Jesus replied, "It is easier for a camel to go through the eye of a needle." (Mark 10:25)
8. When someone showed him a coin with Caesar's inscription and asked, "Is it lawful to pay taxes to Caesar or not?" Jesus replied, "Give to Caesar Caesar's things, and to God, God's." (Mark 12:17)
9. When a woman from the crowd raised her voice and said to him, "Blessed is the womb that bore you and the breasts that you sucked!" Jesus replied, "Blessed rather are those who listen to what God says and do what he says." (Luke 11:27-28)
10. When someone from the crowd said to him, "Teacher, tell my brother to divide the inheritance with me," Jesus replied, "Sir, who made me your judge or lawyer?" (Luke 12:13-14)

These stories are quite similar to large numbers of ancedotes told about Cynics.[15] The Greek penchant for crisp formulation and clever rejoinder was not limited to Cynics, but anecdotes of this type were much more frequent in the Socratic, Cyrenaic and Cynic traditions than in other school traditions, where ethical maxims and truisms were more the rule. A game seems to have been played with the Cynics by those courageous enough to confront them. Since they lived in a kind of negative symbiosis with society, espousing indifference to it but actually dependent upon it, almost any typical situation could be turned into a trap. The trick was to catch the Cynic in some inadvertent compromise, then point out their failure to achieve independence from society. The Cynic revelled in these encounters, taking them as opportunities to expose normal expectations as ridiculous. And the anecdote was a perfect medium for distilling the nature of such exchanges. In order to win, the Cynic had to put an altogether different construction upon things. Strategies ranged from playful put-downs, erudite observations and insights, through biting sarcasm, to devastating self-deprecation, but always with a sense of humour to ease the blow. Here are some examples:

---

15 Cynic anecdotes abound in Diogenes Laertius's *Lives of Eminent Philosophers*. For a discussion of *chreiai* types, with focus upon the Cynic *chreiai*, see Mack, "Elaboration of the Chreia in the Hellenistic School," in *Patterns of Persuasion*, 31-68.

When asked by someone whether he should marry, Bion answered, "If your wife is ugly she will be your bane, if beautiful you will not keep her to yourself." (Diogenes Laertius 4.48)[16]

When censured for keeping bad company, Antisthenes replied, "Well, physicians attend their patients without catching the fever." (Diogenes Laertius 6.6)

When someone said to Antisthenes, "Many praise you," he replied, "Why, what wrong have I done?" (Diogenes Laertius 6.8)

When someone wanted to study with him, Diogenes gave him a fish to carry and told him to follow after him. When for embarrassment the student soon threw it away and left, Diogenes laughed and said, "Our friendship was broken by a fish." (Diogenes Laertius 6.36)

"Most people," Diogenes said, "are so nearly mad that a finger makes all the difference. If you go about with your middle finger stretched out, people will think you mad, but if it is the little finger, they won't." (Diogenes Laertius 6.35)

When someone reproached him for frequenting unclean places, Diogenes replied that the sun also enters the privies without becoming defiled. (Diogenes Laertius 6.63)

When asked why he was begging from a statue, Diogenes replied, "To get practice in being refused." (Diogenes Laertius 6.49)

Crates declared that ignominy and poverty were his native land, a country that fortune could never take captive. (Diogenes Laertius 6.93)

When one of his students said to him, "Demonax, let us go to the Asclepium and pray for my son," he replied, "You must think Asclepius very deaf that he cannot hear our prayers from where we are." (Lucian, *Demonax* 27)

The Greeks measured response by its humour and cleverness, both of which involved a certain logic that allowed the Cynic to get off the hook unscathed. The French classicists Marcel Detienne and Jean-Pierre Vernant have used the term *mētis* (μῆτις), or "cunning intelligence," for the kind of crafty wisdom required.[17] Whereas *sophia* was the wisdom appropriate to conceptual systems and stable orders, *mētis* was the savvy needed for contingent and threatening situations. *Mētis* was the wisdom practised by rhetors, doctors, navigators and actors, as well as any who found themselves threatened by stronger forces or opponents. *Mētis* was the skill required to size up the situation, bend to the impinging forces, feign entrapment, then suddenly shift positions in order to escape or, if lucky, turn the tables and come out on top. In the case of net fighting, for instance, the weaker would feign vulnerability, wait for the

---

16 From the Loeb editions: *Lives of Eminent Philosophers*, 2 vols., trans. R. D. Hicks (Cambridge: Harvard University Press, 1925), and *Lucian*, vol. 1, trans. A. M. Harmon (Cambridge: Harvard University Press, 1913).

17 Marcel Detienne and Jean-Pierre Vernant, *Cunning Intelligence in Greek Culture and Society*, trans. Janet Lloyd (Atlantic Heights: Humanities, 1978).

opponent's overreach, then grab his net and swing it back upon him. The Cynic anecdote is an excellent example of *mētis* in the genre of riposte.

The logic works as follows. A circumstance puts the Cynic on the spot: how can you frequent places that are socially unacceptable (more than likely a euphemism for houses of prostitution)? The first move is to identify the issue underlying the challenge. In this case it is the notion of the socially unacceptable, commonly condensed in the cultural category of things unclean. The second move is to shift orders of discourse and find an example of "entering unclean places" in which contamination does not occur. The sun, for instance, "enters" privies without getting dirty. The clever discorrelation between the two instances of entrance into unclean places creates the humour. Explicit instruction is not the object. The interlocutor may not go away to meditate on theories of things clean or unclean. But he/she may well laugh and let the Cynic go his way, or even catch the point about the limited and arbitrary application of a general category for specific social classifications. As for the Cynic, acceptance of the terms of the challenge, a shift in the orders of application for a category and a momentary confusion in the logic of the situation, results in escape from entrapment.

The anecdotes attributed to Jesus operate by the same logic. In every case a Cynic swerve is characteristic of Jesus' rejoinder. The shifts in orders of discourse are easily identified. In number 1 (above), the issue of contamination is scuttled by shifting from meal codes to medical practice. It is similar to the anecdote about Antisthenes. In number 2 the discrepancy pertains to times when fasting was appropriate and times when it was inappropriate. Number 3 rides on the distinction between two sabbath rules, one a proscription and the other an allowance. In number 4 the incongruous is created by juxtaposing meal codes with a scatological observation. It is similar to Diogenes's response about social and natural contaminations. The put-downs in numbers 5 and 6 ride on the critique of common social values having to do with class. The ambiguity of the terms is used to advantage in statements of contrast, much the same as in the response of Antisthenes when told he was being praised by many. In number 7 there are two twists. One is to shift from the question of ability to a consideration of difficulty, thus appearing to say yes, the rich might be able to enter the kingdom. But the other is to use an example of difficulty so ridiculous as to say no, there is not a chance. In number 8 the political (legal) and the religious (natural) orders are conjoined in a conundrum. As a conundrum the answer is similar to Bion's response to the question about marriage. In 9 two notions of blessedness are set in contrast, but then confused by a shift in the orders of social relationship in view. And in 10, Jesus' anecdote is quite like a large number of Cynic anecdotes in which a student is sternly corrected for some misperception and thrown back upon their own resources for seeing things more clearly and for taking up the Cynic way.

Were we not accustomed to hearing Jesus' words as sharp ethical injunctions coming from the imperious founder of Christianity who steps forth with divine authority in the narrative gospels, the cleverness of these retorts might yet cause a smile or two. They play on the delightful confusion created by the intentional misuse of categories, and they suggest that at some early stage in the Jesus movement playful rejoinder may have been enough to justify an unconventional practice in the face of convention. Turning now to the earlier layers of Q, humour and cleverness, as well as social critique and personal challenge, become even more obvious as the characteristic tenor for the first stages of the Jesus movement.

3. The Aphorisms

I have found John Kloppenborg's work on Q persuasive. The strata he identified in the compositional history of Q as a document I have taken as a written record of the social history of the first followers of Jesus.[18] Kloppenborg was able to identify an earliest stratum of Q by close attention to observations of a redaction-critical kind. The clusters of sayings he identified at this oldest layer, moreover, shared tenor, content and other formal characteristics. I recognized these clusters as small units of rhetorical composition that the Greeks called an elaboration. At the core of each of these blocks is an aphoristic instruction, and these aphoristic maxims, as well as the way in which they were elaborated in the little units of composition, put us in touch with the rules that first governed the Jesus movement. Consider the following:

> How fortunate the poor; they have God's kingdom. (Luke 6:20)
> The standard you use [to judge another] will be the standard used against you. (Luke 6:38)
> Can the blind lead the blind? (Luke 6:39)
> A good tree does not bear rotten fruit. (Luke 6:43)
> Foxes have holes, birds nests, but human beings have no home. (Luke 9:58)
> Everyone who asks, gets. (Luke 11:10)
> Nothing is secret that will not come out. (Luke 12:2)
> Life is more than food. (Luke 12:23)
> The body is more than clothing. (Luke 12:23)
> Are you not worth more than the birds? (Luke 12:24)
> Where your treasure, there your heart. (Luke 12:34)
> Those who exalt themselves will be humbled. (Luke 14:11)
> If salt is saltless, it is good for nothing. (Luke 14:34)
> No one can serve two masters. (Luke 16:13)

---

18 I refer in general to John Kloppenborg's work on Q, a sizable and impressive bibliography, but especially to his major study, *The Formation of Q: Trajectories in Ancient Wisdom Collections* (Philadelphia: Fortress, 1987). My own study is *Lost Gospel* (note 13 above).

These sayings are not unusually clever. Many are simply versions of age-old proverbial lore, and all need some life situation in which to score their point. But they are pungent observations, slightly unnerving, and mildly humorous in the sense that insights about human behaviour and desire have been pressed to the point of extremes, if not absurdity. They illustrate the aphoristic nature of the wisdom attributed to Jesus and bristle with the pointed style of Cynic maxims. The Cynic flavour becomes even clearer if we add to these maxim-like sayings a list of injunctions that recommend a certain kind of behaviour. Consider the following:

> Rejoice when reproached. (Luke 6:22)
> Bless those who curse you. (Luke 6:28)
> If anyone strikes you on one cheek, offer the other as well. (Luke 6:29)
> Give to everyone who begs. (Luke 6:30)
> Do not judge and you will not be judged. (Luke 6:37)
> First remove the stick in your eye. (Luke 6:42)
> Leave the dead to bury their dead. (Luke 9:60)
> Go out as lambs in the midst of wolves. (Luke 10:3)
> Carry no money, bag or sandals. (Luke 10:4)
> Eat what is set before you. (Luke 10:7)
> Ask and it will be given to you. (Luke 11:9)
> Do not be afraid. (Luke 12:7)
> Do not worry about your life, what to eat, what to wear. (Luke 12:22)
> Sell your goods and give to charity. (Luke 12:33)
> Why do you not judge for yourself what is right? (Luke 12:57)
> You cannot be a student of mine if you love your parents more than me.
> (Luke 14:26)

In these sayings both the home and the public arena are regarded as places of encounter with people who live by conventional codes. The Jesus people were apparently taking up what we would call an alternative life-style. And their behaviour was causing a bit of friction. What they were doing was understood to be risky, but worth it. The advice was to be cautious, but also courageous. Take care, don't worry. Just make sure you do it. The question for us is what that was. What were they doing and why? If we analyze the themes that repeatedly occur, a program emerges that looks like this:

> a criticism of the rich and their wealth;
> a critique of hypocrisy and pretension;
> fearlessness in the presence of those in power and authority;
> a challenge to renounce the supports usually considered necessary for human life;
> a call to voluntary poverty;
> a challenge to fearless and carefree attitudes;
> etiquette for unashamed begging;

etiquette for responding to public reproach;
nonretaliation;
disentanglement from family ties;
a strong sense of independent vocation;
concern for personal integrity and authenticity;
a challenge to live naturally at any cost;
a reliance on the natural order;
singlemindedness in the pursuit of God's kingdom;
confidence in God's care.

This list of themes makes a set. The set spells out a program. And the program fits the popular profile of the Cynic in antiquity. The conclusion must be that, were this program the only feature distinguishing the Jesus people, their first-century acquaintances would have thought they were Cynics. They were taking a critical stance against normal patterns of social life. The rules by which most people lived were seen to honour privilege, support ranking and inculcate pretension. To render a critique of the status quo, the Jesus people espoused an alternative life-style. "Why not live differently?" They even developed a philosophical rationale by appealing to the way in which God cared for the natural order in contrast to conventional social arrangements. That also was a possible thought for Cynics. "Live naturally," both said; "Don't be guided by the rules that now govern the social situation. And don't worry. Protecting your own personal sense of integrity is worth it."

4. The Elaborations

The problem with the Cynic hypothesis is not that the core sayings and *chreiai* of the Jesus tradition do not fit the pattern of Cynic discourse. They do. The problem is with the way in which they have been elaborated. All of the sayings of Jesus have been elaborated, taken up into slightly larger units of argumentation, whether in the form of expanded *chreiai* (pronouncement stories), or in the form of compositions that argue for a particular point (as in the "clusters" in Q). This feature of the Jesus traditions is odd, for it makes use of conventional logic to support a rhetoric intended to subvert that logic. Cynic-style rejoinders and aphorisms do not call for elaboration. They make their point by inviting insight. It is maxims, cases, codes and rules that need to be given firm foundation. So a spin of some kind on the teachings of Jesus has to be recognized as characteristic of the direction taken by his first followers. When this slightly later material is compared with the crisp formulations of the earliest period, it is clear that a Cynic-like stance toward the social world was soon left behind. This is true of the second layer of Q where prophetic warnings abound, of the pronouncement stories which get defensive about charges brought against the Jesus people, and of the subsequent developments in Mark,

Matthew, Luke and John, where the teachings of Jesus are intended to be taken very, very seriously.

So now we need to ask, what happened and why? There are two considerations that can help us understand the shift from an earlier Cynic-style discourse to the serious and judgmental tone of the later, more familiar, material. One is that the Cynic-like behaviour of the aphoristic core was upgraded and turned into a code or standard for authentic membership in the Jesus movement. An example is the block of material in Q where the aphoristic injunction to "bless those who curse you," a thoroughly Cynic-like instruction, was turned into the precept to "love your enemies" and underscored with a complete argumentation (Luke 6:27-35). Another example is the shift that takes place in the story about eating with tax collectors and sinners, when the saying about coming to call the sinners rather than the righteous was added to the playful rejoinder about physicians treating sick people (Mark 2:15-17). Embellishments of this kind let us see that the Jesus people were taking themselves seriously as a movement or group in need of standards, codes and definition. This evidence for social formation is important, and marks the difference between the Jesus people and other Cynics. Whereas the Cynics aimed at challenging individuals to live a nonconformist life in the midst of the status quo, and let it rest at that, the Jesus people set out to challenge individuals to join them in a social experiment. They were much more interested in exploring the possibility that a nonconformist life-style might become the basis for new ways of relating to one another in a group of like-minded individuals than they were in merely developing tough individuals of the Cynic variety.

The other clue that helps explain the obvious shift from playful repartee to serious pronouncement is given in the kind of questions the Jesus people came to take seriously. Making a set of these questions, one can see that the Jesus people had become preoccupied with the differences between their association and other social systems governed by customary taboos against cross-cultural, cross-gender and cross-class association. Especially prevalent are the objections they took seriously that came from a Jewish perspective, objections that were grounded in a Pharisaic view of the piety appropriate to Jewish identity. The Jesus people of the slightly later period can be seen busily defending themselves as an acceptable group despite the fact that they did not look acceptable in the light of these and other customary standards for ethnic and national identities. The Jesus people said, in effect, that, yes, they did have tax collectors and sinners among them (including Syrians and women, outcasts and other unlikely sorts) but that that was just the point of their movement. So the Cynic-style subversion of the dominant systems of purity and/or honour-shame was not all there was to the Jesus movement. The Jesus people were looking for something to put in the place of traditional cultural codes that were no longer working in their unruly, fragmentary, multicultural world. They were searching for codes of mutual recognition. They took a Cynic stance as individuals with respect to the world at large, but with respect to one another they were experimenting with a thoroughly social notion. At first, apparently, the best they could do was to take their practice of setting conventional codes on their ear and try to turn inversion into rule. "Think of us as the clean unclean, the honoured poor, those who dance to a different tune." But eventually, of course, more constructive systems had to be crafted.

So a social vision marks the difference between the Jesus people and the Cynics. The Cynics promoted a standard for individual integrity in the midst of the *status quo*. The Jesus people promoted a vision for social experimentation as an alternative to the *status quo*. Some sense of the importance of belonging to a group, a people, must have been there from the beginning of the movement. This sensibility might be traceable to generally Semitic cultural sensibilities in Galilee except that, with Galilee looking less and less like Judaea, the particular Semitic nuances in Galilee have become very difficult to document. But some sense of belonging to a social group seems to have coloured the selection of behavioural characteristics thought to be important at the earliest layer of the sayings tradition. These sayings reveal strong interest in exploring different responses to moments of human encounter with an eye to their effect on human relationships. And a social vision was certainly involved in the early use of "kingdom of God," the only self-designation these people had. The social vision factor does not disprove the Cynic analogy to the challenge addressed to individual persons, but it does show that more was at stake in the Jesus movement than the achievement of personal virtue. The Jesus movement was attractive as a novel social notion.

5. Conclusion

Shall we take the Cynic hypothesis seriously? I see no way around it. But it does clash, not only with the customary portraits of the historical Jesus as a religious reformer (as in any of the otherwise diverse and conflicting roles suggested in recent scholarship), but also with the traditional picture of Christian origins (whether taken from Mark's gospel or Paul's report in Galatians 2). That means we have some work to do. Either we must explain the Cynic-like instructions in relation to the other, more familiar, narrative, kerygmatic and apocalyptic scenarios of Christian beginnings (something I think cannot be done), or we must explain these enhanced views of Jesus' importance as emerging from a Cynic-like Jesus movement for understandable reasons. My own preference is to note the lack of fit between the Cynic data and the gospel accounts, start with the more plausible Cynic hypothesis, and try to make sense of the kerygma and gospel as early Christian mythmaking. If we are able to do it, to explain the many views of Jesus that emerge by means of some theory of mythmaking, our redescription of Christian origins will certainly put the pressure on traditional Christian imagination and faith (beholden as it has been to the narrative gospels as history, with a little interpretive help from Pauline theology). But the reward should be great, for we might be able to say (at last) that our labours have resulted in some real understanding.

I might even try for the peaks again where memory and imagination, mythmaking and social formation put us in touch with the real attraction of the early Christian enterprise—a social experiment driven by a novel social vision. If I ever do get close to a view from the top again, you can be sure I will take some care not to jump for another slide. The Cynic-like data from Q and Mark are as close as we shall ever get to the real Jesus of history. Punkt. And what they tell us, in effect, is that the Jesus of history was not nearly as important for the emergence of Christianity as the intellectual energies generated by his followers while experimenting with a novel social vision. Mythmaking is hard work. It is not the clever insight or the dramatic moment of vision that counts. It is the elaboration.

4. The *Gospel of Thomas* and the Cynic Jesus[1]

John W. Marshall

1. Introduction

Recent years have witnessed a resurgence of historical-Jesus research.[2] Jesus—variously portrayed as healer, charismatic, magician, prophet, revolutionary or reformer—can now add Cynic to his résumé; he is a gadfly, a pesky mutt nipping at the heels of the establishment.[3] For the most part, the case for seeing Jesus as a Cynic rests on three pillars: (1) recent research on and interest in Q which posits the apocalyptic and eschatological elements as secondary; (2) re-evaluation of the social and cultural context of first-century Galilee and Palestine; and (3) comparative materials from Graeco-Roman and particularly Cynic authors. These three pillars are not unrelated. The re-

---

1   The final shape of this study is indebted to the generous input of Elaine Pagels, Michel Desjardins and Pamela Klassen. It was revised with the support of a Social Sciences and Humanities Research Council grant. Helpful criticisms from Canadian Society of Biblical Studies members Terence Donaldson, William Klassen and Dietmar Neufeld also sharpened the argument.

2   See for example Marcus J. Borg, *Conflict, Holiness and Politics in the Teachings of Jesus* (New York: Edwin Mellen, 1984), and *Jesus, a New Vision: Spirit, Culture, and the Life of Discipleship* (San Francisco: Harper & Row, 1987); John Dominic Crossan, *The Historical Jesus: The Life of a Mediterranean Jewish Peasant* (San Francisco: Harper SanFrancisco, 1991); Richard A. Horsley, *Jesus and the Spiral of Violence* (San Francisco: Harper & Row, 1987); Marinus de Jonge, *Jesus, the Servant-Messiah* (New Haven: Yale University Press, 1991); Burton L. Mack, *A Myth of Innocence: Mark and Christian Origins* (Philadelphia: Fortress, 1988), and "Q and a Cynic-Like Jesus" (in this volume); John P. Meier, *A Marginal Jew: Rethinking the Historical Jesus*, 2 vols. (New York: Doubleday, 1991-94); E. P. Sanders, *Jesus and Judaism* (Philadelphia: Fortress, 1985); Geza Vermes, *Jesus the Jew: A Historian's Reading of the Gospels* (Philadelphia: Fortress, 1973), *Jesus and the World of Judaism* (Philadelphia: Fortress, 1983), and *The Religion of Jesus the Jew* (London: SCM, 1993); N. T. Wright, *Who was Jesus?* (Grand Rapids: Eerdmans, 1993). For overviews of historical-Jesus scholarship see Marcus J. Borg, *Jesus in Contemporary Scholarship* (Valley Forge: Trinity Press International, 1994); N. T. Wright, "Jesus, Quest for the Historical," in David Noel Freedman *et al.*, eds., *The Anchor Bible Dictionary* (New York: Doubleday, 1992), vol. 3, 796-802.

3   This is a most irreverent summary of the Cynic Jesus. Mack's portrait (see *The Lost Gospel: The Book of Q and Christian Origins* [San Francisco: HarperCollins, 1993]; *Myth of Innocence*; "Q and a Cynic-Like Jesus") comes closest to it, but F. Gerald Downing (see "Cynics and Christians," *New Testament Studies* 30 [1984]: 584-93; *Jesus and the Threat of Freedom* [London: SCM, 1987]; "The Social Contexts of Jesus the Teacher," *New Testament Studies* 33 [1987]: 439-51; *Christ and the Cynics* [Sheffield: JSOT, 1988]; "Quite Like Q—A Genre for 'Q': The 'Lives' of Cynic Philosophers," *Biblica* 69 [1988]: 196-224; *Cynics and Christian Origins* [Edinburgh: T & T Clark, 1992]) and Crossan (see especially his *Historical Jesus*)—each with individual emphases—agree substantially.

evaluation of first-century Galilee allows Graeco-Roman authors to be brought into the discussion more justifiably and supports a new understanding of Galilean scribal culture, which underlies John Kloppenborg's description of the redactional history of Q.[4]

This essay brings the *Gospel of Thomas* into the discussion of this aspect of the historical Jesus. While *Thomas* has certainly not been absent from discussions of the historical Jesus and the history and character of Q, it has usually received only minimal treatment in discussions of Jesus as a Cynic—partly because it is not as immediately congenial to the case as Q, partly due to ongoing uncritical prejudice against non-canonical materials and partly because of the view of some scholars that *Thomas* is a mid-to-late second-century document.[5]

At a very basic level, it seems easy to predict the results of this study: *Thomas* does not portray a Cynic Jesus; it portrays a gnostic Jesus.[6] Nevertheless, comparison of materials shared by *Thomas* and the canonical gospels, together with consideration of the sayings unique to *Thomas*, suggest that the synoptic tradition increasingly felt the need to set Jesus in relation to the characteristic practices of Cynicism. Comparison of individual sayings within *Thomas* to their canonical parallels suggests that there are important elements of the preaching of the historical Jesus that resist characterization as Cynic. In the effort to understand Jesus as a Cynic, therefore, *Thomas* exerts a moderating influence.

2. The Case for "Jesus the Cynic"

2.1 The Place of Q in the Case for Jesus the Cynic

Among possible sources for understanding the life of Jesus as that of a Cynic, Q has occupied the premier position. Because it is earlier than Matthew or Luke, one can more easily argue that at least parts of Q go back to the historical Jesus.

---

4   John S. Kloppenborg, "The Formation of Q Revisited: A Response to Richard Horsley," in David J. Lull, ed., *Society of Biblical Literature 1989 Seminar Papers* (Atlanta: Scholars Press, 1989), 212.

5   Helmut Koester (especially in "One Jesus and Four Primitive Gospels," *Harvard Theological Review* 61 [1968]: 203-47, and "Apocryphal and Canonical Gospels," *Harvard Theological Review* 78 [1980]: 105-30) has been one of the most influential opponents of the latter two views.

6   See the arguments that *Thomas* cannot easily be categorized as "gnostic"—especially Stevan L. Davies, *The Gospel of Thomas and Christian Wisdom* (New York: Seabury, 1983); Francis T. Fallon and Ron Cameron, "The Gospel of Thomas: A Forschungsbericht and Analysis," in Hildegard Temporini and Wolfgang Haase, eds., *Aufstieg und Niedergang der römischen Welt* (Berlin: De Gruyter, 1988), part II, vol. 25.6, 4230-36.

John Kloppenborg's study of the genre and composition of Q has won a large following among those who see Q as a primary source for reconstructing a Cynic Jesus.[7] Kloppenborg's method is a redactional analysis based on clusters of sayings.[8] Regarding the composition of Q, he posits three major recensions: (1) a primary sapiential layer; (2) a redaction announcing the coming judgment against "this generation"; and (3) the temptation narrative.[9] The second part of Kloppenborg's study plots Q's generic trajectory from instructional collection (Q^1), through *chreia* collection (Q^2) to proto-*bios* (Q^3). In Matthew and Luke, Q completes its generic trajectory as a full *bios*. Here, according to Kloppenborg, Q and *Thomas* part paths in terms of genre; while Q moves toward the *bios*, the incipit of *Thomas* exerts a solidifying influence on the sayings of the collection by establishing an "authorial fiction and specifically calling for interpretation."[10]

Kloppenborg's results have not always been used by others as carefully as they were generated by him. Though it is understandable to assume that the earlier strata are more likely to be authentic, Kloppenborg is careful to note that his primary distinction is literary; he distinguishes between a formative layer of Q and its framing redactions.[11] In some cases, it is possible that a saying in Q^1 which is not an authentic Jesus saying may be framed in Q^2 by an authentic saying. To say that a saying is, from a literary perspective, part of a framing redaction is not to make a direct comment about the historical origin of that saying. With this caution in mind for individual sayings, Kloppenborg suggests that, in general, Q^2 contains an imminent catastrophic eschatology that is a

---

7   John. S. Kloppenborg, *The Formation of Q: Trajectories in Ancient Wisdom Traditions* (Philadelphia: Fortress, 1987).

8   Presuming, for the most part, Lukan order. In *Formation of Q*, 47-51, Kloppenborg surveys scholarship on the order of Q and provides cogent arguments to support this presupposition of his redactional analysis. For a more elaborate discussion of his method, see Kloppenborg, *Formation of Q*, 95-101, and "Formation Revisited," 204-206.

9   It is customary to refer to Q-passages by their Lukan versification. More fully, the three strata Kloppenborg discerns are:
     Q^1 6:20b-23b, 27-49; 9:57-62; 10:2-11, 16; 11:2-4, 9-13; 12:2-7, 11-12, 21b-31, 33-34; 13:24; 14:26, 27, 34-35; 17:33;
     Q^2 3:7-9, 16-17; 6:23c; 7:1-10, 18-23, 24-28, 31-35; 10:12-15, 21-24; 11:14-26, 29-36, 39-52; 12:8-10, 39-40, 42-46, 49, 51-53, 54-56, 57-59; 13:25-30, 34-35; 14:16-24; 17:23, 24, 26-30, 34-35, 37b; 19:12-17; 22:28-30;
     Q^3 4:1-13.
     Kloppenborg does not assign Q 13:18-21, 15:4-7, 16:23 and 17:1-6 to any of the strata (although it is quite unlikely they entered the collection as late as Q^3). For reference, I will use $Q^?$ to designate this group of sayings.

10   Kloppenborg, *Formation of Q*, 327. To comment on the generic relationship of Q and *Thomas* is not to comment on the genetic relationship of those texts. Several "lines of descent" have been proposed, mostly from Q to *Thomas*, but they have been more easily falsified than defended.

11   Kloppenborg, *Formation of Q*, *passim*; "Formation Revisited," 206.

response to a failed mission to Israel and the persecution (real or imagined) that followed in its wake.[12] This stratigraphy draws imminent eschatology away from the centre of our portrait of the historical Jesus and thus disarms one of the primary objections to seeing Jesus as a Cynic (or as highly-Hellenized, in any manner).

2.2 The Vision of Historical Context[13]

Moving in tandem with the new vision of Q which integrates it more closely with Hellenistic literary genres is an interpretation of first-century Galilee as a highly-Hellenized place rather than as a Jewish backwater. This new view is based on the archaeology of Sepphoris, recent re-evaluations of demography and a change of perspective from viewing Galilee through the Jerusalemite lenses (illustrated in John 7:52) to viewing it from within. The kernel of the argument is that Galilee was a highly-Hellenized and densely-populated region. With Sepphoris only six kilometers away from Nazareth, it is argued that Jesus would surely have come into contact with Cynic street preachers there. This possibility (or probability) of contact with Cynics is another piece of evidence in the case for a "Cynic Jesus."

2.3 Literary Evidence (Chreiai)

The favourite literary form of Cynic philosophers, especially in their public preaching, seems to have been the *chreia*. The work of Ronald Hock and Edward O'Neil has set the *chreia* firmly in its context of Hellenistic

---

12 Kloppenborg, *Formation of Q*, 167-68. Mack, *Myth of Innocence*, 318-19, makes a similar argument for Mark 13, although he also adds the destruction of Jerusalem as a significant factor. He expands this idea in his *Lost Gospel*, 204-205; throughout this book, Mack uses Kloppenborg's stratigraphy and treats what Kloppenborg designates as primary in a literary sense as also historically primary. He makes no allowance for authentic Jesus sayings employed in the framing redaction (or in any other source). Kloppenborg, too, has constructed a social history of the "Q people," although he hesitates to draw conclusions about the historical Jesus. See his "Formation Revisited," 211-15; and "Literary Convention, Self-Evidence and the Social History of the Q People," *Semeia* 55 (1991): 77-102.

13 It is easy to synthesize this view of Galilee from the various efforts to re-envision Jesus as Cynic. Mack, *Lost Gospel*, 51-68, gives a summary of the most extreme version of this view. For a contrary (more traditional) assessment of the cultural environment in Galilee during the first century, see Seán Freyne, *Galilee from Alexander the Great to Hadrian, 323 B.C.E. to 135 C.E.: A Study of Second Temple Judaism* (Wilmington: Michael Glazier, 1980); *Galilee, Jesus and the Gospels: Literary Approaches and Historical Investigations* (Philadelphia: Fortress, 1988); "Galilee (Hellenistic/Roman)," in *The Anchor Bible Dictionary*, vol. 2, 898; "Galilean Questions to Crossan's Mediterranean Jesus" (in this volume).

(progymnasmatic) education.[14] Burton Mack and Vernon Robbins have also shown the relevance of the *chreia* for interpreting the canonical gospels.[15] Although the focus of much of their work is form-critical and rhetorical-critical, Mack especially emphasizes the affinities between this literary form as it appears in the gospels and in sources about and by Cynics.[16]

2.4 Comparative Materials

Gerald Downing has done the bulk of the work on comparing Cynic materials with the canonical gospels, assembling an extensive collection of parallels.[17] Although Downing differentiates what he considers strong from weak parallels, the quality of even the strong parallels varies considerably. For instance, the parallel he offers to Q 6:27-29, 35 is striking:

> Love your enemies, do good to those who hate you, bless those who curse you, pray for those who abuse you. If someone slaps you on the cheek, offer the other also. (Q)
> A rather nice part of being a Cynic comes when you have to be beaten like an ass, and throughout the beating you have to love those who are beating you as though you were father or brother to them. (Epictetus)[18]

On the other hand, the "strong" parallel he offers for Q 4:2 is merely perplexing:

---

14 Ronald F. Hock and Edward N. O'Neil, *The Chreia in Ancient Rhetoric*; Volume 1: *The Progymnasmata* (Atlanta: Scholars Press, 1986).

15 Burton L. Mack and Vernon K. Robbins, *Patterns of Persuasion in the Gospels* (Sonoma: Polebridge, 1989); Burton L. Mack, *Anecdotes and Arguments: The Chreia in Antiquity and Early Christianity* (Claremont: Institute for Antiquity and Christianity, 1987), *Rhetoric and the New Testament* (Minneapolis: Fortress, 1990), *Myth of Innocence, Lost Gospel*, "Cynic-Like Jesus"; Vernon K. Robbins, *Jesus the Teacher: A Socio-Rhetorical Interpretation of Mark* (Philadelphia: Fortress, 1984).

16 Mack, *Anecdotes and Arguments*, 42; *Myth of Innocence*, 181-92; *Lost Gospel*, 115-18; "Cynic-Like Jesus," 33.

17 See especially F. Gerald Downing, *Christ and the Cynics: Jesus and Other Radical Preachers in First Century Tradition* (Sheffield: JSOT, 1988). Without explanation or argument, in *Jesus and the Threat of Freedom* (London: SCM, 1987), Downing excludes all non-canonical Jesus material. In *Cynics and Christian Origins* (Edinburgh: T & T Clark, 1992), 123-42, Downing occasionally treats *Thomas* in contrast to Q, but never in itself and never with the idea that *Thomas* could be of direct or positive relevance for reconstructing the historical Jesus. For comparison of gospel materials with progymnasmatic materials, see Mack and Robbins, *Patterns of Persuasion*, and Mack, *Anecdotes and Arguments*. Regarding the other dimension of the comparison, Downing's "common Cynicism" is too nebulous a concept to apply with control or discrimination to any public philosopher or preacher in the Roman Empire.

18 Downing, *Christ and the Cynics*, 24. The Cynic passage from Epictetus comes from *Discourses* 4.5.2.

... for forty days, tested by the Adversary. For those forty days he ate nothing
at all, and when they were over, he was hungry. (Q)
Once when Diogenes was bathing in the Craneion, Alexander came and stood
over him and said, "Ask any boon you like." "Stand out of my sunlight,"
snapped Diogenes. (Diogenes Laertius)[19]

Although he depends on Kloppenborg's *The Formation of Q*, Downing does not
differentiate between the various strata of Q. This may be due in part to the
shifting nature of Downing's argument. His assertions vary between claiming
that Jesus' self-presentation was Cynic-like[20] to merely observing that *some*
early Christians and *some* non-Christian preachers would have sounded alike to
some hearers.[21] Such a qualified case is as easy to make as it is difficult to
refute. Nevertheless, in spite of those parallels where Downing reaches too far,
the comparative materials make a strong case that Jesus must *also* be seen in the
context of popular Hellenistic wisdom and social criticism.

2.5 Synthesis of the Case for the Cynic Jesus

Downing has been the most active proponent of the Cynic Jesus, although in
North America Mack may be the most well known. With more subtle reasoning
and more support than a summary allows, their arguments for a Cynic Jesus
accord with the following description.

Jesus was an itinerant preacher. Galilee, the area in which he concentrated
his preaching, was a fully Hellenized region, with two major Hellenistic towns
(Sepphoris and Tiberias). Cynic preachers were a part of public culture there
and Jesus, throughout his adult life, would certainly have come into contact with
them. His preaching followed their model: he challenged the *status quo* with
incisive intellect and wit, he advocated freedom from the cares of the world,
and from material possessions. He often spoke (or was at least often recorded)
in characteristic Cynic style (using *chreiai*). His crucifixion was either
incidental[22] or in reaction to the counter-cultural force of his Cynic teaching.[23]
In any case, as Q and *Thomas* show, it was quite possible for early Jesus
traditions to develop without any interest in his death (or resurrection).

Proponents of a Cynic Jesus understand the development of Jesus literature
to support this picture. Q developed from an earliest sapiential layer to include
the proclamation of an imminent apocalyptic judgment; that is, its earliest

---

19 Downing, *Christ and the Cynics*, 15. The Cynic passage from Diogenes Laertius comes
    from *Lives of Eminent Philosophers* 6.38.
20 See, e.g., *Threat of Freedom*, x, 131; "Social Contexts of Jesus," 449.
21 "Cynics and Christians"; *Christ and the Cynics*, ix.
22 Mack, *Myth of Innocence*, 107.
23 Downing, *Threat of Freedom*, 77.

stratum is more characteristically Cynic than its later strata.[24] The model of Christian preaching in Q^1 (e.g., 10:2-12) is Cynic-like.[25] Mack's picture (*A Myth of Innocence*) of the development of the Jesus traditions in Mark concurs. He argues that Cynic-like sapiential teaching was the earliest part of the Jesus tradition, and that the apocalyptic elements of the Jesus tradition entered from a Pauline, Hellenistic "Christ-cult" (which bore little relation to the historical Jesus or the Jesus-movement), as part of the "Mark-people's" reaction to their loss in the conflict with the synagogue.

3. The Contribution of the *Thomas* Tradition

While almost everyone who has argued for a Cynic Jesus has acknowledged that *Thomas* has some relevance to the case, none has given it its due. Most are quick to use *Thomas* to validate the existence of Q by offering it as an extant example of the sayings tradition that makes no reference to the death of Jesus. Mack makes only passing references to *Thomas*, and Downing dismisses non-canonical material out of hand. Indeed, in his discussion of the genre of Q, Downing takes great pains to distance it from *Thomas* in terms of genre.[26] James Robinson, however, has made a strong case for seeing *Thomas* as essential to understanding the development of Jesus traditions.[27] Although "new" Jesus material is the most sensational element of *Thomas*, Robinson suggests that its primary value may lie in the way those materials which *Thomas* shares with the canonical gospels can provide new comparative material for redactional analysis. Such a task is the primary focus of this paper.

There are several questions at issue in the case for a Cynic Jesus which *Thomas* can address: (1) the role and character of eschatology in the preaching of Jesus; (2) the role of the kingdom (of God, of heaven, of the Father or just "the kingdom") in Jesus' preaching and its relationship to eschatological traditions; (3) affinities with Cynicism of sayings attributed to Jesus, in either style or content, and the history of the transmission and the elaboration of those sayings.

---

24 Kloppenborg's assessment of the generic trajectory of Q *(Formation of Q*, 322) contradicts this view.

25 Leif E. Vaage, *Galilean Upstarts: Jesus' First Followers According to Q* (Valley Forge: Trinity Press International, 1994), especially 17-39.

26 Downing, "Quite Like Q," 223-24. Downing's content-centred view of genre deserves severe critique. For a more historically-oriented critique of Downing's look at the genre of Q, see Christopher M. Tuckett, "A Cynic Q?" *Biblica* 70 (1989): 349-76.

27 James M. Robinson, "The Study of the Historical Jesus After Nag Hammadi," *Semeia* 44 (1988): 45-55.

3.1 Introductory Concerns

Before moving to analysis of individual logia, a number of basic concerns need to be addressed about the character and provenance of *Thomas*.[28] *Thomas* has several important differences from Q. *Thomas* is more purely a sayings source than Q in its final form (although Q^1 contains as little narrative as does *Thomas*). *Thomas* also has a longer period of independence than Q. Since Q is distilled from Matthew and Luke, its period of independent development is at most thirty years; *Thomas*'s period of development as a written source, on the other hand, may be as much as 350 years. Although POxy 1, 654, 655 confirm slightly different versions of some of the sayings (in different order) at around 200 CE, it is possible that some otherwise unattested sayings could have been added as late as the very copy that was buried at Nag Hammadi.

Although there have been recent and persuasive attempts to claim a tight structure for Q, no such attempts have been persuasive for *Thomas*.[29] An unattested saying could be added at almost any time without leaving a discernible seam in the stream of *Thomas*.[30] As yet, scholars have been unable to propose a plausible stratigraphy for *Thomas* which has gained widespread acceptance.[31] There may not be one. The model for the formation of *Thomas* may be continuous sedimentation rather than well-defined strata, although that too is undemonstrable. Accompanying this continuous accretion might be redaction of sayings already in the collection. More important than "dating" is assessing the role of individual sayings within the Jesus tradition. Helmut Koester has argued strongly that at least some of the sayings in *Thomas* precede

---

28 On dating *Thomas* (or traditions within *Thomas*) to the second half of the first century, see Helmut Koester, *Introduction to the New Testament*; Volume 2: *History and Literature of Early Christianity* (Philadelphia: Fortress, 1982), 150-54, and "Introduction," in Bentley Layton, ed., *Nag Hammadi Codex II, 2-7* (Leiden: Brill, 1989), 38-49; Fallon and Cameron, "Gospel of Thomas," 4224-30; Davies, *Gospel of Thomas*, 4; James M. Robinson, "On Bridging the Gulf from Q to the Gospel of Thomas (or Vice-Versa)," in Charles Hedrick and Robert Hodgson, Jr., eds., *Nag Hammadi, Gnosticism, and Early Christianity* (Peabody: Hendrickson, 1986), 127-75. On the genre of *Thomas*, see Robinson's "LOGOI SOPHON: On the *Gattung* of Q," in James M. Robinson and Helmut Koester, *Trajectories Through Early Christianity* (Philadelphia: Fortress, 1971), 71-113, and "On Bridging the Gulf," 164-75.

29 On Q's structure, see especially Kloppenborg, *Formation of Q*, 323. See Fallon and Cameron, "Gospel of Thomas," 4205-7, for a survey of proposals on the structure of *Thomas*.

30 E.g., Davies (*Gospel of Thomas*, 149-55) sees *Thomas* 114 as just such an addition.

31 Crossan's stratigraphic proposal (which he admits is in need of improvement) is that there is a "James" stratum that is earlier and consists of the material that is also attested in the synoptics, and a "Thomas" stratum, composed of unattested and therefore secondary material (*Historical Jesus*, 428). This proposal implies a canonical bias that belies Crossan's methodological introduction (xxvii-xxxiv) and reverses the hierarchy of stratification and attestation that is so crucial to his method (xxxi, 427-50).

their extant versions in Matthew and Luke.[32] Crossan has made a similarly persuasive case for some of the parables that *Thomas* shares with the synoptics.[33] For these reasons, I treat the logia of *Thomas* individually in understanding the relevance of *Thomas* to the picture of Jesus as a Cynic, rather than comparing *Thomas* as a whole to other sources about Cynics. I have organized the relevant sayings attributed to Jesus in *Thomas* into types.

3.2 Binary Logia

"Binary logia" discuss the future (either the cosmic future or the future of the individual) in terms of binary categories (4, 5, 6, 11, 14, 22, 41, 47, 62, 70, 89, 106). Within the group of binary logia there are several strategies for relating the binary opposites: reversal, union, correspondence and reification (of the division). The development and modification of the binary logia in *Thomas* become clear when the logia are seen in comparison with their canonical counterparts. *Thomas*'s redactional tendency to transform binary sayings into sayings about a primordial unity, in combination with the indications that *Thomas* has incorporated versions of the binary sayings that have not undergone the editorial touch of the synoptic tradition, suggests that those sayings embodying a *reversal* of binary antitheses derive from traditions prior to the redaction of *Thomas* and the canonical gospels, and as such are more likely to derive from the historical Jesus.

> LOGION 4
> [4:1]Jesus said, "The person old in days will not hesitate to ask a little child seven days old about the place of life, and that person will live. [2]For many of the first will be last, [3]and will become a single one."[34]

Logion 4:2 has parallels in Q[2] 13:30 and Mark 10:31,[35] suggesting three lines of transmission: Q, Mark and *Thomas*. In each of its five instances

---

32 Helmut Koester, *Ancient Christian Gospels: Their History and Development* (Philadelphia: Trinity Press International, 1990), 86-96; "One Jesus and Four Primitive Gospels," 225-26.

33 John Dominic Crossan, *Four Other Gospels: Shadows on the Contours of Canon* (Minneapolis: Winston, 1985), 35-62.

34 English translations (as well as the Coptic text on which they are based, and the versification within individual logia) of *Thomas* are from Marvin Meyer, "The Gospel of Thomas: Text & Translation," in John S. Kloppenborg *et al.*, *Q-Thomas Reader* (Sonoma: Polebridge, 1990), 128-58.

35 The Q parallel to *Thomas* 4:2 is part of what Kloppenborg designates as Q[2]. The *Thomas* saying has a transmission history separate from the redaction of Q which serves as a polemic against "this generation." The saying thus illustrates nicely the distinction between what is a secondary redaction *in its literary position* in Q, but not necessarily secondary with regard to the history of the tradition.

(including those in Matthew and Luke), the saying is appended as a concluding aphorism to a separate discourse. In the case of the canonical traditions, it is appended to a discourse on imminent eschatology. Matthew 20:16 takes the saying from Mark 10:31 and appends it to the climactic end of Q, which describes how those who remain faithful to the Son of Man will judge the twelve tribes of Israel in the coming kingdom. In *Thomas*, however, the saying concludes a discourse about the old person learning from an infant about "the place of life." This is part of *Thomas*'s preference for protology rather than eschatology. The first/last saying seems to be a free-floating unit which authors/compilers attach to other sayings to add emphasis and to set the message within a theological program of reversal.[36] The nature of that reversal, however, is determined by the saying to which the first/last adage is attached. Logion 4:3 changes the emphasis again from reversal to union. The mixture of teachings on reversal with others on union in logia 5 and 6 suggests that "and will become a single one" is an addition to logion 4 within the *redaction* of *Thomas* (and not prior to that redaction). Comparing *Thomas* 4 to the canonical instances of the first/last saying suggests that it was a Jesus tradition about reversal independent of the imminent apocalyptic eschatology of Mark 10 and Q^2.

LOGIA 5 & 6

[5:1]Jesus said, "Know what is before your face, and what is hidden from you will be disclosed to you. [2]For there is nothing hidden that will not be revealed."
[6:5]"For there is nothing hidden that will not be revealed, [6]and there is nothing covered that will not be disclosed."[37]

Logia 5 and 6:5-6 have parallels in Q^1 12:2 and Mark 4:22. In Q, the saying provides a rationale for the belief that their enemies, those who persecuted and killed the prophets and apostles sent by the wisdom of God, would be exposed as such. Luke (12:2, from Q) directs the force of exposure against the Pharisees, and Matthew (10:26, par. Luke) against those who chase the twelve out of the synagogues. In Mark, the setting is much different; the saying is part of the parable collection (Mark 4). There is no indication that it

---

36 So Koester, *Ancient Christian Gospels*, 148. Somewhat similar is the widely attested phrase "whoever has ears, let them hear," although the first/last phrase has more definite content.

37 The best parallel Downing (*Christ and the Cynics*, 66) can cite is: "The Cynic's only shield is his self-respect. If he doesn't use that (and that only), he'll find himself naked and disgraced in public. This is his house and his front door, the attendants at his bedroom door, and his protective night-time darkness. He ought to have nothing of his own that he wants to hide. Otherwise he's gone off, he's destroyed the Cynic that was, the public figure, the free man, he's started to be afraid about externals, he's begun to feel the need for concealment. And he couldn't keep anything concealed even if he wanted to. Where or how could he possibly hide himself?" (Epictetus, *Discourses* 3.22.14-16).

should fortify Jesus' disciples as they face specific hardships. For this reason, it seems that Matthew and Luke, following Q, position the saying in the service of their redactional concerns about the persecution of members of their movement. In *Thomas* 5, the hidden/manifest saying functions as a rationale for a command to "know what is in front of your face," whereas in *Thomas* 6 it is a rationale for obeying *Thomas*'s negative version of the golden rule. Although both *Thomas* 5 and 6 share word for word the first portion of the saying, only logion 6, in common with the synoptic tradition, uses the doubled form of the hidden/manifest contrast. The variety of imperatives for which the hidden/manifest saying provides the rationale (in *Thomas*, Q, Matthew and Luke), as well as its presence in the parable collection in Mark 4, suggest that, like the first/last saying, it circulated widely and in a variety of literary settings under Jesus' authority. It too is part of an early tradition of future reversal and is independent of the setting of persecution and animosity that characterizes its Q context.

LOGION 11

[11:1]Jesus said, "This heaven will pass away, and the one above it will pass away. [2]The dead are not alive and the living will not die. [3]During the days when you ate what is dead, you made it alive. When you are in the light, what will you do? [4]On the day when you were one, you became two, but when you are two, what will you do?"[38]

This logion is relevant not only for its eschatological sentiments (discussed in section 3.4 below), but also for its binary character. While the portion about the heavens passing away has many parallels in the canonical Jesus traditions, the portions about the live and the dead and about the two and the one have none. The second riddle is a reification of the division of dead and living. The third riddle connotes more union than division, and the fourth, oddly, discusses division rather than union. One possibility is that the fourth riddle refers to the division of a primordial union (Adam and Eve, perhaps), and looks forward to reunification. The riddles show more concern for future transformation than they do for binary categories as such. The binary sayings of this logion, unattested elsewhere and explicable in terms of the particular protological and soteriological concerns of *Thomas*,[39] are relatively unlikely to be part of the preaching of the historical Jesus.

---

38 Since the binary riddles of this logion are not paralleled in the canonical gospels, Downing (*Christ and the Cynics*) makes no effort to find Cynic parallels for them.

39 On *Thomas*'s protology, see Stevan L. Davies, "The Christology and Protology of the Gospel of Thomas," *Journal of Biblical Literature* 111 (1992): 663-82. In his view (672), the sayings of *Thomas* 11 are protological transformations of "what were originally eschatological pronouncements." On the soteriological significance of the image of consumption in *Thomas*, see logia 6, 7, 14, 27, 60, 104 and 107.

LOGION 14

[14:1]Jesus said to them, "If you fast, you will bring sin upon yourselves, [2]and
if you pray, you will be condemned, [3]and if you give alms, you will harm
your spirits. [4]When you go into any country and walk from place to place,
when the people receive you, eat whatever they serve you and heal the sick
among them. [5]For what goes into your mouth will not defile you; rather, it is
what comes out of your mouth that will defile you."[40]

Logion 14:5, on defilement, has parallels in Mark 7:15 and Matthew 15:17-
18. In those cases, the saying is set in the context of controversy with Jewish
leaders over purity protocols and the relevance of Jewish law and tradition in
general. In *Thomas*, the association with food laws is still present in the
admonition that the disciples should eat whatever is set before them, but explicit
controversy with Jewish leaders is absent. The sections of logion 14 before the
defilement saying are paralleled in the synoptic tradition, but are not associated
with the saying. The saying is not so much a reversal adage as a correspondence
adage; it asks that the inner and the outer correspond. Like binary sayings
within logia 4-6, it seems to have circulated freely as a rationale for various
ethical imperatives.

LOGION 22

[22:1]Jesus saw some babies nursing. [2]He said to his disciples, "These nursing
babies are like those who enter the kingdom." [3]They said to him, "Then shall
we enter the kingdom as babies?" [4]Jesus said to them, "When you make the
two into one, and when you make the inner like the outer and the outer like
the inner, and the upper like the lower, [5]and when you make the male and
female into a single one, so that the male will not be male nor the female be
female, [6]when you make eyes in the place of an eye and a hand in the place
of a hand, a foot in the place of a foot, an image in the place of an image, then
you will enter [the kingdom]."[41]

Among the sayings, logion 22 looks like a magpie, picking up any
contrasting pair it comes across. The first parts of the logion, concerning
children taking precedence over adults, is familiar from *Thomas* 4, Luke 18:15-
17, Matthew 19:13-15 and Mark 10:13-16. Logion 22:4-7 has no parallel in the
canonical gospels. Galatians 3:28, however, expresses a similar sentiment, as
do *Thomas* 114, the *Gospel of the Egyptians* 5, *2 Clement* 12:2-6 and the
Martyrdom of Peter 9. The concern of logion 22:4-5 seems to be the union of
binary antitheses and the appropriate placement of things—a hand in the place

---

40   See section 3.5, below, for a discussion of the implications of 14:1-4. On the internalization
     of defilement, the closest parallels Downing (*Christ and the Cynics*) cites are from Philo,
     although there are also relevant materials in Epictetus and Diogenes Laertius.

41   Downing (*Christ and the Cynics*) cites no parallels.

of a hand, etc. (22:6). Over the course of the whole logion, the movement is from reversal to union, and then to correspondence. Judging from the way desultory sets of pairs get tacked on to the end of this logion, the first parts of the saying (22:1-2) are probably the oldest element of the tradition, with the movement to union and correspondence being a secondary elaboration (although perhaps before the redaction of *Thomas*).

LOGION 41

[41:1]Jesus said, "Whoever has something in hand will be given more, [2]and whoever has nothing will be deprived of even the little that person has."[42]

This simple logion has close parallels in Q^2 19:26 and Mark 4:24 (and parallels). In Q, it concludes the long parable of the entrusted money. In Mark 4, it is one of the short sayings (4:21-25) in the midst of the parable collection. Luke reproduces this small sayings group in 8:16-18, even though it duplicates sayings that Q sets in different contexts. Matthew 13:12 uses the Markan version as part of the interpretation of the parable of the sower. Like the hidden/manifest saying, this *Wanderlogion* seems to have been a free-floating unit used to provide an argumentative rationale in different contexts. Unlike the hidden/manifest saying, however, it speaks not of reversal, but of a reification of the division.

LOGION 47

[47:1]Jesus said, "A person cannot mount two horses or bend two bows. [2]And a servant cannot serve two masters, or that servant will honor the one and offend the other. [3]No person drinks aged wine and immediately desires to drink new wine. [4]New wine is not poured into aged wineskins, lest they break, and aged wine is not poured into a new wineskin, lest it spoil. [5]An old patch is not sewn onto a new garment, for there would be a tear."[43]

Logion 47 is a collection of binary sayings that has no parallel as a group. Some of the constituent sayings, however, have parallels in the canonical gospels. Logion 47:2 finds a parallel in Q 16:13. Logion 47:4-5 is paralleled by Mark 2:21-2 (and parallels). Within Q, the Two Masters saying is not strongly bound to its immediate context. In Matthew (6:24), it is set within a series of aphorisms in the Sermon on the Mount. In Luke (16:13), it is the pithy conclusion to the parable of the dishonest steward. Here, contrary to Kloppenborg's assessment that Luke reflects the original order of Q, Matthew's

---

42 Downing (*Christ and the Cynics*) cites no parallels.

43 For 47:2, Downing (*Christ and the Cynics*, 81) offers the following parallel: "Every slavery is hard to bear. But think of someone who happens to be a slave in a household with two or three masters, and imagine that they differ in age and character, say, a stingy old man and his young sons intent on drink and extravagance" (Dio 66.13).

order probably should be preferred because Luke's placement of the saying is editorially explicable. In Mark and Matthew the wine and patches sayings are cast as a response to questions by the disciples of John about whether to fast; in Luke it is a "parable" without context. Although their sparser attestation makes these sayings more difficult to assign to the earliest Jesus tradition, their call for an ethical radicalism and their sharp distinction between the old and the new, together with the absence of the imminent eschatology which characterizes the redaction of Q^2 and Mark, contributes to their coherence with the other early aphorisms of the Jesus tradition.

LOGION 62
62:1Jesus said, "I disclose my mysteries to those [who are worthy] of [my] mysteries. 2Do not let your right hand know what your left hand is doing."[44]

Logion 62:2 is paralleled only by Matthew 6:3. The saying is as enigmatic in *Thomas* as it is in Matthew. *Thomas* treats it as one of the "mysteries" of Jesus and makes no effort to explain it, while Matthew uses it as a rationale for giving alms without ostentation. Within the group of binary sayings, its theme is the maintenance of division. It is difficult to determine how far back in the Jesus tradition this saying goes.

LOGION 70
70:1Jesus said,"If you bring forth what is within you, what you have will save you. 2If you do not have that within you, what you do not have within you [will] kill you."[45]

This logion has no parallels, canonical or non-canonical. There is nothing about it to suggest that it goes back to the historical Jesus, especially considering *Thomas*'s redactional concern with learning what is within oneself. Much more widely-attested Jesus traditions suggest that what is within will necessarily come out, and that what comes out is not necessarily good.[46] Logion 70 illustrates a tendency within *Thomas* to construct binary sayings in terms of union rather than any of the other logical options.

LOGION 89
89:1Jesus said, "Why do you wash the outside of the cup? 2Do you not know that the one who made the inside is also the one who made the outside?"[47]

---

44 Downing (*Christ and the Cynics*) cites no parallels.
45 Downing (*Christ and the Cynics*) cites no parallels.
46 See, e.g., *Thomas* 14:5 and Mark 7:15 (on defilement); Q 11:34-36 (on the light within); *Thomas* 89 and Q 11:39b-41 (inside and outside of the cup); Matthew 23:27-28 (tombs with filth inside but whitewashed outside); *Thomas* 5, 6b, 33 and Q 12:2-3 (whispered indoors and shouted outdoors).
47 Downing (*Christ and the Cynics*) cites no parallels.

Logion 89 has parallels in Q^2 11:39b-41. Q sets the saying in the context of an extended harangue against the Pharisees. Matthew and Luke do not change this context significantly. *Thomas*, however, records the saying without reference to conflict with the Pharisees, even though other sayings do contain this animosity (*Thomas* 39 and 102). It appears that this saying has been transmitted to *Thomas* independently of Q, since it lacks Q^2's redactional emphasis on polemic against other Jewish groups. As such, it is a correspondence saying from a relatively early Jesus tradition.

LOGION 106

[106:1]Jesus said, "When you make the two into one, you will become children of humankind, [2]and when you say 'Mountain, move from here!' it will move."[48]

Logion 106:2 has independent parallels in Matthew 17:20, Mark 11:23 and 1 Corinthians 13:2. The binary saying of 106:1 has a parallel only in *Thomas* 48. The promise to be able to move mountains (or, in Luke 17:6, trees) on the basis of faith had wide currency in the traditions of the Jesus movement. It is not necessary here to make a judgment about whether it goes back to the historical Jesus. The point is that *Thomas* demonstrates its redactional concerns in making the ability to move mountains the reward for union of a binary pair. This union concern is paralleled in *Thomas* 48, where the promise is made on the condition that two make peace in a single house.

Analysis of the binary logia of *Thomas* has several implications for understanding the content of the preaching of the historical Jesus. Reversal sayings which are associated with an imminent eschatology in the canonical tradition circulated prior to the introduction of that motif by the authors of the gospels and of Q^2. The transmission history of the binary sayings in *Thomas* also supports the assertion that traditions of conflict between Jesus and groups such as the Pharisees have been added or significantly amplified by the authors of the gospels and Q^2. The sayings which emphasize a union of binary pairs (4:3; 11; 22; 70; 106) are less well-attested across the Jesus traditions and often show themselves to be modifications to earlier sayings which did not originally emphasize the theme of union. Distinct from all these movements is a trajectory of binary sayings that reifies division (41; 62). The resulting picture of the binary sayings of Jesus, illuminated by *Thomas*, is primarily of sayings which speak of some form of future reversal. As they move into *Thomas*, some of them undergo redaction which transforms the reversal concern into a concern with the unification of the contrasting terms.

---

48 Downing (*Christ and the Cynics*) cites no parallels.

3.3 Kingdom Logia[49]

Kingdom logia are sayings that concern "the kingdom" or "the kingdom of the Father." Their relevance for the Cynic hypothesis is that *Thomas* shows this very early type of Jesus saying without the connections to that imminent catastrophic eschatology with which it is so often embellished in Q and the canonical gospels.

3.3.1 "Where is the Kingdom?"

Logia 3 and 113 share the image of people seeking the kingdom in a spatial or temporal location, so that Jesus must enlighten his audience with the observation that the kingdom is to be realized in their midst. The independent canonical parallels to these sayings are Mark 13:31, Q^2 17:23-28 and Luke 17:20-21. The Markan passage is set within the synoptic apocalypse, while the Q passage is set within a thematically similar section on the apocalyptic coming of the Son of Man. The passage unique to Luke is woven into Luke's discourse on the catastrophic coming of the kingdom. Luke 17:21, speaking of the kingdom rather than of Christ and claiming that it "is among you" (ἐντὸς ὑμῶν ἐστιν), is the closest parallel to *Thomas*'s theme of the already-realized kingdom. Comparison of these logia with their synoptic parallels shows how even the kingdom sayings, which, in Mark 13 and Q^2, are tightly integrated into the works' apocalyptic eschatology, circulated apart from those settings without that apocalyptic interpretive overlay.

3.3.2 "The Kingdom of the Father is Like..."

All but two of the eight sayings in *Thomas* which start with "Jesus said, 'the kingdom [of the Father] is like . . .'" have canonical parallels. For the most part there are few differences that can be attributed to redactional concerns. *Thomas* shares only some of the parables of the kingdom collected in Matthew 13 from Q and other sources. The presence of parallels to *Thomas* 20, 96 and 107 in $Q^?$ also suggests that analogies to the kingdom circulated widely and independently. The enigmatic comparisons of *Thomas* 97 and 98—a woman with a leaky jar, an assassin practising at home—have no parallels. Although some might argue that their very disturbing nature suggests authenticity, since it is hard to imagine someone attributing such unsavoury similitudes to Jesus, there is no secure way to determine this. The analogies of the kingdom in *Thomas* support the consensus that Jesus spoke of the kingdom in parables, and further

---

49 Kingdom logia include: 3, 20, 22, 27, 46, 49, 54, 96, 97, 98, 99, 107, 109, 113 and 114. There is no concept of the kingdom of God in Cynic philosophy comparable to that in Christianity (but see Vaage, *Galilean Upstarts*, 55-65, for an opposing viewpoint).

indicates that these parables were not originally imbued with apocalyptic eschatology.[50]

3.3.3 "Who Will Enter the Kingdom?"

The last group of kingdom logia addresses the requirements for entering (or knowing) the kingdom. In this group of sayings the *Thomas* tradition exhibits most clearly its distinctive redactional inclinations, in contrast to other Jesus traditions. Logia 22 and 46 deal with the familiar topic of children being the first in the kingdom. Most of the synoptic parallels to this topic are associated specifically with reversal imagery (first/last, humbled/exalted, least/greatest), in addition to the reversal implied by children preceding adults in the kingdom. The *Thomas* version of logion 22 (see above) transforms the theme of reversal into one of union. This move to associate entry into the kingdom with union or unity is also evident in logia 49 and 114, which have no parallels outside *Thomas*; their emphasis on solitariness and transformation of female to male is a distinctive redactional concern within *Thomas*. These logia, when they differ from synoptic parallels or are unattested, show a movement toward the theme of union rather than reversal.

The kingdom logia of *Thomas* suggest that the concept of the kingdom is present in the earliest traditions about Jesus. Some may go back to Jesus himself. *Thomas* presents kingdom sayings which are free of the apocalyptic eschatology of Q^2 and the synoptics, but which may also have a future orientation and the theme of reversal which characterize many early Jesus traditions.[51] This combination of themes (for a strong example, see logion 49) has an eschatological import, regardless of the secondary nature of apocalyptic features in the sayings.[52]

3.4 Protological and Eschatological Logia[53]

Thomas has a definite interest in protology. Logion 18, which is without parallels, is the clearest example: when the disciples ask about the end, Jesus

---

50 *Thomas*, for example, lacks Matthew 13:49-50 and 25:1-13.

51 Pheme Perkins, "The Rejected Jesus and the Kingdom Sayings," *Semeia* 44 (1988): 79-94, also notes the association of kingdom sayings with reversal traditions, but she understands the character of the kingdom sayings in *Thomas* to be a "development" of "the fact that, in the preaching of Jesus, Kingdom language functioned as a messianic proclamation to the disinherited of Israel" (81). I do not share this presupposition about the function of kingdom language in the preaching of Jesus, and my reading of *Thomas* does not support it.

52 Koester, "One Jesus and Four Primitive Gospels," 216, suggests that "the proclamation of the coming kingdom . . . ultimately has its roots in the preaching of Jesus."

53 These logia include: 3, 4, 9, 18, 50, 51, 57, 61, 73, 91, 103 and 113. See Davies ("Christology and Protology") for a fuller discussion on the protological interests of *Thomas*. Davies cogently argues that "light" in *Thomas* functions analogously to *logos* in John and Philo, and thus investigates a much wider range of sayings as protological. I agree with his wider collection of protological materials, but restrict myself here to those which are most explicit.

redirects their question toward the beginning. Similarly, in logion 51 Jesus asserts that looking forward to "the repose of the dead" and a new world is a mistake. Although not as explicitly protological as logion 18, logion 51 (which has affinities with 113) places the critical moment in and before the present, not in the future. Here logion 51 has affinities with logion 113, which treats the question in terms of the kingdom. The most elaborately protological logion is 50, which describes an interrogation during a heavenly ascent.[54] As Stevan Davies says of logia 51, 83 and 84, these sayings "presuppose a metaphysics that is hinted at so briefly and that is so dependent on unclear pronoun references that certainty in regard to their interpretation may be impossible."[55] Detailed description of the protology of such logia may well be impossible, but the high place of protology in *Thomas*'s interests is indisputable.

On the other hand, several logia in *Thomas* lack the catastrophic eschatological overtones of their canonical counterparts. Logion 3 ignores the predictions of tribulation accompanying the return of the Son of Man which characterize its parallels in Mark and Q, and which Matthew and Luke combine to form an extended apocalyptic discourse.[56] The freely-circulating rationalizing statements in logia 4, 5 and 6 serve to endorse much more catastrophic eschatological visions in their synoptic versions. The parable of the sower in logion 9 occurs in the triple tradition (Mark 4:2-9, 13-20 and parallels), but is always accompanied by an interpretation set on the lips of Jesus, which explains that the seeds that were sown upon the rocky ground and wither quickly are those unable to withstand tribulation. This concern with persecution and rejection by the present generation is a concern of Mark, which Matthew and Luke inherit and develop on their own.[57]

The dialogue between Jesus and Salome in *Thomas* 61 lacks any of the eschatological themes that surround the Q parallel to logion 61:1 (Q^2 17:23-4, 26-30, 34-5, 37), and it may well be that the traditional division of *Thomas* into logia is misleading here; it is possible (even probable) that 61:2-5 was set in the collection after 61:1 merely because of the Coptic catchword bed/couch (ϬⲗⲟϬ). As it stands, however, *Thomas* 61 develops the statement of 61:1 into a protological rather than an eschatological discourse. In Q the saying is set within a lengthy discourse about the tribulations accompanying the coming of the Son of Man. Matthew and Luke intensify the apocalyptic character of the discourse. Luke inserts an otherwise freely-circulating reversal saying (17:33: "Those who try to make their life secure will lose it, but those who lose their life will keep it"). Logion 103 similarly lacks an eschatological reference, while

54   Koester, *Ancient Christian Gospels*, 125-26.
55   Davies, "Christology and Protology," 669.
56   *Thomas* 3 has independent parallels in Mark 13:21 and Q^2 17:23-28.
57   On this redactional emphasis in Mark, see Mack, *Myth of Innocence*, 127. Note that the same motif is inherited by both evangelists from Q as well. See Kloppenborg, *Formation of Q*, 167-68.

its counterpart in Q^2 12:39-40 associates it with the coming of the Son of Man. In Matthew and Luke, the Q text rounds off longer discourses concerning the coming of the Son of Man. There are also relevant parallels to the thief image in 1 Thessalonians 5:2 and Revelation 3:3; 16:15. Similarly, the saying about the passing away of the heavens which introduces *Thomas* 11, in contrast to its synoptic parallels, first leads into the theme of reversal, then union. For all of these *Thomas* logia, apocalyptic associations present in the synoptics are lacking.

The eschatological intensity of *Thomas* 57 stands in contrast to the rest of the writing. Its "plot" is closely paralleled by Matthew 13:24-30 but its style is quite different. In *Thomas*, Jesus narrates the story as a series of events, but Matthew communicates it through a more dramatic combination of narrative and dialogue between characters within the parable. Within *Thomas*, logion 57 is notable for the role that future destruction plays in its eschatology. It is no less catastrophic than Matthew. It is difficult to understand the relationship between the parable in *Thomas* and its counterpart in Matthew (there may be no direct relationship at all), but within the literary history of the Jesus tradition, elaboration into a relatively complex combination of narrative and dialogue seems a more likely editorial activity than condensation.[58] The intense eschatology of this kingdom saying is at odds with the tendency within *Thomas* to picture the kingdom without catastrophic eschatology.

In addition to logion 57, *Thomas* contains three eschatological logia with no close parallels. *Thomas* 21 has only slight similarities to Matthew 24:42-44. The very situation of Jesus characterizing his own disciples makes it unlikely that this logion goes back to Jesus. Its metaphors of returning vineyard owner, coming thief, approaching troubles and imminent harvest, crushed up against against each other and capped with the cliché "whoever has ears to hear should hear," suggest that this is a potpourri of different Jesus traditions. It runs counter to most of the protological/non-eschatological interests of *Thomas*. It also includes the theme of the disciples as children, a relatively late motif in the Jesus tradition, developed more fully in gnostic traditions. For these reasons, one could speculate that it is a relatively late addition to *Thomas*, put in its current place because of the parallel between Mary's question and the question of the disciples in the preceding logion. *Thomas* 37 makes use of a similar nakedness motif in an eschatological (although not a catastrophic) context. These sayings may represent an eschatological countercurrent within *Thomas*.

Logion 111 is relevant, not only for the imminent eschatological imagery, but also for what seems to be a comment, in 111:2, by the collection's editor.

---

58 Note, however, that John G. Gager, "The Gospels and Jesus: Some Doubts about Method," *Journal of Religion* 54 (1974), 244-72, argues that condensation may be characteristic of the oral transmission of traditions.

The image of the heavens and the earth being rolled up connotes a catastrophic eschatology in other contexts, but here it is very present-oriented. The promise that "the one who lives in the living one will not see death" orients the logion to the collection's strong emphasis on the present, as logion 1 describes it. The editorial comment in 111:2 also suggests that 111:1 was put into the *Thomas* collection with this emphasis in mind.

The protological and eschatological logia in *Thomas* display a redactional movement toward protology. As far as can be discerned, none of the sayings incorporated into the *Thomas* collection have a catastrophic eschatology based on the coming of the Son of Man, as in Q^2 and Mark 13. Alongside this trajectory is a smaller group of logia (21, 37, 111) which describe a somewhat catastrophic future, but which still lack a returning figure or conflict with "this generation." Some of these may have been added relatively late in the course of *Thomas*'s development.

3.5 Specific Logia in Relation to Cynicism

There are several logia in *Thomas* which bear some relation to the practices advocated by Cynics or to the literary forms that characterize writing about Cynics. Following are two groupings of these logia.

3.5.1 Logia of Cynic-Like Practice

Within several logia of *Thomas* is an anti-materialist ethic. *Thomas* 42 puts it most simply: "Jesus said, 'Become passersby.'"[59] Logion 76 conflates sayings traditions found in Q^1 (Q 12:33-34) and Matthew (Matt 13:45-46) to form an exhortation to seek what is enduring rather than what is perishable. A Cynic would concur. Logion 14:1-3 censures religious practice in a way that might also seem Cynic-like, but *Thomas*'s attitude to religious practice is not to be defined only by the negative attitude in sayings like this. Logia such as 27 ("sabbath as sabbath") suggest that there was also an urge to spiritualize religious practice without removing it from the "actual" practice, or the terminology and history of the practice. Here, *Thomas* has much more in common with Philo than with the Cynics.

Logia 14:4 and 86 have close canonical parallels which play a significant role in the case for understanding Jesus as a Cynic. They suggest a practice of itinerancy that closely parallels Cynic circuit-preaching. In the case of Logion 86, there is no significant difference between the words of Jesus in *Thomas* and those in Matthew and Luke. The exact verbal agreement between the Matthean

---

59 This brief logion raises difficult problems for translation, but none of the many possible renderings removes the obvious connotation of asceticism and itinerancy.

and Lukan versions of the saying, the close translation that obviously underlies the Coptic of *Thomas* and its position in Q[1] suggest that this saying was rigidly fixed quite early in the tradition. The use of "Son of Man" with no titular implication, especially when *Thomas* eschews (or merely lacks) any other saying with this title, also suggests that this saying might have formed before the heavenly Son of Man figure was integrated into the Jesus tradition. Logion 86 in *Thomas* is an early witness to the value placed on itinerancy in the earliest layers of the Jesus tradition. Logion 14:4 parallels the mission speech in Q[1] 10:2-12.

Although these sayings witness to an early tradition of itinerant mission, the relation of the itinerants to Cynicism is complex. Both Matthew and Luke agree that those sent out are not to carry a bag (πήρα); Luke does not mention a staff or tunic, but Matthew says not to take "two tunics . . . nor a staff" (μηδὲ δύο χιτῶνας . . . μηδὲ ῥάβδον). The staff, satchel and "doubled tunic" were the identifying garb of Cynics.[60] It is also possible that Q and Mark recognized similarities to the itinerancy of the Cynics and sought to differentiate the itinerants of the Jesus movement.[61] *Thomas* 14:4, however, shows no knowledge of these issues; it merely advocates itinerancy and the cleanness of all foods. Furthermore, because of the relevance of Jesus' words to his disciples for establishing authority and authoritative models of practice in the early Christian movements, it is difficult to ascribe a mission speech to the historical Jesus with any confidence. The logia about Cynic practice suggest that the early Jesus traditions shared with Cynicism a tendency toward itinerancy and an antipathy to material things, which a Cynic would characterize as "indifference," but *Thomas* lacks the urge to define its audience in relation to Cynicism that may be present in Q and Mark.

3.5.2 Logia of Cynic Literary Style

The primary constituent unit (comparable to the logia of *Thomas*) in writings about Cynics is the *chreia*, i.e., a brief response to a situation which reveals something about the respondent's character.[62] Examining the role of *chreiai* in order to gain insight into the character of the historical Jesus is problematic. The remembrances reveal more about their author/compiler than about Jesus.

---

60 E.g., Diogenes Laertius 6.22. See the Loeb edition: *Diogenes Laertius: Lives of Eminent Philosophers*, trans. R. D. Hicks (Cambridge: Harvard University Press, 1966-70), vol. 2, 24-25.

61 In so doing, however, they opened the door to seeing the missionary activity of the early church as Cynic-like.

62 For a more extensive discussion of definition, including ancient definitions and discussions of *chreiai*, see Hock and O'Neil, *Chreia in Ancient Rhetoric*, 23-27; Mack, *Anecdotes and Arguments*, 4-15; and Mack and Robbins, *Patterns of Persuasion*, 11-13.

Nevertheless, a comparison of parallel sayings in *Thomas* and other Jesus traditions suggests that there is a movement in the canonical tradition toward casting the sayings of Jesus in *chreia* form. I suggest that this is evidence of a slight "Cynicizing" tendency in the canonical tradition about Jesus.

There are many types of *chreiai*.[63] Most of those in *Thomas* are question *chreiai* (12, 18, 20, 21, 24, 37, 43, 51, 52, 53, 72, 91, 104, 113, 114). Comparison of these logia with their synoptic parallels reveals that their parallels are also set in question and response form. There is no evidence that *Thomas* took a saying that circulated simply as a saying of Jesus and turned it into a question *chreia*. The only two non-question *chreiai* in *Thomas* are logia 60 and 100. Logion 60 has no parallel in the synoptic tradition, so it is impossible to discern movement toward or away from a *chreia* form (the content of the logion also has little to do with the content of Cynic preaching). Logion 100 is more apropos. In *Thomas*, it is a "mixed" *chreia*.[64] In Mark, Matthew and Luke the question about taxes is set in a more elaborate dialogue form, which may suggest an elaboration of the original *chreia* according to the exercises in the progymnasmata.[65] In any case, there is nothing to suggest a tendency in *Thomas* to create *chreiai*.

The last comparative evidence includes sayings which are set in *chreia* form in the synoptics which have non-*chreia* parallels in *Thomas*.[66] A few examples will suffice. Mark 12:28-34 is a series of *chreiai*, of which 12:31 and 12:34 are paralleled separately in *Thomas* 25 and 82. Mark seems to have created a *chreia* dialogue from sayings that circulated freely, and not in the form of *chreiai*. Q 9:57-58 is a simpler *chreia* than those in Mark 12:28-34 and has a closer parallel in *Thomas* 86. What Luke and Matthew set as a classic question *chreia* (both employ a participial introduction), *Thomas* simply sets as a saying. The most extensive example is Q 12:22-31, which Mack has shown quite clearly to be an argument created under the principles of *chreia* elaboration in the progymnasmata.[67] *Thomas* 39 preserves as a simple saying that which the Q discourse extensively elaborates. If there is any tendency among the Jesus traditions to create *chreiai*, it is found in the synoptics, although some of that process must be attributed merely to the narrative genre of the gospels.[68]

---

63 See Hock and O'Neil, *Chreia in Ancient Rhetoric*, 27-35; Klaus Berger, "Hellenistische Gattungen im neuen Testament," in Hildegard Temporini and Wolfgang Haase, eds., *Aufstieg und Niedergang der römischen Welt* (Berlin: De Gruyter, 1984), part II, vol. 25.2, 1096-1103.

64 "Mixed *chreiai*" combine both events and speeches. See Hock and O'Neil (*Chreia in Ancient Rhetoric*, 27-28) for a more extensive discussion of this form.

65 Hock and O'Neil, *Chreia in Ancient Rhetoric*, 35-41; Mack and Robbins, *Patterns of Persuasion*, 31-67; Mack, *Anecdotes and Arguments*, 15-28; *Rhetoric and the New Testament*, 43-47.

66 I have chosen a few examples from the *chreiai* listed in Berger, "Hellenistische Gattungen."

67 Mack, *Lost Gospel*, 121-23.

68 In the judgment of James G. Williams, "Parable and Chreia: From Q to Narrative Gospel," *Semeia* 44 (1988): 85-114, none of the *chreiai* in Q appear as such in *Thomas*.

4. Conclusion

4.1 The Contribution of the Gospel of Thomas

Thomas exercises a moderating influence on the case for seeing Jesus as a Cynic. Analysis of the binary logia suggests that the earliest and most reliably-attested material among these logia emphasizes the motif of reversal: the first will become last and the last, first. The kingdom logia are part of the earliest strata of the Jesus tradition and are demonstrably independent of the apocalyptic eschatology which characterizes much of their context (and therefore exerts a significant influence on their meaning) in Q^2 and the synoptics. They were often associated (and thus generated their meaning in conjunction) with reversal sayings. The eschatological and protological logia illustrate a tradition in transition from an interest in eschatology to a focus on protology, but the "eschatological beginnings" of this tradition had roots independent of the imminent eschatology of Q^2 and Mark 13 and their developments in Matthew and Luke. The resulting picture of the historical Jesus is one of eschatological preacher, proclaiming a coming kingdom and a coming reversal.[69] This is only one part of the entire picture of the historical Jesus implied by *Thomas*, which in turn would be only one angle on Jesus among several. Nevertheless, it evinces a portion of Jesus' preaching for which the Cynic model has little explanatory power.

In comparison with Cynic practice and Cynic literary forms, three findings emerge: there is an element of itinerancy and world rejection in the earliest Jesus traditions for which Cynicism may well provide a helpful context; there is a tendency within the synoptic branch of the Jesus traditions to "Cynicize" the literary forms in which Jesus' teaching emerges; and Q takes some care to differentiate the missionary practice of the Jesus movement from Cynic practice. Thus the historical Jesus is likely to have been somewhat less of a Cynic than he is portrayed in the synoptics.

4.2 The Wider Context of Criticism

At this point it is possible to step back from *Thomas*, to integrate the results of the close investigation of its logia and to offer some criticism of the case for a Cynic Jesus in light of a wider view of the Jesus traditions. Although it is necessary to add *Thomas* to the sources for evaluating Cynicism as a model for understanding Jesus, *Thomas* does not tell the whole story. In addition to the questions that are raised by *Thomas*, some general problems linger for the case of a Cynic-like Jesus.

---

69 Koester's interpretation of this element of Jesus' teaching (*Ancient Christian Gospels*, 156) seems to characterize Jesus as a Bultmannian existentialist.

Sometimes the case for understanding Jesus as a Cynic is stated in terms of appearances: "whether or not Jesus was a Cynic, he would certainly have looked like one." To whom? Jesus was Jewish, spoke Aramaic and lived in a thoroughly Jewish milieu. Who, then, would look at such a man, would listen to such a man speaking in Aramaic, and say "There is a Cynic"? Downing is far too eager to dissociate the audience of the gospels from Judaism, and then project the characteristics of his construction back onto Jesus' own audience. Similarly, Crossan's formulation, "peasant Jewish Cynic,"[70] covering all the bases, designates an unattested hybrid unlikely to be recognized as such in first-century Galilee or Judea. By the time Christianity was addressing itself in large measure to Gentiles who had little understanding of Judaism (even if one places this development as early as 65 CE), Jesus had come to be associated either with the role of "son of God" and the apocalyptic eschatology of the synoptic tradition or with Q^1's and *Thomas*'s image of a teacher of wisdom. In the case of Q^2, there is a slight tendency to "Cynicize" Jesus by using the *chreia* form.

Jesus' healings and the rural location of his other activities also blunt the force of the Cynic model. *Thomas* has little interest in the actions of Jesus, and so has little information to contribute to these facets of Jesus' life. That he was reputed to have healed, and that his activities were primarily rural, however, are well established.[71] Downing's remark that some Cynics were interested in health and that they preached everywhere does little to answer the strong objections raised by these questions.[72] Similarly, the strong presence of women among Jesus' followers has no Cynic precedent; Downing's citation of Pseudo-Crates' fictional correspondence with Hipparchia is insufficient.[73] To these objections one might add Jesus' association with John the Baptist (who, in the story of the Cynic Jesus, bears the weight of the apocalyptic and eschatological materials for which there is no room in the Cynic Jesus' satchel).[74] Although Cynicism provides a helpful comparative model for understanding itinerancy, the reason Jesus is not explicitly described as a Cynic in the first century is that he was probably not seen as one in the first century.

---

70 *Historical Jesus*, 421.
71 See Crossan, *Historical Jesus*, 310-13, on the very early place of healing and wonder-working in the Jesus traditions.
72 Downing, "Cynics and Christians," 585-86; *Cynics and Christian Origins*, 131.
73 Downing, *Christ and the Cynics*, 5.
74 Terence Donaldson made this observation in his response to an earlier oral form of this paper at the Canadian Society of Biblical Studies meeting in Calgary, 1994.

5. The Galilean Jewish Jesus: Context

William E. Arnal

The title of Seán Freyne's paper is eminently descriptive. It signals his use of the methodology on which he has built his reputation, i.e., the careful social, cultural and economic description, and analysis, of Roman Galilee. The title also signals the rather novel element of this paper: the effort to bring that scholarship to bear on the reconstruction of the historical Jesus, particularly that offered, recently and with considerable impact, by John Dominic Crossan.[1] The basic crux of this juxtaposition is the contrast between the generality with which Crossan situates Jesus in a broadly "Mediterranean" environment and the specificity with which Freyne is able to describe the particular locale in which Jesus surely lived and taught.

The contrast is indicative of two larger trends or currents in historical-Jesus (and, generally, New Testament) scholarship. On the one hand, there is the "Jewish Jesus," a historical Jesus understood in terms of his location in a first-century Jewish religious context. Proponents of this current (Geza Vermes and E. P. Sanders come immediately to mind) tend to equate Judaism (and Jesus, as a Jew) with the insulated image of this religious tradition conveyed by both rabbinic and intertestamental Jewish elite literature. On the other hand are those who, without denying that Jesus was in fact a Jew, minimize the extent to which this observation helps us to understand him, and seek instead to contextualize him within a broader Roman, Hellenistic or Mediterranean milieu. Freyne's work to date locates him within the first current, while Crossan falls squarely within the second. A Jesus whose relevant historical context is Galilee—and even more specifically, Galilee as reconstructed and described by Freyne—will emerge distinctively as "a Jew." A Jesus whose relevant historical context is the entirety of Roman antiquity, as is Crossan's, will be less so.

The "Jewish Jesus" controversy in recent scholarship has some methodological corollaries. Typically, those who adopt a more cosmopolitan or Hellenistic Jesus will make greater use of extra-canonical early Christian writings, especially the *Gospel of Thomas*, while proponents of a more circumscribed Jewish Jesus tend to rely more exclusively on the synoptic gospels for their data. The debate also raises the rather venerable issue of the dichotomy between "Judaism and Hellenism." Both parties in the dispute, to be sure, acknowledge that first-century Judaism was very much part of the Hellenistic world and strongly influenced by it, so a strict dichotomy will no longer do. But different implications are drawn from this conclusion. For Jewish Jesus proponents, the Hellenization of ancient Judaism means that we

---

1   See especially John Dominic Crossan's *The Historical Jesus: The Life of a Mediterranean Jewish Peasant* (San Francisco: HarperSanFrancisco, 1991).

cannot rule out "Greek-sounding" conceptions as inauthentic when they appear in the teachings or behaviour of first-century Jews such as Jesus. For those who advocate a broader cultural milieu for Jesus, this Hellenization indicates that we cannot reify "Judaism" and consequently treat it as a contextually-significant culture-in-itself within the larger context of the Roman Empire. The reader will also note that the arguments surrounding "apocalypticism," a burning issue in several of the papers in this volume, are not irrelevant to this debate.

Freyne's paper is an effort to breach the boundary between these two currents, and to take seriously the portrait of Jesus offered by Crossan, with the critical qualification that it be supplemented and revised by situating Jesus within his *specific* historical context: first-century *Galilee*. In a paper that, in exemplary fashion, touches clearly on nearly all the issues endemic to this debate, two of Freyne's critiques of Crossan merit special attention. The first of these is Freyne's charge that Crossan does not pay sufficient attention to the activities of the Galilean tetrarch Antipas, whose activities—including especially the founding (or re-founding) of two major urban centres in Galilee (Sepphoris and Tiberias) just prior to the emergence of the early Jesus movement—must have had a direct and immediate bearing on Jesus and his original audience. The second striking point made by Freyne—it is not exactly a critique—is the suggestion that the "Cynic" Jesus favoured by Crossan is a more plausible figure in an urban rather than a rural environment. This consideration leads in turn to the suggestion that it is the (urban) composers of Q, rather than Jesus himself, who are responsible for the Cynic-like tone of the Sayings Gospel. Of all of the important questions and issues raised in this paper, these two appear most likely to bear fruit in future scholarship, and may point to the resolution of some of the thornier issues plaguing the "quest" today.

Freyne, then, attempts to steer a middle course between two equally untenable extremes: an image of Jesus relying on a no-longer-believable dichotomy between "Judaism" and "Hellenism," and an image that might deny the distinctiveness or relevance of his Judaism altogether (Ernest Renan comes to mind). His reconstruction of Jesus remains rooted in the third-quest tendency to use the synoptic records to locate Jesus and his teachings in the context of Jewish *religious* debates. The discussion not only offers an excellent introduction to the relevance of Galilean socio-political life for reconstructing the historical Jesus; it also illustrates remarkably well the current scholarly debate around the Jewish religiosity of Jesus.

6. Galilean Questions to Crossan's Mediterranean Jesus

Seán Freyne

1. Introduction

In this paper I would like to engage in an exercise of intertextual reading of a kind. I read John Dominic Crossan's book, *The Historical Jesus: The Life of a Mediterranean Jewish Peasant*, with great enjoyment and not a little profit, as I hope will emerge from this discussion.[1] It would be naïve, however, to suggest that I was a disinterested reader. At every step of the way I found myself interacting in the light of my own preoccupation with many of the themes and issues with which he has dealt in such a lucid and challenging way. This paper is then a report on the light that has been generated for this critical reader by rubbing Crossan's book against my own perspective on Jesus and his ministry (to borrow Harold Bloom's image for the reading process in which I have been engaged). Although disagreeing with him in many fundamental respects, I have been forced to revise and sharpen my own construal of Jesus by critically interacting with his persuasively-argued positions. In the book's preface the author asks those colleagues who disagree with his moves to replace them with better ones. I am not sure that my moves are better, nor would I be certain by what criteria I could come to such a judgment. But my moves are certainly different, for reasons which will become explicit as my argument develops.

2. Some Queries about Crossan's Categories

2.1 The Question of Sources

I have followed the work of the Jesus Seminar from a distance—some might say a safe distance—and was therefore familiar with the meticulous concern for bedrock tradition that has marked the discussions of its members. Crossan has clearly been one of the main fashioners of the rigorous methodology that has been developed, and the present study aims to put the results of that methodology to the test.[2] While the logic of his approach might appear to be impeccable in dealing with individual items of the Jesus tradition, I do have

---

1   John Dominic Crossan, *The Historical Jesus: The Life of a Mediterranean Jewish Peasant* (San Francisco: HarperSanFrancisco, 1991).

2   See John Dominic Crossan, *Four Other Gospels: Shadows on the Contours of Canon* (Minneapolis: Winston, 1985); and "Materials and Methods in Historical Jesus Research," *Forum* 4/4 (1988): 3-24.

serious reservations about its advisability when it comes to building an edifice from the scattered bits and pieces that eventually get the red, or even the pink, votes. Only those items that have a double attestation from the earliest stratum will be used in the reconstruction, we are told, and on the whole this stringent criterion is followed. But how realistic is this almost squeamish concern with bedrock and whence this almost obsessional desire for unimpeachable criteria? The elaborate stratification of all the early Jesus traditions, canonical and non-canonical alike, is of course a matter that could be debated as regards details. I could not help but note in passing that all of Crossan's "stratum one" material is either extra-canonical or not very helpful in the quest for Jesus (the Pauline material). Mark finds himself relegated to stratum two, and even then supplanted by *Secret Mark*. At least the 19-century questers were kinder in their judgment of Mark. At all events the difficulties with claiming that only the earliest documents can serve as genuine sources in historical reconstruction have been exposed for a long time now. No amount of refinement of criteria can overcome the epistemological problems inherent in such an approach.

Rather than entering into debate on matters of detail I would prefer to query the very model that is being used—stratification—which is drawn from archaeology and shows a predilection for so-called hard facts. In dealing with a living and oral tradition I suspect that it is an unhelpful, and in the end a potentially damaging, model in identifying literary sources for historical writing. Reminiscences, quotations of pithy sayings, reports of incidents and the like all occur in lived and living contexts. Nothing is frozen in time, awaiting the arrival of the modern historical critic with his or her trowel to release it from the later "fill" that has obscured it from view for centuries. In his concern to arrive at bedrock Crossan freely admits that he may well be ignoring important pieces of evidence from other strata, just because they do not meet his rigid criteria. But surely that is being methodologically correct to the point of distorting the picture from the outset by limiting the field of vision. Indeed, if one were to follow Crossan's methodology to its logical conclusion—that is, use only material from stratum one—it would be difficult to locate Jesus anywhere, certainly not in Galilee. In the end I found myself wondering whether the "atopicality" which is so important a feature of Crossan's Jesus[3] was the result of the minimalist position adopted from the outset with regard to the appropriate sources, or, conversely, whether the image of such a figure already created a predilection for a certain kind of evidence.

My own approach to the issue of the sources for the historical Jesus begins in quite a different place. While I am well aware that the canonical gospels represent choices, often the ideological ones of the second century, it is they and not the other gospels that have shaped Christian self-understanding down

---

3   Crossan, *Historical Jesus*, 345-48.

through the centuries. The synoptic portrait does after all pre-date Schweitzer by two millenia, contrary to what some of proponents of the extra-canonical Jesus seem to think. This does not mean that other, extra-canonical, portraits should not be considered, even when they appear to conflict with the canonical accounts in a fundamental way. Stephen Patterson is surely correct in objecting to using *Thomas* only when its traditions can be shown to corroborate the traditional accounts.[4] However, there are a number of critical questions to be addressed before one can go to the other extreme and postulate a minimalist common core of sayings which were subsequently developed by *Thomas* and the synoptics along different trajectories, and claim that in that core "we can catch a glimpse of that common beginning, extremely important for understanding who Jesus was."[5] There seems to be an assumption among those who seek to limit themselves to such an early stratum (be it best represented in *Thomas* or the first stratum of Q) that the existence of such a putative wisdom portrait of Jesus means that that portrait was the only one available to the tradents of that particular set of traditions. As E. P. Sanders remarks in another context, there may have been genre constraints which allowed for only certain aspects to be included in a particular document. Even more fallacious would be the assumption that these people were opposed to that about which they do not speak.[6] It is possible to imagine a situation in which collections of wisdom sayings, accounts of Jesus' mighty deeds and a primitive passion story were utilized in different contexts by the same people, and at an early stage in the tradition (see, e.g., 1 Cor 11:23-25; 15:3-6). If one is attempting to escape "the tyranny of the synoptic portrait of Jesus," as one member of the Jesus Seminar puts it, then one must likewise be careful not to become slave to a tyranny of the "earliest stratum" either.[7]

In my book, *Galilee, Jesus and the Gospels*,[8] I took as my starting point for enquiry the very specific setting of Galilee as a way of exploring the traditions about Jesus, since it plays a determining role in shaping the plots of all four canonical gospels. In view of the methodological difficulties associated with the

---

4   Stephen J. Patterson, *The Gospel of Thomas and Jesus* (Sonoma: Polebridge, 1993), 221-25.

5   Stephen J. Patterson, "The Gospel of Thomas and the Historical Jesus: Retrospectus and Prospectus," in David J. Lull, ed., *Society of Biblical Literature 1990 Seminar Papers* (Atlanta: Scholars Press, 1990), 614-36, especially 622.

6   E. P. Sanders, *Jewish Law from Jesus to the Mishnah* (London: SCM, 1990), 322-25.

7   Charles W. Hedrick, "Introduction: The Tyranny of the Synoptic Jesus," *Semeia* 44 (1988): 1-8; Burton L. Mack, "All the Extra Jesuses: Christian Origins in the Light of Extra-Canonical Gospels," *Semeia* 49 (1990): 169-76. John S. Kloppenborg, "Literary Convention, Self-Evidence and the Social History of the Q People," *Semeia* 55 (1991): 77-102, especially 79-81, is aware of the problem of moving from text to social entity, but still believes that the document was canonical for the group and hence mirrors its social world.

8   Seán Freyne, *Galilee, Jesus and the Gospels: Literary Approaches and Historical Investigations* (Philadelphia: Fortress, 1988).

search for the earliest stratum and in an attempt to see how literary and historical concerns might co-operate in gospel studies I decided to experiment with the notion of narrative realism as applied to the final redactions of the evangelists. In choosing to experiment in this way I realized that I was leaving myself open to the charge of confusing the realism of narrative fiction with historical fact. My own criticism of the experiment five years later would be to say that I did not carry through with sufficient rigour my initial insight of allowing the individual writers' different social worlds to emerge, before attempting to show that each in their different ways and despite their other immediate concerns paid their debt to the past of the real Jesus in the real Galilee through the various traces of that past that were available to them. Paul Ricoeur has clarified considerably the overlap between narrative fiction and history writing and has indicated how a consideration of this overlap might assist in freeing us from the objectivist fallacy, without thereby abandoning a critical historical perspective. Because both enterprises are mimetic, re-presenting the world of human affairs through emplotment, both involve an active imagination. In the case of history writing the events, characters and situation to be emplotted are present only insofar as individual historians can imaginatively revivify the past through its remaining traces. In other words, all history writing engages in the metaphorical mode, generating a perception of likeness between a present account and the real past, a past which has gone forever and can only be imagined.[9] All history writing is interpretation, and the past is only mediately accessible to us despite our most rigorous efforts to recover "objective" sources.

I am not of course suggesting that the gospels are purely fictional narratives, nor am I advocating a return to a naïve conflation of the various accounts, as though all we had learned from form and redaction criticism can now be abandoned. But it cannot be doubted that the intentions of the authors of our texts were historical, since they have left traces of those intentions indelibly printed in their works—Luke most explicitly, but all, by implication, in their adoption of the narrative mode. In accomplishing their task they had, we know, their sources, and today we can identify these sources with a reasonable amount of certainty. Equally, however, they had their imagination and their convictions, which caused them to wonder about the past in the light of the present and the future. In putting their questions to the past they created the past, but not in a way that violated that metaphorical likeness which is essential to all rendering of the past in the narrative mode, whether fictional or historical.[10] At least that is the hypothesis that we today are called on to test as

---

9   See in particular Paul Ricoeur, *Time and Narrative*, 3 vols., trans. K. McLaughlin and D. Pellauer (Chicago: Chicago University Press, 1984-88), esp. vol. 3, 104-240.

10 Here I am indebted to the reflections of Ben F. Meyer, building on Bernard Lonergan's theory of human cognition, in "The Challenge of Text and Reader to the Historical-Critical Method," in W. Beuken, Seán Freyne and Anton Weiler, eds., *The Bible and its Readers* (London: SCM, 1991), 3-12.

historically-conscious readers of these works. We render our debt to their past by taking seriously their intentions which they have left for us to decipher in and through those texts.

It will be obvious that by taking seriously as my starting point the narrative mode of the gospels, rather than any putative earliest stratum, my starting point and therefore also, presumably, my end result will be very different from Crossan's. At least I can enter Galilee freely as by right, and I cannot as easily abandon it for a Mediterranean atopicality which Crossan's Jesus finds more congenial. This will also mean a considerable difference of emphasis in two important respects. Because my focus throughout is on Jesus in Galilee I will not be happy with merely painting a "background" of Palestinian life and then constructing an image of Jesus that is never made to engage seriously with that world. If the impact of Jesus' socio-religious vision and movement is to be properly elucidated and evaluated, the values inherent in the embattled brokerage of Galilee and the brokerless kingdom of Jesus' teaching will need to be brought into direct and critical confrontation with each other. Second, in view of his use of an image from archaeology to establish his literary methodology, Crossan could have paid more attention to the account of Galilean social life that is now emerging from the application of the methods of the "new archaeology" to Galilee. Not that these stones will speak with one voice! Yet in many instances they present us with aspects of Galilean social life that are just as challenging to the gospel portraits as are the extra-canonical gospels. The critical correlation of both the literary and archaeological remains is then an essential prerequisite for anybody interested in locating the real Jesus in the real Galilee.[11]

2.2 Where is the Fox?

"Foxes have holes and the birds of the air have nests" (Q 9:58), as Jesus remarked, not directly referring to Antipas, I take it, despite Theissen's imaginative uncovering of the reed of Tiberias.[12] Nevertheless, Antipas was a fact of life in the Galilee of Jesus, and I find his almost complete absence from Crossan's book strange but predictable in the light of Crossan's tendency to atopicality. The omission is all the more significant in view of the fact that the

---

11 See my "Archaeology and the Historical Jesus," in John R. Bartlett, ed., *Archaeology and Biblical Interpretation* (London: Routledge, 1997), 117-44.

12 Q texts are cited by Lukan versification. Gerd Theissen, *The Gospels in Context: Social and Political History in the Synoptic Tradition*, trans. Linda M. Maloney (Minneapolis: Fortress, 1991), 26-39, adduces numismatic evidence to argue that Q 7:24's enigmatic "reed shaken by the wind" is a deliberate reference to the Galilean tetrach, Herod Antipas, whose first coinage portrayed a reed on the obverse. One could argue analogously that the reference to the fox's hole in Q 9:58 is in fact intended to refer to Antipas's royal residence. [Eds.]

reign of Antipas in Galilee had a direct bearing on the situation of the local peasants to whom the message of Jesus was addressed.

What difference did Antipas make? In previous discussions I have espoused the view that the reign of Antipas provided a buffer for Galilee from the excesses of Roman provincial rule and that conditions under him should not be confused with those obtaining in Judaea after the deposition of Archelaus or with those in Galilee itself on the eve of the first revolt. In this regard Crossan's ignoring of the archaeological evidence shows up particularly, since so much of the data points to regional differences and their importance in terms of trade and commerce, language, religious affiliations and social conditions generally. It is not that we have suddenly discovered that Galilee was not Jewish at all. It is a matter of sensitively estimating the way in which Jewish faith was lived and expressed in everyday life in a region that was both part of *Eretz Israel*, yet cut off from its main cultic centre and so forced to develop its own brand of Jewishness in response to the social factors operating there at different periods.

It so happens that Jesus' career coincided with the emergence for the first time of a local Galilean ruler, somebody who had been frustrated in his ambition to succeed his father as king of the entire land and who yet operated with a relative degree of independence as tetrarch. The fact that there was no protest in Rome calling for his deposition may or may not be significant. The aniconic coins of Antipas show a sensitivity to Jewish religious concerns, unlike his palace which was destroyed in 66 CE, ostensibly because of its representations of the human form.[13] Josephus contrasts him unfavourably with his brother Philip in terms of the administration of justice in their respective territories.[14] The pre-emptive strike against John the Baptist shows that Antipas could be ruthless. It also raises sharply the question of how Jesus avoided a similar fate at his hands. If the scenario suggested by Crossan's adoption of Ted Robert Gurr's model of a peasantry suffering from decremental deprivation[15] is to be evaluated, close attention will need to be paid to the shifting social world of Antipas's reign, especially as this was symbolized in the emergence of Sepphoris and Tiberias as administrative centres in Lower Galilee. As I will argue later, this shift provides us with the most immediate context for understanding the factors that gave rise to the Jesus movement and the strategies which it adopted.

2.3 Mediterranean and Cynic or Galilean Jewish and Apocalyptic?

"Mediterranean" has replaced "Hellenistic" or "Graeco-Roman" as the "in" umbrella-term among those who are social-scientifically literate in NT studies,

13   Josephus, *Life* 66.
14   Josephus, *Antiquities* 18.106-108.
15   Crossan, *Historical Jesus*, 218-22.

largely due to the influence of Bruce Malina and the Context Group. I do not wish to deny the advantages of employing categories that will aid us in better understanding the social codes and values that were operative in cultures other than our own. As an instrument in historical investigation, however, it could become a very blunt tool indeed if it were to mean that all historical, cultural and social differences were to be obliterated. The issue surely is to find out how far generalized categories apply in particular contexts, or how far they must be modified (or abandoned entirely) in the light of contrary evidence. In terms of Crossan's Jesus the question is whether "Mediterranean" is more important than "Jewish" in the subtitle, and even more specifically whether *Galilean* Jewish does not introduce another dimension of particularity that will also have to be considered. Administrative Galilee did not reach the Mediterranean Sea, and indeed a culture that could describe its largest inland water complex as a sea rather than a lake suggests that its orientation was not directly toward the west.[16] The history of Judaism, especially in the land of Israel in the Second Temple period, was one of resisting any easy assimilation to the universal values that were then in circulation. Fergus Miller has drawn our attention to the ways in which the Semitic cultures of the East, including the Jews, adopted and adapted Hellenistic influences.[17] It was by no means a one-way process, nor did the older local indigenous people become absorbed in a pan-Hellenistic culture that shared a common ethos and value system. There are far too many examples—both ancient and modern, some heroic, some tragic—of resistance by the "little tradition" to the "great tradition." Certainly, if we are going to use the category "Mediterranean" for Jewish peasantry it will need to be refined and defined carefully. Anyone who has read Josephus's *Life*, for instance, must be aware of just how distinctive Jews in Galilee regarded themselves to be, even as they were participating in aspects of the larger world in their own midst, such as trade and commerce. The fact that archaeological data, especially coins, point to strong trading links between Tyre and Upper Galilee[18] no more means that a cultural continuum existed between this city and the Galilean rural hinterland, than that Arab traders who look for U.S. dollars today are thoroughly imbued with all aspects of American culture.

---

16 Gerd Theissen, "'Meer' und 'See' in den Evangelien: Ein Beitrag zur Lokalkoloritforschung," *Studien zum Neuen Testament und seiner Umwelt* 10 (1985): 5-25.

17 Fergus Millar, "Empire, Community and Culture in the Roman Near East: Greeks, Syrians, Jews and Arabs," *Journal of Jewish Studies* 38 (1987): 143-64; U. Rappaport, "The Hellenization of the Hasmoneans," in Menahem Mor, ed., *Jewish Assimilation, Acculturation and Accommodation: Past Traditions, Current Issues, Future Prospects* (Lanham: University Press of America, 1991), 1-13; Louis Feldman, "How Much Greek in Jewish Palestine?" *Hebrew Union College Annual* 57 (1986): 82-111.

18 Joyce Toby Raynor and Ya'akov Meshorer, *The Coins of Ancient Meiron* (Winona Lake: Eisenbrauns, 1988).

   Crossan's acceptance of Overman's view that Lower Galilee was urbanized proves to be an important step in the development of his argument.[19] Undoubtedly, Lower Galilee, especially around the lake, was more culturally mixed than was Upper Galilee/Golan, as has been shown by various archeological surveys.[20] This difference is no doubt attributable to the trading and other links that were possible in the Valley region as a result of the ease of communications between the various city territories and across the lake. These links provided a natural outlet for any surplus production as well as markets for the pottery and fish industries which we know were developed in Lower Galilee.[21] Not all of the region's cities, however, were the same. One must make a very clear distinction between the ethos in Caesarea Philippi, in autonomous cities such as Scythopolis, Tyre and Ptolemais, and the Herodian administrative centres of Sepphoris and Tiberias. As regards the former, relations were never far from strained, and clashes could easily erupt between the non-Jewish inhabitants and their Jewish neighbours.[22] Their avowedly Gentile ethos which can be documented from inscriptions as well as the literary sources marks them off as an essentially hostile environment for Jews. Sepphoris and Tiberias were different, however, and even though there probably were some non-Jewish elements in the population from the start, neither town shared the Gentile ethos of the autonomous cities, certainly not in the early part of the first century CE. Antipas was careful not to offend the Jews with his coinage, and he had no desire to propagate Gentile culture actively in the Jewish part of his realm. Despite the essentially Jewish ethos of these cities it is my conviction that the hostility shown to them by the Galileans according to Josephus's *Life* was not due to the circumstances leading up to the revolt but was inherent in the very nature of the relations of these centres with their rural environs. In sociological terms, despite their Jewishness, they were heterogenetic rather than orthogenetic, and their overall impact on Galilean peasant life must be judged accordingly.[23]

---

19 Andrew Overman, "Who were the First Urban Christians? Urbanization in First Century Galilee," in David J. Lull, ed., *Society of Biblical Literature 1988 Seminar Papers* (Atlanta: Scholars Press, 1988), 160-68.

20 Eric M. Meyers, James F. Strange and Dennis Groh, "The Meiron Excavation Project: Archaeological Survey in Galilee and Golan 1976," *Bulletin of the American Schools of Oriental Research* 230 (1978): 1-24; Dan Urman, *The Golan: A Profile of a Region during the Roman and Byzantine Period* (Oxford: Oxford University Press, 1985).

21 David Adan-Bayewitz, *Common Pottery in Roman Galilee: A Study of Local Trade* (Ramath Gan: Bar-Ilan University Press, 1993); David Adan-Bayewitz and I. Perlman, "The Local Trade of Sepphoris in the Roman Period," *Israel Exploration Journal* 40 (1990): 153-72; M. Nun, *Ancient Anchorages and Harbours around the Sea of Galilee* (Kibbutz Ein Gev: Kinnereth Sailing Co., 1988).

22 Josephus, *War* 2.457-65.

23 Seán Freyne, "Urban-Rural Relations in First-Century Galilee," in Lee I. Levine, ed., *The Galilee in Late Antiquity* (New York: Jewish Theological Seminary of America, 1992), 75-91.

Could these and other lesser centres have been the bearers of a popular Cynicism—that pervasive and quintessentially Mediterranean philosophy for coping with the inequalities of life within an agrarian society?[24] This is what Crossan's book strongly implies and it has been argued or assumed by a number of recent studies. In my view this is extremely unlikely, especially for the rural peasants. I agree with Gerald Downing that Burton Mack assumes too readily that Galilee was just the right kind of environment for the transmission of popular Cynic ideas.[25] Downing himself mounts an impressive case for a broad social basis for Cynic ideas in every place from the law courts to the street corners. His analysis of Q persuasively shows a strong Cynic influence in terms of both form and content—with a few important exceptions to be discussed presently. The core of his argument is that Cynic influence is so pervasive in early Christian writings (Mark, special Matthean material, James and 1 Thessalonians, as well as Q) that the most plausible explanation is that this influence emanated from Jesus himself, rather than that a Jewish Jesus was later "Cynicized" by different groups in various social settings. There are still enough gaps in our knowledge of the social milieu of Galilee to allow for a Cynic presence there at a popular level, to the extent that it was natural and possible to present "characteristically and distinctively 'Cynic-friendly' ideas and attitudes and practices" and that these were "readily communicable" in that setting.[26]

Downing's position is well-argued and nuanced. He is aware that there are counter-arguments but in his view they lack both the scope and the force of his own position. Yet Downing avoids any sweeping generalizations. He is aware of the tensions between town and country that might block an easy spread of "urban" ideas among country folk; he repeatedly refers to "the Jewish pallette," "older native Jewish influences" on Jesus, and the teaching material "unmistakably drawing its colour from Jewish sources." Thus, Downing is well aware of the distinctively Jewish dimension of the Jesus tradition. The question, then, is whether both strands—the Jewish and the Cynic—go back to Jesus and if so how that particular amalgam is best expressed in the light of all the circumstances. Will Jesus be seen as more "Jewish" than "Mediterranean"?

In my opinion it is unrealistic to assume that close proximity to an urban culture means that the population as a whole was likely to be imbued with the attitudes and values, alleged or real, of those centres. Why would certain strata of the population adopt those attitudes and values, and why would they abandon older ones? Those older values were, as I have argued elsewhere, grounded in

---

24 Crossan, *Historical Jesus*, 72-88.

25 F. Gerald Downing, *Cynics and Christian Origins* (Edinburgh: T & T Clark, 1992), 146 n. 7, referring to Burton L. Mack, *A Myth of Innocence: Mark and Christian Origins* (Philadelphia: Fortress, 1988), especially 72-74.

26 Downing, *Cynics and Christian Origins*, 148.

the Jewish theocratic ideal that was built on the realities of land, Temple and Torah.[27] As a result of the archaeological evidence, I am now dubious about my earlier views that an old Israelite presence was maintained in Galilee over the centuries. The pentateuchal traditions, however, did function to legitimate the inclusion of the northern regions within *Eretz Israel* once the possibility of a Jewish national state emerged under the Hasmoneans. Archaeology is helping to identify those sites in the Galilee/Golan where new Jewish foundations occurred in the late-Hellenistic period. The presence of ritual baths (מקוות), the nature of the art work and the absence of any signs of Gentile worship in Galilean Jewish sites of the first century (as distinct from the evidence from the surrounding city territories where several non-Jewish inscriptions have been found) all point to the essentially conservative nature of the Jewish settlements in Galilee (Upper and Lower) in religious terms even when the archaeological evidence points at the same time to trading links with those non-Jewish centres.[28] It is difficult not to see in this attachment to the Jewish way of life a legitimation for the peasants in terms of access to the resource of the land. Despite a Galilean-flavoured critique of the Jerusalem priesthood and its cult-centre (*1 Enoch* 14:18-22; 15:3-7),[29] when all was said and done, that cult-centre supported a symbolic universe which could on the whole rely on Galilean peasants' loyalty to the very end.[30]

It was in Jerusalem's interest to foster those links. The visits of scribes to Galilee described by Mark (3:22; 7:1) fit into a larger pattern of such visits by influential Jerusalemites such as Johanan ben Zakkai or the delegation sent to unseat Josephus in 66 CE. Synagogue remains from the pre-70 period are meagre for the whole country, but that does not obviate the presence of the synagogue as an institution of both prayer and instruction in first-century Galilee. Moreover, if Downing can point to second-century characterizations of Christians as Cynics as an argument for a trajectory going back to Jesus, then one is equally entitled to argue from the migration of Jews to the north in the wake of the Bar Cochba revolt that there was a Jewish trajectory in Galilee going back well beyond Jesus. Indeed the tensions between the rabbinic teachers and the synagogue leaders that are echoed in later Jewish writings suggest that the synagogue had had an independent life of its own in the region before the

---

27 See Seán Freyne, *Galilee from Alexander the Great to Hadrian, 323 B.C.E. to 145 C.E.: A Study of Second Temple Judaism* (Wilmington: Michael Glazier, 1980); and *Galilee, Jesus and the Gospels*.

28 Eric M. Meyers, "Galilean Regionalism as a Factor in Historical Reconstruction," *Bulletin of the American Schools of Oriental Research* 221 (1976): 93-101; Eric M Meyers, Ehud Netzer and Carol L. Meyers, "Sepphoris: Ornament of all Galilee," *Biblical Archaeologist* 49 (1986): 4-19.

29 George Nickelsburg, "Enoch, Levi, and Peter: Recipients of Revelation in Upper Galilee," *Journal of Biblical Literature* 100 (1981): 575-600.

30 Josephus, *Life* 63.

advent of the sages and was determined to maintain such a role for the ordinary people.[31] This phenomenon provides the context for Bruce Chilton's targumic studies, in which he finds echoes of what later came to be the Palestinian Targum in the language, content and style of Jesus' sayings.[32] Clearly, then, the Cynics had their competitors in the Jewish villages of Galilee.

Downing concedes one important element in the Q material that finds no parallel in the Cynic tradition: the notion of eschatological judgment (Q 3:17; 6:20-23; 10:12-15; 17:23-27), a theme, as is well-known, that is pervasive in Jewish apocalyptic writing. One might have expected that an apocalyptic, rather than a sapiential, understanding of Jesus' kingdom language would therefore have suggested itself to Crossan. Following Mack and others, however, and in line with the Cynic hypothesis generally, he opts for a decidedly this-worldly understanding of the kingdom as the one that would suggest itself most naturally to the peasants, "a kingdom of the nobodies and the destitute, a kingdom performed rather than just proclaimed."[33] Leaving aside the issue of the social situation of the peasants that this statement presupposes, one would have to query its probability in the light of the arguments just presented for a vibrant and conservative Jewish practice in Galilee, especially when an unlikely hybrid, Jewish Cynicism, has to be constructed in order to support such a claim. It is, of course, based on the analysis of Q that has now become almost standard, namely its division into a sapiential stratum followed later by an apocalyptic one,[34] and its interest in the present rather than in any future, other-worldly, kingdom. It would seem, then, that this interpretation of the kingdom is forced on Crossan as a result of his rigorous adherence to the stratification of the Jesus tradition, even though he has difficulty in finding the right label for the particular mix he thereby creates: "Call it, if you will, Jewish and rural Cynicism rather than Graeco-Roman Cynicism."[35] There are, however, no examples of this "rural Cynicism" that can be drawn on, but there *is* a tradition of proverbial wisdom from the ancient Near East which is much older than Cynicism, and had to do with trying to understand and cope with the vagaries of life, often with those of life in the country. Centuries earlier, the Jewish religious tradition had shown itself sufficiently flexible to be able to incorporate this tradition into its own theocratic framework, and the rabbinic writings

---

31 Lee I. Levine, *The Rabbinic Class of Roman Palestine in Late Antiquity* (Jerusalem: The Jewish Theological Seminary of America, 1985), esp. 38-42.

32 See, e.g., Bruce Chilton, *A Galilean Rabbi and his Bible: Jesus' Use of the Interpreted Scripture of his Time* (Wilmington: Michael Glazier, 1984).

33 Crossan, *Historical Jesus*, 292.

34 Largely based on the work of John S. Kloppenborg, *The Formation of Q: Trajectories in Ancient Wisdom Collections* (Philadelphia: Fortress, 1987), and the adoption of his hypothesis (for the most part) in the subsequent work of Mack and Crossan. [Eds.]

35 Crossan, *Historical Jesus*, 340.

indicate that it also was not incompatible with their world-view. Perhaps such a precedent might have suggested a more adequate framework for interpreting the presence of the sapiential elements in both Jesus' teaching and Q, while doing far greater justice to the Jewishness of both Jesus and Galilee. On the analogy of the international character of proverbial wisdom this would not at all preclude the inclusion of Cynic aphorisms—if such wisdom was in fact current in Galilee—but would place it within a comprehensively Jewish theocratic framework. To suggest that the Cynic world-view shaped Jesus' self-understanding would, in my opinion, be both theologically questionable and historically implausible.

Part of the problem has to do with the understanding of apocalypticism as being totally other-worldly and future-oriented, and therefore lacking an ethical impulse for the present. But as Chilton, Malina and others have recently emphasized from quite different perspectives, the distinction between present and future as it has become a received orthodoxy in New Testament scholarship (especially German) is a creation of our modern thinking rather than a genuine reflection of Jewish thought processes. Chilton in particular emphasizes the eschatological nature of the notion of the kingdom of God in the Targumim as referring to God's definitive, yet present, intervention on behalf of his people now.[36] Confirmation of this understanding comes from the very setting in which the Targumim functioned, namely the synagogue service, where the prayer—the eighteen benedictions—celebrated God's triumph over Israel's enemies as a reality that could be experienced now in and through cultic performance.[37] Surely this setting is as close as we can reasonably hope to come to an appreciation of how common people, even peasants, might have whetted their appetite for the arrival of God's kingdom. Even when one moves from this setting, where an eschatological understanding of God's rule in the present could be affirmed and experienced, to a more thorough-going apocalyptic symbolization of the event, the collection of Jewish apocalypses which now constitute *1 Enoch* shows how the circles in which this material was developed and transmitted could integrate this-worldly wisdom, Hellenistic cosmic

---

36 Bruce Chilton, "Kingdom Come, Kingdom Sung: Voices in the Gospels," *Forum* 3/2 (1987): 51-75.

37 See the important study of Thomas Lehnhardt, "Der Gott der Welt ist unser König: Zur Vorstellung von der Königsherrschaft Gottes im Shema und seinen Benediktionen," in Martin Hengel and Anna Maria Schwemer, eds., *Königsherrschaft Gottes und himmlischer Kult im Judentum, Urchristentum und in der hellenistischer Welt* (Tübingen: J. C. B. Mohr, 1991), 285-307, who shows that the central declaration of the synogogue liturgy, Deuteronomy 6:4, was interpreted in terms of God's kingship which was first experienced at the Red Sea (Exod 15:18). This connection provided the context for the association of the kingship of God and the acceptance of the requirements of the Torah in the rabbinic literature. Thus an eschatological and an everyday understanding of kingdom was quite feasible within a thoroughly Jewish context.

speculation, and varied expressions of the divine-combat myth. Far from being some utopian fantasy of the future, this synthesis was directly addressed to coping with the challenges that Hellenism as an economic and cultural force was posing even from within Judaism itself.[38] Philo of Alexandria and the Book of Wisdom are the Jewish witnesses that Mack and Crossan can adduce for their sapiential (i.e., Cynic-Stoic) understanding of the kingdom as applying to the individual who has achieved inner self-control through wisdom.[39] Yet even if one were to allow for such an intellectual understanding in certain circles in Galilee, the individual's participation in the world process is ultimately dependent on the creative and sustaining power of God, whereby he alone is king of the cosmopolis, and he is the one on whom all human kingship depends.[40] In other words, behind the Philonic philosophical expression of the individual wise person as king stands a thoroughly Jewish theocratic conception that cannot disguise its true parentage.

3. Jesus in a Jewish Galilee

My critical reading of Crossan's book has helped me to sharpen my understanding of how a Galilean setting and a more grounded Jewish Jesus would lead to a very different construal than that which a broadly "Mediterranean" perspective offers. It is my opinion that a less rigid approach to the question of sources and a greater attention to the real social world of Galilee has a better chance of doing justice to the historical Jesus, however inaccessible that figure may still remain. I now propose to develop my own alternative construal in a more positive way, once again treating first geography, then politics and finally theology.

3.1 Galilean Geography and Jesus

Taking the gospel narratives as a starting point, one is immediately confronted with the geography of Jesus' activities, especially their Galilean geography.

---

38 Martin Hengel, *The "Hellenization" of Judaea in the First Century after Christ*, trans. John Bowden (London: SCM, 1989), 45-52, with copious bibliographical references to the Hellenistic influences in Jewish apocalyptic literature in the notes; see also Margaret Barker, *The Older Testament: The Survival of Themes from the Ancient Royal Cult in Sectarian Judaism and Early Christianity* (London: SPCK, 1987), 83-103. Both texts show that ethical wisdom and apocalyptic kingship motifs were by no means incompatible.

39 Burton L. Mack, "The Kingdom Sayings in Mark," *Forum* 3/1 (1987): 3-47, especially 11-21; Crossan, *Historical Jesus*, 282-92.

40 See Naoto Umemoto, "Die Königsherrschaft Gottes bei Philon," in *Königsherrschaft Gottes*, 207-56; and James G. Williams, "Neither Here nor There: Between Wisdom and Apocalyptic in Jesus' Kingdom Sayings," *Forum* 5/2 (1989): 7-30. The latter directly addresses Mack's proposal in a manner with which I would concur, by suggesting that genres such as wisdom and apocalyptic were not pure types mutually excluding each other.

Much has been made of the symbolic intentions of the different evangelists in terms of their references to geography. Such symbolism need not, however, obliterate all actual reference, especially in a context in which the land and its different regions had definite religious associations from Israelite experience and history (see Isa 8:23). Yet when one compares the gospels' geography with the accounts of Palestine with which Roman writers such as Strabo, Pliny and Tacitus provide us, not to speak of Josephus and the rabbinic writings, there is a stark contrast. Despite various inaccuracies and confusions that are easily attributable to the absence of maps or any other technical aids, there is a far greater sense of place in these non-biblical writers and a keener interest in the natural resources.[41] Josephus has a very clear sense of boundaries, distances between various places and the length of time required for journeys between different destinations, as well as the topography of certain key sights—all information we would expect from somebody who had been active in the field as a military and political commander. In the rabbinic writings, on the other hand, geographical interests are directly related to halachic ordinances to do with the observance of tithing laws in terms of the provenance of various products. That these discussions were not purely academic emerges from such notices as that of Josephus concerning John of Gischala's exploitation of his co-religionists' desire to obtain native oil,[42] as well as the mosaic floor in the synagogue at Rehov in the Bethshean valley, which has a most detailed description of the borders of Israel in the north, especially the border between Tyre and Galilee.[43]

Despite the comparative vagueness of the gospels' geography, the evangelists are well-informed about the regional and territorial dimensions of Palestine. These facts, however, do not directly impinge on their story in terms of the natural resources of land, the political boundaries or the demands of religious *halacha*. Such a combination of informed background with the absence of any very immediate or explicit interest in details does not allow us to dismiss the geographical notices of the gospels as mere window dressing, but summons us rather to discern what precisely the intentions of these notices might be. For example, does the fact that Jesus is depicted as moving freely between Galilee and its environs reflect the situation in Mark's own day or does it tell us something about Jesus' own attitudes as they were remembered—and how might one go about answering such a question in historical terms? Even more intriguing is the question of why there is no mention of either Sepphoris or Tiberias, the former refurbished and the latter founded during Jesus' life-time,

---

41 Menachem Stern, ed., *Greek and Latin Authors on Jews and Judaism* (Jerusalem: Israel Academy of the Sciences and the Humanities, 1974-84), vol. 1, 305; vol. 2, 21.

42 Josephus, *Life* 74.

43 Jacob Sussman, "The Inscription in the Synagogue at Rehob," in Lee I. Levine, ed., *Ancient Synagogues Revealed* (Jerusalem: The Israel Exploration Society, 1981), 146-53.

and both playing such a significant role in the commercial and administrative life of Galilee, as Josephus makes abundantly clear.

The excursions of Jesus to outside territories in Mark are generally attributed to the evangelist's interest in Gentiles. There are, however, certain problems with this position from a purely historical perspective. On the assumption that Mark was written during or immediately after the Jewish War, easy movement between Galilee and the surrounding non-Jewish territories would be highly improbable. The insistence of the inhabitants of Tarichaeae that the refugee noblemen from Trachonitis should be circumcised[44] show just how fraught local relations were in that period. This is not surprising in the aftermath of the Jew/Gentile hostilities that had broken out in the territories of the Greek cities of Palestine immediately prior to the revolt.[45] In such a climate would Mark have presented a Jesus figure who seemed so indifferent to such tensions? Perhaps so. One can think of several reasons why such a presentation might have been significant at that juncture, especially if the gospel was directed to Christian communities in Galilee or southern Syria, as has been suggested. On the other hand, such a cavalier attitude to religious and social boundaries could only have been extremely provocative to Jews in the region.[46]

What if we were to think of such inter-regional movements some thirty years earlier? How well do they fit the situation then? Palestine, like other regions of the Mediterranean world, seems to have enjoyed the relative peace of Tiberius's reign. In Galilee, Antipas had political quarrels only with the Nabateans. The Phoenician city territories, the territory of Herod Philip and the Decapolis would all be accessible to Jewish traders and craftspeople, and the Herodian cities of lower Galilee were certainly less likely to be unfriendly to Gentiles than they were later. The archaeological data mentioned earlier is highly relevant here; recent analysis of common household pottery in the Roman period shows a thriving export industry of wares from Kefar Hanania to the surrounding cities, especially in the Golan, but also to Ptolemais and Caesarea Philippi. Significantly, however, no wares emanating from Galilee are found in sites south of the Nazareth ridge.[47] The presence of Tyrian coinage in upper Galilean sites points to commercial movement in that region also. In other words, both the political realities and the material remains make the kind of free movement between Jews and Gentiles in the north more plausible for the period of Jesus than for the period of Mark. The material remains show that while such movement was a fact of everyday life, religious and ethnic differences such as

---

44 Josephus, *Life* 113.

45 Josephus, *War* 2.457-65.

46 See Howard Clark Kee, *Community of the New Age: Studies in Mark's Gospel* (Philadelphia: Westminster, 1977); Ched Myers, *Binding the Strong Man: A Political Reading of Mark's Story of Jesus* (Maryknoll: Orbis, 1988).

47 Adan-Bayewitz, *Common Pottery in Roman Galilee*.

those operating between Jews and Samaritans did affect trading patterns. When the political and religious climate was right, Jews had long since learned how to live their traditional way of life among Gentiles and to deal with them on a daily basis. The hostility that operated between Jew and non-Jew in the Hellenistic city territories prior to the Great Revolt was another matter.[48]

These observations do not necessarily mean that Mark is describing things as they actually happened. The story of the Syro-Phoenician woman who came to Jesus is pre-Markan. However well it fits Mark's interest in Gentiles, he cannot remove the Jewish bias of the story which suggests that Jesus' interest in visiting such places was not to "go to the Gentiles," but rather to "the lost sheep of the house of Israel."[49] Such a conclusion would naturally depend on a much broader analysis of Jesus' intentions, but Mark's careful presentation of his visiting the territories and villages of the surrounding cities, but not the cities themselves, may point to the evangelist's awareness of the real purpose of such excursions. Mark also intimates that Jesus, despite his healing powers, was not welcome to the people of Gerasa, who on hearing of his successful exorcism of the "legion" of demons asked him to depart their territory (Mark 5:17). In other words, the Markan narrative does not totally dilute the Jew/Gentile divide in cultural as well as religious terms in its handling of Jesus' movements, even when we might assume that it was in its own theological interests to do so.

Such a conclusion only makes Mark's complete silence concerning Sepphoris and Tiberias all the more baffling. If the reason for the omission is the lack of success that Jesus had in such centres, we might have expected a series of woes against them similar to those expressed against Chorazin, Bethsaida and Capernaum. On the other hand, if Jesus was prepared to visit Gentile territories to address Jews living there, why exclude these cities from the ambit of his activities, since both were thoroughly Jewish in character in the first century, despite some minority Gentile presence? Reading the gospels with the complete picture of Galilee as the intertext, one suspects that the silence is not just an omission, but very deliberate. It seems impossible for anyone to have conducted the kind of activity attributed to Jesus in lower Galilee without having to encounter in some way these two Herodian cities and their spheres of influence. Perhaps a consideration of the political and economic roles of these centres will help to explain the enigma that our geographic considerations have thrown up.[50]

---

48 Aryeh Kasher, *Jews in the Hellenistic Cities in Eretz-Israel* (Tübingen: J. C. B. Mohr, 1990), especially 268-87.

49 Theissen, *Gospels in Context*, 61-80.

50 See my "Jesus and the Urban Culture of Galilee," in Tord Fornberg and David Hellholm, eds., *Texts and Contexts. Biblical Texts in their Textual and Situational Contexts: Essays in Honour of Lars Hartman* (Oslo: Scandinavian University Press, 1994), 597-622.

3.2 Antipas and Galilee

Our discussion of the geographic realities of Jesus' activities as they are reflected in the gospel narratives raises the question of the Herodian cities of Lower Galilee in a particularly acute manner. The usual ways of posing the question of Jesus' relation to Sepphoris are in my view far too simplistic, focusing as they do on the psychological or personal impact that growing up beside such a centre, or possibly plying his trade there as an artisan (τέκτων), might have had on him.[51] To pose the question in this way is to fall into the 19th-century Liberal trap of psychologizing Jesus. What is forgotten is that both centres were new foundations, and as such they symbolized and embodied rapid social change in Galilee as a whole under Antipas.[52] Such a claim might appear to be unwarranted in view of Antipas's rather phlegmatic character as it comes across in the gospel portraits, especially Luke's, and because Josephus does not give the same detailed account of his reign as he does of his father's. Antipas had hoped to succeed his father. Foiled in that hope, he was all the more likely to have thrown himself into the task of proving himself to the Romans, never relinquishing the hope of kingship. Indeed, the expression "residence of a sovereign" (αὐτοκρατορίς) as applied to Sepphoris and the calling of Tiberias after the emperor shows how much he kept Roman imperial patronage in his sights. Rome allowed him a personal income of 200 talents, in the collecting of

---

51 Richard Batey, *Jesus and the Forgotten City: New Light on Sepphoris and the Urban World of Jesus* (Grand Rapids: Baker, 1991), although attractively presenting some of the recent archaeological evidence for Sepphoris, assumes but does not prove that close association with a place means sharing its ethos and values. Equally, Overman, "Who Were the First Urban Christians?" and Douglas Edwards, "First-Century Urban/Rural Relations in Lower Galilee," in David. J. Lull, ed., *Society of Biblical Literature 1988 Seminar Papers* (Atlanta: Scholars Press, 1988), 169-82, and "The Socio-Economic and Cultural Ethos of the Lower Galilee in the First Century: Implications from the Nascent Jesus Movement," in Lee I. Levine, ed., *Galilee in Late Antiquity* (New York/Jerusalem: The Jewish Theological Seminary of America, 1992), 53-73, although using the evidence (especially the gospels) more critically, are both in danger of operating with the same assumptions. The classic expression is that of Shirley Jackson Case, "Jesus and Sepphoris," *Journal of Biblical Literature* 45 (1926): 14-22.

52 I wish to express my thanks to Chris Seeman, who shared with me his Masters thesis from the University of California at Berkeley: "The Urbanization of Herodian Galilee as an Historical Factor Contributing to the Emergence of the Jesus Movement." This impressive study has helped me to appreciate more clearly the importance of these centres as new foundations pointing to far-reaching social changes of a rapid nature in Galilee. See also my "Herodian Economics in Galilee: Searching for a Suitable Model," in Philip Francis Esler, ed., *Modelling Early Christianity: Social-Scientific Studies of the New Testament in its Context* (London: Routledge, 1995), 23-46. (Note also the work of Jonathan L. Reed, "Population Numbers, Urbanization, and Economics: Galilean Archaeology and the Historical Jesus," in Eugene H. Lovering, Jr., ed., *Society of Biblical Literature 1994 Seminar Papers* [Atlanta: Scholars Press, 1994], 203-19, especially 214-18. [Eds.])

which he had need of a well-disciplined, loyal and efficient administrative bureaucracy—tax-collectors, notaries, judges, military personnel, store and market managers—in short, a whole range of retainers, who could ensure that he and his court would reap the full benefits of a relatively fertile region within an agrarian economy. Antipas's reign, therefore, marked the rapid development of the Galilean economy along lines that were directly opposed to the Jewish patrimonial ideal, as this had been enshrined in the Pentateuch, upheld by the prophets and re-enacted by reformers such as Nehemiah (Neh 5:1-11).

Sepphoris and Tiberias shared a common ethos as administrative centres whose population was that of the retainer class for the most part, without excluding wealthy landowners as a native aristocracy. Josephus paints a picture of the mixed character of the population of Tiberias at its foundation—people from every quarter and background being brought together either by force or with blandishments of gifts of land in return for loyalty to Antipas,[53] thus presumably violating Jewish law not merely in terms of building the city on a burial ground, but also in forcibly appropriating the land of others. When Josephus arrived in the region in 66 CE he was confronted with a combination of Herodian land-owning residents with estates across the lake; various officials at the Herodian court such as Justus of Tiberias, a man well-educated in Greek ways; and the service classes, "sailors and destitutes," as the aristocratic Jerusalemite describes them.[54] The trappings of a Greek city ($\pi\acute{o}\lambda\iota\varsigma$), with its council ($\beta\text{o}\upsilon\lambda\acute{\eta}$) and chief magistrate ($\check{\alpha}\rho\chi\omega\nu$), should not disguise the fact that Tiberias had a subordinate position within the Herodian administrative framework from the outset. Even that role had been diminished when Nero transferred it to the territory of Agrippa II in 54/5, thus ceding primacy in banking, market and other administrative functions to its rival Sepphoris, something that Justus bemoans. It would be a mistake to think of either place being on a par with other cities in the environs where the epithet "free and autonomous" meant much more in developing their own ethos and life-style. It was only in 66 that Sepphoris struck its first coins and Tiberias had to wait until 100 CE, that is, after the end of the Herodian dynasty, before it enjoyed the same privilege by favour of Trajan.[55]

Since land was the primary resource in antiquity generally, and in Galilee in particular, the issue of Herodian land policy is crucial to the case being argued here. The question is whether or not there was an appreciable move away from small family-run holdings in which reciprocity was still the basic mode of exchange, toward a situation of land use as a revenue-generating resource. In previous studies I have maintained that on the basis of the literary

---

53 Josephus, *Antiquities* 18.36-38.
54 Josephus, *Life* 32-38.
55 Ya'akov Meshorer, *City Coins of Eretz Israel and the Dekapolis in the Roman Period* (Jerusalem: The Israel Museum, 1985), 33, 36.

evidence (Josephus, the gospels, Jewish writings and the Zenon papyri) land-ownership patterns in Galilee were mixed, including both large estates such as Beth Anath and small, family-run holdings that were part of the traditional Jewish ideal (1 Macc 14:10; cf. Neh 5:1-11).[56] Undoubtedly, pressure had been exerted on these latter since the onset of the Hellenistic age, as increased taxation and narrow yield margins left the small landowner increasingly vulnerable. Once a person was caught in the situation of having to borrow money, thus mortgaging their holding, it was extremely difficult for them to recover.[57] The *Similitudes of Enoch*, which most commentators date to the Herodian period, reflect this situation in their repeated condemnation of "the kings, the governors, the high officials and the landlords" (*1 Enoch* 38:4; 46: 3-5; 48:8; 53:5; 62), and in their insistence that the holy and just ones will "possess the earth." Clearly, the reality was that pressures on peasant ownership had increased considerably. Recently David Fiensy has produced the most up-to-date study of the topic of land-ownership in Herodian times in which he challenges my views about the persistence of the small landowning class on the basis that the evidence does not allow us to decide between ownership of land and leasing. Yet later in the same work he acknowledges that the small landowners bore the brunt of the tax burden, which was considerable.[58] To some extent the issue is academic in this context, as on either reading of the evidence the tension between two very different systems was real and growing.

The intensification of the market which is represented by the emergence of Sepphoris and Tiberias as administrative centres within an agrarian economy brought about considerable changes in the lives of Galilean peasants. In such a climate it is the small landowner who is most vulnerable since there is no protection built into the system to guard against a bad harvest, illness or some other catastrophe.[59] By contrast, leaseholders may be fortunate enough to be protected by a benign landlord in a culture where magnanimity was a pivotal value in the context of patron-client relationships. Archaeological evidence suggests that the single holdings were not large—an average of six to nine acres has been estimated—and hence there was little possibility of increased output

---

56 Freyne, *Galilee from Alexander the Great to Hadrian*, 156-70; *Galilee, Jesus and the Gospels*, 155-67.

57 Benjamin Isaac, "The Babatha Archive: A Review Article," *Israel Exploration Journal* 42 (1992): 62-75, esp. 72, notes that in the village of Engedi there was both crown property and private property side by side. Document 11 from the cache relates how a centurion stationed in the town had made a loan of 60 denarii of Tyrian silver to a local Jewish resident who pledged his courtyard should he be unable to repay the loan. Fortunately in this case the borrower was able to do so, according to documents 19 and 20, suggesting somebody engaged in commercial activity rather than farming.

58 David Fiensy, *The Social History of Palestine in the Herodian Period* (Lewiston: Edwin Mellen, 1991), 55-57.

59 Moses I. Finley, *The Ancient Economy* (London: Chatto and Windus, 1973), 108.

through more intense labour or specialized production.[60] In all probability, many engaged in mixed farming (vines, olives, grain) in an effort to meet the family's basic dietary requirements. The demands of the tribute, other taxes and religious dues had first to be met, and in the case of grain crops the following year's seed requirements had to be set aside. This meant scarcity for domestic use, with low nutrition resulting in a high incidence of illness and infant mortality.[61] In such conditions the reciprocal system of exchange with its in-built concerns for all members of the extended household or clan is more favourable to the poor than is the market economy which functions in favour of the ruling elite and to a lesser extent their administrative retainers. The tensions between these two types of economic systems and the increasing dominance of the latter in Herodian Galilee were likely to generate the social situation that many gospel parables depict: day labourers, debt, resentment of absentee landlords, wealthy estate owners with little concern for tenants' needs, exploitative stewards of estates, family feuds over inheritance, etc. In these vignettes we catch glimpses of both systems in operation and the clash of values inhering in their co-existence, a topic we shall presently address.

In light of this picture we can readily understand the hatred that the Galilean peasants displayed for both cities in 66 CE. Crossan's analysis has helped considerably in sorting out what happened then, and the mediating role that Josephus played in Galilee.[62] In Judaea/Jerusalem the Zealot takeover turned what was at first a political rebellion under the control of the aristocracy into a social revolution that turned the lower classes, clergy and laity alike against the ruling priestly aristocracy. A similar situation also existed in Galilee, except that the aristocracy was, for the most part, Herodian rather than priestly, and beneath them the upper echelons of the retainer class were equally hated. In this situation the Jerusalemite, Josephus, was able to mediate between the rival factions, acting as a broker between them until Vespasian put an end to both the rebellion and the possibility of social revolution. But that was in 66 CE and many things had changed in Palestine since the twenties, when the intensification of the social changes associated with the development of an agrarian market economy came to Galilee, disrupting older relationships and the values associated with them. Such changes were clearly and unambiguously embodied in the two urban foundations, which from the start must have been

---

60 See Fiensy, *Social History of Palestine*, 94-96, who gives a table of the various estimates, based on current archaeological evidence.
61 For an excellent account see Gildas H. Hamel, *Poverty and Charity in Roman Palestine: First Three Centuries C.E.* (Berkeley: University of California Press, 1990), especially chap. 3, "Causes of Poverty: Physical Environment and Human Labor," 94-141; also Douglas Oakman, *Jesus and the Economic Questions of his Day* (Lewiston: Edwin Mellen, 1986), 57-72.
62 Crossan, *Historical Jesus*, 193-96.

experienced as heterogenetic by the peasant population in a way that Jerusalem was not, despite that city's frequent exploitation of peasant loyalties to its cult centre. Since the Jesus movement's rise coincided with the emergence of Sepphoris and Tiberias in this role and since Jesus appears to have adopted a deliberately negative attitude to both, at least as his activity is described in the gospels, we are surely provided with the most immediate and specific setting in which to understand the movement's appearance and strategy.

3.3 Jesus in the Galilean Social World

The argument in the preceding section is that coincident with the arrival of the adult Jesus in Galilee from the Jordan, or wherever, there were obvious signs present of an intensification of market-oriented agricultural production, sharply at odds with the Jewish theocratic ideal. This older ideal still continued to appeal to many, especially the Galilean peasants, despite the erosion of its vision and its basic values among the ruling, priestly elite. Josephus, who himself came from that elite background, makes no attempt to hide this stark reality.[63] It could well be that there were already in Galilee those who were critical of the Jerusalem cult-centre and its priesthood. But they certainly do not appear as an organized circle or network within the region in the way that the Essenes had functioned in Judaea. It is only in the Jesus movement that we find such an organization. The task now is to show that it was with an essentially Jewish understanding of history and from a decidedly Jewish hope of restoration and renewal that Jesus and his movement mounted their critique of both value-systems, Herodian and theocratic alike. I do not believe that what began as a set of insights for coping with life (which is what Cynicism of a popular kind essentially was, *pace* Crossan's best efforts to make it capable of generating an organized counter-cultural life-style[64]) could have been transformed into the kind of apocalyptically-inspired renewal movement with a radical social agenda in such a short space of time, and with only the memory of a discredited teacher of aphorisms to inspire it.

In the first part of this paper I argued that kingdom language and imagery addressed to peasants in Galilee was much more likely to have been received in Jewish eschatological terms than in the purely Cynic mode that Crossan and others have claimed, irrespective of how one seeks to introduce a Jewish colouring to what was in essence a decidedly un-Jewish world-view. The levels of practice and attachment to the Jewish theocratic ideal were too vigorous and too developed for such a diluted version to have had any wide-scale currency, least of all among the peasants. The social setting I am now proposing as most

---

63 Josephus, *Antiquities* 20.181, 206-10.
64 E.g., Crossan, *Historical Jesus*, 128.

immediate and significant for the historical Jesus' activity (as distinct from the setting of Q or *Thomas*), namely, the need to resist the changing values and attitudes represented by the rise of Sepphoris and Tiberias, requires, it seems to me, something other than a strategy for coping with life, though of course in many instances, in the ancient as well as in the modern world, that is all that is possible. If we are going to use material as well as cultural factors in our attempt to explain (as distinct from merely to describe) the Jesus movement and its emergence in this particular place (Galilee, not Judaea or Idumea) and at this particular time (the reign of Antipas rather than 66 CE), then we must attempt to show how its strategy and approach fit into the totality of life in that society and how precisely it was aimed at alleviating the perceived condition of alienation resulting from the new developments under Antipas. Which of the following alternatives was likely to be better news for Galilean peasants threatened with loss of land and the kinship values associated with it, without any redress: to hear that if they honoured what was best they would be like kings, and would have the freedom "to dare to be different,"[65] or to be reassured that the advent of God's reign which was occurring now in their midst (ἐντὸς ὑμῶν of Luke 17:21) would mean the reversal of all the dominant values which were currently destroying their lives at every level? The former merely accepts the *status quo* and hopes to alleviate its most baneful effects; the latter calls for envisioning the world differently. It is the dramatic suddenness of the changes which were occurring in their midst that in my opinion called forth the latter rather than the former understanding as the more adequate way of addressing the situation.

How did Jesus propose to confront this situation in the light of his kingdom language and praxis? Crossan's open commensality is a good place to start. There can be no doubt of the radical social dimensions of such a programme. Its real point, however, is lost, or at least considerably weakened, unless we locate it in a social world in which its political implications are seen in all their immediacy. To espouse table fellowship with tax-collectors and sinners (which probably should be taken to mean women[66]) is not just to incur the condemnation of those whose program is based on Temple purity, but rather throws down the gauntlet to the very institutions on which the current repressive system was based in terms of both its patriarchal value-system and retainer class structure. As a result of his meals with such "undesirables," Jesus was accused of being a winebibber and a glutton, a friend of tax collectors and sinners (Luke 7:33; Matt 11:18). Such an accusation takes on its full vilificatory force only when it is heard against the critique by orthodox Jewish circles of the Herodian

---

65 This is Mack's approximation of what kingdom language in the Cynic mode would have meant on the lips of Jesus ("The Kingdom Sayings in Mark," 17).

66 Kathleen Corley, *Jesus, Women and Meals in the Synoptic Gospels* (Peabody: Hendrickson, 1993), 103-108.

court. According to Josephus one of the complaints of the Jewish delegation in Rome seeking an end to Herodian kingship had to do with the bribery and corruption of those sent to collect the tribute and the corruption of their wives and daughters in drunken orgies.[67] Such an ethos is at least evoked by the legendary story of Antipas's birthday, with its local Galilean colouring (Mark 6:21-28). Thus, as a way of discrediting him, Jesus' religious opponents accuse him of subscribing to the value-system of the Herodian life-style. For such a charge to have any power it had to have some basis in fact. In the same context, however, Jesus aligns himself very definitely with John the Baptist, by unfavourably contrasting "those who are clothed in fine garments" and are to be found in "the houses of kings" with the desert figure, John the Baptist, possibly his own mentor. Theissen's identification of the reed of Tiberias with Antipas gives real political point to Jesus' encomium of John,[68] despite their own contrasting strategies: John's ascetic life in the desert, and Jesus' traveling through the villages and subtly undermining the Herodian value system by sharing inclusive meals with both the peasants (including the womenfolk) and the retainers (Luke 7:24-28, 31-35; Matt 11:7-11, 16-19). According to Fritz Herrenbruck, retainers enjoyed positions of high status and wealth in Palestine, as well as being integrated socially and religiously into Judaism.[69] The tax collectors, however, whom Jesus was likely to encounter in the Galilean towns would not be from the upper echelons of their profession; those would have been found in Sepphoris and Tiberias. By bringing together these two different strands of the Galilean population who were disaffected in terms of the prevailing ethos, Jesus was not fomenting an atmosphere of hatred and hostility toward Sepphoris and Tiberias. His struggle in the name of God's kingdom had to be directed elsewhere, namely, to those for whom it was good news to hear that that kingdom had come now and that it was the very antithesis of human kingship, based on lording it over others.

One could also read the evidence concerning Jesus' attitudes to possessions, money and the family in a similar vein. The very founding of Tiberias and the allotment of land to the inhabitants must have meant some displacement. Similarly, the pressure on the private landowner meant the break-up or diminution of the small holdings, leading to the intra-family feuding about property and inheritance rights that are echoed in the parables of Jesus. For those who were exposed in this way to the harsh realities of life and who had the will to resist there were few enough options open—from landowning or leasing or day-labouring, to slavery or banditry. All of these possibilities remained within the existing structures. Not even banditry, which was the most

---

67 Josephus, *Antiquities* 17.304-309; *War* 1.511.
68 Theissen, *Gospels in Context*, 26-42.
69 Fritz Herrenbruck, "Wer waren die 'Zöllner'?" *Zeitschrift für die neutestamentliche Wissenschaft* 72 (1981): 178-94.

violent response to the unequal situation, had any alternative to put in its place, but was simply reactive.[70] By contrast, Jesus' vision of shared goods and rejection of the normal securities, including money, which apart from land was the most important commodity in the market economy, although utopian in its intention, did provide an alternative vision. This vision viewed the world of human relations, based on status maintenance, in a very critical light and instead allowed for oppressors and oppressed to relate as equals. In proposing such an ideal Jesus was not seeking to revert to the *status quo ante* for Israel as stated in the Pentateuch, but was operating within the prophetic framework of adapting the received tradition to the demands of a new situation, and doing so in the name of God's final prophetic word to Israel.

A similarly radical stance can be discerned in his dealing with the crisis facing the family within the new situation. Thomas Carney has remarked that the family unit bonded by factors other than economic ones is singularly ill-equipped for the market-economy which calls for specialized skills and the maximization of resources.[71] Under such pressures kinship values can easily be eroded. Josephus, relying as he was on his status as a Jerusalem priest to win the support of the Galilean country people, repeatedly appeals to kinship (ὁμοφυλία) in order to appease their hostility toward the Jewish retainer class in Sepphoris and Tiberias, with, it must be said, only limited success. Jesus, by contrast, challenges the absolute nature of kinship values, which can of course legitimate great inequalities, proposing instead an ideal of community based on love, forgiveness and shared reciprocity. Once again one can detect a subtle, yet firm, critique of the prevailing patriarchal family structure, which was one of the cornerstones, not just of the Herodian vision, but also of the theocratic systems that were competing with each other in Palestine generally, and specifically in the Galilee of Jesus. Family imagery and values are appropriated to the new, fictive social configurations that were emerging around Jesus and in his name, even as he refused to endorse certain aspects of the existing family reality, recognizing instead that adherence to his way would be disruptive of those set patterns, with their economic and social rootedness in the past.

Not everybody in Jesus' putative audiences or who benefited from his healing was ready for such a message. The threat to land ownership was real and the signs of rapid change were now very tangibly emanating from the new cities. Yet as long as a tenuous link could be maintained with the old ways, many were uncertain about the new—at least such a radically new—vision. The Galilean peasantry, who in 66 CE were still prepared to bring their tithes to Josephus and his colleagues and support him rather than any native person as

---

70 Richard A. Horsley, "Bandits, Messiahs and Longshoremen: Popular Unrest in Galilee around the Time of Jesus," in *Society of Biblical Literature 1988 Seminar Papers*, 183-99.

71 Thomas F. Carney, *The Shape of the Past: Models and Antiquity* (Lawrence: Coronado, 1975), 149-51.

leader, show how powerfully the old symbol system of Temple and land still functioned. An idealization of the destitute and a declaration that in the new economy theirs was the kingdom of heaven was only likely to resonate on any large scale with those who were already destitute. The relative failure of the Jesus movement as an inner-Galilean Jewish renewal movement must be judged not only in terms of the absence of any clear evidence, archaeological or literary, of a widescale Christian presence there in the first century, but also in terms of the extent to which the Herodian and the theocratic systems, each vying with each other for control of the resources, were still in place in 66 CE.

My starting point in the gospel narratives does not require the existence of Q, at least in the refined form in which modern North American scholarship has been able to identify this putative document and the group for whom it functioned as a foundation myth. Yet I do have to acknowledge that the sayings tradition came to the evangelists by some channels and circulated independently in others also—Q, *Thomas*, the *Apocryphon of James*, oral traditions. Since John Kloppenborg's stratification of Q is the currently-accepted one among most scholars, I am happy to explore how his profile might correlate with my proposals in light of the social situation that I have postulated for Jesus. Kloppenborg does not seek to identify his earliest sapiential stratum directly with Jesus—in contrast, for example, to Harnack's vision of Q. It represents a studied production within a known sapiential genre. Thus, we can see in Q a stage at which the Jesus tradition was already shaped by various factors, social as well as theological (the words of Sophia incarnate), within a circle of "petite bourgeoisie." These figures are to be identified with village administrators rather than the rural peasants. The social disruption caused by the transfer of political jurisdiction in Galilee under Nero in the fifties would have represented difficulties for this class and affected their social standing; it is these circumstances that can be discerned in their shaping and transmission of the Jesus material which they had inherited. The apocalyptic element in Q comes at the stage in which this group, who originally had no need to create social boundaries, now feels the need to do so because of pressure from their rejection by the local Pharisees.[72] Although Kloppenborg does not suggest this, the circumstances immediately prior to the revolt and the anti-Jewish feelings in the surrounding city territories might have been the catalyst for this second step in the Q-people's social formation.

The situation envisaged in this scenario represents a rather different stage in the social transformation of Galilee than that which Jesus encountered in the twenties. I have maintained that Jesus' message was addressed both to landowning peasants (the majority of the population of lower Galilee) and to the

---

72 Kloppenborg, "Literary Convention." See also his "'Easter Faith' and the Sayings Gospel Q," *Semeia* 49 (1990): 71-99.

lower levels of the retainer class. I have claimed that his message was eschatological in tone ("after whom there would be no other," as Ben Meyer puts it) and apocalyptic in inspiration, involving a total renewal of the social order based on a reversal of the existing value-system. In contrast, the situation envisaged by Kloppenborg—the need to cope with changing fortunes within a particular class—is not quite so drastic. In my opinion a radically transformative statement about what was called for would have been required if Jesus had any hope of receiving a hearing across the class divisions and in light of the different social pressures under which each lived. If Q as reconstructed by Kloppenborg indicates that some of the lower retainer classes were attracted to Jesus' social program, including its Cynic-sounding elements, thereby causing dissension in their own ranks (i.e., with the Pharisees), Josephus's *Life* would seem to suggest strongly that most of the land-owning peasants, despite their hostility toward the Herodian centres, were not so impressed. No doubt the call to abandon all, trusting the gracious providence of God, proved to be a stumbling block for those who already experienced that care while holding on to their own plot of *Eretz Israel*. The Jesus tradition had retained a memory of Jesus' refusal to take on the role of popular kingship in Galilee, when the ordinary people expected this from him in view of his words and actions (John 6:14-15 and possibly Mark 6:45). Perhaps it was this refusal and the rejection of the violence that it would have involved that caused the disillusionment of the country people with Jesus. Someone who had established his authority among them as prophet, healer and teacher and who in the name of God's kingdom had proposed a radically different life-style and set of values, might have been expected to engage in military action.[73] Jesus' refusal to do so explains at once his avoidance of the cities, and the failure of the country peasants to heed his proposal. Since his message was grounded in his own experience as a religious charismatic, it was to another urban centre that he directed his gaze, Jerusalem, the cult centre that continued to have such a hold on the village people of Galilee, despite its co-operation in the oppressive economic value-system represented by the Herodian centres in their midst.

If the Jesus movement does not appear to have attracted widespread popular support among the peasantry, despite the social role of his healing acts, what of the attitude of others within the social hierarchy? Overt opposition in Galilee seems to have emanated in religious rather than political circles, and that might appear to weaken my case for seeing the Herodian value-system as Jesus' primary target. Nevertheless, the Herodians and the Pharisees are linked together more than once in Mark's account in deciding to kill him and as representing an alliance dangerous for his followers (Mark 3:6; 8:15; 12:13). Despite the avoidance of Sepphoris and Tiberias it can scarcely have been a

---

73 See, e.g., Josephus, *Antiquities* 17.271-72; *Life* 66-67, 134-35.

matter of Jesus being on the run constantly from Herodian aggression, as Luke seems to suggest (Luke 13:31). The fate of the Baptist shows that one could not hide forever, even from Antipas. There would be nothing incompatible about Herodian retainers also belonging to the scribal class or being adherents of Pharisaic ideals.[74] Perhaps, then, opposition that appears to be religious is in fact politically inspired as well. True, Jesus' words and actions were directed at the peasants in the villages, whose loyalties to the Temple, we have argued, were still largely intact. It was they who were under the greatest pressure from the new economic developments and it was among them that he might have hoped for the most enthusiastic response. Inevitably, then, his opponents came not primarily from the Herodian elite but from those religious elements whose status with the people was most threatened by his presence. This would explain why the most serious charge against him in a Galilean setting is religious, namely the charge that he was in league with Beelzebul because of his healings. According to Mark, the charge came from Jerusalem-based scribes, whereas Matthew attributes it simply to Pharisees (Mark 3:22; Matt 12:24). That such visits represented the formal control of the Jerusalem Sanhedrin over Galilean affairs has been challenged recently by James McLaren, who argues that the existence of a permanent council or Sanhedrin in charge of strictly Jewish affairs throughout the country may well be a perception drawn from later sources.[75] This would not preclude visits by influential Jerusalemites such as Johanan ben Zakkai on their own initiative, but the situation in 66 CE of a formal appointment of a representative governor would have been exceptional. This would mean that internal Galilean factions were the real opponents of Jesus, even if Mark wants to have the opposition coming from Jerusalem as part of the Galilee/Jerusalem tension which structures his gospel. As a professional class, the scribes were local village officials who would have known at first hand the real impact of Jesus' presence and would have been opposed to it as undermining their own status within the theocracy and their accommodation with the Herodian establishment. The role of a popular healer/exorcist/teacher was inevitably viewed with suspicion, especially in a climate in which religious authority was highly structured, exclusively patriarchal and centralized. Characters such as Hanina ben Dosa and Jesus were either domesticated or vilified. What made Jesus' behaviour particularly threatening was the fact that it was performed in the name of Israel's God, whose kingly rule, he declared, was already breaking into history and manifesting itself in the new social configurations that he sought to establish. These violated the strictly-defined internal boundaries of the Israelite community based on the purity laws which

---

74 Anthony J. Saldarini, *Pharisees, Scribes and Sadducees in Palestinian Society* (Edinburgh: T. & T. Clark, 1988), esp. 284-87.

75 James S. McLaren, *Power and Politics in Palestine: The Jews and the Governing of their Land 100 BC-AD 70* (Sheffield: JSOT, 1991).

were legitimated by the Jerusalem Temple. Thus, Jesus' Galilean actions could be seen as an attack on "this house" (*Thomas* 71), which did not have to await the incident in Jerusalem to be seen by the more astute as threatening to the religious elite.

4. Conclusion

I do not expect that my account will win over many Cynics or doubting Thomases. I have, however, been able to identify my differences with Crossan. These differences primarily concern my interest in recognizing the distinctive ethos of Galilee and the social transformation that was occurring there during the reign of Antipas. It is this situation which provides the best context for explaining the emergence of the Jesus movement and the particular form of social critique that it embodied. For me this perspective has the advantage of taking seriously the Galilean indicators of our narratives, by attempting to follow the historical trajectories that they suggest. One should not minimize the difficulties inherent in such a construction in view of the many gaps in our knowledge of that society. The dangers of creating a social world to fit our own perceptions of the main character are all too obvious. Nevertheless, the use of archaeological as well as literary evidence can help to ground our best guesses. The value of such an exercise is that it also grounds Jesus' career in a particular historical and social context (contemporary liberation theologians have shown us how *theologically* important that insight is).

My hunch is that Crossan's Jesus and my own are not total strangers. His is perhaps more witty, more enigmatic and less socially engaged, although definitely counter-cultural. Does that say something important about the two of us, I ask myself. There is, however, a more deep-seated difference between us, I suspect, that has emerged in my insistence on the Jewishness of Galilee and the eschatological intent of Jesus' kingdom talk. I believe that there are good historical reasons for both claims. The theological implications of those claims interest me now. My insistence on the eschatological nature of Jesus' career arises from my concern regarding the claims to ultimacy that Christian faith makes in terms of Jesus. Such a claim is offensive to the modern mind, but then nobody—least of all Jesus or Paul—ever said that Christian claims should be inoffensive. In the absence of an eschatological dimension to Jesus' utterances it would be impossible to see how any christological claims could be grounded in his earthly life, which is precisely the issue that gave rise to the quest for the historical Jesus in the first place as both an ecclesial and an academic exercise. Even if Christology can be grounded in the earthly Jesus, the adequacy of its contemporary formulation will have to be debated in the light of feminist, liberationist, ecumenist and other critiques of the Christian tradition. The claim to ultimacy for those who call themselves Christian, however, cannot be abandoned in any critical retrieval. By the same token it is difficult to imagine how an adequate political and ethical agenda could be formulated in the name of Christian faith without the connection with the historical Jesus being maintained, since that connection points directly to the earthly career of Jesus in its radical engagement in the struggles of the oppressed as an integral part of Christian faith itself.

My second concern, to maintain and affirm the Jewishness of Jesus, is likewise theologically motivated, even if at first sight it might seem to be at odds with the case I have just argued in regard to the ultimacy of Christian faith-claims. To water down the Jewishness of Galilee and thereby to deny the Jewishness of Jesus not only has the potential for anti-Semitism, as Walter Grundmann's 1941 book on Jesus the Galilean shows,[76] it also involves a refusal to acknowledge that the Christian understanding of God is grounded in the Jewish religious experience. With the collapse of the classical forms of theistic belief and without any replacement possible in our postmodern climate, the Jewish understanding of God which Christians share has an important contribution to make in the current debilitating climate that passes for Western culture. To attempt again to experience a sense of God, active within history, hidden and mysterious, yet present and living, a God who suffers because it is God's nature to care, to care ultimately about the whole of God's creation, especially its most fragile and broken elements—to retrieve such an understanding of God is for me what is ultimately at stake in a Jewish Jesus. In our post-Auschwitz humility, when Christians want to continue to claim the ultimacy of Jesus, it is the ultimacy of the God of Jesus that they are affirming, not another God who supersedes this God of Israel. The dangerous memory of the Galilean Jesus, engaged as he was in a kingdom-praxis within the very concrete confines of his own social world, ensures that that God is never reduced to a metaphysical abstraction, but is always again to be discovered in the midst of human need, especially when authentic human community is threatened by ideologies of greed or power.

In declaring what is at stake for me theologically in the quest for the historical Jesus, I run the risk of destroying the credibility that my historical reconstructions may merit. Yet I am convinced that the present "third wave" quest for the historical Jesus is no more free of presuppositions than any of the other quests that went before it. Nor could it be otherwise, no matter how refined our methodologies. If we are all prepared to say at the outset what is at stake for us in our search for Jesus—ideologically, academically, personally—then there is some possibility that we can reach an approximation to the truth of things, at least for now. Even that would be adequate.

---

76 Walter Grundmann, *Jesus der Galiläer und das Judentum* (Leipzig: Georg Wigard, 1941).

7. Socio-Rhetorical Interests: Context

Willi Braun

Historical-Jesus research is much like any other historical research: an operation that retrospectively tries to describe and disseminate a present perception of some exempla—events, activities, persons—located in the past. Historians, including Jesus historians, are not detached and isolated technicians of a positivistic data-gathering craft that would merely dust off and present the past with the greatest possible semblance to how it actually was. Influenced by postmodern shifts in historiographical sensibilities, Jesus historians are becoming increasingly aware that the "past" is not just sitting back there, ripe and waiting to be plucked; the "past" is pliable and subject to shaping by the historian, as Albert Schweizer demonstrated with abiding instructiveness nearly a century ago. The "past" (the historical Jesus) is selectively identified from items in an "archival" record; by applying complex value judgments and evidentiary standards, these items are then counted as evidence or assigned a factual status; the valued items, now counting as evidence or facts, are then interpreted in relation to each other by some explanatory schema of coherence and meaning generated by the creative intellectual activity of the historian. *Et voilà*, an image of the past (the historical Jesus) is put in place.

Each of these constructive operations—selection, valuation, explanation—of representing the past, however, is deeply embedded in the contemporary social, institutional and disciplinary settings that furnish the historian not only with the motivations and aims but also with conceptual and analytic tools for "doing history" in the first place.[1] The historical Jesus would hardly exist as a figure of continuing interest, most certainly not in the reshapable and displaceable forms he has taken on in the history of Jesus research, apart from the socio-political and intellectual warrants for his existence that are inherent in the modern discourse about the historical Jesus. It is this insight that is behind Jonathan Z. Smith's claim that "there is no primordium—it is all history."[2] And, insofar as the shape of the "past" (the historical Jesus) is a lever in

---

[1] This reciprocal embedding and shaping of "past" and "present" in historical description is a basic feature of socio-rhetorical criticism, a model of analysis articulated best by Vernon Robbins. For a succinct description of the model, see Vernon K. Robbins, "Social-Scientific Criticism and Literary Studies: Prospects for Cooperation in Biblical Interpretation," in Philip Francis Esler, ed., *Modelling Early Christianity: Social-Scientific Studies of the New Testament in its Context* (London: Routledge, 1995), 274-89; cf. Robbins, *Exploring the Texture of Texts: A Guide to Socio-Rhetorical Interpretation* (Valley Forge: Trinity Press International, 1996), and *The Tapestry of Early Christian Discourse: Rhetoric, Society and Ideology* (London: Routledge, forthcoming).

[2] Jonathan Z. Smith, *Imagining Religion: From Babylon to Jonestown* (Chicago: University of Chicago Press, 1982), xiii.

negotiating the terms of modern discourse, the "past" (the historical Jesus) is also a rhetorical category and tool. As for the ancient Athenian orators, "history . . . become[s] rhetoric,"[3] proof-by-exemplum in discourse whose general economy turns in large part on the desire to elicit persuasion for and assent to its own cosmotrophic or soteric interests.[4]

The three essays in this section may be seen both as exhibiting and as commenting on the complex and ambiguous relationship between the Jesus of history and the scholars' Jesus who is made and remade in the history of talk about Jesus. None of the papers offers a new and complete image of the first-century Galilean Jesus. Nor is that their aim. Rather, they deal more with the ways scholars have gone, and perhaps ought to go, about the business of Jesus research and what is at stake in the various approaches taken. Gregory Bloomquist and Wendy Cotter set their focus on specific dossiers of the earliest traditions about Jesus and reassess their evidentiary value either for our description of "Jesus' historical consciousness and/or aims" (Bloomquist) or for disclosing their claims within a first-century Mediterranean world-view (Cotter). In Halvor Moxnes' essay, the way the historical Jesus is approached becomes the focal topic of self-conscious analysis; the essay is a commentary on the cultural situations in which the recently-surging spate of Jesus research (the "third quest") is located, on how these situations are productive in redescriptions of the past (Jesus) and what interests these redescriptions might serve in the present.

1. Bloomquist: Is Jesus Hidden Behind a Rhetorical Stance?

Gregory Bloomquist's gambit is to destabilize the widely-operative view in Jesus research that the historical Jesus can be identified and described from sayings and actions that scholars have more or less consensually attributed to him. Drawing on classical and modern theories and methods of rhetorical analysis, Bloomquist's central argument is this: once we have uncovered the sayings and actions of the historical Jesus by means of the most reliable tools for doing so, we may not yet have before us data that disclose an accurate

---

3   Ian Worthington, ed., *Persuasion: Greek Rhetoric in Action* (London: Routledge, 1994), 127.

4   I am here alluding both to Jonathan Z. Smith's statement that "religion," for which we might substitute "Jesus," is the result of the imaginative activity in "the scholar's study" (*Imagining Religion*, xi), and to Gregory Alles's suggestion that this imaginative activity is manipulative, i.e., rhetorical. Imaginative manipulation, Alles further suggests, is either *cosmotrophic* (from τρέφειν, "to sustain or nurture"), supporting the present "order of things," or *soteric*, negating and wanting to overturn the established order of things (Gregory D. Alles, *The* Iliad, *the* Ramayana, *and the Work of Religion: Failed Persuasion and Religious Mystification* [University Park: Pennsylvania State University Press, 1994], 104-106).

picture of who Jesus really was. Rather, between the saying and the real character who said it may stand a figure who speaks in the guise of an assumed rhetorical persona who has learned the arts of rhetorical self-presentation by means of speech and social gestures. Specifically addressing John Dominic Crossan's recent life of Jesus as a Mediterranean Jewish peasant,[5] Bloomquist asks if the "peasant" Crossan has constructed may in fact not be a peasant at all, but someone—an anti-urban urban intellectual, Bloomquist suggests— deliberately taking on the speech and social gestures of the peasant for rhetorical purposes.

The question is imaginative and Bloomquist has shrewdly chosen his sample saying (Q 6:20, the blessing of the poor) on which to test his question. He demonstrates well that in Mediterranean rhetorical practice, espousals of the ideal of poverty and valorizations of the poor are neither a reliable guide to the socio-economic status of the rhetor nor necessarily telling that an argument on the blessedness of the poor is aimed at a poor audience; his audience may just as well have been the economically and politically well-positioned Jewish elite—in which case, Bloomquist suggests, the aim of the rhetorical Jesus may have been to shame and cajole the custodians of the "upper structures of power in Hellenistic Judaism" to give up their patterns of "abusive patronage" and adjust their political, economic and social activities in accordance with the values of Jesus' romantic-pastoral social vision.

Readers will have to judge if the "rhetorical Jesus" can be kept alive on the evidence and arguments Bloomquist provides and, if so, what is at stake for how we (including Bloomquist himself) imagine Jesus and his message. The image of Jesus as a rhetor is deeply consistent with the rhetorical culture that marked Mediterranean societies of his time. It is equally consistent with the manner in which the early followers of Jesus exerted their claims about him.[6] The argument thus has an immediate kind of appeal as a corrective to the tendency to immunize Jesus from the rhetorical practices of his day. But Bloomquist's agenda appears to include more than making a corrective point on methodology. His freshly-minted "rhetorical Jesus" is currency that allows him to bid for a reticently-stated proposition: to move Jesus out of the company of Crossan's peasants and their peasant-empowerment project (the "brokerless Kingdom of God") and into the company of Virgil, Luke and other urban elites

---

5   John Dominic Crossan, *The Historical Jesus: The Life of a Mediterranean Jewish Peasant* (San Francisco: HarperSanFrancisco, 1991).

6   See Burton L. Mack, *Rhetoric and the New Testament* (Minneapolis: Fortress, 1990); Burton L. Mack and Vernon K. Robbins, *Patterns of Persuasion in the Gospels* (Sonoma: Polebridge, 1989); Vernon K. Robbins, "Progymnastic Rhetorical Composition and Pre-Gospel Traditions: A New Approach," in Camille Focant, ed., *The Synoptic Gospels: Source Criticism and the New Literary Criticism* (Leuven: Leuven University Press/Uitgeverij Peeters, 1993), 111-47; and Robbins, *Tapestry of Early Christian Discourse*.

for whom "the poor" are allies in arguments for adjusting—but not eliminating—the patronage-client system and its systemic need for the poor.

2. Cotter: What Do the Miracle Stories Claim About Jesus?

Wendy Cotter's reassessment of the claims of the Jesus miracles begins on the assumption that miracle stories presume a cosmology—an image of the physical architecture of the universe that locates the realms of the gods and human beings, and structures the modes of contact between them. By the first century, indeed considerably earlier, the classical Greek and Ancient Near Eastern model of the three-tiered structure of the universe, in which humans and gods lived in relative proximity to each other in the middle (earthly) enclave and met each other in designated "sacred" spaces (mountain, temple, civic or national cult), was outdated. A new image of the universe's structure, the Ptolemaic cosmos, had replaced the old model in the popular conception of cosmic architecture.

The reasons for re-imagining the cosmos were multiple and make an interesting story in themselves, but for the purpose of appreciating Cotter's essay, it is important to know that this cosmic remodelling in the early Hellenistic era was linked to the perceived emigration of the gods from the earthly realm to their now distant retreat in the ethereal, superlunar regions of the cosmic sphere. Left behind in the terrestrial, sublunar regions and separated from the superlunar gods by a chasm of cosmic space patrolled by elemental and demonic powers, humans had to fend for themselves in the chancy "anthropologized"[7] muck of life under the moon.[8]

A primary challenge imposed by this new cosmology and the absence of the gods was thus the need to redraw the links between humans and gods or, to use terms Cotter prefers, to re-imagine the transcendence-immanence connection. This singular challenge was met in diverse ways, ranging from the rational piety of the philosophers, the secret initiations of the mystery cults, gnostic myths of salvation, to a variety of popular divination practices.[9] Increasing burden was placed on religious specialists, mediator figures who functioned as mobile brokers between human groups and the gods.[10]

---

7 Jonathan Z. Smith, "The Temple and the Magician," in his *Map is not Territory: Studies in the History of Religions* (Chicago: University of Chicago Press, 1978), 187.

8 See Ptolemy, *Tetrabiblos* 1.2.1; and Luther H. Martin, *Hellenistic Religions: An Introduction* (Oxford: Oxford University Press, 1987), 6-10.

9 See Georg Luck, *Arcana Mundi: Magic and the Occult in the Greek and Roman Worlds* (Baltimore: Johns Hopkins University Press, 1985). The most coherent description of the great variety of Hellenistic religious practices is provided by Martin, *Hellenistic Religions*. In addition to providing an introductory-level survey of "the profuse religious data" (155), Martin argues that common assumptions and principles organized the profusion of practices; he thus speaks of Hellenistic religions "as system" (155-63).

10 Smith, *Map is not Territory*, 187-88, describes one of the effects of the change in cosmology as the shift from a fixed site (sacred place) of access to the divine to a mobile site (religious specialist).

It is against this "cosmological backdrop" and its religious challenges that Cotter explains the significance of the Jesus miracles. This move allows her to criticize two of the major commentary traditions on early Christian miracle stories, and it permits her to recontextualize these stories' claims within analogous and therefore comparative material from Graeco-Roman sources roughly contemporary with the Christian stories. Her analysis results not only in a corrective description of how the miracle stories, although often appropriating ideas and images from the Jewish scriptures, relate to the Roman culture in which these stories arose, but also in diminishing their oft-supposed testimonial value concerning early Christian apocalypticism and, of emphasized concern to Cotter, in a revision of their claims concerning Jesus' relationship to divinity.

Although Cotter does stress the authorizing function and propaganda value of miracle stories, she does not describe or locate either of these functions with precision. Readers may well ask if all early Christians were equally drawn to the narrative-rhetorical genre of miracle story as a means of identifying Jesus and themselves and, if so, why to this genre and not to others. Vernon Robbins recently argued that thaumaturgic rhetoric, although "deeply embedded in Hellenistic-Roman discussions and traditions about what it is possible and impossible for gods to do,"[11] proceeds from more *specifiable* values and takes a more *particular* cultural stance than Cotter's essay brings to light. A few years earlier, Burton Mack attempted to link the production and use of miracle stories to the social-formational needs of a particular group of Galilean Jesus people for whom a "miracle gospel" served as a means of articulating its own social values against competing Jewish and Graeco-Roman norms.[12] These socio-rhetorical studies of the Jesus-miracles thus are part of the modern project in which Wendy Cotter's article profitably participates.

3. Moxnes: Jesus-Study as Self-Study?

When Albert Schweizer ended his exposé of the "roll-your-own Jesus" efforts reflected in the 19th-century Lives, he paused wishfully to project that in the future Jesus would not be someone to whom "the religion of the present" would ascribe "its own thoughts and ideas."[13] Historical description, he thought, is too determined by the cultural givens of the historian's location, so that the description of the historical "other" ends up a replication of the describer.

---

11 Vernon K. Robbins, "Interpreting Miracle Culture and Parable Culture in Mark 4-11," *Svensk Exegetisk Årsbok* 59 (1994): 74.

12 Burton L. Mack, *A Myth of Innocence: Mark and Christian Origins* (Philadelphia: Fortress, 1988), 208-45.

13 Albert Schweitzer, *The Quest of the Historical Jesus: A Critical Study of its Progress from Reimarus to Wrede*, trans. W. Montgomery (New York: Macmillan, 1968 [1906]), 398-99.

Jesus, therefore, can only be domesticated, not encountered, by historical inquiry. Encounter, thought of as an intersubjective meeting, is "direct" and attributable to "a mighty spiritual force [that] streams forth from Him and flows through our time also."[14] In retrospect, Schweitzer's distinction between historical description and religious encounter preoccupied and set the shape of the "new quest," as Halvor Moxnes points out in his essay, and signalled increasingly deliberate divorce proceedings between theology-driven and history-based approaches in Jesus research.[15] Has this divorce been finalized in the output of recent ("third quest") Jesus scholarship? If so, and Moxnes does not appear to think it has, what are the intentions and interests behind the latest stage of historical-Jesus scholarship?

This is one of the central questions that Moxnes pursues in a style more interrogative than assertive. He observes that "theological issues" and "theological intentions" are less dominant in the third quest, but he also points out, referring to Crossan's charge, that "history" and "biography" nonetheless may be disguised categories of and sites for a religious quest for a meaningful Jesus. The intellectual and institutional loyalties of current Jesus scholars may not be as obviously linked to official church theologies, but this does not mean that these scholars are not engaged in implicit theological commentary and rhetoric, whether cosmotrophic or soteric. As other essays in this volume show, the stakes and consequences are usually not a matter of indifference.

Another issue threaded through Moxnes' commentary concerns the "emphasis on methodological awareness" coupled with "a growing methodological diversity" that marks current scholarship. He does not offer a full explanation of the reasons for and nature of this awareness, nor ask if and how methodological awareness and diversity might be related, although he advocates the former and is not much troubled by the latter, perhaps reflecting his own hermeneutical stance that prefers particular locality over universality, both for Jesus and the Jesus historian. His bare comments on this issue are nonetheless important, for they imply a host of other questions having to do with historiography (writing the "other") itself and so link Jesus scholarship to intensely debated questions in the history of religions generally.[16] Moxnes' essay may not fully identify all of these questions, but it does enough to effect a reason for pause to think about what constitutes a history/life of Jesus, why one would want to continue to participate in the recovery of the historical Jesus and what interests one serves or criticizes in so doing.

---

14 Schweitzer, *Quest of the Historical Jesus*, 399.
15 This has its parallel in the increasing divergence, in this century, between theological and history-of-religions approaches to the study of religion generally, culminating in "the great divorce" between them. Alles, *The* Iliad, 158, attributes the announcement of this divorce to Joachim Wach.
16 See, e.g., Alles, *The* Iliad; and Ernest Gellner, *Postmodernism, Reason and Religion* (London: Routledge, 1992).

8. The Rhetoric of the Historical Jesus

L. Gregory Bloomquist

1. Introduction

In her recent book, *On Looking into the Abyss: Untimely Thoughts on Culture and Society*,[1] Gertrude Himmelfarb takes on contemporary deconstructionism and postmodern scholarship, which she sees as celebrating relativism and anarchy over the search for truth. This criticism is tendered not because such scholarship recognizes that any historical work is "necessarily imperfect, tentative and partial," but because it celebrates partial and imperfect truths and thus denies reality and truth itself.[2] Himmelfarb argues that contemporary postmodern historiography has lost sight of the goals of accuracy and knowledge, and has replaced these goals with imagination, inventiveness and creativity, resulting in a blurring of the lines between history and fiction.[3] She further notes that in the postmodern understanding all historical texts are "indeterminate and contradictory, paradoxical and ironic, rhetorical and metaphoric."[4] According to Himmelfarb, this understanding leads to a state of affairs in which any event can be relativized. For her, the schools of historiography that aim at an understanding of everyday life or private life may be able to convey what "normal" life looked like in a period, but cannot get at the more deeply-rooted questions of good and evil which underlie these events.[5]

I would certainly agree with Himmelfarb that much postmodern historiography errs on the side of a denial of facticity *per se*. To this extent, it is important to heed Himmelfarb's words of caution. I would also contend, however, that it is precisely the imaginative attention that can be paid to the "rhetorical and metaphoric" nature of, in this case, statements *of* Jesus that will in fact lead us to a better and more truthful understanding of the historical figure of Jesus. In fact, it is precisely the lack of this imaginative approach that leaves the study of the historical Jesus confined to the ideological and theological pseudo-history of positivism.

2. Thesis

There is an assumption that underlies much historical-Jesus research, that once we have discerned the *ipsissima verba Jesu* or even, by the criterion of

---

1   Gertrude Himmelfarb, *On Looking into the Abyss: Untimely Thoughts on Culture and Society* (New York: Alfred A. Knopf, 1994).
2   Himmelfarb, *Into the Abyss*, 134-35.
3   Himmelfarb, *Into the Abyss*, 138-41.
4   Himmelfarb, *Into the Abyss*, 140.
5   Himmelfarb writes specifically on the way in which the Holocaust can be undermined in terms of the enormity of evil involved by looking at the "normal" life that was going on at the same time (*Into the Abyss*, 142-61).

coherence, the content of Jesus' words and/or deeds, we will have then obtained an accurate picture of the historical Jesus. I would argue, however, that while we can indeed obtain some critical certainty regarding the words and even deeds of the historical Jesus, these selfsame words and deeds must then be understood in terms of how the Jesus of history wanted to present himself. The historical Jesus' words and deeds do not give us a picture of the historical Jesus but rather a picture of the *rhetorical* Jesus.

3. Method

The axiom upon which this study is based is that historical-critical study of early Christian literature is able, at least to some extent, to cut through the layers of built-up tradition in order to arrive at the probable words and deeds of the historical Jesus. These findings are in themselves inadequate in order to understand the historical Jesus, since their end result will primarily be the words and deeds of the rhetorical self-presentation of Jesus. A subsequent, necessary step in historical-Jesus study will be to examine the resulting findings in order to determine the rhetorical significance of these words and deeds as their necessary and immediate interpretive context.

In order to examine and support this contention successfully, the following steps are necessary. First, I would need to show that there is in fact a difference between a rhetorical figure and an historical figure in antiquity. Second, I would need to take a sampling of those words and deeds that are consensually agreed to be those of Jesus in order to provide a body of material for analysis. Third, I would need to examine the conclusions arising from a study of this list and note whether scholarship has in fact taken into consideration the problem of the rhetorical Jesus in light of these words and deeds. Fourth, I would need to note the probable rhetorical self-presentation that is elicited by those words and deeds. Finally, I would need to draw conclusions concerning the possible agreement or dissonance between the rhetorical and the historical Jesus.

Given that the above method is impossible to carry out fully in a brief essay, I will limit my work here to one text rather than to the sampling of texts that would make this work more convincing. As such, what I present here should be viewed as a "testing of the waters" or a "sampling of a sampling," not as a final, scientific product. I will discuss one relevant parallel situation from which historical-Jesus research can profit in terms of the overall presentation of the problem, namely, the question of the historical and rhetorical Socrates; and I will take one text which is agreed by both conservative and radical scholars to have been uttered—in some form—by the historical Jesus: the blessing of the poor in Q 6:20[6] and *Thomas* 54.

---

6   Q texts are cited by Lukan versification.

4. Exegesis

4.1 The Historical and the Rhetorical Socrates

4.1.1 The Sources for Our Knowledge of Socrates

Two, probably three, different presentations exist of Socrates. First, there is the highly unfavourable but contemporary portrait of Socrates given by Aristophanes, largely in the *Clouds*, first produced in 423 BCE (almost 25 years before Socrates' execution). Second, there are the highly favourable but late portraits of Socrates given by Plato and Xenophon. Were we to ask in terms of the popular understanding which picture of Socrates is that of the historical Socrates, the average person and even many classicists would of course adduce the posthumous picture drawn of Socrates by Plato. To think of Socrates as a scoundrel and rhetorical cheat grates on our Western sensibilities. Thus, A. R. Lacey's question is indeed pertinent: "do we judge our conception of Socrates by what we find in the sources or do we judge the sources by what we think we already know about Socrates?"[7]

The point is crucial for our purposes, for we need to ask where we would be more likely to find authentic words and deeds of Socrates: in the earlier, contemporary depiction or in the later, possibly mythified depiction? While it is fair to say that we do not have a favourable contemporary who gleans Socrates' words for us, it is also the case that an unfavourable contemporary such as Aristophanes would have his words subject to public scrutiny and investigation. Plato in his dialogues and Xenophon in his history (both of whom, although later contemporaries of Socrates, assert that they knew him[8]) portray Socrates as the preeminent, wise teacher of the day,[9] a far cry from Aristophanes' buffoonish presentation, and do so on the basis of his words ("Socratic discourses"[10]), although it is believed that Socrates himself, like Jesus, wrote nothing.[11]

4.1.2 Assessing the Evidence for our Knowledge of Socrates

How do we then assess the sources by which we in fact know all that we know of Socrates? How do we determine what Socrates actually said and what he

---

7   Alan Robert Lacey, "Our Knowledge of Socrates," in Gregory Vlastos, ed., *The Philosophy of Socrates: A Collection of Critical Essays* (Garden City: Doubleday, 1971), 22.

8   Xenophon, *Memorabilia* 3.6.1, in which Plato is also mentioned.

9   See Lacey, "Socrates," 22-49; 31-32 n. 19, deals with other testimonies to Socrates from antiquity.

10   But are these discourses historical or literary *genera* of the day (Lacey, "Socrates," 32)?

11   Lacey, "Socrates," 22-25.

actually meant? One school of historiography argues *prior melior* (earlier evidence is better evidence). According to this school, Aristophanes' account of Socrates as rogue ought to be accepted as the historical one because it is the only one that is contemporary with the man himself. Such accounts would be written "from a fresh memory and for an audience familiar with Socrates himself and before any tradition could have arisen of the 'Socratic discourse' as a literary genre that could take liberties with history."[12] Thus, there are those who find in the contemporary portrait of Socrates given by Aristophanes, especially in his comedy *Clouds*, an accurate picture of the historical Socrates. Another school of historiography points out that, while Aristophanes' picture of Socrates is contemporaneous with the historical Socrates, it need not, for that reason alone, be an accurate picture of the historical Socrates. This school might be called the *prior melior ad propriam* (early evidence is indeed better evidence . . . for authorial bias on the part of the observer). Accordingly, since the earliest contemporary accounts of Socrates may stem "from non-philosophers or those out of sympathy with Socrates,"[13] they are in actual fact better witnesses for the historical reality of those biases than for an accurate picture of the historical Socrates.

In the case of Socrates, there is good reason to argue that this latter school (*prior melior ad propriam*) ought to be given more credence than the school for which earlier utterances and deeds are necessarily better and more objective evidence (*prior melior*) for pointing to "what actually happened." There are good grounds for skepticism regarding Aristophanes' contemporary portrayal of Socrates, even if that contemporary portrayal echoes certain words or deeds of the historical Socrates. First, in terms of the comedic style of the day, Aristophanes himself presents us with his own agenda in his portrayal of Socrates. Historians are rightly skeptical of biased arguments, even when they are contemporary. Second, it is unclear whether the Aristophanic Socrates is in fact the "final" Socrates. It is possible that *Clouds* depicts an earlier, less mature Socrates.[14] Third, we do not know whether Socrates himself was Aristophanes' target or whether he suffered from guilt by association. It is possible that Aristophanes was not attacking Socrates but "the subversive tendencies of the Sophistic movement, the apparent absurdities of Ionian 'science,' or just 'long-haired intellectuals' in general."[15] Fourth, even if Socrates himself was Aristophanes' target, Aristophanes may have captured Socrates in comedic spirit in terms of Socrates' own agenda as it was perceived

---

12 Lacey, "Socrates," 25.
13 Lacey, "Socrates," 25.
14 This position is discussed by K. J. Dover in his introduction and commentary, *Clouds* (Oxford: Clarendon, 1968), xlix.
15 This suggestion is discussed by Dover, *Clouds*, xlix-l, and by Lacey, "Socrates," 25-26.

by the Athenians of his day, namely, the subversion of traditional Athenian values.[16]

There is also a fifth possibility that has been overlooked, namely, that Socrates may well have presented himself rhetorically in such a way that he was pictured accurately by Aristophanes (as one who subversively called attention to a decadent society) but that he did so for reasons that Plato best adduces in his portrayal of Socrates (to exalt justice). If this is the case, then in actual fact it would be Plato's later picture of Socrates that more accurately grasps the historical Socrates, understood in terms of the rationale behind his rhetorical self-presentation, as well as his other intentions, underlying character, genius and social embodiment. What allows us to make this conjecture? It is well known that public speaking and public writing came under the heading of rhetoric,[17] and that there were many different schools of rhetoric. From all reports, both favourable and unfavourable, we are aware that Socrates was known as a rhetor. Perhaps, then, the difference between the two presentations of Socrates concerns how he is perceived to have used his rhetoric.

4.1.3 Implications for the Study of the Historical Jesus

It is not inappropriate at this point to ask a pertinent question regarding studies of the historical Jesus. While we can safely talk of rhetoric in the case of Socrates, can we talk of rhetoric in the case of Jesus? There is obviously no definitive answer to this question. What we can say for the moment is that there is no *a priori* reason why Jesus may not have engaged in some deliberate rhetorical self-presentation.

We can then ask whether, although many studies of the historical Jesus assume the *prior melior* position regarding Jesus' statements, there is not a danger in taking authentic words of Jesus as they were heard and remembered by his contemporaries as indications of the historical Jesus—in other words, of his intentions, social embodiment and underlying character. Instead, they should perhaps be taken as rhetorical self-portrayals of Jesus, meant to project his historical intentions in a way that is only decipherable once the rhetoric has been understood. Furthermore, if there is in fact something to the contention that Jesus' rhetorical self-portrayal took shape in the form of a kind of Cynicism,[18] then we shall have further evidence of his attempt to make a public statement in the rhetoric not only of speech, but also of action and dress. In order to examine this possibility further, I will look at one logion generally

---

16 A position discussed by Dover, *Clouds*, 46-49.

17 See Benjamin Fiore, "Rhetoric and Rhetorical Criticism," in David Noel Freedman *et al.*, *The Anchor Bible Dictionary* (New York: Doubleday, 1992), vol. 5, 710-19.

18 See, for example, Burton L. Mack, *A Myth of Innocence: Mark and Christian Origins* (Philadelphia: Fortress, 1988); "Q and a Cynic-Like Jesus" (in this volume).

considered to be a statement by Jesus himself, with the assumption, not that this gives us immediate access to Jesus, but rather that it gives us immediate access to his rhetorical self-portrayal.

4.2 An Utterance of the Historical Jesus: The Blessing of the Poor (Q 6:20 and Thomas 54)

4.2.1 General Agreement on the Historicity of this Saying

Conservative scholars do not doubt that the statement found in Luke 6:20 (par. Matt 5:3) reflects a statement made by the earthly Jesus. The famous English evangelical preacher, D. Martin Lloyd-Jones, argued that the words stemmed from the experience of the incarnate Jesus ("It is the God-Man speaking"), who, in his life, acts out of this experience.[19] Furthermore, according to Lloyd-Jones, there is no difference between the two expressions of this utterance, with Matthew 5:3 giving the essential meaning of Luke 6:20. Or again, while Robert Guelich understands "the Sermon on the Mount . . . , above all, in terms of its role in Matthew's Christological portrait,"[20] he also argues that "the Beatitude to *the poor* and the theme of Isa 61:1 are part and parcel of Jesus' earthly ministry. . . . Both the Beatitude and the application of Isa 61:1 to Jesus have their most natural *Sitz im Leben* in his ministry to *the poor* rather than in early Christian prophecy."[21] Furthermore, Guelich strives to show that, while at first reading Matthew's version of the beatitude might be construed to be more spiritual, this is not the case.[22] Finally, among conservative scholars, I. Howard Marshall, whose commentary stands out for its technical and scholarly mastery,[23] suggests that the Lukan beatitudes are different from those of Matthew—although the two different traditions behind Matthew and Luke possibly go back "to two separate, but closely related traditions of the teachings of Jesus"[24]—and stand closer in some way to the historical Jesus. According to Marshall, "by his addition of the woes and various small modifications Luke has brought out the social concern inherent in the message of Jesus."[25] Noting

19 D. Martin Lloyd-Jones, *Studies in the Sermon on the Mount* (Grand Rapids: Eerdmans, 1960), vol. 1, 50.
20 Robert A. Guelich, *The Sermon on the Mount: A Foundation for Understanding* (Waco: Word, 1982), 25.
21 Guelich, *Sermon*, 71-72. In so concluding, Guelich quotes favourably E. Percy, *Die Botschaft Jesu: Eine traditionskritische und exegetische Untersuchung* (Lund: Gleerup, 1953), 108.
22 Guelich, *Setting*, 75.
23 I. Howard Marshall, *The Gospel of Luke: A Commentary on the Greek Text* (Grand Rapids: Eerdmans, 1979).
24 Marshall, *Luke*, 247.
25 Marshall, *Luke*, 246.

that the concern expressed in Luke 6:20 is "one of the constant themes of the message of Jesus" and "is in no sense a limitation of the promise of salvation to a specific circle of people," Marshall thus takes to task Ernst Bammel's denial that this beatitude is an authentic saying of Jesus.[26] Marshall does suggest, however, that the historical Jesus did not speak here about poverty as such, but rather about the poverty or homelessness of "those who are ready to be persecuted for the sake of the Son of Man," namely, the disciples.[27]

On the other side of the theological and ideological divide stands the work of Rudolf Bultmann and that of the Jesus Seminar. Bultmann considers several Q logia (6:20-21; 7:22b-23; 10:23-24; and 12:8-9), including this one, in all likelihood to be authentic sayings of Jesus. He can affirm this based on the claim that these logia are clearly not the result of apocalyptic fancy but the "original utterances of a prophetic personality."[28] In the case of the Jesus Seminar, the "blessing of the poor" found in Q 6:20 and *Thomas* 54 is also considered to be an authentic statement of the historical Jesus.[29] In fact, the statement "Congratulations, you poor!" received the Seminar's "second highest weighted average of all the sayings attributed to Jesus."[30] Furthermore, in commenting on this Jesus logion, the authors state that "there is no question about Jesus' consorting with the poor, the hungry and the persecuted. He announced that God's domain belonged to the poor, not because they were righteous, but because they were poor. This reverses a common view that God blesses the righteous with riches and curses the immoral with poverty."[31]

---

26 Marshall, *Luke*, 249, noting E. Bammel, "πτωχός," in Gerhard Kittel and Gerhard Friedrich, eds., *Theological Dictionary of the New Testament* (Grand Rapids: Eerdmans, 1968), vol. 6, 906.

27 Marshall, *Luke*, 249.

28 Rudolf Bultmann, "The Study of the Synoptic Gospels," in F. C. Grant, ed. and trans., *Form Criticism: A New Method of New Testament Research* (New York: Harper, 1962), 56-57, cited in Barry W. Henaut, *Oral Tradition and the Gospels: The Problem of Mark 4* (Sheffield: JSOT, 1993), 39. According to Henaut, Bultmann is too quick to leap to his conclusion that the logion Q 6:20 must be from the historical Jesus. In his view, "the beatitude form (Q 6.20-21) is not unique to Jesus, nor is the concern for the poor and hungry." Henaut implies that the statement in Q 6:20 could be the product of "the theological world of Q, Matthew, Luke, and Thomas."

29 David Aune notes that, of the fifteen aphoristic beatitudes in the canonical Gospels and the thirteen in *Thomas*, there is only one beatitude that is paralleled in the two bodies of literature, namely, Q 6:20 and *Thomas* 54 (Henry Wansbrough, ed., *Oral Tradition and the Aphorisms of Jesus: Jesus and the Oral Gospel Tradition* [Sheffield: JSOT, 1991], 227-28). Aune also points out that the logion is found in Polycarp, *Phil.* 2:3.

30 Robert W. Funk, Roy W. Hoover and the Jesus Seminar, *The Five Gospels: The Search for the Authentic Words of Jesus* (New York: Macmillan, 1993), 504. According to the authors, "it was exceeded only by the sayings concerning giving up one's coat and shirt and turning the other cheek, Luke 6.29, which were given the highest weighted average."

31 *Five Gospels*, 504.

Thus, there is widespread scholarly agreement that this logion is one of Jesus' own statements. In order to explore its meaning I turn now to one of the text's interpreters, John Dominic Crossan.

4.2.2 Crossan's Position

One prominent example of contemporary historical-Jesus research's willingness to accept that the critically-discernible words of Jesus (ascertained through criteria of authenticity) yield a picture of the historical Jesus is found in John Dominic Crossan's *The Historical Jesus: The Life of a Mediterranean Jewish Peasant*.[32] Crossan's book is a learned and wide-ranging overview of the field of historical-Jesus research prepared from the vantage point not simply of a literary analysis but especially cultural and economic anthropology. According to Crossan, Jesus was a kind of Jewish Cynic[33] or magician,[34] who spoke out of a peasant background.[35] The key social element in Jesus' activity was that he proclaimed an egalitarian "free healing and common eating" in which God was the provider and for which Jesus would be "neither broker nor mediator" but rather the proclaimer of "the brokerless kingdom of God."[36]

In this context Crossan devotes significant attention to Q 6:20. He notes especially that the original logion must be understood in the context of the ancient understanding of "beggary" or "destitution" (πτωχός), a situation that would be exemplified in Jesus' own Cynic life-style. As evidence of this contention, Crossan points to Aristophanes' *Plutus* (*ca.* 388 BCE) in which the personification of poverty distinguishes between destitution and mere poverty.[37] He further underscores this distinction by citing three studies: Arthur Hands' *Charities and Social Aid in Greece and Rome: Aspects of Greek and Roman Life*,[38] Moses Finley's *The Ancient Economy*[39] and Gildas Hamel's *Poverty and Charity in Roman Palestine, First Three Centuries C.E.*[40] In Hands and Finley,

---

32 John Dominic Crossan, *The Historical Jesus: The Life of a Mediterranean Jewish Peasant* (San Francisco: HarperSanFrancisco, 1991).

33 Crossan, *Historical Jesus*, 421; cf. also 72-88.

34 Crossan, *Historical Jesus*, 421; cf. also 137-67, although note also that the rabbinic texts cite "magicians" who are later contemporaries of Jesus, rather than possible earlier prototypes.

35 Crossan, *Historical Jesus*, 421-22.

36 Crossan, *Historical Jesus*, 422.

37 In his commentary on *Plutus*, Karl Holzinger says that Poverty is furious to be compared with πτωχεία (*Kritisch-exegetischer Kommentar zu Aristophanes' Plutos* [Vienna: Hölder, Pichler, Tempsky, 1940], 181).

38 Arthur Hands, *Charities and Social Aid in Greece and Rome: Aspects of Greek and Roman Life* (Ithaca: Cornell University Press, 1968).

39 Moses I. Finley, *The Ancient Economy* (Berkeley: University of California Press, 1973).

40 Gildas H. Hamel, *Poverty and Charity in Roman Palestine, First Three Centuries C.E.* (Berkeley: University of California Press, 1990).

Crossan finds that the "poor" are those who lack the wealth and thus the leisure of the aristocratic class, being forced to work the land that they have. Unlike the fate of the destitute, the class of labourers who possess no land at all and probably no savings whatsoever, the lot of small-plot farmers could from time to time be spoken of highly in the literature of the period.[41] It is in Hamel that Crossan finds that which allows him to correct what he sees as the move of later gospel writers away from the original meaning of Jesus' words. According to Hamel, the rich—understood as the wealthy land-owners who were at leisure—and the poor—those who owned land but were forced to work it themselves—were at least in the same economic game; the beggar was not even on the playing field. The later gospel writers, when confronted with Jesus' blessing of precisely this destitute class, found themselves forced to spiritualize the meaning.[42] Thus, Crossan suggests that πτωχός in Q 6:20 would better be translated "destitute" and that Jesus thus spoke not of a kingdom of the poor but of the destitute.[43] According to Crossan, this picture—which fits Gerhard Lenski's view of the stratification of agrarian societies[44]—shows Jesus speaking about a kingdom of the "unclean, degraded, and expendable," not a kingdom of the "peasant or artisan."[45] Not surprisingly, Crossan argues that, by making the phrase speak of spiritual poverty, Matthew later relegates this logion "to the confines of normalcy if not banality."[46]

4.2.3 Critical Assessment of Crossan's Position on the Poverty/Destitution Distinction

Although the poor/destitution distinction is standard in classical antiquity, it appears that it was not clearly drawn. Aristophanes' Athens provides some clarification. Vincent Rosivach argues that the "poor," about whom the Athenians talked a good deal, was a wide classification that included both the destitute and those who "were still only barely making it."[47] At odds with the contention that "destitution offers a fairly clear bottom line (nothing), while 'poverty' is merely a state below that which one regards as real wealth," stands the contention that Athens was a class-conscious society, in which there were only two classes and where "the primary indicator of class was wealth or its absence."[48] The poor were a social class that included the many professionals classed as poor and servile (including those who worked in trades, crafts,

---

41 Crossan, *Historical Jesus*, 272.
42 Crossan, *Historical Jesus*, 272.
43 Crossan, *Historical Jesus*, 271-73.
44 Gerhard Lenski, *Power and Privilege: A Theory of Social Stratification* (New York: McGraw Hill, 1966).
45 Crossan, *Historical Jesus*, 273.
46 Crossan, *Historical Jesus*, 270.
47 Vincent J. Rosivach, "Some Athenian Presuppositions about 'The Poor,'" *Greece and Rome* 38 (1991): 190.
48 Rosivach, "Athenian Presuppositions," 190.

shopkeeping and farming),[49] as well as the indigent. True, it was theoretically possible for the working "poor" to rise above their poverty to wealth and leisure;[50] practically speaking, however, it was next to impossible.[51] When it did happen, Rosivach notes, it was almost always seen as being through dishonest means and as the result of criminal acts,[52] as is the case with Blepsidemus's response to Chremylus in Aristophanes' *Plutus* (382-385). Rosivach suggests that "there is sufficient evidence that Athenians included the indigent among the poor." Moreover, he maintains that it is inaccurate to view the passage in Aristophanes' *Plutus* as distinguishing πτωχοί from the πένητες, since, "properly speaking, all non-wealthy, including beggars, were *penētes.*"[53]

When we turn to the literature of Hellenistic Judaism, the distinction occasionally breaks down as well. For example, why would the third-century BCE translator of the Septuagint of Psalm 39:18 translate the Psalmist as saying that he is both πτωχὸς καὶ πένης? Surely, if the two are distinguished in degree he might say he was πένης, καὶ πτωχός , but not the reverse.[54] Would we say: "I am destitute, nay even relatively poor"?

The distinction between the poor and the destitute is not as clear as Crossan makes it out to be. One implication of this assessment is a re-opening of the question about the intended target of Jesus' words in Q 6:20. While the audience of Jesus' pronouncement may in fact be the homeless and indigent, my analysis suggests that it could also be the small-farm peasant, considered poor in an absolute sense. Moreover, if the antique distinction was in fact between rich and poor, as opposed to rich, relatively poor and indigent, then Jesus' pronouncement may have been addressed implicitly to the wealthy as a hortatory, cautionary or eschatologically-loaded logion. We shall examine this possibility below.

4.3 Implications of the Rhetorical Re-Assessment of the "Blessing of the Poor"

4.3.1 The Rhetorical Jesus

Amos Wilder, with his *Early Christian Rhetoric*, has brought rhetoric to the attention of North American New Testament scholars.[55] His book makes

---

49 Rosivach, "Athenian Presuppositions," 192-93.

50 Nevertheless, according to Rosivach, "rising from the thetic to the zeugite class was not the same as going from poor to rich" (Rosivach, "Athenian Presuppositions," 197 n. 12).

51 "There is little to suggest that poor people could ever escape their poverty simply by working hard" (Rosivach, "Athenian Presuppositions," 197 n. 10).

52 E.g., Aristophanes, *Clouds* 920-21 (cited in Rosivach, "Athenian Presuppositions," 197 n. 10). Rosivach alludes to numerous examples from Athenian antiquity (190-91, and corresponding notes).

53 Rosivach, "Athenian Presuppositions," 196 n. 5.

54 Cf. also Septuagint of Pss 40:2; 69:6; 71:13.

55 Amos Niven Wilder, *Early Christian Rhetoric: The Language of the Gospel* (Cambridge: Harvard University Press, 1971).

significant assumptions. For example, he contends that earliest Christian speech, "including that of Jesus," is "naïve, it is not studied; it is *extempore* and directed to the occasion, it is not calculated to serve some future hour."[56] Wilder's words seem primarily directed to show that early Christian utterances were "dynamic, actual, immediate, reckless of posterity,"[57] and as such not intended to be literary monuments. Wilder further contends that this primitive situation did not continue, but that "the uncalculating oral speech and dialogue of Jesus and his first followers gave place in part to memorization and repetition, and eventually to writing and later to the greater formality of publication."[58] In his view, rhetoric and stylization take on increasing importance decade by decade.

These contentions reflect widespread thinking on early Christian speech. The one regarding the primitive nature of Jesus' speech has significant implications for New Testament scholarship. While the kind of immediacy about which Wilder speaks does not indicate absence of rhetorical artistry, it does imply a certain subordination of rhetorical artifice to either the long-hewn skill of the rhetor who is able to rise to any occasion on the basis of years of experience, or a conscious or unconscious inattention to rhetoric, characteristic of the less-trained rhetor.

The dominant position in recent historical-Jesus study is the latter. Utterances of the historical Jesus—either in abundance, among conservative scholars, or scant, among the more radical—are not examined for their rhetorical sophistication; almost inevitably they are taken at face value as affording a direct link to the historical Jesus, his intentions and his setting. Is this a fair assumption? Is it so obvious that Jesus spoke in a primitive and unmediated fashion and did not use rhetorical artifice? There does not appear to be anything in the authentic words of Jesus that would lead us to believe that a classical rhetor is at work[59]—although the incarnation of Hellenistic rhetoric in Hellenistic Judaism remains for the most part virgin territory for New Testament scholarship. Neither is there anything that discounts the possibility of rhetorical presentation. In fact, Wilder himself seems to contradict his own assessment of the primitive nature of Jesus' words when, speaking of Jesus' parables, he compares Jesus favourably with those highly literary groups from antiquity, "the prophets and the apocalyptists" who, like Jesus, use "tropes or extended images to unveil mysteries."[60] By this statement it does not appear that

---

56 Wilder, *Rhetoric*, 20-21.

57 Wilder, *Rhetoric*, 21.

58 Wilder, *Rhetoric*, 23-24.

59 Wilder, *Rhetoric*, 29, comments that "early Christian speech and rhetoric" were not "diffuse or verbose." This suggestion appears to be diametrically opposed to that of C. Clifton Black, "An Oration at Olivet: Some Rhetorical Dimensions of Mark 13," in Duane F. Watson, ed., *Persuasive Artistry: Studies in New Testament Rhetoric in Honor of George A. Kennedy* (Sheffield: JSOT, 1991), 66-92.

60 Wilder, *Rhetoric*, 80.

Wilder simply means the metaphorical nature of Jesus' speech, since he goes on to speak of the "rhetorical perfection of the parables of Jesus";[61] even if one should argue that Jesus' speech was not indebted to the apocalyptic but to the sapiential tradition,[62] this would only change the form of rhetorical speech, not make it primitive or "naïve."

What is probable, then, if not absolutely certain, is that rhetoric in some form was part of Jesus' practice. We can ask further whether this rhetoric would have been one that was not entirely foreign to the rhetoric of the handbooks and Hellenistic examples of children's education throughout the eastern Mediterranean. Is there a compelling reason to argue that Jesus would have been able to escape the atmosphere of Hellenistic culture and education?[63] There is a growing chorus of voices that would like to see the earliest Jesus movement—perhaps traceable as far back as Jesus himself—dependent to some extent at least on a Hellenistic movement such as Cynicism. Jesus' ideas may not simply have been bucolic intuition, pulled from the air on a heavy day of haying.

4.3.2 The Rhetorical Nature of Aristophanes' Presentation and its Implications

One of the main failings in Crossan's approach to the question of the poor in antiquity concerns his disregard for the rhetorical context of the material from which he draws his evidence. In a recent article, Normand Bonneau, Kevin Coyle and I warned that scholars often misunderstand the texts of antiquity as "referential as in a one-to-one adequation between word and idea in modern science. Ancient texts are not clear windows offering an unimpeded view of reality. . . . Ancient texts contain information, but the information is always coloured by rhetoric, by the author's intent to persuade an audience."[64] The contemporary historian often misuses texts from antiquity, looking to them as to a river from which to pan gold, and thus disregarding the context that yields the motherlode.

---

61 Wilder, *Rhetoric*, 88.

62 A possibility made more probable in light of the ascription to Q of an earliest sapiential layer. On the history of the interpretation of earliest Q as a sapiential document, see now James M. Robinson, "The Q Trajectory: Between John and Matthew via Jesus," in Birger A. Pearson *et al.*, eds., *The Future of Early Christianity: Essays in Honor of Helmut Koester* (Minneapolis: Fortress, 1991), 173-94.

63 For example, according to Wilder (*Rhetoric*, 26), to say that Jesus spoke Aramaic is a "truism." This does not at all appear to be the case anymore. As Robert Kraft wrote in a 1994 discussion of this matter on the IOUDAIOS computer-discussion list: it may be that the few Aramaic logia of Jesus preserved in the Gospels were in fact preserved precisely because they were so extraordinary.

64 L. Gregory Bloomquist, Normand Bonneau and J. Kevin Coyle, "Prolegomena to a Sociological Study of Early Christianity," *Social Compass* 39 (1992): 231.

It is in this way that Crossan misses the point that the distinction between destitution and poverty in the *Plutus* is not primarily economic but rhetorical. The point is not lost on Rosivach, who notes that "the word *ptōkhos* is rarely used to describe actual beggars; rather it is used most often in two clearly rhetorically governed contexts, first to elicit sympathy in describing people who have lost everything and second as an exaggerated synonym for *penēs*, particularly as a term of abuse."[65] In fact, when we turn to the play itself we find that the locus of Crossan's discussion is in actual fact a rhetorical contest (ἀγών) between Poverty and Chremylus.[66] In this contest, Poverty is presented in rags and with a sickly look,[67] rhetorical devices that are "guaranteed to distract the spectators and perhaps bias them against her from the start." Penia's arguments are presented in such a way that the audience knows that she will lose the contest to Chremylus, acting on behalf of Plutus, and that ultimately Plutus will be restored to his rightful state.[68]

Crossan's attention to the "upbeat" nature of Poverty's description of poverty attends to that which is both fleeting and conventional at the outset of the contest, since "the speaker is Penia—Poverty herself—, who naturally wishes to put the best possible light on the condition she personifies."[69] In Aristophanes' *Plutus* the reign of Poverty is undone by the rightful restoration of Wealth. Chremylus, who suggests that all poverty is the same, is presented as speaking rightly; not Poverty, who tries to counter Chremylus's attacks by arguing that poverty and destitution are really two separate realities.[70] While it is true that the rhetorical struggle is in fact won by Chremylus, it would be wrong to view all of Poverty's argumentation as false. In fact, within the play Poverty provides an astutely conceived critique of Athenian society. It is Poverty who sets forth "an alternative picture of a life where the *penēs* is just, a good fighter, and self-sufficient economically."[71] Poverty's best argument with Chremylus is intended to make it look as though her model is the perfect Aristotelian state of "self-sufficiency"[72] and that she alone can ensure that the

---

65 Rosivach, "Athenian Presuppositions," 196 n. 5.

66 See A. M. Bowie, *Aristophanes: Myth, Ritual and Comedy* (Cambridge: Cambridge University Press, 1993), 285.

67 Bowie, *Aristophanes*, 285.

68 Anne H. Groton, "Wreaths and Rags in Aristophanes' *Plutus*," *Classical Journal* 86 (1990): 19.

69 Rosivach, "Athenian Presuppositions," 189.

70 Bowie, *Aristophanes*, 284-91. Bowie points out that at various points Poverty can be seen to be making accurate or at least insightful—"Penia's prognostications are not quite accurate as far as the play is concerned" (288)—remarks concerning human nature.

71 Bowie, *Aristophanes*, 290.

72 Bowie paraphrases Aristotle (*Politics*, 1328b 2-23), according to whom "a perfect state must perform certain services and must contain elements to perform those services: food, arts and crafts, arms, property, religion, a system of justice are all essential for if any of these services is missing it cannot be totally self-sufficient" (Bowie, *Aristophanes*, 289).

city does not succumb to the degradation of the poverty-less society of the Cyclopes.[73] In this way, she warns against "the general availability of wealth and the lack of the need to work" which would mean "that no social or economic interchange would be required," thereby pointing to the "cost and even undesirability" of universal wealth.[74]

Coming as it does in the mouth of Poverty and in the context of comedic genre, this double-edged sword of implicit criticism of "golden age" ideologies is surely intended as a satiric jab by which all orders of society are leveled and in which the best defence of the Athenian social order comes not from the "better" gods nor from the best citizens but from Poverty. Surely this social critique does not reflect a "cult" of the poor among Athenian intellectuals. According to Rosivach, we actually find Athenian conceptions of the poor that suggest that the poor are incapable of certain vices because

> they lack the financial means to indulge in whatever one would indulge in the absence of self control (cf. e.g., Aristoph. *Wealth* 563-564). *Hubris*, on the other hand, is the "besetting sin of the rich." It implies a freedom of choice which is denied to the poor who . . . do the bad things they do because their poverty makes them do them. . . . In sum, just as the poor . . . lacked the financial resources necessary for aristocratic *megaloprepeia*, in a similar fashion, in the view of our sources, they also lacked the moral *grandeur* needed for *hubris*.[75]

These points, made in the rhetorical context of comedy, are intended not to be viewed as false, but rather as truths that are askew. Thus, while it is true that the poor are often perceived to be wise and the wealthy proud, this is not as it should be. Aristophanes, from his aristocratic vantage point, was not so much looking to exalt the poor as he was to show that his aristocratic colleagues had lost their focus. Yet to take the texts at face value, as yielding evidence of the actual state of the Athenian economy, not only leads to popular misconceptions of that state, but also to errors regarding the rhetorical intent of Aristophanes' speech.

4.3.3 Implications for the Rhetoric of Jesus

It is certainly possible, as Crossan suggests, that in Q 6:20 Jesus is primarily exalting the destitute in order to show that theirs is the kingdom of God. Such a picture of God becoming the patron of the poor would, in fact, parallel the Roman imperial proclamation of the Emperor as patron of those who had

---

73   Bowie, *Aristophanes*, 286-87.
74   Bowie, *Aristophanes*, 290.
75   Rosivach, "Athenian Presuppositions," 196.

nothing. According to Zvi Yavetz, "with the commencement of the Principate the emperors became in a sense *patroni* of the entire urban *plebs*."[76] Furthermore, such a situation appears to add evidence to Crossan's contention of a division between the poor and the destitute. In Tacitus's work the honourable *plebs* is distinguished from the despised. The honourable, called by Tacitus *pars populi integra*, were those who remained "within the structure of the *clientela* of large aristocratic homes which were not completely destroyed in the civil war" and depended on their aristocratic masters by observing *fides* towards them;[77] the *sordida plebs*, on the other hand, were those whose sole patron was the emperor.[78] As Yavetz himself notes with regard to the imperial practice, Augustus's claim to be the urban *plebs'* patron appears to have had less to do with magnanimity on the part of Augustus than it did with the Emperor's desire "to restrict the private *clientela* of the senatorial aristocracy."[79] Not surprisingly, Augustus's claim to *tribunicia potestas* brought him into conflict with the aristocracy: "although the emperor was not officially referred to as *patronus* of all the *plebs*, there was a clear conflict between his influence and the patronage exercised by individual senators."[80] According to Yavetz, Augustus was thus able to curb "the influence of all who attempted to obtain clients in one way or another from among the common people."[81]

If the parallel applies, one must ask whether the rhetorical Jesus' primary audience was in fact the poor (or the destitute as distinguished from the poor) or whether the rhetorical Jesus' primary audience was the aristocratic elite, including the teachers of the law and the priesthood. If the latter be the case, then and only then can Jesus be seen to have been engaged, as Crossan suggests, in a task similar to Aristophanes' in the *Plutus*: shaming the wealthy by proclaiming a reversal.

4.3.4 Rhetorical Impersonation: When the Rich Become Poor

In his understanding of Jesus' background, Crossan helpfully points to the prophetic elements in Jesus' speech and notes that Jesus acts as a magician-prophet in his proclamation. The rhetorical analysis of Jesus' speech would lead us to believe that, in fact, Jesus did engage in some kind of prophetic challenge to the leaders of his day. But what does this lead us to conclude about Jesus' own social background?

---

76 Zvi Yavetz, *Plebs and Princeps* (Oxford: Clarendon, 1969), 152.
77 According to Yavetz, their economic position may have actually improved as a result of their allegiance (*Plebs*, 97).
78 Yavetz, *Plebs*, 152.
79 Yavetz, *Plebs*, 97.
80 Yavetz, *Plebs*, 97, citing Tacitus, *Historia* 2.92.
81 Yavetz, *Plebs*, 97.

As I have noted above, contemporary historians have often made a one-to-one equation between the discernible words of the historical Jesus and his social background. Thus, if Jesus' words can be found to reflect the speaker's peasant background, the speaker must have been from the peasant class. Little consideration seems to have been given to the rhetorical impersonation that all public address implied in antiquity, and still does in many parts of the world today. In an earlier work, *The Function of Suffering in Philippians*, I argued that impersonation, or taking on a role (προσωποποιία), was an important element in any rhetorical presentation.[82] Two examples help to clarify this point. According to Quintilian an oration will be unsuccessful when it does not agree with the person or thing which it is supposed to fit.[83] To make sense and to convince the hearer, one must take on the part of the one who is being depicted. And in the *Plutus*, Aristophanes need not be viewed as speaking only through one actor, but rather through various actors at various times, even Poverty, in his desire to point to the reversal at work in his world. In that play, then, we have examples of the rich becoming poor, at least in rhetorical self-presentation, to make a point.

Rhetorical self-ascription of poverty is actually quite extended throughout antiquity, although its presence need not indicate a belief in the power of poverty or the good nature of the poor. In Athens there is evidence that the wealthy would make much of the plight of the poor, not as a means of social analysis, but as a means of providing themselves with an opportunity to show themselves to be beneficent and to affirm their superiority to the poor.[84] Citing Demosthenes and Lysias, Rosivach notes that it was a rhetorically well-accepted custom for speakers in the public courts to parade "their generosity to poor individuals to gain the respect and good will of the jurors who represent the community as a whole. In this public sense at least the one-to-one charity discussed here was the counterpart on the personal level of *philotimia*, the public benefaction of individual wealthy Athenians which was expected to call forth the gratitude of the *polis* as a whole."[85] Furthermore, as noted above, the poor were often depicted as wise and the wealthy as proud in order to restore the proper order of things, namely, the role of the aristocratic class as proper leaders. That such an ascription is possible is all the more likely given the leveling of the distinctions in ancient Athenian society to two: wealthy and poor.

Evidence of the rhetorical ascription of poverty in cases where "real" (economic) poverty is not the case is perhaps most notably found in Solon. In

---

82   L. Gregory Bloomquist, *The Function of Suffering in Philippians* (Sheffield: JSOT, 1993).
83   Quintilian, *Institutio oratoria* 3.8.51.
84   Rosivach, "Athenian Presuppositions," 193-95.
85   Rosivach, "Athenian Presuppositions," 195.

Plutarch we read that Solon classed himself among the poor rather than the rich, for which Plutarch finds proof in the following fragment:

> For often the evil are rich, and the good poor,
> But we will not exchange with them
> Our virtue for their wealth, since one abides always
> While riches change their owners every day.[86]

This rhetorical self-ascription appears to have been part of Solon's social critique that "the troubles of Athens in his time were due to the rapacity of the rich," who "sometimes went beyond their legal rights."[87] Thus, Solon sets himself over against the "nobility" who are "extracting from the poor whatever could be turned into silver, or . . . selling the poor themselves as slaves."[88] This especially concerned the ἐκτήμοροι, the class of workers of the land, a class into which, Andrewes notes, Aristotle consigns the whole mass of the poor.[89] In the case of Solon, while the specific measures he took are unclear, it appears that his action caused a serious reversal, leaving this class "in full possession of the land they had been working . . . in effect creating a considerable class of free smallholders."[90] Whatever the result, the fact remains that Solon's self-designation of poverty was not intended for an audience of the poor but for an audience of the wealthy, and for their judgment.

If rhetorical impersonation implied that the speaker would have to adopt the rhetorical guise most suited to the message, there is no reason to argue that Jesus was a peasant simply because he argued "the peasant's case." As in the case of the well-known figure from antiquity, Solon, Jesus could easily have adopted the "garb of the poor" in order to make his rhetorical point.

As we have seen in our discussion of Crossan's work, his understanding of Jesus' "blessing of the poor" is that Jesus was declaring the "destitute," those who had no hope at all in the world, blessed. Other authors have also pointed to the radical nature of Jesus' blessing. Howard Clark Kee says that this blessing is part of Jesus' proclamation of God's "eschatological reversal of roles" that is "vividly set out in the familiar words of the Beatitudes, which promise joy to those now sorrowing, satisfaction to the hungry, vindication to those now oppressed, and participation of the 'poor' in the kingdom (Lk 6.20-

---

86 English translation from the Loeb edition: *Plutarch's Lives*, trans. Bernadotte Perrin (Cambridge: Harvard University Press, 1914), vol. 2, 409-10 (taken from the "Life of Solon" 3.2).
87 Anthony Andrewes, *Greek Society* (London: Penguin, 1971), 117.
88 Andrewes, *Greek Society*, 117.
89 Andrewes, *Greek Society*, 115.
90 Andrewes, *Greek Society*, 117.

23)."[91] The preaching of Jesus thus pictured is one of a radical egalitarianism, characteristic of a new "golden age."

But more needs to be said. As Crossan notes, the blessing is not on poverty as such but on making oneself poor for the sake of the kingdom—or, in the extreme, begging for the sake of the kingdom.[92] These are not, then, the words of those desperate from hunger but the words of one who has willingly undergone hunger for the sake of the greater good of the kingdom. It would then be more likely that Jesus' preaching concerning the "blessing of the poor" picks up and modifies the language of imperial patronage: "the poor are not now being cared for by you, nobility or Jewish patrons, and I say this to your shame." Jesus' words may have extended to talk about caring for the poor, but as clients of God, not as clients of the Emperor.

4.3.5 What Does Jesus' Rhetoric Suggest about him and his Message?

If what I have suggested is tenable, it seems safer to speak not first about the historical Jesus, but rather about the rhetorical Jesus. What we will then discuss in more detail will be the rhetorical Jesus' proclamation and its purposes. It further appears to me that we can speak less confidently about Jesus' history and message. While some—such as Gertrude Himmelfarb—may fear that this will constrain us to be silent on every point of history regarding the historical Jesus, I believe that, to the contrary, we will begin to engage in an imaginative historiography concerning Jesus, a practice which Himmelfarb has so eloquently denounced. For what we will have to do is to determine the historical-Jesus' point of departure from the rhetorical Jesus' self-presentation. And this will allow us a variety of hitherto unsuspected imaginative possibilities.

Let us imagine the discernible words and deeds of Jesus as the not-improbable rhetorical presentation of a first-century Hellenistic Jewish rhetor who used Jewish peasant language. We will need to begin to ask ourselves a number of questions: Why would he have done so? What purpose did he have in mind? Did he do so consciously or unconsciously? Even if we assume that the peasant community was his immediate audience, was it his rhetorical audience? As will be clear, there are a number of possible answers.

Clearly, to whichever audience Jesus sought to speak, he would have needed to communicate, and if Jesus sought to communicate his message to peasant multitudes he would have needed to communicate to them in their language and in their images. It is also possible that Jesus neither stemmed from

---

91 Howard Clark Kee, *Miracle in the Early Christian World: A Study in Sociohistorical Method* (New Haven: Yale University Press, 1983), 157. See also Halvor Moxnes, *The Economy of the Kingdom: Social Conflict and Economic Relations in Luke's Gospel* (Philadelphia: Fortress, 1988), 74.

92 Crossan, *Historical Jesus*, 272-73.

the peasant milieu nor sought to speak to the peasants of that milieu. Jesus might well have been one of those intellectuals who at various points throughout human history have imagined a "golden age," sometimes embodied in a picture of universal wealth and abundance, sometimes embodied in what is understood to be a return to the land. Such anti-urban, romantic movements have arisen at various stress-points in human history, but are usually the ideological domain of urban intellectuals themselves who have grown weary of urban life, not the domain of peasants who know nothing else. As in the case of Virgil, this golden age will be a time of return to the ideal patron-client relationship, as opposed to the aberration found in the abusive patronage of the aristocracy. Whether this patron-client relationship is between God and the poor or is simply a righting of the patron-client relationship of the aristocracy vis-à-vis the poor remains to be determined. Radical reversal does not necessarily mean the reversal of the position of the destitute with all others who have possessions or standing, but the possibility of the fundamental righting of social roles. In either case, the question would be better set in the context not of the extremes of poverty—as Crossan suggests—but of the claims of patronage.

Furthermore, if we take seriously the conclusions at which scholars such as Crossan and others have arrived concerning the non-apocalyptic nature of the preaching of Jesus, one possible result is that the rhetorical situation of Jesus' message may have been largely one of "prophetic" or "comedic" challenge to the structures of power in Hellenistic Judaism. Seen in this way, Jesus' blessing of the poor would have been intended to challenge the wealthy to see that their political and social activity was in fact itself a reversal of the way things should be. As such, Jesus' words would have a satiric spin.

5. Conclusion

I have argued that any examination of the words and deeds of Jesus must contend with the reality that what we will uncover is not the historical Jesus but the rhetorical Jesus, the rhetorical self-presentation of the historical Jesus. I have argued further that this contention has implications for understanding the message of Jesus. In the case of the "blessing of the poor," Q 6:20 and *Thomas* 54, we may want to withhold assent to Crossan's contention that the logion is further evidence of Jesus' message of actual, radical reversal, directed to a peasant audience by a peasant preacher. As I have indicated, a rhetorical analysis may lead to the conclusion that we are dealing with a social reformer whose rhetorical intent is to shame the wealthy in their already active involvement in a reversal of the way things were originally intended.

This approach to Jesus begins with an early picture of Jesus, since it is a word from Jesus himself. Being early, however, only means, as it does in the case of the picture of Socrates in Aristophanes, that it is a better picture of the rhetorical self-presentation of Jesus; it is not necessarily a better picture of

Jesus' historical consciousness and/or aims as such, but can be used to arrive at that consciousness or those aims. Furthermore, we may want to qualify our language in order to allow for the possibility that later gospel writers may actually be reflecting the intention of the historical Jesus precisely by going behind the brief glimpses we historical-critical scholars obtain of the mask of the rhetorical Jesus. It may very well be that the later Lukan focus on the "blessing of the poor" as an indication of how the Christian apostles should act vis-à-vis the poor is in actual fact a better understanding of Jesus' message than our own critically-determined one.

More strikingly yet, it may be that the rhetorical situation or form-critical *Sitz im Leben* for his statements is in fact picked up by Matthew, whom Crossan accuses of being banal and normal in his redaction of the blessing. It is Crossan himself who suggests that *Thomas* prepares the way for the Matthean version when he notes that "for *Thomas*, physical poverty was spiritual riches; physical riches were spiritual poverty."[93] If, in actual fact, Jesus' rhetorical self-presentation was primarily directed to and intended to be heard by the rich, and then subsequently his own followers, the call to a life-style that enabled the original patron-client relationship to function smoothly would have been a clear interpretation of the message: "blessed are the poor."

---

93 Crossan, *Historical Jesus*, 273.

9. Cosmology and the Jesus Miracles[1]

Wendy Cotter

1. Introduction

The significance of any miracle story is immediately controlled by the cosmology presupposed as its backdrop. Once such a basic lens is affixed, it generates the expectation of a particular set of images appropriate to that cosmology. Only allusions and stories understood to share a similar world-view are admitted as resources for contextualization. In the case of the Jesus miracles, the two cosmologies most often presumed by academics for this backdrop, both Jewish, are the biblical and the apocalyptic world-views. Yet the presence of either cosmology cannot remain unargued or taken for granted, since neither represents the ordinary stance of the Mediterranean populace in the Imperial period. This paper addresses the assumptions that continue to justify the supposition that one of these two cosmologies undergirds the miracle stories, it presents the main differences between these cosmologies and those more typical of the Graeco-Roman world and it discusses the impact on miracle interpretation when the Graeco-Roman world-view is allowed to stand as its backdrop.

2. Septuagint Allusions Interpreted by Septuagint Cosmology

When a miracle story involving Jesus holds an allusion to the Septuagint, scholars usually conclude that the writer of the narrative intends to signal that the full meaning of the story will be found by focusing on that Septuagint reference. A distinction, however, needs to be established between the meaning these Jewish texts held when they were first composed and the meaning they would have held in the first century CE. It was Hermann Gunkel who warned the "history of religions" scholars one hundred years ago that no matter how pure an ancient text they might unearth behind first-century allusions, if any "influence" were to be posited, the content and meaning of that text had to be available to a first-century audience and it had to be understood as interpreted through first-century eyes.[2] For Gunkel, the old dichotomies of "Palestinian" and "Hellenistic" were presumed to hold in the Imperial period, and thus a

---

1   This paper relies on research from my 1991 dissertation, "The Markan Sea Miracles (Mk 4:35-41; 6:45-52): Their History, Formation and Function in the Literary Context of Greco-Roman Antiquity" (Ph. D diss., University of St. Michael's College).

2   Hermann Gunkel, *Die Wirkungen des heiligen Geistes der populären Anschauung der apostolischen Zeit und nach der Lehre des Apostels Paulus* (Göttingen: Vandenhoeck & Ruprecht, 1888). In English, see *The Influence of the Holy Spirit*, trans. Roy A. Harrisville and P. Quanbeck II (Philadelphia: Fortress, 1979), 5.

"Jewish mind" could not be represented by the larger Hellenistic world-view. We now consider such divisions untenable since we see the entire Mediterranean, including Palestine, as Hellenized. Yet although we are now agreed that a common cultural influence was shared throughout the Mediterranean world, we have yet to take seriously the implications of Hellenization on the first-century Jewish understanding of the cosmos. If this cosmology or world-view is overlooked, the Septuagint references are interpreted in their most ancient significance and in the context of other biblical texts. This means that in the end the first-century Jesus story is interpreted by ignoring the dominant first-century cosmology.

Paul Achtemeier's study of Mark 4:35-41 demonstrates the effects on a miracle story's interpretation when a cosmology from remote antiquity is allowed to control the meaning of a miracle. Achtemeier claims that in order to understand the story of Jesus "stilling the storm," one needs to approach it from the perspective of a "Semitic mentality."[3] He holds that the reader should be familiar with the ancient Canaanite deities Marduk and Tiamat, and the myth of a war between the great Lord of the Land, Marduk, and the Mistress of the Sea, Tiamat. Triumphing over her, Marduk takes full dominion of the earth and sea and brings the cosmos to peace. Since this myth is an ancient creation story, Achtemeier, consistently enough, interprets the meaning of the Stilling of the Storm to be creation "achieved by overcoming the forces of evil."[4]

Following the principle set down by Gunkel, we need to ask for evidence that this ancient legend was even available to, let alone commonly known by, Jewish people in the first century. The answer in this case is clear: no first-century Jewish texts either directly allude to these myths or recount them. They are known in our own day through the archaeological findings of our modern age. Had Achtemeier probed the popular entertainment literature of the first century he would have seen an abundance of sea-storm stories in which the hero shows his character during a sudden threat to his life. In the first century, such stories serve as metaphors, the sea representing the uncertainty of life in the sublunar region.[5]

---

3 Paul J. Achtemeier, "Person and Deed: Jesus and the Storm-Tossed Sea," *Interpretation* 16 (1962): 170. In other studies, Achtemeier shows more sensitivity to Graeco-Roman perspectives.

4 Achtemeier, "Person and Deed," 170.

5 For examples of sea storms in romances see Apuleius, *Metamorphoses*; Achilles Tatius, *Clitophon and Leucippe*; Xenophon, *An Ephesian Tale*; and Heliodorus, *An Ethiopian Romance*. For an excellent treatment of Graeco-Roman stories of adventure and romance, see Richard Pervo, *Profit with Delight* (Philadelphia: Fortress, 1987), esp. 12-57, and n. 182. See also Pamela Thimmes, "Convention and Invention: Studies in the Biblical Sea Storm Scene" (Ph.D. diss., Vanderbilt University, 1990); for sea storms in odes, Horace, *Odes* 1.3, 5.13-16; in historical adventure, Herodotus, *Histories* 7.34; Diodorus, *History* 4.48, 5-6; Dio Chrysostom, *The Euboean Discourse* 7; Plutarch, "Caesar" 38.3-4; Josephus, *Life* 3.13-16.

Achtemeier also needs to prove the very existence of a "Semitic mind." In this regard, one is reminded of the religious paintings in the third-century CE synagogue in Dura Europos. Far from being a large city under Greek domination, Dura was "an undistinguished frontier town" in Syria serving as an army outpost. The Jewish community there seems to have consisted of "merchants providing supplies to the army."[6] Yet in the synagogue, hero-figures such as Moses, Samuel, David and Ezekiel are painted in the contemporary Roman dress of the late second century CE. The clothing sports the insignia and status signs of the period.[7] As Michael Avi-Yonah observes, the "cycle of images . . . elaborated [at the Dura Europos synagogue] was based mainly on Greek mythological representations (Adam and Eve and the Serpent as Jason and Medea with the dragon, Noah as Danae, Jonah as Endymion, etc.)."[8] In other words, these murals portray ancient Jewish myths as *Greek* myths. This evidence hardly suggests a community with a "Semitic mind," nor even one wishing to appear culturally distinct at all.

When, therefore, Septuagint allusions appear in the Jesus miracles, we cannot make a special interpretive appeal to a closed system of biblical allusions understood in terms of their pre-first-century CE import. We need to keep the world of Jesus and the gospel writers clearly in focus. Similarly, the long lists of "Septuagint allusions" within the miracle traditions generated by modern interpreters need to be tested within a first-century context. Moreover, whether clear allusions to the Septuagint occur or not, the entire framework of a miracle story, with *all* its allusions, must be set against the cosmological backdrop of the first century.

3. The New Cosmology and Life in the Sublunar Sphere

By the third century BCE, the "bowl over a plate" Near Eastern model of the cosmos (i.e., the sky fitting down over the flat earth) for the most part had been

---

6 Joseph Gutmann, "Programmatic Painting in the Dura Synagogue," in his (edited) *The Dura-Europos Synagogue: A Re-evaluation (1932-1972)* (Missoula: AAR/SBL, 1973), 140.

7 For example, in the scene of Moses before the burning bush the hero wears the Roman *dalmatica* which was introduced in the third century CE by the emperor Heliogabalus, himself a native of the Middle East. Two narrow *clavi* run down each shoulder. Earlier, such insignia indicated a man of the *equites* rank. In the third century it seems to have lost this meaning, so we cannot be sure what these *clavi* meant to the onlooker. Over his *dalmatica* Moses wears a *pallium*, the Roman version of the Greek ἱμάτιον. The nicely-barbered hair, mustache and small beard indicate a well-groomed man of the third century. For an itemized description of Moses' attire see Alfred Rubens, *A History of Jewish Costume* (New York: Funk and Wagnalls, 1967), 18. For the history and significance of the *dalmatica* see B. Payne, G. Winakor and J. Farell-Beck, *The History of Costume* (New York: Harper Collins, 1992), 108-109, where one also finds (112) a photograph of an ancient senatorial *dalmatica* with broad *clavi* signifying senatorial rank.

8 Michael Avi-Yonah, "Goodenough's Evaluation of the Dura Paintings: A Critique," in Gutmann, *The Dura Europos Synagogue*, 128.

replaced by the new concept of an "orb within an orb."[9] The earth was now imagined as a sphere at the very center of an enormous orb whose outermost carapace was fixed with the stars, with the planets circling the earth at graduated distances from its surface. The "dome" was removed, and the earth, thought to be a sphere, stood open to the heavens which encircled it.[10]

These cosmological observations led to a variety of new theological theories and assumptions. Philosophers noted that the area extending from the moon to the outermost carapace of stars (the superlunar region) was characterized by peace, predictability and harmony. In contrast, the area from the moon's orbit to the surface of the earth (the sublunar region) was the only one in the cosmos where Divine Nature (φύσις) met with the vagaries of Chance (τύχη), the sector of the cosmos where one found famine, disease, war and death.[11] The implications were clear: if misery was to be found only in the region beneath the moon, one could not expect any deity to make a dwelling there. Thus the old presupposition of constant divine immanence on earth received a serious blow. Lucretius the Epicurean (94-55 BCE) states the case this way:

> The very nature of divinity must necessarily enjoy immortal life in the deepest peace, far removed and separated from our troubles; for without pain, without danger, itself mighty by its own resources, needing us not at all, it is neither propitiated with services nor touched by wrath. Here [on Earth] if anyone decides to call the sea Neptune, and corn Ceres, and to misapply the name Bacchus rather than to use the title that is proper to that liquor, let us grant him to dub the round world Mother of the Gods, while he forbears in reality . . . to infect his mind with base superstition.[12]

If the gods do exist, then, their distance from us makes futile our prayers for help in our petty situations beneath the moon.

The Stoic concept of the cosmos answered this challenge with the idea that Divine Nature was the sacred force responsible for the entirety of the cosmos. In the Stoic view, all patterns and all manifestations of nature, including all human events, express the divine force. Thus even those situations which seem

---

9   For this insight I am indebted to Luther H. Martin's *Hellenistic Religions: An Introduction* (New York: Oxford University Press, 1987).

10   Aristotle, *Meteorologica*; Lucretius, *On the Nature of the Universe* 5.430-590; Cicero, *On the Nature of the Gods* 2.6.16; 22.58; Pliny the Elder, *Natural History* 6.32-40; 12.59-16.80; 63.154-165; 105.224. Notice how Philo interprets Genesis 1:1-2:4 according to the new cosmology in *On the Account of the World's Creation Given by Moses* 1-24. See also Milton K. Munitz, *Theories of the Universe* (New York: Free Press of Glencoe, 1957); John Louis Emil Dreyer, *A History of Astronomy from Thales to Kepler* (Cambridge: Dover, 1953); A. W. H. Adkins, *From Many to One* (London: Constable, 1970).

11   See Samuel Sambursky, *The Physical World of Late Antiquity* (London: Routledge and Kegan Paul, 1962), 62-98.

12   Lucretius, *On the Nature of the Universe* 2.646-57.

wicked are only apparently so. Everything works together to fulfil holy destiny, holy fate. Thus, Stoicism affirmed omnipresent divine immanence.[13] Virgil captures this concept in Anchises' speech: "a spirit within [the cosmos] sustains, and mind, pervading its members, sways the whole mass and mingles with its mighty frame."[14] The new cosmology had introduced doubt that life beneath the moon was subject to patterns and not to any personalized divine causality, a doubt which Stoicism aimed to assuage.

This doubt is the point of dramatic difference between the cosmology of remote antiquity and Hellenistic cosmology. To state the matter rather baldly: in remote antiquity the cause of an act was always the will of a god (provided it were not magic), while in much of the Hellenistic world the causality of any event was not at all certain. The rise of agnosticism and the prevalence and popularity of literary satires jibing at "superstition" are evidence of this shift in perspective.[15] Such public expressions of doubt would not have been expected in the world of remote antiquity. But by the first century CE the Mediterranean world had had 300 years for the dissemination and absorption of the new cosmology. One of the results was increased complexity in the representation of divine immanence. The idea of God Most High directly visiting a populace beneath the moon belonged to the folk stories of old. Divine involvement in the sector beneath the moon was more usually envisioned through a mediator figure, a divinely-empowered hero who brings order to the sublunar world.

3.1 The Divine Hero

Alexander the Great, through his own historiographers and biographers, promulgated the idea of himself as divinely empowered. One example of this propaganda is found in a reference from his biography by Callisthenes of Olynthes (ca. 356-323 BCE). Although this work is no longer extant in its entirety, most modern historians grant that it was known to all subsequent biographers of Alexander.[16] The following reference is drawn from Eustathius, a 12th-century CE commentator, discussing Homer's description of Poseidon, the Lord of the Sea: "Then gambolled the sea beasts beneath him [Poseidon] on every side from out of the deeps, *for well they knew their Lord*, and in gladness

---

13 A. A. Long, *Hellenistic Philosophy: Stoics, Epicureans, Sceptics* (London: Duckworth, 1986); Sambursky, *Physical World*; R. M. Wenley, *Stoicism and its Influence* (New York: Cooper Square, 1963); Jean Pépin, "Cosmic Piety," in A. H. Armstrong, ed., *Classical Mediterranean Spirituality: An Encyclopedic History of the Religious Quest* (New York: Crossroad, 1986), vol. 15, 408-435.

14 Virgil, *Aeneid* 6.726-27.

15 See Plautus, *The Rope* 289-415; Petronius, *The Satyricon* 114; Juvenal, *Satires* 12.77-82; Lucian, *On Salaried Posts in Great Houses* 3.1.

16 This work (not the *Alexander Romance* attributed to a Pseudo-Callisthenes) is no longer extant and must be recovered from the references in Strabo, Plutarch and others.

the sea parted before him."[17] Eustathius recalls Callisthenes' description of Alexander crossing the Pamphylian Sea, and quotes Callisthenes: "*It [the Sea] did not fail to recognize its Lord*, so that arching itself and bowing it may seem to do obeisance."[18] It is clear that Callisthenes is granting to Alexander an obeisance that ordinarily belongs to Poseidon, yet he does not expect his audience to view Alexander as Poseidon himself. Instead, Callisthenes says that the Sea recognized Alexander's divine empowerment. He is not to be impeded in his fulfilment of his heavenly mandate as Lord of earth and sea.

After Alexander's death, his followers continued to impress the notion of his divinity on the imagination of the Mediterranean world. Susan Walker and Andrew Burnett discuss Alexander's representation as a deity:

> Certain gestures, symbols and items of clothing reveal the likening of Alexander to various Gods, both Greek and oriental. The enormous eyes gazing up to heaven and the star that appeared on some portraits were marks of deification; some early portraits showed him in the aegis of Zeus, while posthumous portraits had rams' horns over his ears, a characteristic of the god Zeus Ammon, his reputed divine father. . . . [A] chariot drawn by elephants or an elephant-scalp recalled the god Dionysus, conqueror of the east, and evoked Alexander's triumphs in India.[19]

These portrayals demonstrate the ways that the idea of a divinely-empowered hero, subsequently divinized himself, was now pressing the popular imagination of the western Mediterranean world.

The Roman conquerors were not unaware of the propaganda value of a leader's portraiture on coins and public monuments. Augustus had to protest against the abundance of statues raised in his honour and he publicly denounced divine honours of any kind. But the very necessity of such legislation is proof enough that the idea of a divinely-empowered leader was already popular in his day.

> Augustus imposed restrictions on the use of his image, allowing some Greek cities with the tradition of emperor worship to build temples dedicated to him with the goddess Roma, while refusing to allow temples in places where Roman sentiment might be offended. The most important of these was in Rome itself, where the new policy was inaugurated in a spectacular fashion

---

17 *Iliad* 13.27-29 (emphasis mine).

18 This is reported by Eustathius in his comment on the *Iliad* 29 (emphasis mine). See *The Lost Histories of Alexander*, trans. Lionel Pearson (London: Basil Blackwell, 1960), 37. See also Felix Jacoby, *Die Fragmente der griechischen Historiker* (Leiden: Brill, 1962), vol. 2, B.650.

19 Susan Walker and Andrew Burnett, *The Image of Augustus* (London: British Museum, 1984), 4.

with the destruction and melting down of eighty silver statues of Augustus.
. . . . The use of silver was considered inappropriate for images of living
persons, and should be reserved for the gods.[20]

Despite Augustus's efforts, representations of him alluding to divine
empowerment remain. The Boston Museum of Fine Arts holds a sard intaglio
which depicts Octavian pulled across the waves by four horses, the classical
Homeric image of Poseidon. This gem was carved in 31 BCE to commemorate
Octavian's triumph at Actium.[21]

The application of Poseidon's typical activity to Augustus does not identify
him as Poseidon any more than Callisthenes meant to communicate such an
identity for Alexander. The message is that Augustus has been granted authority
over the cosmos, including the sea. The sea recognized Augustus's heavenly
authorization and would not obstruct his war plans. Thus nature demonstrates
its subservience to the one chosen by heaven to guide the destiny of the world.

Just as Augustus is not Poseidon, neither is he Zeus, or God Most High.
According to the new cosmology, the hero's command over Nature is one
expression of empowerment by God. The obedience of the elements are a
testimony that they recognize that authorization. Of course, in the larger
Mediterranean world, a hero capable of ordering the elements would be readily
granted the status of a "god." In Jewish circles the hero would be understood
as a divinely-empowered mediator. When Philo praises Augustus to the
emperor's great-nephew, Gaius Caesar, he uses the metaphors of a man
miraculously ordering calm to a storm and healing a pestilence without a
petition to a deity to describe Augustus's independent exercise of authority,
which resulted in the *pax*.[22] (This is also evidence that the idea of a hero
calming a storm on his own is already "alive" from the 40s of the first century.)
Later, in Nero's reign, Calpurnius Siculus (ca. 50-60 CE) composed a poem
meant to honour the young new prince. One shepherd says to another: "Do you
see how the green woods are hushed at the sound of Caesar's [Nero's] name?
I remember how, despite the swoop of a storm, the grove, even as now, sank
sudden into peace with boughs at rest. And I said, 'A god, surely a god, has
driven the east winds hence.'"[23] In this case the divinity of Nero is directly
confessed.

It is this independent action on earth, the direct response of nature to the
authority of the hero, that separates heroes of the Graeco-Roman world from
those most common to the world of remote antiquity. In this context, the mere

---

20 Walker and Burnett, *Image*, 17.
21 Moses Hadas, *Imperial Rome* (New York: Time, 1965), 69.
22 Philo, *Embassy to Gaius* 144-45.
23 Calpurnius Siculus, *Eclogue* 4.97-100. Translation, by J. Wight Duff and Arnold M.
    Duff, taken from *Minor Latin Poets* (Cambridge: Harvard University Press, 1954), 252-53.

claim of Jesus taking authority over nature would not necessarily have led first-generation Christians to the conclusion that Jesus was literally the embodiment of the Most High. The obedience of the elements to Jesus who "stilled the storm," for example, would not have been sufficient to support their belief in Jesus as creation's Lord. Rather, in the Imperial period such a demonstration would suggest that Jesus had received an authorization acknowledged by the elements. His mission on earth was not to be resisted.

3.2 The Function of Septuagint References in Jesus' Miracles

When a Jesus story contains a Septuagint reference it is usual for scholars to seek the meaning of the miracle, at least in part, by exploring the meaning of the biblical passage in its original context, but also against the backdrop of Graeco-Roman ideas. For instance, two major biblical texts feature in Mark 4:35-41. First, the main parts of the plot, with the two exceptions of the cause of the storm and Jesus' ordering the wind and sea to silence, seem to rely on Jonah 1:4-6, 15-16. Common narrative elements would include the suddenness and severity of the storm, the futility of those on board to save the ship, the sleeping protagonist, the protagonist being scolded, the protagonist giving the solution of the puzzle and the sudden calm of the sea.[24] This overlap, however, does not indicate that the meaning of Jesus' action depends on the Jonah story—the miracle itself is the very place where the stories diverge. The Jonah story requires the sailors to throw him into the wild sea, to throw him back to God. The Jesus story states that the awakened Jesus orders the wind and sea to be silent and that the elements obey. The act of calming a storm could be seen as an example of the Most High's cosmic power (Pss 29:3; 89:25; 107:29; Nah 1:4).[25] If we were to interpret this miracle story in light of the cosmology of remote antiquity, it would imply that Jesus is in fact the Creator God. But the new cosmology already informs us that the hero—Jesus in this case—is known by the elements, which must then obey him. It affirms that Jesus' empowerment must be seen and understood in the context of Jewish revelation.

Here we see that a Christian community would give to Jesus literally what Philo grants to Augustus metaphorically:

---

24 These similarities have already been observed by Rudolf Bultmann, *The History of the Synoptic Tradition*, 2nd ed. (New York: Basil Blackwell, 1968 [1963]); Rudolf Pesch, *Das Markusevangelium* (Freiburg: Herder, 1980), vol. 1, 278; E. Lohmeyer, *Das Evangelium des Markus* (Göttingen: Vandenhoeck & Ruprecht, 1937), 90; and in particular O. Lamar Cope, *Matthew* (Washington: Catholic Biblical Association of America, 1976), 97.

25 C. F. D. Moule, *The Gospel According to Mark* (Cambridge: Cambridge University Press, 1965), 42; Alan Richardson, *The Miracle Stories of the Gospels* (London: SCM, 1941; repr. 1963), esp. 90-92; and Denis E. Nineham, *The Gospel of St. Mark* (London: Adam and Charles Black, 1963), 146-47.

> The whole human race exhausted by mutual slaughter was on the verge of utter destruction had it not been for one man and leader, Augustus, whom men fitly call the averter of evil. *This is the Caesar who calmed the torrential storms on every side*, who healed pestilences common to Greeks and barbarians, pestilences which descending from the south and east coursed to the west and north sowing the seeds of calamity over the places and waters which lay between them.[26]

Both Jesus and Augustus are credited with the type of salvific activity which Psalm 107:28-32 reserves for God himself:

> Then they cried to the Lord in their trouble
> and he brought them out from their distress;
> he made the storm be still,
> and the waves of the sea were hushed.
> And they were glad because they had quiet,
> and he brought them to their desired haven.
> Let them thank the Lord for his steadfast love,
> for his wonderful works to humankind.
> Let them extol him in the congregation of the people,
> and praise him in the assembly of the elders.

In the Jesus miracle, then, the obedience of the wind and the sea would not necessarily communicate that Jesus is the Most High or creation's Lord. But certainly we could expect a first-generation Christian audience to see in Jesus' power a testimony to his divine authorization: nature recognizes his cosmic *imperium* as its Lord. The allusion to the Septuagint therefore signals the class of power Jesus is intended to have—that is, cosmic authority—as it obviously identifies the source of that power with the God revealed in Jewish scripture.[27]

What, then, is the function of the allusion to the Jonah story? Certainly it places the Jesus story in dialogue with Jewish material and, in this case, a prophetic tradition. Moreover, it accommodates the popular theme of the sea storm. In particular, however, it emphasizes the point that Jesus clearly outshines Jonah. Thus the similarities with the Jonah story only serve to emphasize the superior status of Jesus over this prophet. The same might be said of Mark 6:30-44, where Jesus feeds the 5,000 in the wilderness. The Septuagint allusion recalls 2 Kings 4:42-44, where Elisha produces 120 loaves of barley and some fresh ears of grain. As portrayed by the gospels, Jesus' miracle far surpasses that of Elisha. Thus the more exalted status of Jesus is asserted to anyone conversant with the Elijah traditions.

---

26 Philo, *Gaius* 144-45 (emphasis mine). Translation, by F. H. Colson, taken from *Philo* (Cambridge: Harvard University Press, 1972), vol. 10, 72-75.

27 My dissertation ("The Markan Sea Miracles") deals with this miracle in a more detailed manner.

Allusions to a Septuagint passage in a miracle story do not allow the scholar to find the whole meaning of the miracle there. We have already seen that the first-century lens accommodates a divinely-empowered hero acting in ways reserved for the Most High without in fact implying that the hero actually is God Most High. The particular act authorized by the hero will situate his relative importance in the world. In the Stilling of the Storm, Jesus' command to the wind and the sea would suggest to a first-century audience that he is Lord of the sea. Metaphorically, since the sea symbolizes life's unsettled and dangerous character, Jesus' authority as Lord of the sea signals to the attentive listener that just as surely as he commands the elements such as wind and sea, so too he has control over life-threatening events. These interpretations are possible because Jesus' act of calming a storm is seen with the symbol system and the cosmological nuancing appropriate to the first century.

This understanding of how the Septuagint would function in first-century Christian miracle stories is well supported by what we have already seen in our examples of contemporary political propaganda. Homer's description of the Lord of the sea, Poseidon, features the sea-beasts pulling him across the waves, "for well they knew their Lord, and in gladness, the sea parted before him." Callisthenes was alluding to this religious text in his description of Alexander's crossing of the Pamphylian Sea. The Roman jeweller who carved the intaglio made the allusion visual in his depiction of the triumphant young Octavian of 31 BCE being pulled across the sea by horses. Gaius Caligula's five-mile bridge across the Bay of Baiae is another example of a desire to appropriate a deity's image to emphasize Lordship. Gaius had ordered Roman ships to be lashed together end to end in order to construct this bridge, and on two days he made triumphant crossings of the bridge, first attired in a breastplate and riding a charger, then riding a chariot in a mock triumph. Because the water remained calm throughout the exhibition, Gaius was convinced that Neptune feared him.[28] In effect, using artificial means Gaius could boast that he had ridden across the water dryshod. Neptune's subservience to his plan was interpreted to mean that he too recognized him as Lord. In none of these examples does the leader's supremacy mean that he is, in fact, Poseidon/Neptune. The idea is that the hero has been divinely empowered over earth and sea by Heaven, and that the elements, including the sea, know it. Nothing must interfere with the authority of the hero who carries cosmic *imperium*.

In the same way, the Septuagint allusion locates the religious tradition in which Jesus and his message is to be understood and interpreted. But these texts must be seen through the lens of the first century, which had its own ideas of mediated Lordship and cosmic *imperium*, ideas which were foreign to the world of remote antiquity.

---

28 Dio Chrysostom, *Roman History* 59.17.11.

4. Apocalyptic Cosmology and the Jesus Miracles

Robert Grant's 1952 book, *Miracle and Natural Law*, perfectly epitomizes the dichotomy many scholars presume between the ordinary world-view of the Graeco-Roman Mediterranean world and the apocalypticism accepted by most Christian communities.[29] Although the title suggests an integration of the two topics, they are in fact two separate essays. The first correctly clarifies the change in cosmological ideas in the Graeco-Roman period. The second explains that Christian miracles show no influence from that Graeco-Roman world-view because "the New Testament reflects Old Testament ideas of miracles."[30] For Grant, biblical ideas in the first-century Christian communities are to be equated with apocalypticism; he presumes that a first-century "Jewish" world-view would have been apocalyptic in character. Of course, once it is asserted that Christians did not share the ordinary world-view of their day, then a contextualization of Christian miracle stories may not include the typical narratives common to that world, and the backdrop is immediately confined to apocalyptic texts and apocalyptic world-views. Thus, the dark view of the world saturated with sin, under the unbridled control of Satan and doomed to destruction is presupposed in interpreting the Jesus miracles. The meaning is always the same: Jesus' manifestation of power in the individual miracle spells the end of Satan's control, the promise of the coming salvation from sin's control and the assurance of liberation from the dark forces that hold the entire cosmos in slavery. Those who have held this position include C. J. Cadoux, C. H. Dodd, Alec Burkill, Paul Achtemeier, Reginald Fuller and Howard Kee.[31] With respect to the Stilling of the Storm, Dodd, for instance, states: "The raging sea is a symbol of primaeval chaos and so of returning chaos at the end. . . . [The] tradition which underlies the pericope had at some stage been influenced by apocalyptic conceptions and had absorbed some of their imagery."[32] Reginald Fuller holds that the "power of Yahweh is present in Jesus, as it was in the original act of creation. The chaos of the world is being

---

29 Robert M. Grant, *Miracle and Natural Law in Graeco-Roman and Early Christian Thought* (Amsterdam: North-Holland, 1952).

30 Grant, *Miracle*, 154, which echoes Richardson, *Miracle Stories*, 90.

31 Cecil John Cadoux, *The Historic Mission of Jesus* (London: Lutterworth, 1941), esp. 17; C. H. Dodd, "The Appearances of the Risen Jesus," in Denis E. Nineham, ed., *Studies in the Gospels* (Oxford: Basil Blackwell, 1955), 26; T. Alec Burkill, "The Notion of Miracle with Special Reference to St. Mark's Gospel," *Zeitschrift für die neutestamentliche Wissenschaft* 50 (1959): 38; Reginald Fuller, *Interpreting the Miracles* (London: SCM, 1963), 41; Howard Clark Kee, *Miracle in the Early Christian World: A Study in Sociohistorical Method* (New Haven: Yale University Press, 1983). An exception is Karl Kertelge (*Die Wunder Jesu im Markusevangelium* [München: Kösel, 1970]) who, although he does not discuss non-Jewish parallels to the Jesus stories, at least provides references to them in his copious footnotes.

32 Dodd, "Appearances," 26.

restored to its pristine order. . . . The theological point of this story is that in Jesus, God is asserting his sovereignty over the uncanny realm of Satan."[33] Paul Achtemeier states its significance in this way: "Both [the exorcism of Mark 1:21-28 and the storm in Mark 4:35-41] are dealt with in the same way because it would appear that both are caused by the same element: the enemy of God and Christ, the demonic."[34]

The serious difficulty with each of these treatments is that they presume an apocalyptic world-view. The miracle has not been allowed to stand against a backdrop of sea adventure stories common to the first-century Mediterranean world. If it had, these scholars would have noted that the storm simply arises as the sea storms in the adventure accounts often do. Jesus' command to the elements need not be a sign that they are possessed. Rather, the point of surprise for those on board is that the wind and sea obey Jesus; the submission of the sea does not necessitate an appeal to an apocalyptic world-view. The longing to claim that the elements recognize a hero is easily found in the Imperial propaganda of the ordinary Graeco-Roman world. If, then, we wish to interpret the miracle story against an apocalyptic background, we must be able to point to some unusual features that cause it to diverge from ordinary contemporary ideas about the sea and the other elements of the cosmos; there must be some sign that the author of the miracle story presumes an evil world saturated with sin. An apocalyptic world-view simply cannot be presumed, and then applied as an interpretive tool.

The need to test the world-view presumed by the author of a Christian miracle story is especially important in the case of exorcism stories. One scholar who has attended to this necessity is Graham Twelftree, who examines the evidence of exorcisms—both Jewish and non-Jewish—throughout the Graeco-Roman world.[35] Although Twelftree is particularly interested in what might be said about the actual exorcistic practices of the historical Jesus, his treatment allows us to note that it is possible for an exorcist to perform successfully without any sign of an apocalyptic world-view. The two exorcisms of Apollonius of Tyana, for example, attend to the unhappy condition of the possessed and liberate them. But there is no hint from the narrator, Philostratus, that Apollonius's power over the demons marks the beginning of Satan's overthrow.[36] Philostratus does not give any indication that he or Apollonius expects an imminent end to a sinful cosmos. If a Jesus exorcism is told in roughly the same manner, we should not immediately assume that the Christian author holds an apocalyptic world-view. Our point is not that an exorcism story

---

33   Fuller, *Interpreting*, 54, 59.
34   Achtemeier, "Person and Deed," 176.
35   Graham H. Twelftree, *Jesus the Exorcist: A Contribution to the Study of the Historical Jesus* (Tübingen: J. C. B. Mohr, 1993); see especially 23-28.
36   Philostratus, *The Life of Apollonius of Tyana* 3.38; 4.20.

cannot express apocalyptic expectations, but only that in order to do so, some formulation in the account must diverge from ordinary exorcism accounts of the Graeco-Roman world and signal that the world is now being saved from the grip of satanic power.

Some scholars look for their evidence in the eschatological Jesus sayings. Gerd Theissen supports his position that the exorcisms assume an apocalyptic world-view by reference to four eschatological sayings: Mark 3:24-26; Mark 3:27; Luke 10:18; and Matthew 12:28. He notes that in each case an exorcism story occurs in close proximity to each of these sayings. In this view, therefore, "the starting point for an eschatological interpretation of the miracles is the exorcisms." This reasoning leads him to the following conclusion: "Because Jesus casts out demons he can proclaim that the end has entered into the present. . . . Because the negative web of evil has already been broken it is possible for salvation to come in individual instances. Because individual instances of salvation occur, the presence of the end can be proclaimed here and now."[37] But Theissen's argument is a surprising one for a form critic, since sayings and miracle stories represent two discrete genres and cannot be presumed to be dependent on each other to facilitate mutual interpretation. The proximity of an eschatological saying to an exorcism story is a secondary choice made by the evangelist, not by the composers of the particular sayings or stories. Theissen has also failed to note that the sayings of Jesus are not of one type, but hold various perspectives on the world. To set aside the four particular sayings he does is a product of his own theory, not the impression fostered by the sayings tradition taken as a whole.

5. Conclusion

This treatment has suggested two major implications which derive from the observation that a proper interpretation of the miracles demands that any cosmology presumed for their backdrop must begin with the one most common to the Mediterranean world of the first century. First, our guild has only slowly come to appreciate the dramatic differences between that dominant Hellenistic cosmology and the one prevalent in remote antiquity. As a result, the interpretation of Jesus' miraculous activity has tended to be made in the light of an ancient Jewish lens which allowed only the Most High, and not a designated hero, to command any cosmic change. Second, many scholars have presumed that a Jewish first-century lens is equivalent to an apocalyptic world-view. They also assume that this cosmology represents the earliest Christian lens

---

37 Gerd Theissen, *Urchristliche Wundergeschichten: Ein Beitrag zur formgeschichtlichen Erforschung der synoptischen Evangelien* (Gütersloh: Gerd Mohn, 1974)—English translation: *The Miracle Stories of the Synoptic Tradition*, trans. Francis McDonough (Philadelphia: Fortress, 1983), 279-80.

everywhere around the Mediterranean Sea. I have argued that such a position stands on untested assumptions or on highly selective groupings of Jesus' sayings.

The foundational character of cosmology, coupled with the scholarly misunderstanding of its typical first-century form, suggests that all the Jesus miracles should undergo a re-examination. Each story must be tested individually for the world-view it evinces. Since both Septuagint ideas of the cosmos and apocalypticism represent uncommon world-views in the first century CE, such perspectives must be proven to be intended by the author on the basis of internal evidence. Only then can the contextualization of the story be accomplished responsibly, since relevant parallels will then be gathered on the basis of a similar world-view. Biblical allusions as well as references contemporary with the first century will thus be viewed in accord with authorial intent.

10. The Theological Importance of the "Third Quest" for the Historical Jesus

Halvor Moxnes

1. New Wine in Old Wineskins?[1]

As this century comes to a close, have we come full circle in the study of the historical Jesus, returning to the beginning of the century when Albert Schweitzer wrote *The Quest of the Historical Jesus*? This may seem a strange proposition since Schweitzer's criticism of liberal theology and its quest has long been accepted. But the question was sparked by John Dominic Crossan's criticism of recent research, with accusations similar to those levelled against 19th-century questers: "It is impossible to avoid the suspicion that historical-Jesus research is a very safe place to do theology and call it history, to do autobiography and call it biography."[2] A much-heard accusation against liberal theology is that it described Jesus in its own image; that made me curious about possible connections or similarities with contemporary Jesus research. In many ways the present situation within biblical studies, in terms of methods as well as results, is very different from that at the beginning of the century. These differences owe most to the domination of form and redaction criticism in the period between the beginning of the century and the present.

Historical-Jesus research may be a special case, with the "third quest" exhibiting similarities with the first. One similarity appears in the optimism of such studies. There is now less fear of producing "lives of Jesus" than there was in the period between the first and third quests; correspondingly, there has been a mushrooming of "Jesus" books in our day as there was in Schweitzer's. Another similarity appears in the context in which historical-Jesus studies are carried out. Both late-19th- and late-20th-century quests have shown more interest in Jesus and society than in relations between Jesus and the church.

---

1 Since my contribution to the 1993 seminar, a number of relevant new publications on the historical Jesus have appeared—in particular, works by E. P. Sanders (*The Historical Figure of Jesus* [London: Allen Lane, 1993]), John Dominic Crossan (*Jesus: A Revolutionary Biography* [San Francisco: HarperSanFrancisco, 1994]) and Richard A. Horsley (*Galilee: History, Politics, People* [Valley Forge: Trinity Press International, 1995]). Also important in this regard is Luke Timothy Johnson's *The Real Jesus: The Misguided Quest for the Historical Jesus and the Truth of the Traditional Gospels* (San Francisco: HarperSanFrancisco, 1996). The discussion of various approaches to the study of the historical Jesus ought to be seen within the larger context of changes in historical scholarship, especially concerning the question of "meaning" in history. I have attempted to do this in "Den historiske Jesus: Mellom modernitet og postmodernitet?" *Norsk Teologisk Tidsskrift* 96 (1995): 139-56.

2 John Dominic Crossan, *The Historical Jesus: The Life of a Mediterranean Jewish Peasant* (San Francisco: HarperSanFrancisco, 1991), xxviii.

The third quest, as its name reveals, follows two others. The first quest, by which I mean historical-Jesus research (mostly in Protestant Germany) around the turn of the century, saw Jesus within the context of society at large, and not only within the Church. What has usually been termed "the new quest of the historical Jesus"[3] I shall speak of as the "second quest." Coming from within the Bultmannian tradition, it had to defend the legitimacy of the very question of "a historical Jesus." Central to this second quest was raising the question of the historical Jesus so that the preaching (κήρυγμα) about Jesus Christ should not become detached from the historical Jesus. The situation in which this "new quest" arose explains its explicit theological interest focusing primarily on the question of continuity (or not) between the historical Jesus and the proclaimed Christ of the church. The third quest is clearly less dominated by theological issues.

Some third-quest scholars even explicitly deny any theological intentions.[4] There is an interest in describing Jesus as an historical person, without relating that image to questions about Christology. This may be because renewed interest in the historical Jesus has arisen outside the specific context of an "inside reaction" to a dominant German Protestant (Bultmannian) tradition. Rather, it is the result of a much more varied intellectual situation; initially at least it also was much more of an American enterprise. Moreover, its scholarship is often done outside a specific church-oriented context. Although Jewish interest in the historical Jesus also existed earlier, there is now a considerable Jewish contribution, and Jewish and Christian scholars are showing more similarities in approach and results.

Although the third quest clearly exhibits less interest in issues traditionally spoken of as theology within a church context, is "theology" present in a different and broader sense, in terms of "meaning" and "relevance"? With fewer direct links to a church context, it may become more important for biblical scholars to be aware of the *general* context within which we find ourselves. The public sphere continues to exhibit considerable interest in Jesus. This interest, for example, contributed significantly to the success of Robert Funk's "Jesus Seminar," with its much publicized votes on the historicity of words of Jesus.[5]

The public interest is of varying character. It is found both inside and outside a Christian context. Within a "New Age" setting, for instance, Jesus is a "holy man" among other Eastern holy men and women. Within Islam—especially in Egypt—there is also growing interest in Jesus as a holy

---

3   James M. Robinson, *A New Quest of the Historical Jesus* (Missoula: Scholars Press, 1979 [1959]).

4   E.g., E. P. Sanders, *Jesus and Judaism* (Philadelphia: Fortress, 1985).

5   I might add, however, that I think the Seminar's votes on the authentic words of Jesus is an exercise more typical of the interests of the second quest.

man. Scandinavia, my own context, provides another example. Two books about Jesus appeared in 1992 written by prominent intellectuals.[6] Alvar Ellegard claimed that the traditions about Jesus were all a forgery; Villy Sørensen, in the tradition of the 19th century, spoke of Jesus as the epochal figure of our ("Western") culture. Perhaps representing rather outdated points of view, they nevertheless accurately reflect a European intellectual tradition which has often been quite critical of established Christianity. We should also not forget that many churches in Latin America, Africa and Asia have interpreted the gospels and spoken of Jesus in ways that draw heavily upon an image of Jesus in his historical life in Palestine. Thus, it does not seem irrelevant to ask whether we are again in a situation in which historical-Jesus studies are related to general cultural, religious and social contexts more than to specific theological and church-oriented ones.

2. The Question of Genre in the Study of the Historical Jesus

Are we also on our way to a situation where the fear of "Jesus-biography" or concern for "objective" history does not dominate so much? This question is prompted by an observation about the genres of studies of Jesus and the perspectives of their authors. In his introduction to *The Historical Jesus*, Crossan sees the present situation as a problem.[7] He finds the large variety of pictures of Jesus an "academic embarrassment" and calls for more concern for questions of theory and method. And it is in the stringent execution of clearly-delineated methods (exemplified by his own book) that he sees the solution to this problem of diversity. But is it really a problem? Is it not more a result of this new stage in historical-Jesus scholarship, and indeed in historical scholarship in general, that we speak not of *the history* of Jesus, but rather *histories* of Jesus? The emphasis on methodological awareness of which Crossan speaks has become increasingly important, but a consequence of this heightened awareness is a growing methodological diversity.

There can, for instance, be a connection between history and rhetoric. Crossan's book is itself an example of that. Its title—*The Historical Jesus*—is succinct, and the book's cover presents it as "the first comprehensive determination of who Jesus was, what he did, and what he said," giving the impression of "objective history." But then suddenly the subtitle breaks this pattern, with a vivid and stimulating, but certainly contestable, phrase: "the life of a Mediterranean Jewish peasant." This evokes memories of the "life of Jesus" series, with a further characterization of him as "peasant," a term that

---

6   Alvar Ellegard, *Myten om Jesus: Den tidigaste kristendomen i nytt ljus* (Stockholm: Bonniers, 1992); Villy Sørensen, *Jesus og Kristus* (Copenhagen: Gyldendal, 1992).

7   Crossan, *Historical Jesus*, xxviii.

creates an expectation that we shall now read the story of somebody who lived his life as a peasant in a Jewish village.

Other authors also give the impression of their awareness of the diversity of presentations of Jesus in the way they describe their studies. Paula Fredriksen's *From Jesus to Christ* in its subtitle announces "the New Testament images of Jesus," and retains the term for her effort to reach the historical Jesus of Nazareth: "toward a historical image of Jesus."[8] In a similar way Marcus Borg in *Jesus: A New Vision* contrasts "the popular image" of Jesus with the "dominant scholarly image" before proceeding to spell out a "new historical image of Jesus."[9] Borg explains the primary categories that he uses when he sketches his portrait of Jesus. This makes it possible for him to criticize a former scholarly consensus; still, he presents his alternative not as historical "fact," but as an attempt to "recover the vision of Jesus."[10] This way of clarifying one's method and at the same time speaking of "image" bespeaks the historian's task. It is predictable, and not a *problem*, that we cannot reach "the historical Jesus," but instead must construct "the historian's Jesus."[11]

3. Jesus and Society

In what way does the quest for the historical Jesus describe and understand his social context? Is the emphasis put upon "general" or even "universal" elements, or on concrete and particular historical factors? The emphasis changes not only the historical picture, but also to a large extent its possible use and relevance. A comparison between the "first quest" and the "third quest" will point to several differences.

3.1 Jesus the Religious Personality in a Universal Society

A characteristic example of historical-Jesus scholarship at the beginning of the century, "unreformed" by Schweitzer's criticism, is the article "Jesus Christus" by Wilhelm Heitmüller, in the first (1912) edition of *Die Religion in Geschichte und Gegenwart*.[12] Heitmüller defines the task for the scholar who wants to place Jesus within history: it is most important to grasp the character of Jesus' personality, and particularly its religious aspects. Jesus' teaching, according to

8   Paula Fredriksen, *From Jesus to Christ* (New Haven: Yale University Press, 1988).
9   Marcus J. Borg, *Jesus, a New Vision: Spirit, Culture, and the Life of Discipleship* (San Francisco: Harper, 1987), 14.
10 Borg, *New Vision*, 17.
11 Robinson, *New Quest*, 31.
12 Wilhelm Heitmüller, "Jesus Christus," in *Die Religion in Geschichte und Gegenwart: Handwörterbuch in gemeinverständlicher Darstellung* (Tübingen: J. C. B. Mohr, 1912), vol. 3, 343-410.

Heitmüller, closely reflected his religious personality. Consequently, it is not, as commonly held, the Kingdom of God that is the central point of Jesus' teaching. The emphasis on the Kingdom must be ascribed to the earliest Christian communities. A study of Jesus' own teachings, however, must proceed from that which is always of basic importance in religion: conceptions of God and the relations between God and humanity. The result is, not unexpectedly, an emphasis on ethics; moreover, Heitmüller finds that the main characteristic of Jesus' ethical stance is its individualism. He notes the correspondence between human relations to God, which are solely concerned with the individual, and relations to other human beings, which are not. Considering "life in God" to be completely individualistically determined and all other human institutions of less importance, Heitmüller speaks in a general way of "family, society, state, culture."

The way in which Heitmüller uses these terms to describe Jesus' surroundings seems more appropriate to Protestant Germany in the early-20th century than to Palestine in the first. When we realize how these social institutions were not only accepted but highly valued by liberal Protestants, it is obvious that Jesus' negative attitude to them is a problem. Jesus did not share a belief in an independent value of the family, the state or culture. Heitmüller rejects various ways to "explain away" this uncomfortable fact, and ends up with the suggestion that Jesus' expressions are paradoxical, directed at the individual. Although Jesus presents the individual with ethical demands, disconnected from various forms of social contexts, his words do not aim at a rejection of the desultory forms of human fellowship.

This approach, abounding with anachronistic elements in its description of the social scene, places Jesus in an ahistorical limbo where the presupposed context is really early-20th-century Germany. But it makes the discussion of the historical Jesus directly relevant for Heitmüller's own time, for important elements in contemporary society. Jesus' ethical stance was described so as to address the individual in a way that questioned, but did not seriously threaten, the recognized social and political institutions of a modern European society.

3.2 Jesus the Peasant in a Particular Society

It is illuminating to see recent trends in the study of Jesus in his social setting against this example of the *status quaestionis* 80 years ago. Although some interest was shown in the social location of Jesus in the "second quest" (especially in the political attitudes and actions of Jesus), social setting has become a central issue in the third quest. Representatives of this new emphasis include Gerd Theissen, Willy Schottroff, Wolfgang Stegemann and Seán Freyne in Europe; Marcus Borg, Paul Hollenbach, Richard Horsley, Douglas Oakman and now also John Dominic Crossan in the United States. Several common elements distinguish newer studies from Heitmüller's: highlighting Jesus' acts, not only his teaching; prioritizing a Jewish (at times eschatological) orientation to Jesus' proclamation; insisting on a kingdom related to community, not just to the individual; linking the religious, the social and the economic; and setting first-century social structures and groups in their particular historical context, using appropriate methods and models.

Over against an image of Jesus as the unique religious personality, speaking to individuals in an abstract social context of "family, state, and culture," one can use Crossan's "Mediterranean Jewish peasant" as an example of the third quest. Each of these words demands explanations and raises questions: "Was Jesus really a peasant?" "What did it mean to be a Jewish peasant in the first century?" "What is special about being a Mediterranean peasant?" I will use Crossan's subtitle to highlight some of the more promising directions of current research, using as examples three recent books: Seán Freyne's *Galilee, Jesus and the Gospels*, Douglas Oakman's *Jesus and the Economic Questions of his Day* and Richard Horsley's *Jesus and the Spiral of Violence: Popular Jewish Resistance in Roman Palestine*.[13]

Freyne's book situates Jesus in the context of Galilee, not just Palestine in general. He takes regional differences seriously in terms of history and the varying degrees of Hellenistic influence. This study and his earlier book, *Galilee from Alexander the Great to Hadrian*,[14] stand within a larger group of historical studies of areas and regions in late antiquity (as well as the Middle Ages) where presentations of the ecological basis, control of land and produce, and social relations contribute to a more comprehensive picture of history. Fernand Braudel's work, *The Mediterranean and the Mediterranean World in the Age of Philip II*,[15] is one of the most impressive examples of this type of study. Thus, modern biblical scholarship shares the movement from an individualistic and primarily political or religious history toward one that is multi-dimensional.

The broader picture that emerges from such an inquiry is also more difficult to handle. If the past is presented with more variety and diversity, all the more must the picture be focused and explained with the help of appropriate methods and models. If these models are not made explicit, unconsciously the material will be arranged in ways that conform even more to preconceived models appropriate for our own society.

---

13 Seán Freyne, *Galilee, Jesus and the Gospels: Literary Approaches and Historical Investigations* (Philadelphia: Fortress, 1988); Douglas E. Oakman, *Jesus and the Economic Questions of his Day* (Lewiston: Edwin Mellen, 1986); Richard A. Horsley, *Jesus and the Spiral of Violence: Popular Jewish Resistance in Roman Palestine* (Minneapolis: Fortress, 1987).

14 Seán Freyne, *Galilee from Alexander the Great to Hadrian, 323 B.C.E. to 135 C.E.: A Study of Second Temple Judaism* (Wilmington: Michael Glazier, 1980).

15 Fernand Braudel, *The Mediterranean and the Mediterranean World in the Age of Philip II*, trans. Sibn Reynolds, 2 vols. (New York: Harper and Row, 1972).

It is particularly in this respect that Oakman's book is a valuable contribution. The economic questions of Jesus' day were different from those that we think of as the most important today (e.g., those related to the stock market, gross national product). The economy had not yet become a separate sector of society with its own rules and a power-base separate from political and social forces. Ancient economies were much more embedded in the social structures of family, kinship and politics. The undisputed economic base in antiquity was production from the land. To understand a first-century Jewish peasant, one needs to know something about the land in Palestine, the modes and types of production, the distribution and ownership of land, the social and economic structure of farming, control over the crop and distribution of surpluses. The system that Oakman describes is one of (rich) landowners and brokers who served as links to tenants and smallholders. In this system the elite extract the surplus of a crop produced by peasants. Their relations can be categorized under the rubrics of patrons, brokers and clients. This economic system is best studied by means of the category "reciprocal exchange," developed in social anthropology by Marshall Sahlins.[16] Various forms of exchange fall under different categories: generalized reciprocity, i.e., giving with no (or with delayed) expectation of return; balanced reciprocity; and negative reciprocity, i.e., getting something for nothing, sometimes with force.

In what sense can one say that Jesus was a peasant? Oakman discusses this issue more thoroughly than Crossan, with references to the lively discussions of the term's definition among social scientists.[17] According to one definition of "peasant," which limits its application to those who cultivate the land, Jesus, as an artisan, cannot even be considered a peasant. According to another definition, however, "peasantry" denotes "the common situation of a whole range of rural groups who are occupationally diversified," but who operate within the framework of dominant peasant economy, and face the same situation of having little control over their political and economic situation.[18] In this latter respect Jesus was a peasant, because he "stood within the same structural relationship to the powerful as other villagers and artisans of his environment." This means that Jesus' "fundamental world of values and his fundamental interests and loyalties were shaped within and oriented towards the village."[19] Read with this insight, many of Jesus' parables are not "pastoral" in a romantic sense, but steeped in those economic questions that Jewish peasants experienced. Oakman's study is really a book about "peasant economics," that is, economic issues seen "from below," not from the perspective of the political elite.

---

16 See, e.g., Michael Sahlins, *Stone Age Economics* (Chicago: Aldine-Atherton, 1972).

17 Douglas E. Oakman, "Was Jesus a Peasant? Implications for Reading the Samaritan Story (Luke 10:30-35)," *Biblical Theology Bulletin* 22 (1992): 117-25.

18 Oakman, "Was Jesus a Peasant?" 118.

19 Oakman, "Was Jesus a Peasant?" 120-21.

In order to understand the social and economic situation of peasants in the time of Jesus, one must know what changes took place in the first century, changes whereby the political elite consolidated more land in larger estates, creating a heavy downward pressure on small landowners and tenants. Small landholders were often turned into debtors and even forced from their land. This development is part of the story told by Richard Horsley. Like Oakman, he focuses on village relations and structures.[20] Horsley puts Jesus within the context of popular Jewish resistance to Roman rule in Palestine and sees him as the leader of a non-violent, "social revolution." Of particular interest to us is the way in which Horsley focuses upon the local village community as the centre of Jesus' efforts for renewal. This situates his book within the context of studies of the structure, social organization and mentality of peasant villages.[21]

Horsley interprets Jesus' exhortation to forgive debts within this larger picture of village society. In the most general terms, it is part of the scholarly consensus that Jesus was concerned with the poor, that he taught that there should be no great difference between rich and poor. But this issue cannot remain on a general level. In order to understand specific sayings such as those about the cancellation or forgiveness of debt, it is imperative that we understand their social context. The Lord's Prayer shows the significance of remission of debts for Jesus' concept of the kingdom. Using village society as the primary context for Jesus, Horsley finds that by forgiving debts Jesus aims at a renewal not primarily of the individual, but of the local communities. His works and words aim to renew Israel by preaching and enacting the kingdom started in and focused on relations in the village. This activity can partly be described as a restoration of traditional community patterns (e.g., cooperation), but there were also elements critical of such traditions, for instance the introduction of egalitarian rather than hierarchical social relations.[22]

Finally, Crossan's introduction of "Mediterranean" into his title opens up a broader range of issues. It is not primarily a political term. It must be understood, rather, in light of the use of "Mediterranean" within social anthropology to indicate an area of study that has gained prominence in the last twenty to thirty years. Its focus is the Mediterranean area as a socio-cultural unity in terms of a specific configuration of the value system associated with honour and shame.[23] A number of studies on the gospels have appeared over the

---

20 Horsley, *Spiral of Violence*.
21 Classic works in this field include: Robert Redfield, *The Little Community* (Chicago: University of Chicago Press, 1955); and Julian Pitt-Rivers, *The People of the Sierra*, 2nd ed. (Chicago: University of Chicago Press, 1971 [1954]). See also Teodor Shanin, ed., *Peasants and Peasant Societies*, 2nd ed. (Oxford: Basil Blackwell, 1987).
22 Horsley, *Spiral of Violence*, 209-84.
23 Jean G. Peristiany, *Honour and Shame: The Values of Mediterranean Society* (London: Weidenfeld and Nicholson, 1966); David G. Gilmore, ed., *Honor and Shame and the Unity of the Mediterannean* (Washington: American Anthropological Association, 1987).

last several years using the anthropology of the Mediterranean area as a major model.[24] The question that naturally arises, as it did in my study *The Economy of the Kingdom*, concerns the role of Jesus in this Mediterranean world.[25] Compared to the image of the "unique religious personality," does Jesus disappear behind the focus on groups and structures? Has the unique individual been replaced by a social movement? I think not. Models from social and economic anthropology are necessary to understand the type of societies that existed in Galilee and Palestine, and in order to identify types of social interaction and exchange. With these models, we may more correctly describe the social structure within which Jesus lived, and the types of alternatives he outlined in his words and works.

But these models do not explain the changes that took place, and the motive force behind new movements. The alternatives that Jesus envisaged were not just a return to traditional "peasant economics." Here were also breaks with tradition in terms of critiques of the system of village hierarchy, patronage, traditional systems of honour and shame, purity and impurity. That Jesus and his influence can be described by using known categories allows us more clearly to see his influence and the changes that he introduced—all these within a first-century context, not a modern one.

4. The Universal and the Particular

The titles alone of books such as *Jesus and the Spiral of Violence: Popular Jewish Resistance in Roman Palestine, Jesus and the Economic Questions of his Day* and *The Historical Jesus: The Life of a Mediterranean Jewish Peasant*, strike a very different note from older lists of books on Jesus with their stereotypical, general titles. They point to the specific political, economic and cultural location of Jesus and emphasize the distance between him and us, not only in time and place but also in culture. Moreover, with the cultural distance and specific location also comes the particular, that which cannot so easily be generalized and directly applied to the contemporary situation.

At the beginning of this century, Heitmüller said in very general terms that Jesus did not set independent value on the family, the state or culture. In making that statement, it was obvious that Heitmüller was thinking of the social institutions of his own times. Eighty years later, Horsley draws much more specific and nuanced conclusions, distinguishing between Jesus' attitudes to

---

24 See, e.g., Bruce J. Malina, *The New Testament World: Insights from Cultural Anthropology* (Atlanta: John Knox, 1981); Bruce J. Malina and Jerome H. Neyrey, *Calling Jesus Names: The Social Value of Labels in Matthew* (Sonoma: Polebridge, 1988); Bruce J. Malina and Richard L. Rohrbaugh, *Social Science Commentary on the Synoptic Gospels* (Minneapolis: Fortress, 1992).

25 Halvor Moxnes, *The Economy of the Kingdom: Social Conflict and Economic Relations in Luke's Gospel* (Minneapolis: Fortress, 1989), 166.

different "institutions." In his view, Jesus was concerned with the restoration of the people, and that meant "renewal of the fundamental social-political form of traditional peasant life, the village."[26] On the other hand, Horsley finds no indication "that Jesus saw any role for the ruling institutions of his society."[27] Moreover, in contrast to Heitmüller, Horsley does not use a vocabulary that implies the "sameness" of Jesus' situation and our own.

Hermeneutics (notably in its Bultmannian version) has focused on those elements that are considered to be "the same" across temporal and cultural divides. This "sameness" need not be existential, but can also be institutional. The Danish philosopher Villy Sørensen stands within this tradition when he says that Jesus' reevaluation of dominant values is always valid because there is a perpetual conflict between the more or less artificial norms which uphold social institutions and the "natural values" which uphold life.[28] This is the conflict between (self-) interest and love. Likewise, Crossan makes a similar sweeping statement when he says that Jesus' actions are a challenge not only to Judaism and the patterns of Mediterranean patriarchal society, but to "civilization's eternal inclination to draw lines, invoke boundaries, establish hierarchies, and maintain discriminations."[29]

Such generalizations, however, do not do justice to all the insights about the historical Jesus that have been gained in the third quest. We are again faced with a Jesus "not in our image." It is not the similarities, but the differences, between "then" and "now" which these new methods and presentations emphasize.

Hermeneutics stands in need of renewal. A dialogue with other studies also facing the strangeness and distance of their subject may prove useful. Two areas of particular interest are history and social anthropology. In the words of the anthropologist Emiko Ohnuki-Tierney, "the two disciplines share 'the distancing of the self' as a basic tenet. . . . The past makes us think about the present reflexively. . . . Scholars in both disciplines choose the cultural other as their object of investigation, and their work often results in the reflexive examination of self."[30] Thus, historians and social anthropologists combine two processes: to study "the other" in his or her historical "otherness," and to think of the "self" reflexively, that is, with the insight provided by the study of the "other." Consequently, the very act of "reading" historically implies a hermeneutical process in which one analyzes the present situation just as carefully as Jesus'. The "particular past" must encounter the "particular present."

---

26 Horsley, *Spiral of Violence*, 324.
27 Horsley, *Spiral of Violence*, 325.
28 Sørensen, *Jesus og Christus*, 239.
29 Crossan, *Historical Jesus*, xii.
30 Emiko Ohnuki-Tierney, ed., *Culture Through Time: Anthropological Approaches* (Stanford: Stanford University Press, 1990), 1-2.

At the turn of this century the eschatological Jesus shattered an image of the "ethical" Jesus adaptable to the contemporary cultural situation. Is the "peasant Jesus" now threatening to do the same? To be confronted with a Mediterranean peasant from the first century is an experience that cannot easily be translated into general principles. I suspect that the encounter is as much of a cultural shock now as the encounter with the "eschatological Jesus" must have been then. Jewish eschatology represented a challenge in terms of an experience of the world that was totally alien to the "modern world." Likewise, a (de-romanticized) "peasant" Jesus represents a cultural world that has a totally different construction of reality than that of a postmodern, Western society.[31]

---

31 Let me again thank Edith Humphrey for her insightful comments on an earlier draft of this paper, and also say how grateful I am for the invitation to participate in this seminar, which turned out to be an exceptional experience of open exchanges of views, respectful and listening attitudes to colleagues and a serious consideration of the existential aspects of our scholarly work. As a celebration of the fiftieth anniversary of the Canadian "Learneds," the 1993 seminar was conducted in a spirit that bodes well for the next fifty years of that community of scholars. Congratulations and thanks to Peter Richardson and Michel Desjardins and their colleagues in the Canadian Society of Biblical Studies.

11. Academic Engagement: Context

Sandra Walker-Ramisch

The two papers which follow represent a radical methodological and substantive challenge to the historical-Jesus project as it continues to be conducted within the discourse of traditional historical criticism. Schaberg's work reframes the project within feminist critiques of ecclesiastical, social and academic patriarchy, and challenges the hegemony of androcentric scholarship which continues to be impervious to those critiques. LeMarquand's paper reframes the Jesus debate within the critical discourse of post-colonialism which challenges the ethnocentrism of Western historical-Jesus research and its implicit claims to universal validity. These papers draw attention to the ways in which feminist and African scholars, among others, are bringing new and challenging concepts and interpretive categories to historical reading, and in doing so are "taking ownership" of biblical interpretation. This growing body of scholarship emerging "on the margins" has to date been consistently excluded by the dominant scholarly canon.

Methodologically, feminist scholars such as Jane Schaberg and the African scholars discussed by Grant LeMarquand call into question the scientific (*wissenschaftliche*) ideology of disinterested or disengaged scholarship and its claim to value-neutrality. Both recognize that the socio-cultural location and experience of every researcher is a variable—a heuristically-valuable variable—in any historical reconstruction. The researcher's subjectivity has a shaping influence at the outset on the questions asked and the identification of problems. For example, only in the context of the African quest for the historical Jesus is the "non-Africanness" of Jesus problematized, and only in the context of feminist quests does Jesus' relationship with women become a defined area of investigation. The social location of the researcher also has an impact on the perception and judgment of what counts as data and which data are judged significant. The traditional assumption has been that prejudice (pre-judgment) enters only at the level of interpretation and explanation, and that when personal prejudices are controlled, the objective evidence is allowed to "speak for itself." Feminist scholarship, liberation theology and postmodernism in general have discredited this myth of "objective data." Much of feminist historical reconstruction builds on evidence that has been overlooked, ignored, suppressed or erased by androcentric biblical scholarship. Finally, the subjectivity of the researcher is a significant variable in the language, concepts and theories employed in classifying and explaining evidence. A powerful illustration is the introduction of gender as an analytic category in feminist biblical scholarship which has profoundly reshaped our reading of biblical texts.

Substantively, the quest for the historical Jesus represented in the following two papers is a quest solidly engaged with contemporary social conditions. The feminist quest is explicitly advocatory, aimed at the transformation of contemporary social relations and institutions, and the transformation of the rhetoric of androcentric scholarship. The African quest, according to LeMarquand, is "unabashedly confessional" and has "an urgent and practical purpose." Disinterested, disengaged scholarship is radically at odds with the feminist and African quests for a "useful" Jesus, quests carried out within the context of political struggles.

The challenge from the margins is fundamentally an epistemological one. For the politically-engaged quest represented by the following papers, knowledge is understood to be grounded not in objective empirical evidence but in the concrete and diverse historical experiences of oppression. There can be no extra-discursive, raceless, disinterested, genderless observer. The historical-Jesus project is a site of epistemological struggle and the production of truth, and the critical questions connected to it are how knowledge is constituted and generated, who are deemed knowers and why, how knowledge claims are adjudicated, and what the material conditions and discursive strategies are which enable the privileging of one discourse and the structuring of positions of marginality for the "deviant other." When the quest for the historical Jesus is seen as a site of epistemological struggle, the need for a critical awareness of the ideological and ethical impact that we and our writings have on society becomes acute. This demands a self-consciousness regarding the forms of knowledge and the types of power-relations which shape disciplinary practice. As Elisabeth Schüssler Fiorenza has so eloquently argued, historical-critical scholars who consider androcentric texts as their data, and who consider their own androcentric language and interpretation to be detached from contemporary interests, legitimate and perpetuate the political and academic *status quo*.

I would like to end by addressing directly the academic, ecclesiastical and public reactions to Jane Schaberg's work, which she describes in the following paper. These reactions range from vehement censure to personal verbal and physical violence. Why? Her work is an exemplary application of historical-critical methods. It is also an exemplary application of feminist theory and method. What she finds by a combination of these two discursive fields is historical evidence which suggests the existence in early Christianity of competing traditions regarding the conception and birth of Jesus, traditions for which no theological elaboration is extant, and which were ultimately erased by the patriarchal Church. Her work and the reaction to it reveal two sites of epistemological struggle: one, the challenge to the modern myth of disinterested scholarship through methodological control and its material manifestations in forms of institutional power; and two, the complex and contentious issue of sexuality and virginity in Christianity. The former I have discussed above. The latter will be the subject of my closing remarks.

Sexuality and virginity have meant different things in different periods of Christian history and, more significantly from a feminist perspective, they have meant different things to men and women. Men, however, have given them a discourse, a discourse which represents male experiences of sexuality and salvation. The virgin Mary, *virgo intacta*, who did not transmit sin through semen, is patriarchy's normalized image of virginity and motherhood, and the perfected icon of the patriarchal church. Schaberg's feminist historical work has not only retrieved the censured traditions; it has suggested what profound theological meaning and emancipatory power those traditions might have had for women in the past and might still have for women today. These traditions, Schaberg notes, could not have been passed on within a patriarchal form of Christianity, which depends upon the definition of women as other, as deviant and as subordinate, for its survival. The violence of the reaction to her work is evidence enough that social, ecclesiastical and academic patriarchy today struggles to retain its power to "name reality," to marginalize difference and to erase "deviance."

12. A Feminist Experience of Historical-Jesus Scholarship

Jane Schaberg

1. Introduction

In this paper, I originally intended to explore the contribution of feminist New Testament criticism to historical-Jesus research, to identify the precise nature of this contribution in terms of the major questions feminist criticism asks, the rethinking it demands and the challenges it poses. I wanted also to address the issue of what seems to me its present ineffectuality, its lack of contribution: that is, the ignoring, censoring, dismissing, silencing and trivializing of feminist scholarship, as well as its appropriation without attribution, which is a form of silencing.

What I had in mind was an analysis of the use and non-use of Elisabeth Schüssler Fiorenza's articles and books, especially *In Memory of Her*,[1] in the monumental historical studies of Jesus in the last decade: those of John P. Meier,[2] E. P. Sanders,[3] Burton Mack,[4] John Dominic Crossan,[5] James H. Charlesworth[6] and Richard Horsley.[7] My aim was to spotlight the areas in which one would have expected Schüssler Fiorenza's work to have made a difference, or at least to have been a serious dialogue partner. In fact, this is not

---

1 Elisabeth Schüssler Fiorenza, *In Memory of Her: A Feminist Theological Reconstruction of Christian Origins* (New York: Crossroad, 1983). There is no book-length feminist study of the historical Jesus, and none that I know of in process. This fact is intriguing in itself, as was the strangely flat discussion in the "Historical Jesus Section" at the 1991 AAR/SBL meeting on "Feminist Perspectives on the Historical Jesus." Panelists were Elisabeth Schüssler Fiorenza, Rosemary Radford Ruether and Karen L. King. Jacquelyn Grant was listed but did not appear.

2 John P. Meier, *A Marginal Jew: Rethinking the Historical Jesus*, 2 vols. (New York: Doubleday, 1991-94).

3 E. P. Sanders, *Jesus and Judaism* (Philadelphia: Fortress, 1985). While Schüssler Fiorenza's book may not have been available to Sanders during the writing of his 1985 book, her articles were already widely published.

4 Burton L. Mack, *A Myth of Innocence: Mark and Christian Origins* (Philadelphia: Fortress, 1988).

5 John Dominic Crossan, *The Historical Jesus: The Life of a Mediterranean Jewish Peasant* (San Francisco: HarperSanFrancisco, 1991).

6 James H. Charlesworth, *Jesus Within Judaism* (New York: Doubleday, 1988); Charlesworth, ed., *Jesus' Jewishness: Exploring the Place of Jesus in Early Judaism* (New York: Crossroad, 1989).

7 Richard A. Horsley, *Jesus and the Spiral of Violence* (San Francisco: Harper and Row, 1987); *The Liberation of Christmas: The Infancy Narratives in Social Context* (New York: Crossroad, 1989); *Sociology and the Jesus Movement* (New York: Crossroad, 1989).

the case in almost all of the works mentioned above.[8] So I wished also to raise the question of the effect this studied ignorance or dismissal of her work—that of the most eminent feminist New Testament critic—has on the field, especially what impact it has on other feminist critics.[9] "State of the art" discussions in other fields such as psychology, literature and history usually feature analyses of how feminist studies have changed them. Why have they not changed this field?

I also wanted to discuss the popular and critical reception of my own book, *The Illegitimacy of Jesus: A Feminist Theological Interpretation of the Infancy Narratives*,[10] not as an exercise in vanity and self-promotion—or at least not only that—and not simply because the response to a work is inordinately interesting to its author. It rather seemed to me that certain aspects of that response are well worth studying for what they reveal of publishing and bookselling matters, the gap between the academy and the church, patriarchal images of women and the attempt to control these images, and the reception of feminist scholarship and ideas. The personal, that is, would be discussed as the political.

As I worked toward a preliminary draft, however, there was a kind of escalation and intensification of audience response to my own work on the infancy narratives, on the figure of Mary Magdalene, and on the Gospel of Luke for the *Women's Bible Commentary*.[11] I decided to do something different: to bring this recent experience of mine, in which I have struggled to keep my career on track, to bear on illustrating some aspects of the situation in which feminist New Testament scholarship attempts to make its contribution. What follows is a paper more personal than I had first intended.

2. Reactions to my Works

Since the publication of *The Illegitimacy of Jesus* (1987), I have had responses that are both abusive and supportive, but I was unprepared for the latest round of reactions. It was initially a result of an article I did on Mary Magdalene for

---

8 Horsley's work is the sole exception.

9 I am thinking, *inter alia*, of Winsome Munro, Maryanne Tolbert, Amy-Jill Levine, Ross S. Kraemer, Mary Rose D'Angelo and Luise Schottroff. Marcus J. Borg ("Portraits of Jesus in Contemporary North American Scholarship," *Harvard Theological Review* 84 [1991]: 1-22) discusses Schüssler Fiorenza's work along with his own and that of Sanders, Mack and Horsley as part of a "third quest." Borg notes that her book was published while his *Conflict, Holiness and Politics* was in press. He says, "I would now incorporate most of her feminist insights" (13 n. 52), but does not elaborate.

10 Jane Schaberg, *The Illegitimacy of Jesus: A Feminist Theological Interpretation of the Infancy Narratives* (San Francisco: Harper and Row, 1987; New York: Crossroad, 1990).

11 Carol A. Newsom and Sharon H. Ringe, eds., *The Women's Bible Commentary* (Louisville: Westminster/John Knox, 1992).

a feminist issue of Hershel Shanks's popular journal, *Bible Review*. The Associated Press picked up as "news" the information that "Mary Magdalene was not a whore," and many newspapers across the country carried it—much, I thought, as they carry news from the Jesus Seminar, and with what I imagined to be the same result, in terms of both furious and supportive/interested readers responding.

This Associated Press article led to efforts on the part of the *Detroit Free Press* to interview me about my work. I determined that the first *Free Press* writer who contacted me did not have the training or interest to do a piece on my work, and I said no; I was then approached by the *Free Press* religion editor, David Crumm, and after meeting with him thought (naïvely) that he would indeed want to, and be able to, focus on the academic work in a careful and accurate way and give some wider hearing to basic feminist positions and issues. Each of us in the field has decisions of this kind to make about the public hearing and impact of our work, decisions which raise questions about different routes of access to the general public, and about our understanding of the aims of our work. Ten hours of interviews were conducted, in an extremely respectful and serious manner, focusing on the published works, which the editor took with him and read perceptively.

The result was disconcerting. The *Free Press* ran a profile not of the work but of an angry, uncredentialed, loose-cannon feminist, dogmatically preaching "the gospel according to Jane" on everything from Mary's rape to abortion rights, while threatening to sue her university. Statements taken out of context, embroideries, lack of attention to argumentation and detail, and flip remarks were used to hype the piece. In the profile, the Jesuit Vice-President of Academic Affairs was quoted as defending academic freedom, but insisting that my "basic teaching on the birth of Jesus really does cut to the core of our faith. Her interpretation is not the position of this university, and I would say 99 percent of the people at this university disagree with her on this." He also insisted that the university is not a fundamentalist institution.[12]

The article let the wild dogs loose. The phones began ringing at the University, at my house and at the Archdiocese of Detroit (since the University of Detroit Mercy is a Jesuit university), and the mail piled up. The Vice President for Public Relations told me that in the first week alone the university had lost over $200,000 in donations and been written out of two substantial wills (it is rumoured to be a million dollars now). My later attempts to find out from the department of public relations about the "cost" of the article and how the letters were running, pro and con, was met with the decision to give me no further information. One of my friends, an alumnus of the university, said in the wake of this controversy that "a poor university can't afford academic

---

12 *Detroit Free Press*, February 14, 1993.

freedom." Seven hundred angry phone calls were said to have come in to the administration and Board of Trustees. Many of the calls to me were hostile. They expressed religious outrage at my ideas, and called me whore, feminazi, queen of crapola, pseudo-intellectual, delusional, bitch, blasphemer, heretic, spiritual cancer, satanic, lesbian and sicko. They asked about my ethnic identity, insisted I had no place on the faculty of a Catholic university, should not be honoured as chair and asked for my resignation or firing, and—in a couple of cases—even my death. The supportive callers asked where they could find the *Illegitimacy of Jesus* book, which is not carried by local bookstores. Letters to me ran about eight positive to one negative. They were from abused women asking for my help, gay men expressing their alienation from the church, young fathers contemplating their daughters' fate, women who felt rage at being silenced, men and women who had hope or no hope for the future of Christianity, old men with shaky handwriting protesting the second-class status of women, and other scholars. Many remarked that the article had helped them see how the tradition could function to create compassion for the most powerless members of our society.

A week or so later, Archbishop Adam Maida of Detroit was asked on a cable television show about my "controversial theories" which include "allegations Mary was not a virgin and that she may have been a rape victim, that Jesus may have been illegitimate, and that Mary Magdalene was actually a respected woman in her time whose reputation fell victim to a male-dominated patriarchal church." The questioner asked how the church combined academic freedom and traditional Catholic beliefs in a Catholic learning institution. "Among the many things we need to ensure is that those who teach and come to Catholic universities will somehow live out that faith," said Maida: "Those who teach must be faithful to the magisterium of the church." When asked if he was saying "that a professor at a Catholic university has to stand by the Catholic codes and that there is a point where you would cut them off," Maida answered, "I don't get involved in the internal administrating of the university, but if there is someone who was speaking a heresy, I would have to challenge that." The student newspaper subsequently strongly defended my academic freedom in an editorial, and called for the administration to have the courage to do likewise. It insisted that students "have the right to be exposed to new ideas, even if the new ideas are contrary to that which is accepted by the administration and its alumni."

Two members of the university's Board of Trustees, representing the sponsoring religious orders (Jesuits and Sisters of Mercy) issued a formal statement and gave an interview to the *Michigan Catholic*. They affirmed that the university is "solidly Catholic," and stated that they have faith especially in the "Catholicity" of the religious studies department (whose full-time members [they did not note] include two Presbyterians, a self-styled "lapsed Unitarian," a Jew, two Jesuits, a layman of Catholic background and myself). They remarked that as a tenured profesor I am protected by civil law and university policy against sanctions for holding unpopular views. "Unless there were indications of a breakdown in professional standards of scholarship, it would not be the business of the university's sponsors to even attempt to interfere, both religious superiors said. Even if there were a concern about the integrity of a particular professor or department, it would primarily be a matter for the university's administration and board, they said."[13] They stressed that my "controversial ideas only became known several years after [I] came to U[niversity] of D[etroit Mercy]" but that I also have "other views that are right down the line with Catholic teaching" (these were not identified). The fact that I am departmental chair, they insisted, was not an honour or a position of power. My views, they stated, "will be subject to and balanced by the review and critique of her professional colleagues." ("Sources" at the university reported to me privately that a draft of this statement had included the claim, based on a telephone interview with someone who was not named, that my work was not respected by my scholarly peers.) Furthermore, they added, these views "are not representative of the theology and religious studies curriculum, nor of the university as a whole. Certainly our congregations, represented by twenty-six Jesuits and fourteen Sisters of Mercy on the university's faculty, administration and board of trustees are committed to our Catholic faith, an important feature of which has always been devotion to Mary, the Mother of Christ." Promising that "new courses in Catholic theology will soon be added to the many now available" (a reference to a new Chair in Catholic Theology promised by a donor), they expressed their confidence that the university community shared their commitment "to maintain and enhance the Catholic identity of the university."

In a subsequent treatment by the student newspaper, the Vice-President of Academic Affairs asserted: "As a single faculty member, she doesn't represent the belief of the entire university." The *National Catholic Reporter* reduced the *Michigan Catholic* article to six inches. *The Wanderer* printed a summary and interpretation of the *Free Press* article, and added that despite my "unorthodox views and negative reactions to my work by other faculty, students, and alumni," I was securely tenured and would sue if fired.

There was a broad and interesting range of faculty reaction at the university. Several faculty members declared themselves in the "1 percent" of those who agreed with me: many said they were shocked by the lack of administrative support; most disturbingly, several said they could not voice their views publicly because they were not yet tenured and/or they hoped for promotion. A letter was drafted by a supportive colleague but not sent, looking for support from other scholars, ending with this paragraph: "We are sorry to be sending

---

13 *Michigan Catholic*, February 26, 1993.

this letter to you anonymously. However, this is still life for some feminist scholars in some places." Letters supportive of me and attempting to correct misperceptions in the article were sent to the *Free Press* by the one untenured woman in my department, Gloria Albrecht, and by directors of the Ethics Institute, Student Life and Campus Ministry. The newly-founded Women's Studies Program judged it more prudent, in view of its extreme financial vulnerability, to say nothing. A few professors let me know that, with the bad publicity, I had endangered the jobs of all and hurt the university's image. One person in a faculty meeting with the vice presidents raised the question of whether the university's "Mission Statement" could be used in retaining or dismissing faculty, as well as in hiring; the answer given was yes.

Two members of the university's philosophy department wrote a letter to the *Michigan Catholic* challenging the claim that the university "is indeed a fine Catholic university," claiming that it is "time that Catholic universities question both the reality and the legitimacy of the 'American university tradition'" of academic freedom. They noted that the lack of review or criticism of my work by my department indicated that "there is no evidence of balance in that department." They also stated that the university has no "theology curriculum" and no theology department or program, "nor has it established a unified core curriculum which would, by academic means, transmit the cultural, intellectual, and theological heritage of the Catholic faith. Faith seeking understanding, the hallmark and reason for being of a Catholic university, is conspicuous by its absence at UDM." They called for serious examination of the university's character: "If it is to be another private, secular institution, even with a few trappings of Catholicism, it will have no reason for being and will deserve to die."

My union's newsletter ran a paragraph "in support of our colleague," stating simply that the 1940 Statement on Academic Freedom and Tenure published by the AAUP "is an elegant articulation of our position: 'The common good depends upon the free search for truth and its free exposition. Academic freedom is essential to these purposes and applies to both teaching and research.'" The dean said he was working with President Fay on a piece on academic freedom for the OpEd page of the *Free Press*, but this piece never appeared.

Archbishop Maida then sent out a letter and an article to all the Roman Catholic parishes in his area. The letter was read from some pulpits on a Sunday in March and the article published in parish bulletins. Referring to the interview with me in the *Free Press*, Maida remarked that I had expressed "a number of personal and professional opinions regarding various Church teachings." He went on to set the people straight: "As you know, the virginal conception of Jesus is a dogma of paramount importance in our faith. It is integral to the faith of the Church that Jesus truly is the Son of God. It was through the direct intervention of God, through the Power of the Holy Spirit, that the Word became flesh in the Virgin Mary. Both the Gospels of SS. Matthew and Luke attest to this fact as does Church teaching over the centuries." His article then expressed his desire and obligation to clarify the church teaching, since the article in the *Free Press* "may have confused many of our people." He asked in the article that the *Michigan Catholic* "give greater attention to making itself a medium for ongoing adult education and formation," and mentioned that just now Pope John Paul II is issuing in English the *Universal Catechism of the Catholic Church*. He anticipated that in the weeks and months ahead his office for Religious Education and Catechesis would hold special workshops regarding the catechism, which "will serve as a ready and sure reference point for those involved in the teaching ministry."

He said that the many calls and letters he had received suggested that many people were deeply troubled by the article on me in the *Free Press*. He insisted that the sponsors' statement in the *Michigan Catholic* "made the point that the University of Detroit/Mercy is truly a Catholic university, holding all the teachings of the Catholic faith, including belief in the virginity of Mary, the Mother of Jesus" (the statement in the *Michigan Catholic*, however, did not make that point). Maida distinguished "three aspects of Mary's virginity as taught in our Catholic tradition: A. Her virginal conception of Jesus by the 'power of the Holy Spirit'; B. The virginal birth of Jesus; C. The lifelong virginity of Mary after the birth of Jesus."

Maida finds contemporary relevance in these teachings. He states that the virginal conception has profound implication for our own daily faith life, since by it Jesus inaugurated a "'new creation' and 'new birth' for all those who are children of adoption according to the Holy Spirit by faith," and "foreshadowed our own hope that God will fulfill His promise to us with a birth to external [eternal?] life." Maida finds that these three teachings "all have a connection with our daily lives of faith and even with our understanding of our Christian morality as we face issues of abortion and euthanasia. These teachings remind us of the dignity and value and mystery of [God's] presence in and through every human life. He intervened in an extraordinary way with the conception and birth of Jesus; although not in the same way, He continues to bless us with every human birth and life."

Maida's letter to the pastors of the archdiocese linked "two matters of recent and urgent importance": "respect for life issues" (the controversy over assisted suicide; the "Freedom of Choice Act" reintroduced in the United States Congress forbidding states to restrict abortions before fetal viability; Right to Life educational fund, activities and banquet) and "our church's teaching on the virginal conception of Jesus." "In a very real way, these two topics of respect [for] life and belief in the virginal conception of Jesus go hand in hand. When we begin to question and even deny Church teachings, then the basis of our moral teachings is also jeopardized. Morality and dogma clearly and directly interconnect and interrelate."

A "representative sample" of several dozen letters to the *Michigan Catholic* applauded Maida for his courage and dedication, and chastised me for my "bizarre revelations" and heretical views. The UDM sponsors' disavowal of me also reminded readers of "the similar case involving the Catholic University of America's tolerance of theologian Fr. Charles Curran" and of Rome's successful demand for his ouster.

At a vicars' meeting, when asked why he did not respond through the *Free Press* to the article regarding me, Maida answered that he "chose not to challenge in the public area with condemnation and accusation." He said he is currently serving on a committee of six bishops and six presidents of Catholic universities, examining the papal document *Ex corde ecclesiae*, which deals with Catholic institutions of higher education and their relationship to the church. This document, he said, has different applications in different cultures. They are just at the point of defining its application in the United States, but until they complete this study the relationship and activities between these institutions and the church hierarchy is not clear. He did not want to preempt the results of this study, and hence stayed within the confines of the church in making his reply.

A class at Orchard Lake Seminary in canon law discussed the topic of how many canons I had broken with my writings, and discussed the necessity of teaching orthodoxy. I was advised to hire a lawyer who knew about issues of tenure, academic freedom and church-university relations. I was urged by various people to ignore all this and let it blow over, not to fight back, not to be defensive, to look carefully at what I want to accomplish and not to go public unless necessary, since I could get hurt.

Outside my university and outside church circles, many regarded the flap with bemused or irritated puzzlement, as an absurd argument over matters of no importance: "Who in their right mind would care about whether or not Mary was a virgin or the Magdalene a whore? There are important and serious issues to focus on here in Detroit." Recognizing the seriousness of this incident, however, Professor Pamela Milne of the University of Windsor circulated a letter to scholars in the Society of Biblical Literature, asking for letters of support for feminist scholarship in general, and, if possible, for my own work, to be sent to President Fay and the Board of Trustees. These letters put my work into perspective within the discipline and expressed grave concern about academic freedom at my university. Copies sent to me from professors in many major universities and seminaries and from the executive committee of the Women's Caucus of the Society of Biblical Literature were the main source of personal support for me during this period, alongside the support of colleagues and many readers, students and alumni/ae who wrote and called.

Elisabeth Schüssler Fiorenza told me of the *New York Times'* request that she write an OpEd piece this past Christmas (1993). Using my work and those of other feminists on the Infancy narratives, she argued that "to place the agency of Mary, the 'single' mother, into the center of our attention interrupts the androcentric Christmas phantasy . . . a move dangerous in the eyes of both ecclesiastical and political authorities."[14] This piece was rejected by the *Times* as too controversial. She discussed the resistance to her using my book in classes at Harvard, the impossibility of any feminist theologian being tenured in Germany, the targeting of Rosemary Radford Ruether by right wing, anti-feminist Christian groups (especially the attacks spearheaded by the author of *Unholy Rage*), and Schüssler Fiorenza's own decision to address the phenomenon of the attack on feminist scholarship as the topic of her talk at the Women-Church Convergence Conference in April 1993, mentioning my experience in Detroit and that of Chung Hyun-Kyung in Korea.

This harrassment is not merely a quaint tempest in a Roman Catholic teacup. We remember that members of the Inclusive Language Lectionary in the 1980s received death threats in the mail, and were put under FBI protection. We remember that the 1992 *Women's Bible Commentary* has been met with frantic and condescending reviews in Britain.[15] We remember also farther back the charges of heresy, trials and retrials, suspensions and controversies that shaped many of our major academic institutions, such as my own alma mater, Union Theological Seminary, in its defence of Charles Briggs in the 1890s.[16]

3. Attitudes and Implications

To summarize: the response of my institution's administration was to distance itself from me and my work by public statements and internal silence. The response of the faculty was divided. Those who spoke in public support of my academic freedom or work were few; others remained silent out of fear or lack of interest, or expressed anger about the economics of this incident. The archdiocese of Detroit went on the offensive against my "ideas and opinions" on cable TV, in the Catholic press and from the pulpit. The feminist scholars contacted recognized—as many of them put it—that "this could happen to any one of us." They mobilized support for me, recognizing also that this is all the protection each of us has.

The situation for me now is tentative. I believe that I will not be fired (although my university is under censure from the AAUP for firing tenured faculty in the mid 1970s and again in 1992). I believe that some students will boycott my classes, and others will be attracted to them. So life goes on as usual, but what has changed is my understanding of my position in my

---

14 Elisabeth Schüssler Fiorenza, "Born of Woman," unpublished manuscript, 1992.
15 See, e.g., Susan Brooks Thistlethwaite, "The Bible and the Feminists," *Christianity and Crisis* 53 (Feb. 1, 1993): 20-23.
16 Robert T. Handy, *A History of Union Theological Seminary in New York* (New York: Columbia University Press, 1987), chap. 4.

university. I know I am far more isolated and vulnerable than I had thought, that my support comes from an outside network of feminist scholars, men and women. I got a quick glimpse of the abyss of endless, fruitless litigation and unemployment that would open under my feet as it has under the feet of other feminist scholars. Most importantly, I got a glimpse of the fanaticism and power with which patriarchy clings to images of women it creates—images of virgin and redeemed whore—and a glimpse of the uses to which these images are put to control women.

I tried in *The Illegitimacy of Jesus* to analyze the ideas/feelings associated with the doctrines concerning the virginity of Mary, and to speculate about the reasons for the tenacity with which some, especially Roman Catholics, hold this image of the Virgin Mary, Mother of God—a figure Julia Kristeva calls "one of the most powerful imaginary constructs known in the history of civilization."[17] I will not repeat that discussion here. But excerpts from my recent negative mail make aspects of the ideology clear. "You belong to the group of women who believe they can do with their bodies what they wish. Not so." "If females are so compasionate, why do they murder 1.5 million unborn a year in the US alone? Is it compassion for their own selfishness? Maybe you are not glad you were not aborted. Do you think you should have been?" "Only an egomaniac would put themselves in the position of knowing more than the great theologians of the church, such as St. Augustine, St. Thomas Aquinas, St. Benedict and too many others to enumerate."

The most revealing of these remarks have to do directly with rape: the possibility that Mary was raped is called "garbage" fed to young, impressionable adults, is modernistic rubbish and feminist babbling of radical propagandists, the "infiltration of Satan's influence," sick teaching and heresy. "Mary could not have conceived by rape or her child Jesus would have been an imperfect human and would not have been suitable ransom to make possible the release from sin and death for us (I Tim. 2:5-6). Mary needed to be a virgin so that it would be clear that Jesus was the son, not of an imperfect man, but of God." "The angel . . . called Mary 'highly favored one.' Would a God of love and justice announce to a highly favored one if He knew rape was to be involved?" "You are nuts! How dare you say those dirty things about Our Lady." "Have you talked to yourself and other women about having a baby after this kind of abuse? Don't you think that this will have an effect on her? God forbids this kind of thinking. Many have tried to pervert the gospel of Jesus Christ including his own people." "You propose that Christ was the bastard Son of a rapist. If that was the case, why are there 300 prophecies of His birth, including the fact that conception would be a sacred event." "Your theories about rape and illegitimacy are a terrible dishonor of Mary and Jesus."

---

17 Julia Kristeva, *Tales of Love* (New York: Columbia University Press, 1987), 237.

"I cannot stand to think of rape and Mary in the same breath." "It is disgusting to think that God would allow Mary to be raped." "What amazes me is how you can believe that the Creator of the universe would choose any one less than a pure, inviolate being to become the vehicle for the entrance of His Son upon earth." "You are associating Mary with the lowest of the low, in claiming that she was raped and had an illegitimate child." "How could the Son of God be the child of a raped woman and a rapist?" "God kept Mary and Jesus pure from the revolting, shameful things you write about." A typical one regarding Mary Magdalene is: "Dear Heretic, Mary Magdalene may not have been a whore but you certainly are one! I won't keep you from your work. I'm sure you have other saints to smear and unborn babies to kill. Signed, A White Male (the cause of world strife)."

These letters, including Maida's, tell us what we already knew: that the general public is ignorant of the basics of historical criticism, and proud of it; that it serves the interests of the clergy and hierarchy to keep the general public in such ignorance and unable to think for themselves; that there are some loonies out there, with a great interest in religion; that fundamentalism is a powerful and often cruel force; that feminist concerns and perspectives are not studied, but reduced to slogans, and perceived by many as immoral; and that debate can swirl around books and articles never read.

The response tells us also: (1) that sexism and misogyny are deeply rationalized, theologized and spiritualized; (2) that societal attitudes about sexual assault assume the culpability of the victims and draw strength, we may suppose, from repression and guilt; (3) that hatred and blame are directed most particularly against the female victims of male violence, and also against the children who come from such violence; (4) that the official doctrines regarding Mary denigrate normal women, implying their hearts are divided and their humanity spoiled; (5) that these doctrines, however, draw on, and at the same time obscure, the human need for a feminine dimension of the divine; and (6) that fundamentalists and the ultra-orthodox see, as liberals often do not, that biblical and traditional images of women go hand in hand with the denial of women's rights to control their own bodies and lives. Further (it would take another paper to explore this), these popular outpourings are not so far removed from some scholarly sensibilities (see, for example, the distaste with which John Meier approaches the issue of the illegitimacy tradition, "usually not mentioned in polite company or in polite books"[18]).

We are led to ask—and have been asking for a long time—whose are these doctrines and dogmas? Once it is realized that women had no part in making them, what force do they have for women and for men? Whose ideas are these of honour and shame? Whose ideas are these of salvation, purity and history?

---

18 Meier, *Marginal Jew*, vol. 1, 222.

4. Conclusion

The personal incident I have detailed above is political. Feminist scholars will recognize in it the dangers that attend our work; the lack of public and professional knowledge of and respect for this work; our numerical and social isolation in almost all university departments throughout the world; the shocking lack of institutional and psychological support; the danger attendant on our focus of attention on certain texts and certain issues, especially those concerning sexuality;[19] the danger also in even following good feminist methodological procedure and speaking personally in or about one's scholarly work; the responses, negative and positive, to feminists' work and persons; the caricatures and stereotypes of us, and of women in general; the fragility and newness of our networks of support; our need for scholarly community; the lack of a forum for discussion of these realities; the lack of backup support from other institutions, secular or religious; the lack of money for exploration of feminist issues, and the money preventing or impeding it; the importance of this exploratory work.

To focus again on my own university: it constantly claims financial crises, existing in what has been called "America's first Third World city"; has no employment equity policy (which could help bring in feminist colleagues) and no commission on the status of women; virtually no institutional support for the struggling Women's Studies Program which is two years old and twenty years late; and publicizes itself on the basis of an unexamined, traditional Catholic ethos. According to 1992-93 statistics, women make up only 34 percent of the faculty; if we subtract the women teaching in nursing and education (areas which are traditionally female), the remaining faculty is only 25 percent women. My own department, with only two women, is below this, at 22 percent women, up from 11 percent in 1992.

Facts like these exacerbate the difficulties facing feminist scholars. But they also, I think, throw the realities into high relief. This incident I have described—or something like it, or the threat of it—is the context in which feminist New Testament critics pursue their work. That is my major point. It is necessary that scholars in the field of biblical studies take note of this, especially those scholars who want to enter into the feminist conversation. We have to make efforts to change this situation, if we want the conversation to continue.

The current backlash against feminist scholarship is an occasion to observe deep tensions in our social and intellectual fabric. Feminist scholarship is an occasion, not the cause, of a struggle between the forces of social change and

---

19 Even the self-styled "centrist," Raymond E. Brown, has been repeatedly attacked by fundamentalists for his work on the infancy narratives, especially concerning the virginal conception.

the forces of nostalgia, fundamentalism and "business-as-usual." This struggle affects us all.

What has this got to do with historical-Jesus research? A great deal. Let me identify several topics and questions the incident raises for me, and try to relate them to the topic at hand: the contribution of feminist interpretation to the quest for the historical Jesus.

I said above that this experience reveals something about the context in which feminist New Testament critics pursue their work and therefore about the broader context of late-20th-century biblical studies. A major feminist contribution to historical-Jesus research is to insist that the field look hard at this contemporary context, look at the social conditions in which we all work—that is, look at the universities, seminaries, departments, journals, professional organizations, ecclesiastical and social pressures, publishing opportunities, and our classes, meetings and conferences. And there is more. We also need to look at gender representation and roles, at who is speaking and to whom and for how long and about what, at who is silent or marginalized or tokenized or absent. We need to look at the context in which we are engaged in this phase of the quest for the historical Jesus, the present context of our knowledge of the historical Jesus. Feminist criticism challenges us to recognize and try to remedy the lopsidedness, the inequities, the limitations of our knowledge. Otherwise, in the words of Cynthia Ozick, "we make ourselves partly deaf and partly dumb."[20] As feminist scholarship is trying to hear the voices of women who were silenced in the first century, it is itself trying to be heard.

To what degree is historical-Jesus research still influenced by and playing into ecclesiastical, dogmatic concerns and agenda? I have in mind here not only portraits and analyses that serve to bolster traditional doctrines and avoid offending powerful religious leaders and constituencies, but also portraits that intentionally or unintentionally serve the *status quo*, including those which reduce the historical Jesus to someone of little or no religious power or connection to Christianity, reduce the early Jesus movements to nothing but power plays and some kind of vague community creativity in the service of self-survival, and leave today's churches to themselves. We need to study this aspect of our context: why some types of research are attacked and not others. Feminist criticism asks in a new way how we free and protect ourselves from the pressure of these concerns.

Feminist scholarship challenges us as critics to become more conscious of—and to state more openly in our work—who we are, what and for whom we work, where our allegiances, commitments and limitations lie, what our experience has been. It challenges us also to make open use of our experience,

---

20   Cynthia Ozick, "Notes Toward Finding the Right Question," *Lilith* 6 (1979): 25.

to see and to show that where we stand gives us a valid angle of vision and not the only angle. Feminist New Testament scholars have focused on issues they deem important and, in particular, on the question of the nature of the community of first followers of the historical Jesus, on the search for a Jesus who might have been at least welcoming to women, on the women in this movement, on the possibility of an "egalitarian moment," on the possibility of women's contributions to early Christian traditions. Feminist scholarship takes Schweitzer's insights seriously enough to make it clear that we are frankly interested in ourselves and our own usable and non-usable past (as well as our future) as we engage in the search for the all-historical Jesus. But to call feminist interpretation "self-serving"[21] is to ignore the biases and motivations of supposedly disinterested, supposedly culturally-neutral, male interpretation. All of our reconstructions are—at least partially—mirrors. All of our reconstructions have political uses. We need to look at what role the gender of the knower plays in historical-Jesus research.

Feminist interpretation involves a shift in focus of attention—away from the historical Jesus. We have all inherited a focus on specific aspects of the New Testament gospels and the history they come out of and create: titles; individualistic identity questions; the focus on Jesus as Lord, hero, prophet, Cynic, whatever; his actions, his teachings, his death. It is the focus, of course, of the gospels themselves. Feminist interpretation in a sense deconstructs and undermines the quest; it is not so interested in Jesus the individual, as in the relational Jesus, Jesus in his social world, Jesus reforming his social world. To be more specific, feminist critics are interested in the search for the historical women of this movement. Their presence, roles and contributions are of greatest importance to feminist scholars, but apparently of little or no importance to other scholars, even though questions about these women have broad and serious implications. The makeup of the circle of Jesus' companions, for example, must tell us something about the Judaism(s) of this circle, and vice versa. We are interested, yes, in the possibility of an egalitarian Jesus, but it is to the historical women of this movement that one must look in order to explore that possibility: to their Judaisms, their attraction to the movement, their contributions, their life-styles, their silencing, the phenomenon of forgetting. When we do this, we disturb the sleeping lions that guard the androcentric heritage.

One major issue that is central to recent scholarship and strongly debated is the evaluation of apocalypticism: its social/political/religious meaning and value, its role and placement in the formation of the gospels, its relationship to the mentality/social aims of the historical Jesus and the early Jesus

---

21 See Charlesworth, *Jesus Within Judaism*, 201; cf. his edited work, *Jesus' Jewishness* (New York: Crossroad, 1991), 71, on my *Illegitimacy of Jesus*.

movement(s). Apocalyptic aspects of the New Testament passion/resurrection predictions, the stories of the empty tomb and the witness of women merit, in my judgment, much more careful historical and literary sifting than they have so far received. Instead of being dismissed as legend and later accretion, the empty tomb tradition may prove to be ever more central to a feminist understanding of Christian origins. Apocalyptic eschatology, understood by John Collins as the (mystical) experience of transcendence of death,[22] may have not only provided the vision and hope of life and justice beyond the grave, but also fueled the energy and discipline for an egalitarian socio-political experiment. We need today an egalitarian space in which to pursue these questions.

It is too early to see if or how feminist studies will change and reconfigure the discipline of New Testament studies, and if or how it will affect historical-Jesus studies. We can hope now for an enlarged framework of discussion, for an understanding of knowing as a cultural, gendered construct. Feminist criticism, as Adrienne Rich puts it, approaches the old texts from a new direction. Its presuppositions, questions and interests are different from those of non-feminists. It values the experience of women as a source of knowledge and authority. It is bound to come into deep and serious conflict with ecclesiastical, social and scholarly traditions. Its charter is, to use Adrienne Rich's words again:

> To question everything. To remember what it has been forbidden even to mention. To come together telling our stories, to look afresh at, and then to describe for ourselves, the frescoes of the Ice Age, the nudes of "high art," the Minoan seals and figurines, the moon landscape embossed with the booted print of a male foot, the microscopic virus, the scarred and tortured body of the planet Earth [and, we add, the texts with which we deal]. To do this kind of work takes a capacity for constant active presence, a naturalist's attention to minute phenomena, for reading between the lines, watching closely for symbolic arrangements, decoding difficult and complex messages left for us by women of the past. It is work, in short, that is opposed by, and stands in opposition to, the entire twentieth-century white male capitalist culture.[23]

---

22 John J. Collins, "Apocalyptic Eschatology as the Transcendence of Death," *Catholic Biblical Quarterly* 36 (1974): 21-43.

23 Adrienne Rich, *On Lies, Secrets and Silence* (New York: Norton, 1979), 13-14.

13. The Historical Jesus and African New Testament Scholarship

Grant LeMarquand

> And yet for us it is when he is on the cross,
> This Jesus of Nazareth, with holed hands
> and open side, like a beast at sacrifice:
> When he is stripped, naked like us,
> Browned and sweating water and blood in the heat of the sun,
> Yet silent,
> That we cannot resist Him.[1]

1. Introduction: African Biblical Scholarship

This paper examines selected studies of Jesus, representative of the emerging discipline of New Testament studies in Africa. African biblical scholarship, not content to leave Jesus in a first-century context, is compelled by social, political and religious convictions to demonstrate his relationship to contemporary African life. After an overview of the major trends in African biblical scholarship, I turn to the works of selected scholars from South Africa and from sub-Saharan Africa (apart from South Africa) in order to discern what "Western" scholarship might gain from reading this growing literature. My claim is that Westerners may benefit from African scholarship's openness to the differing perspectives from which scholars "read texts" and "do history." It is generally recognized that all scholars are affected by their contexts; it is not so generally recognized that the contexts (social, political, religious) from which we read may actually aid us in understanding the history behind the text. Biases may blind us; biases also have heuristic value.

1.1 The Changing Global Context

For most of the two millennia of Christian history the geographical centre of Christianity has been the northern hemisphere. During this century, however, a remarkable shift has been taking place. Most of the Western world is now secularized, with church membership shrinking drastically and Christian influence, for better or for worse, on the wane. The situation in the southern

---

[1]   Gabriel Setiloane, "I am an African," in John B. Taylor, ed., *Primal World Views: Christian Dialogue With Traditional Thought Forms* (Ibadan: Daystar, 1976), 56-59.

hemisphere is quite different. Particularly in Africa,[2] churches have been growing at an exceptional rate. According to the *World Christian Encyclopedia* there were ten million Christians in Africa in 1900, mostly in Ethiopia, Egypt and South Africa. This amounted to 9.2 percent of the population. By June 1980 the figures had increased to just over two hundred million, or 45.4 percent of the population. The current growth rate of the churches is 3.55 percent, well ahead of the birth rate of 2.7 percent. If this trend continues, there will be four hundred million Christians in Africa by the year 2000, or about 50 percent of its population.[3] Church structures around the world have not yet caught up to this reality. At the Lambeth Conference of Anglican bishops in 1988, for example, the bishops from Canada, the U.S. and England far outnumbered the bishops from Africa, in spite of the fact that there are more Anglican Christians in Nigeria alone than in all three of those Western countries combined.

1.2 The Emergence of African Biblical Scholarship

In a similar way, the world of biblical scholarship, which has traditionally been dependent upon a Christian readership, has not yet caught up to the reality of African Christianity. Is it possible to imagine, for example, attempting to compile a bibliography of Western biblical scholarship, or even Canadian biblical scholarship? The task would be enormous. Yet when I mentioned to a former professor that I was compiling a bibliography of African biblical scholarship he scratched his head for a moment, then responded: "There isn't

---

2   "Africa" here refers to Africa south of the Sahara desert, the region sometimes known as "Black Africa." Although South Africa is something of a special case because of the history of apartheid in that country, this article will include scholarship from that region. Outside South Africa the major centres of biblical scholarship are Ghana and Nigeria in anglophone west Africa, Kenya and Tanzania in east Africa, and Cameroon and Zaire in francophone Africa. Biblical studies are by no means limited to these places. As in Europe and North America, there is diversity among biblical scholars from Africa. Enough African biblical scholars and theologians, however, have pointed to a commonality among people of various language and ethnic groups that we are justified in accepting the unifying factors which distinguish African culture. For a similar view, see: Kofi Appiah-Kubi, "Jesus Christ—Some Christological Aspects from African Perspectives," in Kofi Appiah-Kubi, Rosemary Edet, George Ehusani and Josephine Olagungju, eds., *African Dilemma: A Cry for Life (Papers from the EATWOT West Central African Sub-Regional Conference, 1991)* (n.p.: Ecumenical Association of Third World Theologians, 1992), 58; Osadolor Imasogie, *Guidelines for Christian Theology in Africa* (Ibadan: Ibadan University Press, 1983), 53. Those interested in the cultural and religious world of Africa should consult John S. Mbiti, *African Religions and Philosophy* (Nairobi: Heinemann, 1969), and V. Y. Mudimbe, *The Invention of Africa: Gnosis, Philosophy, and the Order of Knowledge* (Bloomington: Indiana University Press, 1988).

3   David Barrett, ed., *World Christian Encyclopedia; A Comparative Study of Churches and Religions in the Modern World* (Nairobi: Oxford University Press, 1982), 780, 798. It is important to note that Barrett's results were not scientifically acquired. His figures are projections of trends, often based on estimates, rather than scientifically-gathered data.

enough material, is there?" To be sure, the fact that one can make the attempt
to compile a single bibliography on this topic does betray that African biblical
scholarship is only now beginning to emerge.

Nevertheless, although little of their work is known in the West, African
scholars are reading, translating and interpreting the Bible.[4] The discipline of
biblical scholarship has experienced enormous growth in Africa. The desire of
African peoples for self-determination has not been limited to the political
sphere but is evident in all areas of life. As African churches and universities
have grown, so has interest in taking ownership of the interpretation of biblical
texts, rather than simply following the lead of the North Atlantic exegetical
tradition. There is now a steady stream of exegetical work produced by African
scholars. While some of this material is published in Europe or North America,
most African exegesis is published locally. Dozens of journals regularly print
exegetical articles; one journal is devoted entirely to biblical studies.[5] It is
morally incumbent upon scholars in Europe and North America to be informed
about the work of their colleagues in the so-called "third world"; the existence
of such scholarship provides us in the West with an opportunity to obtain a
critical perspective on our own work.[6]

That Africans are taking ownership of the interpretation of biblical texts
does not mean that they are in any way uninformed about the last two centuries
of historical-critical scholarship. Since most African biblical scholars have done
graduate work in Europe or North America, they use the same exegetical tools
as their Western colleagues. Even those who have done most of their training
in Africa have, until recently, mainly been reading North Atlantic scholarship.
In this essay we will see that it is not the application of different tools which
separates African and Western Jesus scholarship, but differing cultural
presuppositions. At least four major issues can be detected in the growing
corpus of African exegesis. This paper sketches these four issues, and explores
how they are shaping Jesus scholarship from Africa.

---

4   See Grant LeMarquand, "A Bibliography of the Bible in Africa: A Preliminary Publication,"
     Bulletin for Contextual Theology in Southern Africa and Africa 2 (1995): 6-40; and
     "Bibliography of the Bible in Africa," *Journal of Inculturation Theology* 2 (1995): 39-139.
     For an overview of the use of the Bible and biblical studies in Africa see Samuel O. Abogunrin,
     "Biblical Research in Africa: The Task Ahead," *African Journal of Biblical Studies* 1 (1986):
     7-24; John S. Mbiti, *Bible and Theology in African Christianity* (Nairobi: Oxford University
     Press, 1986); Nlelanya Onwu, "The Current State of Biblical Studies in Africa," *The Journal
     of Religious Thought* 42 (1985-86): 35-46; Gerald West, *Biblical Hermeneutics of Liberation:
     Modes of Reading the Bible in the South African Context* (Pietermaritzburg: Cluster, 1991).
5   *African Journal of Biblical Studies* is published by the Nigerian Association for Biblical
     Studies (NABIS).
6   Not one of the scholars discussed in this paper, for example, is listed in Craig Evans's
     massive and, in many ways, very helpful bibliographic study: *Life of Jesus Research: An
     Annotated Bibliography* (Leiden: Brill, 1989).

1.2.1 Mission and Colonialism

> When the white men came they told us that our way of praying was
> wrong—one should not pray with one's eyes open but with one's eyes closed.
> So we closed our eyes to pray. When we opened our eyes we had the Bible
> but the white man had the land.[7]

Contemporary African Christians (most biblical scholars in Africa are self-
consciously Christian) have an acute awareness of having been "evangelized,"
of having received the gospel from outside, from the West. They are also aware
that the gospel which came to them from the Western missionary, no matter
how well-intentioned that missionary may have been, was a Westernized gospel.
When Livingston preached in England about the need for missionaries to go to
Africa he did not say that this was just for the purpose of bringing Christianity,
but to bring Christianity and civilization. It has been no simple thing to discern
the difference between gospel and Western culture, between "charity" and
cultural imposition. African biblical scholars are thus concerned to uncover the
Western bias which they find dominates so much of the exegesis they read.
Western scholarship is read and used by African scholars, but with a certain
amount of distrust. The suspicion that the world-view of Europe and North
America has been fused with the exegetical process means that Jesus scholars
in Africa are often cautious about the conclusions of their Western colleagues.

1.2.2 Suffering

It is difficult to summarize the problems of Africa: even a short list of troubles
would include the world's highest birth rate (Kenya), the most displaced peoples
(Sudan, Ethiopia, Somalia), civil war (Rwanda, Angola, Sudan, Somalia,
Zaire), rampant disease (Uganda), tyranny (*passim*) and environmental
degradation (Nigeria). Biblical scholars working in a context of acute and
visible suffering are perpetually challenged to demonstrate the relevance of their
work. In an article on the Lord's Prayer, for instance, Cyril Okorocha states
that the concern of his paper is to question how to "proclaim to a hungry people
that God is their father, and how in the face of that dilemma could we explain
the petition for daily bread, as encouraged by the Lord's Prayer."[8] The desire
for liberation from the suffering of black people under apartheid in South Africa
is the driving force behind most theological and biblical studies from Africans
in that country. The desire for "liberation," however, is not confined to South

---

7   Traditional African anecdote.
8   Cyril C. Okorocha, "God the Father and Hunger in Africa: Give Us this Day Our Daily
     Bread," in David M. Gitari and Patrick Benson, eds., *Witnessing to the Living God in
     Contemporary Africa: Findings and Papers of the Inaugural Meeting of Africa Theological
     Fraternity* (Nairobi: Uzima, 1986), 196.

Africa. From all parts of the continent there is a cry for freedom from dictators, sickness and war. This cry does not escape the ears of African Jesus scholars.

1.2.3 Faith

Western biblical scholarship is now done primarily within the context of the academy. Liberation theology, feminist theology, indeed postmodernism in general, are questioning the assumptions behind the once-normative, "detached" scholarship, but on the whole the biblical scholar's "objectivity" still remains prized. In Africa there is no rift between biblical scholarship and belief. Faith and exegesis go hand in hand. Perhaps the most eloquent (and least polemical) example of this mix is from the preface of Teresa Okure's monograph. After acknowledging the help of parents, supervisors and funding agencies we read an acknowledgement unlike any I have seen in a dissertation written by a Western scholar:

> This litany of acknowledgements would be incomplete without the special mention of Jesus. The statement of the Psalmist applies most aptly in my case: "If the Lord had not been my help," this work would never have seen the light of day (Ps 94:17). Jesus' unfailing help sustained me most tangibly throughout my entire course of study in ways that might be described as miraculous. For the schooling in trust which he provided for me through these trying circumstances, I am deeply grateful to him. It is but a small token of gratitude that I should dedicate this book to his Mother on this feast of her birthday, September 8, as her birthday present.[9]

Most African biblical scholarship is unabashedly confessional. This tendency worries many members of the biblical guild in the West, whose own history—from the confessional to the academic study of religion—provides them with anxieties about the dangers of eisegesis in biblical scholarship which is self-consciously "faithful." No doubt many of those anxieties are well-founded. It must not be assumed, however, that any reading which is explicitly confessional is necessarily "pre-critical." What is implicitly at stake behind claims to objectivity is the taken-for-granted world-view of the interpreter; there is no interpreter (and this is one of the issues African scholars are constantly raising for their readers) who does not have a world-view. There is no presuppositionless exegesis. What distinguishes African scholars is that they tend to be explicit about their presuppositions. Consequently the Jesus which African scholars find reflected in the pages of the New Testament is a Jesus who will help the church in Africa.

---

9 Teresa Okure, *The Johannine Approach to Mission: A Contextual Study of John 4:1-42* (Tübingen: J. C. B. Mohr, 1988), viii.

1.2.4 African Culture

Perhaps the most important matter for recent African scholars is the African cultural context. It has long been noted by Africans and Westerners familiar with Africa that there are similarities between the biblical world and the African world. The establishing of covenants through sacrificial ritual, prophetic itinerancy, the observing of taboos and the importance of proverbial wisdom are only a few of the cultural traditions which Africans share with the Bible. African scholars of the Hebrew Bible in particular have highlighted the continuity (not ignoring the discontinuities) between Africa and the Bible. Some, like Modupe Oduyoye, have attempted to trace genealogical relationships between the Bible and Africa on the basis of linguistic and cultural similarities.[10] Most, like Kwesi Dickson, are content to see analogical relationships between these cultures.[11]

One of the reasons why Africans are so concerned to establish the common ground between the Bible and their culture is precisely because Western missionaries defamed African culture, sometimes labelling it as "satanic." But when Africans learned to read the Bible, it often seemed to them to be very close to the culture about which they had been taught to be ashamed. African scholars attempt to move from the cultures of the biblical periods to the cultures of Africa, and from the cultures of Africa to those of the biblical world, comparing, contrasting, relating the two worlds. Biblical scholarship is often the occasion for Africans to reassess and sometimes reappropriate their non-biblical traditions.

2. Jesus in South African "Liberation" Scholarship

Biblical exegesis, as it is practised by black theologians and a growing number of white theologians in South Africa, is done within a context of political struggle. Black biblical scholars do not ignore their life situation within an oppressive system, which has often used the Bible as a tool of repression. In this section of the paper I examine three South African scholars who, although taking different approaches to the text, all find a Jesus appropriate for their situation.[12]

---

10 Modupe Oduyoye, *The Sons of the Gods and the Daughters of Men: An Afro-Asiatic Interpretation of Genesis 1-11* (Ibadan: Daystar/Maryknoll: Orbis, 1984).

11 Kwesi A. Dickson and Paul Ellingworth, eds., *Biblical Revelation and African Beliefs* (Maryknoll: Orbis, 1969); Kwesi A. Dickson, *Theology in Africa* (London: Darton, Longman & Todd/Maryknoll: Orbis, 1984) (see esp. "Cultural Continuity with the Bible," 141-84); Kofi Appiah-Kubi and Sergio Torres, eds., *African Theology en Route* (Maryknoll: Orbis, 1979), esp. Dickson, "Continuity and Discontinuity Between the Old Testament and African Thought and Life," 95-108.

12 I will not discuss traditional white South African scholarship in this essay. In a pair of articles ("The Ethics of Interpretation—New Voices from the USA," *Scriptura* 33 [1990]:

2.1 Allan Boesak

Allan Boesak affirms the importance, even the centrality, of the historical Jesus for Black theology: "Black theology is not prepared to separate the reality of the historical Jesus from the reality of his presence in the world today."[13] Jesus, he believes, is present and active in today's world but in order to understand his action in our world, "one must begin to understand his acts while he was on earth."[14] Boesak rejects the idea espoused by some that Jesus was literally black, saying that "the literal color of Jesus is irrelevant."[15] What is relevant is that Jesus suffered:

> The historical Jesus of the New Testament has a special significance for those who share the black experience. He was poor, the son of poor people who could not afford to bring the prescribed sacrifice at his birth. . . . Rather, they brought the sacrifice of the poor, two turtle doves instead of the year-old lamb (Lev. 12:6-8; Luke 2:21-24). He belonged to a poor, downtrodden people, oppressed and destitute of rights in their own country and subjugated to

---

16-28; "The Ethics of Interpretation—and South Africa," *Scriptura* 33 [1990]: 29-43), Dirk Smit outlines three stages in the history of white biblical scholarship in that country: "In a first stage, prominent scholars played an important role in legitimizing apartheid and opponents were ostracized from the South African scholarly scene. In a second stage, the socio-political interpretation of the Bible has been strongly rejected, in the name of the ethos of scientific research. At present, in a third stage, the debate between scientific, historical scholarship and committed, socio-politically involved reading, is urgent but diffuse, since it is being argued at so many different fronts" ("Ethics—South Africa," 33). Traditional white South African scholarship has been shaped by and has often supported the structures of apartheid. Until recently some scholars have attempted to use the Bible, especially the stories of the curse of Ham and the conquest of Canaan, to defend Afrikaner nationalism and so-called "separate development"; others have attempted to ignore the societal context in which their scholarship was being done. With regard to Jesus research in white South Africa see especially two articles by A. G. van Aarde: "Recent Developments in South African Jesus Research: From Andrie du Toit to Willem Vorster," *Hervormde Teologiese Studies* 49 (1993): 397-423, and "Recent Developments in South African Jesus Research: From Willem Vorster to Andries van Aarde," *Hervormde Teologiese Studies* 49 (1993): 942-62. These articles show that, until recently, the dialogue partners taken most seriously by white exegetes in South Africa were scholars from the "first world" (of note is that van Aarde uses the phrase "we, as First-World theologians" ["From Willem Forster," 947]) and that the major issue underlying this work was the tension between dogmatic theology and the historical-critical method. Van Aarde's second article shows that what he calls "engaged scholarship" (especially the work of Itumeleng Mosala, see below) is now being taken more seriously.

13   Allan Boesak, *Farewell to Innocence: A Socio-Ethical Study of Black Theology and Black Power* (Kampen: J. H. Kok/Maryknoll: Orbis, 1976/1977), 41.

14   Boesak, *Farewell to Innocence*, 42.

15   Boesak, *Farewell to Innocence*, 42.

countless daily humiliations under the foreign rulers. He lived and worked among the poor. . . . He was one of them.[16]

Jesus' words, for Boesak, are "revolutionary" in the context of the religious tyranny of the high-priests and scribes and the political tyranny of the Romans. "Like a prophet of old he judges [the powerful] with a terrible harshness" but tells the "common" people that God loves them.[17] Boesak has little concern for exegetical method; his reading is a surface reading of the text, a reading which sees a coherence between two worlds: the narrative world of the gospels (which is assumed to be the world of Jesus) and the world of present-day South Africa.

2.2 Itumeleng Mosala

In contrast to Boesak, Itumeleng Mosala argues that the biblical text itself is a product of class struggle. Mosala focuses his attention behind the text, looking for clues to the ideology which produced it. Mosala advocates a hermeneutic which uses an explicitly Marxist materialistic analysis to "liberate the Bible" by exposing not only its oppressive use, but its origins in the struggle against oppression.

Mosala is critical of most South African "Black" theology, especially as represented by Boesak and Desmond Tutu, because of what he considers their uncritical acceptance of the idea of the Bible as the "Word of God." This traditional doctrinal presupposition, he says, leads to an unreflective appropriation of Jesus. He refers, for example, to Tutu's comparison of Steve Biko's death with the sacrifice of Jesus. He does not think that the comparison is totally unwarranted; however, the "point is that the ideological appropriations of Jesus by the various New Testament authors are different and do not all always adequately represent the ideological concerns of *Jesus' own earthly program.* There are, therefore, different approximations of Jesus' ministry by the different discourses of the New Testament."[18]

The New Testament discourse in question for Mosala is Luke's gospel. Opposed to others who have found in this gospel a liberating message for the poor, Mosala finds that the text of Luke treats the poor as a subject, that the text is actually written by and addressed to the rich. "By turning the experiences of the poor into the moral virtues of the rich, Luke has effectively eliminated the poor from his Gospel," says Mosala.[19] Luke's version of the Jesus story is ideologically motivated. The real story of Jesus has been co-opted, the "real

---

16 Boesak, *Farewell to Innocence*, 43.

17 Boesak, *Farewell to Innocence*, 44.

18 Itumeleng J. Mosala, *Biblical Hermeneutics and Black Theology in South Africa* (Grand Rapids: Eerdmans, 1989), 37 (emphasis mine).

19 Mosala, *Biblical Hermeneutics*, 163.

purpose" of the gospel is "to accommodate the gospel of Jesus and its movement to the Roman Empire."[20] This point is not new, of course, and Mosala has a wealth of footnotes to New Testament scholars who would argue similarly that Luke is an apology. What is new about Mosala's work is that he does not shy away from the political implications of his scholarly construct. For him, the gospel is a product of the ruling class, an attempt to tame the oppressed and to keep them controlled. It is only when the oppressed see this ploy and liberate themselves that the Bible will be liberating for them.[21]

Mosala does not go into detail, however, about "Jesus' own program." We have some hints about Mosala's views on this matter: that Luke has co-opted Jesus on behalf of the powerful implies that Jesus was not one of the elite; the period of Jesus' life is characterized by social conflict;[22] stories about Jesus' birth lead us to suspect that he was illegitimate;[23] Jesus' mother was from the "social revolutionary class" as evidenced by the "Magnificat";[24] the followers of Jesus "can only have been a subversive movement."[25] Especially important is Jesus' death:

> the "black struggle" as a hermeneutical category of black theology would begin a reading of Luke's discourse by drawing daggers against his ideological intentions. It would refuse to be drawn into an appreciation of an "orderly" presentation of Jesus and his movement. Luke seeks to clean Jesus up—to make him one of the heroes, a cult leader rather than the failure that his death represented in the face of the repressive and murderous state machinery of "law and order."[26]

Mosala's Jesus is a reflection of what he believes South Africa needs: radical subversion of oppression. Mosala is quite different from most African biblical scholars, not because he believes Jesus to have been a social radical, but because he separates Jesus from the faith context of both the gospel writers and most African gospel readers. For Mosala, Jesus' death, like his "program," was a "failure."

---

20 Mosala, *Biblical Hermeneutics*, 176.
21 This is not the appropriate place to enter into discussion concerning Mosala's own ideology or his opinions about Luke. For discussion of Mosala see Dwight N. Hopkins, *Black Theology, USA and South Africa: Politics, Culture and Liberation* (Maryknoll: Orbis, 1989), 128-29; Anthony C. Thiselton, *New Horizons in Hermeneutics: The Theory and Practice of Transforming Biblical Reading* (Glasgow: Marshall Pickering, 1992), 419-27; West, *Biblical Hermeneutics of Liberation*; and a review of Mosala by Emmanuel Marty in *Africa Theological Journal* 21 (1992): 103-106.
22 Mosala, *Biblical Hermeneutics*, 181.
23 Mosala, *Biblical Hermeneutics*, 166, 169.
24 Mosala, *Biblical Hermeneutics*, 168-69.
25 Mosala, *Biblical Hermeneutics*, 175.
26 Mosala, *Biblical Hermeneutics*, 175.

2.3 Albert Nolan

Albert Nolan's book, *Jesus Before Christianity*,[27] is the most thorough study of Jesus from a South African liberationist perspective. Although a white South African, Nolan is self-consciously in the "liberationist" stream. Nolan's book attempts to take seriously the world of Jesus, the world behind the text of the New Testament. There is little explicit mention of South Africa, although it is clear that an understanding of the suffering of people in South Africa (and other parts of the world) is vital to his work. Nolan says that although his goal is to find "historical truth about Jesus," this is only a means to an end: "The method is historical, but the purpose is not. Despite the consistent use of strict historical criticism and methods of research, our interest is not the academic pursuit of history for the sake of history. This book has an urgent and practical purpose. I am concerned about people, the daily sufferings of so many millions of people."[28] Indeed Nolan makes extensive use of current historical-critical tools. He employs source-critical and redaction-critical insights[29] and even attempts to trace the *ipsissima vox* of Jesus,[30] sometimes using the criteria of dissimilarity[31] and multiple attestation;[32] at times he shows remarkable confidence in the ability of historians to reach assured results.[33]

Nolan admits that historical reconstruction is simply a strategy which he is using in order to achieve a greater goal. He believes that if Jesus can be seen in his historical context, the resulting picture will have an empowering impact on those who suffer from social and political oppression. The gospels were written so that people who lived outside of Palestine would be able to see how Jesus could be relevant in their own situations: "Like them we need a book about Jesus that will show us what he might mean today in our situation."[34]

The picture which emerges is of Jesus as a prophet, challenging the elite, healing the sick, liberating the poor. He dies the death of a political radical: "Jesus suffered and died on a Roman cross because . . . [he] was horrified by

---

27 Albert Nolan, *Jesus Before Christianity* (1st ed.: Claremont: David Philip, 1976; London: Darton, Longman & Todd, 1977; Maryknoll: Orbis, 1978; 2nd ed.: Maryknoll: Orbis, 1992). The changes in the revised edition are confined to the alteration of gender exclusive language. References below are to the first edition.

28 Nolan, *Jesus*, 1.

29 Nolan, *Jesus*, 44, 48.

30 Nolan, *Jesus*, 10, 53.

31 Nolan, *Jesus*, 28.

32 Nolan, *Jesus*, 37.

33 Nolan, *Jesus*, 107: "on no occasion and in no circumstances did Jesus ever claim, directly or indirectly, that he was the Messiah. This is admitted today by every serious scholar of the New Testament, even by those who are inclined to be conservative." Nolan's remark leads one to wonder what kind of Messiah he wants to avoid.

34 Nolan, *Jesus*, 10.

the sufferings of the people, shared in their sufferings and was determined to do something about their plight. Jesus was one of the oppressed struggling to free all who suffered under the yoke of repression. That is the meaning of the cross."[35] Jesus' death, in other words, was a direct consequence of how he lived. His compassion led him to political activism, which led him to conflicts with the authorities (both Jewish and Roman) who put him to death. The one who would follow Jesus does so not by practising some form of orthodoxy but by trying "to live as he lived. . . . [W]e do not need to theorize about Jesus, we need to 're-produce' him in our time and our circumstances."[36]

2.4 Summary

The consistent theme in the liberationist South African studies examined above is the confidence that Jesus was a social radical. The deeds of Jesus—his healings, his action in the Temple, his death on the cross—are seen as embodying elements of social protest. Likewise when these scholars examine the words of Jesus, their primary concern is neither to unearth the "authentic voice" of Jesus (although this is attempted) nor to rank the degree of authenticity of particular sayings, but to reconstruct a probable social context in which to understand parables or sayings. South African scholars approach the text from a variety of perspectives, some using traditional historical-critical tools, some Marxist analysis, others a more narrative approach. The results, however, are similar. The social context of Jesus is consistently seen as one of conflict: Jesus is the subversive opponent of self-righteous religious leaders, oppressive political regimes and life-draining systems of thought. Such a Jesus clearly "fits" the South African context.

3. Jesus Scholarship in Sub-Saharan Africa

African New Testament scholars have produced numerous studies related to the issue of the historical Jesus: a survey of "the quest" from an African perspective,[37] studies of parables and sayings of Jesus,[38] studies of events in the

---

35 Nolan, *God in South Africa: The Challenge of the Gospel* (Cape Town: David Philip, 1988), 61.

36 Nolan, *Jesus*, 139.

37 Samuel O. Abogunrin, "The Modern Search for the Historical Jesus in Relation to Christianity in Africa," *Africa Theological Journal* 9 (1980): 18-29. Cf. the article by a missionary scholar working in Tanzania: Norvald Yri, "I Believe in the Biblical Historical Jesus," *East African Journal of Evangelical Theology* 6 (1987): 23-32 (published in the same year in Leonidas Kalugila and Nancy Stevenson, eds., *Essential Essays on Theology in Africa: Essays Presented to the Rev. Dr. Howard Stanley Olson on his 65th Birthday* [Usa River: The Research Institute of Makumira Theological College]: 18-29).

38 J. O. Ajibola, *The Secret School of Jesus* (Ibadan: Daystar, 1972); David M. Gitari, "The Claims of Jesus in the African Context," *International Review of Mission* 71 (1982): 12-

life of Jesus,[39] studies of titles attributed to Jesus and their relation to his life situation,[40] and studies of Jesus and women.[41] These works all make a serious attempt to understand Jesus in his context, but none are content to leave him there; they seek to show some connection with Africa by underlining the links between a text and the church in Africa, or by arguing that the African tradition helps us to understand the meaning of some aspect of Jesus. The most distinctive work of African Jesus scholars, however, pertains to two facets of the picture of Jesus of Nazareth as portrayed in the gospel accounts: the healing and miracle tradition, and the Jewishness, or rather, the "non-Africanness," of Jesus.

3.1 Healing and Miracle Tradition

Some have noted that Jesus scholarship has often been preoccupied with the words of Jesus.[42] Whether the emphasis on Jesus' words as opposed to his deeds is a latent theological bias inherited from Lutheranism and passed on through Rudolf Bultmann, as has recently been suggested,[43] or whether it is an ethnocentric bias against the miraculous,[44] is not our concern here. For our

19; Chris U. Manus and Fortunatus Nwachukwa, "Forgiveness and Non-Forgiveness in Matthew 12:31-32: Exegesis Against the Background of Early Jewish and African Thought-Forms," *Africa Theological Journal* 21 (1992): 57-77; John S. Pobee, *Who are the Poor? The Beatitudes as a Call to Community* (Geneva: WCC, 1987); Justin S. Ukpong, ed., *Gospel Parables in African Context* (Port Harcourt: Catholic Institute of West Africa [CIWA] Press, 1988).

39 E. Olu Alana, "The Theology of Newness in Jesus' Birth and Burial Narratives," *Caribbean Journal of Religious Studies* 11 (1990): 54-62; Samuel O. Abogunrin, "The Language and Nature of the Resurrection of Jesus Christ in the New Testament," *Journal of the Evangelical Theological Society* 24 (1981): 55-65; A. O. Nkwoka, "Mark 10:13-16: Jesus' Attitude to Children and its Modern Challenges," *Africa Theological Journal* 14 (1985): 100-10; Cornelius Abiodun Olowola, *The Last Week: A Study on the Last Week of Jesus Christ on Earth* (Jos: Challenge, 1988).

40 Samuel O. Abogunrin, "The Three Variant Accounts of Peter's Call: A Critical and Theological Examination," *New Testament Studies* 31 (1985): 587-602; Seth Adom-Oware, "'Who do you say that I am?' (Mt.16:15): A Contemporary African Response," *West African Journal of Ecclesial Studies* 3 (1991): 9-23; George E. Okeke, "The Mission of Jesus and Man's Sonship with God: The Setting of the Problem," *Africa Theological Journal* 9/3 (1980): 9-17.

41 B. Muoneke, "Women Discipleship and Evangelization (Luke 8:13)," *Bulletin of Ecumenical Theology* 4 (1991): 59-69; Emeline Joseph Ng'unda, "The Role of Women in the Synoptic Gospels" (B.D. thesis, Lutheran Theological College [Makumira, Tanzania], 1986); Teresa Okure, "The Significance Today of Jesus' Commission to Mary Magdalene," *International Review of Mission* 81 (1992): 177-88.

42 For example, see E. P. Sanders, *Jesus and Judaism* (Philadelphia: Fortress, 1985).

43 Gregory E. Sterling, "Jesus as Exorcist: An Analysis of Matthew 17:14-20; Mark 9:14-29; Luke 9:37-43a," *Catholic Biblical Quarterly* 55 (1993): 467.

44 Paul W. Hollenbach, "Help for Interpreting Jesus' Exorcisms," in Eugene H. Lovering, ed., *Society of Biblical Literature 1993 Seminar Papers* (Atlanta: Scholars Press, 1993), 119-28.

purposes it is enough to note that African scholars pay a great deal of attention to the gospel portrayals of Jesus' healings and exorcisms. In fact, it is here that we see the greatest difference between scholarship in the West and scholarship in Africa.

The academic world-view of the West after the Enlightenment has left little room for miracles. Several African exegetes have disparaged this Western dismissal of miracles in rather strong language.[45] Abogunrin says, "Western Biblical exegetes think it necessary to reinterpret spiritual forces and demon-possession"; Africa, however, needs a reading of the Bible which emphasizes "the power of Jesus which destroys the power of the devil and delivers from all evil spiritual forces."[46] A large number of Africans, including many who have been educated in the West, still conceive of the world as alive with spiritual beings and forces which cannot be explained by the scientific method:[47] "The majority of African Christians still live in the world of the New Testament, where belief in demons and a host of unseen supernatural powers was potent and real. A Jesus emptied of all the supernatural contained in the Gospels would be meaningless in the African context."[48] Another scholar contends that the deistic world-view of the post-Enlightenment world is one of the greatest stumbling blocks for African biblical scholars: "By the end of the eighteenth century, there seemed little need of the notion of God at all to account for the data of experience."[49] Consequently Western biblical exegesis which finds little need to take the world of the spirits into account is not considered to be beneficial by many in the African context. The African universe is "alive": "spiritual forces both good and evil operated in this world affecting . . . life for good or ill. Indeed, there is a constant interaction between the world of the

---

45 The famous quotation from Rudolf Bultmann, that "it is impossible to use electric light and the wireless and to avail oneself of modern medical and surgical discoveries, and at the same time to believe in the New Testament world of demons and spirits" ("New Testament Mythology," in B. W. Bartsch, ed., *Kerygma and Myth* [London: SPCK, 1953], 4-5), is quoted by one African scholar as evidence of the weakness of Western biblical studies: its "positivistic intellectualism and general scepticism regarding supernatural existence" (A. O. Igenoza, "African *Weltanschauung* and Exorcism: The Quest for the Contextualization of the Kerygma," *Africa Theological Journal* 14 [1985]: 187).

46 Samuel O. Abogunrin, *The First Letter of Paul to the Corinthians* (Nairobi: Uzima, 1988), viii.

47 See, for example, Joseph Martin Hopkins, "Theological Students and Witchcraft Beliefs," *Journal of Religion in Africa* 11 (1980): 56-66.

48 Samuel O. Abogunrin, "The Synoptic Gospel Debate: A Re-Examination in the African Context," *African Journal of Biblical Studies* 2 (1987): 25-51. Also published as "The Synoptic Gospel Debate: A Re-Examination from an African Point of View," in David L. Dungan, ed., *The Interrelations of the Gospels: A Symposium led by M. E. Boismard, W. R. Farmer and F. Neirynck, Jerusalem 1984* (Leuven: Uitgeverij Peeters/Leuven University Press, 1990), 381-407.

49 Nlenanya Onwu, "The Hermeneutical Model: The Dilemma of the African Theologian," *Africa Theological Journal* 14 (1985): 149.

spirits and the world of men in African Cosmology. . . . To a very large extent the biblical worldview is similar to the African worldview. But when we consider the Western and African worldviews, we see features of incompatibility."[50]

Numerous studies of New Testament miracle stories have been produced by African scholars.[51] One representative work is a 1992 article by E. A. Obeng, who analyzes those stories in which Jesus is portrayed as raising people from the dead.[52] The essay is divided into three sections. In Section 1 Obeng categorizes the various forms of miracle stories and limits his study to resuscitation stories.[53] He then (Section 2) investigates the three gospel resuscitation stories from form-critical and redaction-critical perspectives, attempting carefully to distinguish between the life-situation of Jesus and the contexts of the early church and the redactors. He concludes that Western scholars have raised some doubts (to which the text of the triple tradition passage of the raising of Jairus' daughter [Mark 5:35-43, and parallels] and the Lukan story of the widow of Nain [Luke 7:11-17] give legitimacy) about whether or not these people were actually dead, and, therefore, whether Jesus actually raised them. Obeng asserts that for the evangelists Jesus certainly had performed miracles of resuscitation.

For our purposes Section 3 is the most distinctive. Obeng begins by stating that "Jesus' redeeming qualities were not for the benefit of the Jews of the first century only."[54] Africa, he says, is in great need of this message of Jesus' power over death:

> Jesus, the one who raises the dead, must be portrayed to the African as the effective protection against all mystical forces. . . . Every African who has grown up in the traditional environment will no doubt have been aware of the

---

50 Onwu, "Hermeneutical Model," 151-52.
51 For example: S. Cunningham, "The Healing of the Deaf and Dumb Man (Mark 7:31-37), with Application to the African Context," *African Journal of Evangelical Theology* 9 (1990): 13-26; Andrew Olu Igenoza, "Prayer, Prophecy, Healing and Exorcism in Luke-Acts in an African Context" (Ph.D. diss., University of Manchester, 1982), "Medicine and Healing in African Christianity: A Biblical Critique," *African Ecclesial Review* 30 (1988): 12-25, "African *Weltanschauung*"; E. A. Obeng, "The Miracle of the Stilling of the Storm and its Implications for the Church in Africa," *Deltion Biblikon Meleton* 18 (1989): 43-52 (in modern Greek, see *New Testament Abstracts* 34 [1990], #1156); Udobata Onunwa, "The Biblical Basis for Some Healing Methods in African Traditional Society," *East African Journal of Evangelical Theology* 7 (1988): 56-63; Nlenanya Onwu, "'Don't Mention It': Jesus' Instructions to Healed Persons," *African Journal of Biblical Studies* 1 (1986): 35-47.
52 E. A. Obeng, "The Significance of the Miracles of Resuscitation and its Implication for the Church in Africa," *Bible Bhashyam* 18 (1992): 83-85.
53 Obeng, "Miracles of Resuscitation," 84.
54 Obeng, "Miracles of Resuscitation," 91.

harassing reality of these forces. To an outsider, it sounds more like fiction than reality. But the whole psychic atmosphere of African village life is filled with belief in these mystical powers.[55]

Obeng proceeds to show that the denial of the existence of spiritual forces by the mission-founded churches[56] has created a kind of religious schizophrenia among African Christians, who go to church for salvation from sin, but return to traditional religious practices to deal with sickness, evil spirits or troublesome ancestors. "African Independent Churches," on the other hand, have grown because of their willingness to take the African world-view seriously. Obeng concludes by calling the churches to heal. What is needed, he says, is "an all out involvement of the church in Africa, in healing mission, in which many sick people will be treated. . . . What other power is there to counteract this fear [of the power of death] than the name of Jesus?"[57] What Obeng has done is to separate the Jesus of the gospels from the Jesus which Western scholarship considers to be plausible. Once this separation has been performed, Obeng is able to see the Jesus of the gospels as relevant to a very real pastoral issue in the African church.

An effective contrast to Obeng's article is a 1981 study by the Nigerian scholar, P. J. Arowele.[58] Whereas Obeng is concerned that scholarship take seriously the African context of belief in the miraculous and the power of the spirit world, Arowele is clearly worried about the "high degree of credulity to miracle-working among African Christians." Instead of commending the African Independent Churches, as Obeng does, Arowele is concerned that the "hungering" for the miraculous has become a "craze."[59]

When he turns to the New Testament text Arowele does not deny that Jesus healed ("Jesus very likely performed such 'signs'";[60] "he occasionally

---

55   Obeng, "Miracles of Resuscitation," 91-92.
56   See, for example, the opinion of Albert Schweitzer (*On the Edge of the Primeval Forest: Experiences and Observations of a Doctor in Equatorial Africa* [London: A. & C. Black, 1928], 156): "But now, how far does the negroe, as a Christian, really become another man? At his baptism he has renounced all superstition, but superstition is so woven into the texture of his own life and that of the society in which he lives, that it cannot be got rid of in twenty-four hours; he falls again and again in big things as in small. I think, however, that we can take too seriously the customs and practices from which he cannot set himself entirely free; the important thing is to make him understand that nothing—no evil spirit—really exists behind his heathenism."
57   Obeng, "Miracles of Resuscitation," 92-93.
58   P. J. Arowele, "This Generation Seeks Signs: The Miracles of Jesus with Reference to the African Situation," *Africa Theological Journal* 10 (1981): 17-28; also published as "This Generation Seeks Signs: An Exposition of the Miracles of Jesus with a Reference to the African Christian Situation," *Bulletin de théologie africaine* 3 (1981): 247-55.
59   Arowele, "This Generation," 17.
60   Arowele, "This Generation," 25.

performed some astonishing deeds, notably healings"[61]). Arowele relativizes the importance of these miracles, however, in two ways. First, he draws a dichotomy between Christology and history in many of the gospel stories. Some of the stories may draw on reminiscences, but the theological colouring of many of the stories should cause us to be cautious in assuming all of them to be historical. The purpose of many of the stories, he says, is christological: they are legendary accounts written for our theological edification, not to be taken literally.[62] Second, Arowele believes that Jesus was an eschatological prophet first, and only secondarily a healer. When Jesus did perform miracles it was not "to arouse sensation, for profit, to boast of his own personality or even to prove himself the Messiah. Rather, his miracles had a specific (religious) eschatological purpose as 'signs': to complement his proclamation that God would shortly reign."[63] Arowele does not deny that Jesus was a healer. He also acknowledges that "belief in miracle-working meets certain needs of the traditional African mind not catered for in traditional Christianity."[64] He is concerned, however, that some independent churches have become sensationalist and are playing into the anxiety of many modern Africans.

3.2 The "Non-Africanness" of Jesus

Nlenanya Onwu identifies a major problem for some Africans with regard to Jesus: he is not an African.

> The fourth problem of hermeneutics is the man Jesus. It is the problem of understanding him in the African context. Historically Jesus was a Jew, not an African. In view of this it is wrong to label him a "Black Christ," "African Chief," "elder brother," or Africa's "Great Ancestor." Admittedly these different "labels" represent the efforts of some African scholars to relate Jesus to the Africans in African categories or thought patterns.[65]

The depth of the problem of Jesus' particularity is underlined by John Pobee: "Why should an Akan relate to Jesus of Nazareth who does not belong to his clan, family, tribe and tradition?"[66] African identity is communal; societies are

---

61 Arowele, "This Generation," 26.
62 Arowele, "This Generation," 24-26.
63 Arowele, "This Generation," 26.
64 Arowele, "This Generation," 27.
65 Nlenanya Onwu, "The Hermeneutical Model: The Dilemma of the African Theologian," *Africa Theological Journal* 14 (1985): 152.
66 John S. Pobee, *Toward an African Theology* (Nashville: Abingdon, 1979), 81. Cf. Kwame Bediako's attempt to answer Pobee's question by reference to the analogous problem raised by the letter to the Hebrews concerning Jesus' lack of blood relationship to the priestly line: "Biblical Christologies in the Context of African Traditional Religions," in Vinay Samuel

bound together by familial relationships. According to John Mbiti the African world-view can be summarized as "I am because we are,"[67] or, as Pobee says, "I have blood relations; therefore I am."[68]

For Onwu the problem is deepened by the gospel stories, especially in Matthew's version, of Jesus and the Canaanite woman (Matt 15:21-28; Mark 7:24-30). Onwu finds the Matthean redaction of the event to have a "racist colouring"[69] in that it portrays Jesus as having an "exclusivist concern for his own people."[70] In his study of the story Onwu seeks to differentiate between the setting of the story in the life of Jesus and the redactional interests which gave rise to the Matthean version. Onwu rejects the suggestion that Matthew was a Gentile, arguing instead that he was a Jewish Christian from a mixed Jewish and Gentile community who did at times have something of a "Gentile bias" but "has not completely divested himself of his racial prejudice and racial pride . . . [wanting] to sustain the religious ideology of election of some of his Jewish converts."[71]

Onwu takes exception to a number of features in the story. The designation of Gentiles as "dogs," he notes, occurs in the Markan as well as the Matthean version of the story. Onwu hypothesizes that the word entered the story in the oral stage, during which, he suggests, there were controversies between Jewish and Gentile members of the early Jesus-movement. The word "Canaanite" is Matthean redaction. The change from "Syrophoenician" is significant, says Onwu, because it heightens the Jewish exclusiveness of the story. Matthew's term refers to the pre-occupation people of Palestine "who are always spoken of with reproach."[72] The line attributed to Jesus (in Matt 15:24, not in Mark), "I was sent only to the lost sheep of Israel," portrays Jesus as hesitant to help a Gentile. The redactional effect of these features indicates that Jesus was reluctant to listen to this Gentile woman's plea, whereas in the rest of the gospel there is "no evidence of such reluctance to his own people."[73] The historical Jesus, Onwu believes, would not have appreciated Matthew's editing process.

---

and Chris Sugden, eds., *Sharing Jesus in the Two Thirds World: Evangelical Christologies from the Contexts of Poverty, Powerlessness and Religious Pluralism* (Bangalore: Partnership in Mission-Asia, 1983): 115-75; republished as *Jesus in African Culture (A Ghanaian Perspective)* (Accra: Asempa, 1990).

67 Mbiti, *African Religions*, 108.
68 Pobee, *Who are the Poor?* 56.
69 Nlenanya Onwu, "Jesus and the Canaanite Woman (Matt.15:21-28): Toward a Relevant Hermeneutics in African Context," *Bible Bhashyam* 11 (1985): 130.
70 Onwu, "Canaanite Woman," 131.
71 Onwu, "Canaanite Woman," 138.
72 Onwu, "Canaanite Woman," 133.
73 Onwu, "Canaanite Woman," 133.

The exclusivist language of verse 24 put into the mouth of Jesus is doubtful. The tradition comes from Matthew and not from Jesus. . . . [T]hat the historical Jesus could fall so low to share such nationalistic opinion of his nation and age to the extent of addressing a Gentile woman with a contemptuous epithet (v.26) is similarly doubtful and quite inconsistent with Matthew's portrayal of Jesus in his gospel. The statement (v.26) cannot be squared with Jesus' attitude toward the poor and the oppressed of the society.[74]

Onwu's interests, to be sure, are not simply historical: "it is the intention of this paper to . . . show how this pericope confronts us with a challenge to seek [a] relevant hermeneutics that calls for renewed commitment to pluralism that acknowledges the integrity of ethnic groups in Africa and the world."[75] Onwu is clearly unable to accept a picture of a Jesus who is in any way racially exclusive. The pain of racism, as it has been experienced in Africa from the slave trade to apartheid, makes totally unacceptable any suggestion that Jesus of Nazareth was racially-biased. Fortunately for Onwu he has the tool of redaction criticism to help him out of his dilemma, but one must suspect that Onwu's own social context has aided him in his exegetical choices. If Jesus is to be on Africa's side he *must not* be a racial exclusivist.

A very different discussion of this problem comes from Eboussi Boulaga, a professor of philosophy from the Cameroun. He begins his study of the significance of Jesus with the words, "Jesus lived, acted, and spoke in the midst of his own and for his own."[76] For Boulaga Jesus is always "Jesus of Nazareth." He is a child of his place, of his culture, a person with ancestors: "Jesus is not an isolated individual. He is characterized by the bond that unites him to other human beings, by his solidarity with the members of his same tribe and lineage."[77] Boulaga does not doubt that Jesus' mission is "only to the lost sheep of Israel" (Matt 15:24).[78] He was a Jew of his time who interacted with the social and political movements and currents of his era[79] in order to

---

74 Onwu, "Canaanite Woman," 137-38.

75 Onwu, "Canaanite Woman," 130.

76 F. Eboussi Boulaga, *Christianity without Fetishes: An African Critique and Recapture of Christianity*, trans. Robert R. Barr (Maryknoll: Orbis, 1984). Compare the attempt to establish common ground between the historical Jesus and the vast majority of Africa's peoples through the designation "peasant": A. O. Mojola, "Peasant Studies and Biblical Exegesis: A Review with Some Implications for Bible Translation," *Africa Theological Journal* 17 (1988): 162-73.

77 Boulaga, *Without Fetishes*, 131. An important discussion of Jesus' genealogy extends to page 133.

78 Boulaga, *Without Fetishes*, 115.

79 See chapter 4 in which Boulaga describes what he calls the Jewish "movements and currents" of first-century Palestine and attempts to situate the words and actions of Jesus in that context.

restructure his society.[80] This Jewish particularity of Jesus is not a scandal. Rather than making Jesus more distant from the African, the rootedness of Jesus among his own people functions as a type for African Christianity, what Boulaga calls "the Christic model." If Jesus was truly a person of his place, so should African Christianity become truly African.[81] "When we wonder," says Boulaga, "whether Africans, conscious of their identities, their continuities and solidarities, can be Christian, we are asking a question about Christianity's original meaning, at a point further upstream than where dogma begins, as near as possible to its origin."[82] Underlying this discussion is a theological issue: Jesus is God and a human being: "Better, he has been God before beginning to be a human being."[83] It is this christological conviction that points Boulaga to the historical Jesus. Jesus of Nazareth is "God by participation."[84] Just as God (in Jesus of Nazareth) sought to re-structure the Jewish society of the first century, so God seeks to be rooted in the African church and through it to restructure society.

4. Conclusion

It is too easy to dismiss a person's scholarly reconstruction as eisegesis, anachronistic, reading back into the text. If a scholar finds in Jesus a "wordsmith," the fact that the scholar may be an expert in ancient rhetoric does not necessarily mean that the scholarly judgment is wrong. If an Irish Catholic scholar finds Jesus to be a pacifist hippie, we are not obliged to find his or her judgment to be mistaken. These scholars may have been inclined—biased, we might say—to find this kind of Jesus. This does not make their efforts fruitless. "Bias" may in fact have a positive role. Our angle of vision heightens our awareness of certain realities. A bias may alert an historian to possibilities of reconstructing the past which others without a similar prejudice may not have noticed. It is possible that an African perspective may provide a window into the first-century world which Western scholars do not possess.

The quest for the historical Jesus should not abandon the desire for objectivity and accuracy, the concern for methodologically-rigorous historical portraits of Jesus of Nazareth. We should be attentive, however, for help from unusual places. A need-driven, committed, even a confessional quest for a "relevant" Jesus of Nazareth may alert us to possibilities which we in our academic institutions in the North Atlantic world might otherwise ignore. Just because Obeng wants, or needs, to see Jesus as a healer does not mean he is

---

80 Boulaga, *Without Fetishes*, 115.
81 Boulaga, *Without Fetishes*, 159.
82 Boulaga, *Without Fetishes*, 161.
83 Boulaga, *Without Fetishes*, 129.
84 Boulaga, *Without Fetishes*, 117.

necessarily wrong; because Mosala wants to believe that Jesus was a social radical does not mean Jesus could not have been such a person. We post-Schweitzerians may be suspicious of those who find the Jesus they need, but we must at least entertain the possibility that their bias may have sharpened their critical senses and enabled them to see things which are there but to which we in Europe and North America have been blind.[85]

African scholarship sometimes lacks polish: scholars who must spend several hours a day growing food for their families instead of doing research, who teach and write in their third or fourth language, who use Gestetners instead of computers, often produce more than the usually-accepted number of grammatical and typographical infelicities. They also may have a certain sympathy for the text which we have lost. The accents of our African colleagues may not often be ours, but their voices open us to new historical and practical meanings for our common texts.

---

85 Feminism has recently drawn to the attention of biblical scholarship the productive potential of bias. Marxist theory has stressed this point explicitly at least since George Lukács's *History and Class Consciousness: Studies in Marxist Dialectics*, trans. Rodney Livingstone (Cambridge: MIT Press, 1971 [1922]). [Eds.]

14. Recent Concerns: The Scholar as *Engagé*

Leif E. Vaage

1. Subjectivity and the Subject of the Historical Jesus

The following observations are not, in any sense, a neutral review of the preceding essays. One reason is my own inevitable interest in the endurance of those views I find appealing. More importantly, I see no merit in aspiring to the perspective of some "transcendent eyeball" (the term is Ralph Waldo Emerson's), if only because it seems to me that one of the postures still befuddling contemporary efforts to discuss the historical Jesus is precisely the patina of "disinterestedness" or methodologically-engineered inner distance from the governing concerns of a particular relationship—whatever it might be—to the indicated object of inquiry. I see no future, therefore, for a conversation about the historical Jesus mired in debates over "criteria of authenticity" or the search for canons of universal, *viz.*, independent, judgment; although let me hasten to remark that I do believe that the conversation can be markedly improved through increased attention to better procedures of shared inquiry and evaluation.

First, the question of bias or (in the language of Hans Georg Gadamer) prejudice: I agree with Seán Freyne in the conclusion to his paper that if "we are all prepared to say at the outset what is at stake for [each of] us in our search for Jesus—ideologically, academically, personally—then there is some possibility that we can reach an approximation to the truth of things, at least for now"; and with Jane Schaberg, when she writes that feminist scholarship "challenges us as critics [of early Christian literature about Jesus and of modern historical-Jesus research] to become more conscious of, and to state openly in our work, who we are, what and for whom we work, where our allegiances and commitments and limitations lie, what our experience has been," again especially regarding the figure of Jesus; and also with Grant LeMarquand, in his contention that "'bias' may in fact have a positive role. Our angle of vision heightens our awareness of certain realities. A bias may alert an historian to possibilities of reconstructing the past which others without a similar prejudice may not have noticed."

Of interest here is not the old-fashioned epistemological problem of "perspective"—the struggle of so many blind people to describe the elephant they are variously touching—or our inability in three (or four) dimensional space to see anything whole, and hence the need to do so always partially from a particular angle. What captivates, rather, is the social fact of situated discourses and their specific subjects. The oft-touted "subjectivity" of historical-Jesus research is simply a function of the fact that, unlike certain other forms of New Testament scholarship, the link here is still patent between who the particular scholar is, including the social grouping(s) to which she or he belongs, and the preferred form(s) into which the Jesus data have been made to fit. Thus, the more honest and precise we can be about exactly what makes "the historical Jesus" worth discussing and what we hope to gain from *our* "Jesus," the better chance there is that our conversation about the historical Jesus will produce not just scholarly smoke but intellectual fire and human warmth.

This sort of clarification is necessary, in my opinion, even if one wishes to contend that the purpose of historical-Jesus research is merely "knowledge for knowledge's sake" (a conviction with its own social location). Do the authors of the preceding essays indicate clearly why they think that their subject is worth pursuing? Overall, not as much as I believe is required in order to be helpful; although, again, I find the conclusion to Freyne's paper exceptional in this regard. At the same time, Freyne's apparent assumption is that the basis for research into Jesus' life is, even now as it was in the beginning, the enduring desire to make certain christological claims.

The levity of Mack's opening remarks has the virtue of frankness (παρρησία; Mack may not have imagined these statements as more than a couple of "throw-away" comments, but their levity is not without comparative import). The same remarks also implicitly make clear the degree to which debates about the historical Jesus often function as academic junk bonds, suggesting real growth in knowledge but serving mainly as a chance for scholars to engage in intellectual competition with each other. However important and salutary it might be to acknowledge the ludic dimension of (biblical) scholarship, a greater and more explicit sense is necessary, it seems to me, of the social placement of this intellectual "sporting life," i.e., historical-Jesus research in the various cultural setting(s) where it occurs, if the enterprise is not simply to remain either childish in its mindlessness or elitist in its disregard of such broader connections and conceivable contributions.

Schaberg's paper documents in excruciating detail how implicated scholarly research into different aspects of Christian origins still is in institutional and other structures of contemporary cultural concern. In the end, however, she seems to have no particular interest in Jesus *per se* except, perhaps, as the "power source" in relation to which the women's lives in which she professes interest would gain their heightened ideological charge (although one might wish to maintain at this point that every person's life is *a priori* equally worthy of attention, this would not account accurately for why and how only certain [types of] lives tend to be chosen as the focus of our research). In this, Schaberg (like Mack) uses the figure of the historical Jesus or, in her words, "the relational Jesus," as a sort of abstract vanishing point: an essentially arbitrary and absent construct used to paint a picture of something else. In Schaberg's case, this would be the various women involved in the early Jesus movement (for Mack, the intellectual labour of early Christian mythmaking). While such a practice is hardly illegitimate, it is not clear to me how it contributes much to historical-Jesus research itself.[1]

2. The Cynic Analogy and the Scholarly Imagination of Society

I read the essays by Crossan, Mack, Marshall and Freyne as all basically addressing, in different ways, the recent (renewed) comparison of Jesus and the Cynics. Each scholar, with the possible exception of Mack, claims to be doing something else. Crossan is especially interested in listening to householders who supported the Jesus movement "talk back" (in the *Didache*) to their itinerant critics; Marshall is arguing for the underexploited relevance of the *Gospel of Thomas* in historical-Jesus research; Freyne is revindicating the importance of Galilee for the life of the historical Jesus and the need to consider more seriously the specific features of this particular region within the ancient Mediterranean world when determining the kind of man that Jesus likely was. But the underlying purpose of these various discussions strikes me as being, explicitly or implicitly, in order to qualify—by diminishing or eliminating—the import of the analogy with the Cynics that can and has been drawn to Jesus.

Even Mack is finally more interested in those aspects of early Christian literature, including Q, that have to do with the formation of social group identity and not especially, in Mack's words, in the Cynics' offer of "individual integrity" and "the achievement of personal virtue." While Mack sees "no way around" taking "the Cynic hypothesis seriously" and is willing to accept that "the Cynic-like data from Q and Mark are as close as we shall ever get to the real Jesus of history," there is nothing for Mack notably significant about Jesus himself: "the Jesus of history was not nearly as important for the emergence of Christianity as the intellectual energies generated by his followers." Correlatively, the Cynic analogy to Jesus, even as Mack has chosen to define it predominantly in rhetorical terms, is finally not instructive of much: "It is not the clever insight or the dramatic moment of vision that counts. It is the elaboration." Mack's light-hearted rendering of the Cynic persona in antiquity makes Cynicism and, by implication the historical Jesus, in the end just light-weight.

This rendering of Jesus is consistent with Mack's conviction that what New Testament scholars and other historians of Christian origins ought to be investigating is really not the historical Jesus; at least not as though Jesus himself were somehow crucial to the subsequent emergence and development

---

1   See Jane Schaberg's statement: "Feminist interpretation involves a shift of focus of attention—away from the historical Jesus. . . . Feminist interpretation in a sense deconstructs and undermines the quest; it is not so interested in Jesus the individual, as in the relational Jesus, Jesus in his social world, Jesus reforming his social world. To be more specific: feminist critics are interested in the search for the historical women of this movement" (159 above).

of Christianity. Instead, Mack contends, it is the process of mythmaking, whereby Christian culture and its legacy came into being, that ought to be the focus of scholarly inquiry.

Let me return to Mack's characterization of ancient Cynicism. For it is in fumbling Cynicism, I believe, that Mack reveals the limitations of his operative sense—otherwise, much livelier than the understanding of most New Testament scholars—of the social world in which both the historical Jesus and his first followers played out their opening span upon the earth. The same would hold true for the different ways in which Crossan and Freyne endeavour to contain or de-centre the Cynic analogy to Jesus. At stake in these various approximations to the historical Jesus and revealed more clearly in the varieties of resistance to (finding significant) the Cynic analogy to Jesus is the scholarly sense of what was (and is) *personally possible* in ancient (and contemporary) human society.[2]

By "personally possible," I do not mean any sort of modern liberal "individualism." But I do mean to recall that human societies, as far back in time and as diversely situated geographically as we know them, are not composed of mobile mathematical units or cultural clones—even if hegemonic discourses of analysis and description might depict them in these terms—but, rather, of the multiple associations of singular instances of so-called human beings: in other words, particular persons.

That such "personalities" are each socially constructed through the progressive imposition (or "growth" or "maturation") of a larger or smaller set of customary or prescribed cultural "masks" or normative clichés of stereotypical behaviour and speech patterns is already implicitly acknowledged in the use of the term "person" itself.[3] That, furthermore, the "interior" life of each such person—including the historical Jesus—is beyond what we can finally ever "know" is likewise not the question. Rather, if we include in our historiographical repertoire the question of what was "personally possible" in antiquity, we can begin to consider how a given person might have resisted the standard options for social indentification in his or her historical context, or have blended them into a singular combination. Jesus may have been remembered as a person who attempted just that.

---

2   In backing away from the Cynic analogy, some strange bedfellows are made. For example, Mack and Crossan essentially agree that early on in the Jesus movement there was a program: Mack calls it "a social vision" or "a vision for social experimentation as an alternative to the *status quo*." Mack is also in essential agreement with Bloomquist (as is Moxnes) on the "rhetorical Jesus," and it is not clear to me how different their "rhetorical Jesus" is, in the end, from Schaberg's "relational Jesus."

3   The English word "person" recalls the Roman theatrical term, *persona*, which, in turn, recalls the similarly employed Greek expression for face/presence (πρόσωπον).

Not to consider such a question, on the other hand, is minimally to betray the undemonstrated (and ultimately conservative) conviction that any such resistance and innovation is unable to be embodied, at least to any significant or "healthy" degree, in a particular human being. The Cynic analogy to Jesus, however, would suggest that the existing evidence for such resistance and innovation on the part of the historical Jesus need reflect neither an obviously transcendent perspective on human affairs nor a plainly "communitarian" social identity. Rather, it allows the contemporary biographer of Jesus at least to consider the possibility that the historical man was wilfully "deviant" in his social practice and pronouncements; and in so being, defined himself in a specifically countercultural—and wholly human—manner, whose precise delineation would presumably be the proper province of historical-Jesus research. One wonders, however, to what degree continuing scholarly hesitation to run with the Cynic analogy to Jesus is not a reflection of modern academic biblical scholarship's general unwillingness and/or inability to imagine the object(s) of its descriptive labours as genuinely opposed to the institutions of power and the traditions that sustain them, institutions with which such scholarship itself remains allied.

3. The Jewishness of Jesus and the Problem of Identity

Despite everything, I suspect that a majority of scholars and interested readers will still tend to gravitate in their imagination of the historical Jesus in the direction of the type of portrait painted of him by Freyne, namely, Jesus as essentially a "Jew," and furthermore a Jew profoundly marked in some fashion by some sort of eschatological expectation. Thus, for example, even Moxnes at the end of his paper remains finally committed to an "eschatological Jesus" out of fear of committing once again the original sin of 19th-century European liberalism and assimilating our recollection of the historical Jesus to a modern sensibility.

Except for Freyne there is hardly any discussion in these essays of what is at stake and what is to be gained or lost by exploring Jesus' "Jewishness." Rather, most of the preceding essays are interested in some aspect of Hellenistic or Graeco-Roman culture and the way in which this knowledge changes or sharpens our reading of the specific evidence for Jesus. In this, I believe that the essays are simply representative of increasing interest on the part of New Testament scholars and historians of early Christianity in the profound participation by Jesus and his first followers in the general Mediterranean culture of their day.

There is no reason, in other words, as far as I can see, to believe that the focus of these essays on Graeco-Roman parallels and context is meant to deny that the historical Jesus was somehow not really Jewish. Rather, it intends to correct a tendency in modern North Atlantic biblical scholarship, as Jonathan

Smith has demonstrated in his book, *Drudgery Divine*,[4] to use the "Jewishness" of Jesus and early Christianity as an ideological cover for continuing implicit claims to Christian uniqueness and categorical separation. Freyne's reference at the end of his essay to Walter Grundmann's 1941 book, *Jesus der Galiläer*, and other similar efforts between the two world wars to "cleanse" early Christianity of any significant "Jewish" connection, is perhaps representative of an understandable anxiety and obviously remains important to recall. But it is, I believe, really a red herring to suppose that the stress on *other* "family resemblances" between Jesus and the wider world around him inevitably will be anti-Jewish in its outcome.

Moreover, lurking in this concerted defence of the "Jewishness" of Jesus, it seems to me, is an excessively narrow and strangely stereotypical vision of Jewish identity in antiquity (and, by extension, also today). Just as Philo and Josephus, to name but two examples, were plainly full practitioners of the Mediterranean culture around them and, at the same time, equally and fully Jews (even if not always perceived to be "exemplary" Jews by all who lived with them or came after them), so also Jesus, it seems reasonable to consider, may simultaneously have been a member of at least the same two distinguishable but not separate social worlds. Indeed, this can only be denied in principle if we were somehow obliged to imagine (as, in fact, modern capitalist Eurocentric civilizations and their colonizing sciences, including biblical scholarship, have endeavoured to maintain) that persons in antiquity (and, by extension, today) must somehow really and necessarily choose to live in one and only one cultural frame of reference. Such an assumption, I am convinced, simply cannot be sustained as a sufficient description of human social life (however much it may still be apparent as political will).

By not discussing the Jewishness of the historical Jesus, the preceding essays—again excepting Freyne—avoid exploring and/or explaining how their different accounts of the man simultaneously imply alternative visions of the nature of Second Temple Judaism. In Freyne's case, the problem is an understanding of Judaism in Galilee that does not allow, at least on the part of the historical Jesus, for serious deviance from, or variation within, a presumed traditional identity. In other words, despite the importance of these essays, an opportunity has been missed to show how historical-Jesus research might contribute to the construction of a much livelier sense (at least on the part of New Testament scholars and historians of Christian origins) of the social world of Second Temple Judaism in Palestine and Galilee.

---

4   Jonathan Z. Smith's *Drudgery Divine: On the Comparison of Early Christianities and the Religions of Late Antiquity* (London: School of Oriental and African Studies, 1990).

PART TWO: ENDURING CONCERNS

Since its inception, the field of Christian origins, especially the critical study of the historical Jesus, has passed through a series of phases in which first one element, then another, appears to be of paramount gravity for determining the direction of research. Throughout the generations of the "quest," however, several critical issues have persisted. Among them are the relationship between Jesus and the Jewish sects described by Josephus (most particularly the Essenes); the supernaturalism of Jesus' vision of the Kingdom of God (most particularly its eschatological dimension); the grounds for, and character of, the distinction between the Jesus of history and the Christ of faith; and not least the question of bias or tendentiousness among scholars putatively seeking only historical ends.

While the studies in the first major section of this collection tend to focus on more novel and pressing concerns, the following studies provide a retrospective glance at the last century of scholarship, assessing its stances on, and contributions to, these persistent questions. They represent many of the issues that continue to define the quest for the historical Jesus.

15. Jesus and the Dead Sea Scrolls: Context

Terence L. Donaldson

The new surge of popular interest in the old question of the historical Jesus has emerged in parallel with an equally intense public fascination with the Dead Sea Scrolls. The phenomena are not unrelated. The fact that the scrolls have achieved a firm hold on public awareness, while the Nag Hammadi documents—discovered at the same time and of equal importance—have not, is undoubtedly due to the fact that the scrolls emerge from the same era and environment as Jesus himself. In return, a significant factor in the recent growth industry of Jesus research has been the belief that the scrolls shed invaluable light on the social and religious environment in which Jesus is to be located, and that they are able to open up fresh angles of vision on his life, program and impact.

To be sure, this assessment of the scrolls' significance is not universal. Influential scholars, some of whose voices can be heard elsewhere in this volume, would disagree with Wayne McCready's assertion that Jesus likely understood himself within an eschatological prophetic tradition, one shared by the community of the scrolls. Still, a sapiential and non-eschatological Jesus, located within a Cynic-like tradition, has certainly not yet carried the day—which means that it is important for a volume such as this to contain an assessment of the significance of Qumran for the historical investigation of Jesus. This is the issue to which McCready addresses himself in his informative, richly-documented study.

Ever since their discovery, the Qumran scrolls have been used in a range of ways to illuminate the figure of Jesus. At one end, there have been those, such as André Dupont-Sommer and Edmund Wilson in the early days and Robert Eisenman and Barbara Thiering more recently, who argued for some direct connection between Jesus and Qumran—the Jesus movement overlapping somehow with the group reflected in the scrolls, or the distinctive features of early Christianity being derived in some way from Qumran. Such approaches have received public attention out of proportion to their scholarly support, and McCready, quite properly, dismisses them with only brief discussion.

At the other end of the range, the scrolls have been used more generally as a means of illuminating the environment from which Jesus emerged. The assumption is that while there may not have been any direct connection between Jesus and the Qumran community, they nevertheless shared a common social and religious milieu, and represent distinct yet parallel responses to the same set of historical factors. As a result, various elements of Jesus' language, message and activity can be given clarity and nuance by comparing them to similar elements in the scrolls. For the most part, this is the approach taken by McCready. The major portion of the paper is given over to a discussion of similarities and differences between Jesus and the scrolls, the purpose of which is to sharpen the profile of Jesus as he is presented in the Gospels.

But there is an additional element in McCready's stance, representing a position somewhere between the two approaches discussed to this point. While he rejects the notion that there was any direct connection between Jesus and Qumran, he follows Flusser in believing that Jesus "likely was aware of Essenism in its widest definition," and that some of his sayings are to be understood as explicit responses to Qumran positions. This theme runs through the section in which he discusses various "factors of dissimilarity between Jesus and Qumranites."

One final observation is in order here. For the most part, the discussion of "Jesus and Qumran" has tended to proceed on the assumption that Qumran is a known quantity, a secure observation point from which the more indeterminate terrain of the Jesus movement can be viewed. But more recent scrolls scholarship has had the effect of calling this assumption into question. In part this has to do with the reopening of issues once widely seen to be settled; the relationship between the Qumran community and the Essenes, and the archaeological assessment of the ruins, are two cases in point. In part, this has to do with the appearance of hitherto unavailable documents, such as 4QMMT with its intriguing calendrical and halakhic material. With one exception, this new state of ferment in Qumran studies is not thematized in McCready's paper; aspects of it are merely touched on here and there in the footnotes. The exception has to do with the enterprise of basing historical reconstruction on literary description. It has simply been assumed by most researchers, for example, that 1QS is indeed a "Community Rule," in the sense that it describes the functioning of an actual community. Such moves from text to community, common in gospel studies as well, require much more care and consideration than is usually the case, as McCready rightly reminds us in a discussion of the work of Philip Davies, appearing near the beginning of the paper. This cautionary note, together with the recognition of the degree of uncertainty pertaining to the scrolls themselves, should be kept in mind as one reads the remainder.

16. The Historical Jesus and the Dead Sea Scrolls

Wayne O. McCready

1. Introduction

1.1 Jesus and his Jewish Context

David Flusser, in his introduction to *Judaism and the Origins of Christianity*, states one of the central tenets of historical-Jesus research when he notes that "the starting point is a truism: Christianity arose among the Jews—it was once a part of Judaism."[1] Flusser, perhaps more than any other contemporary scholar, is convinced that Jesus and the early Jesus movement were influenced directly by many groups within ancient Jewish society, and especially by those responsible for the Dead Sea Scrolls. Jesus and his immediate followers shared not only a common religious context with these people at the turn of the era, but also borrowed and reinterpreted, as well as consciously rejected, Qumranite ideas and practices.[2]

---

1   David Flusser, *Judaism and the Origins of Christianity* (Jerusalem: Magnes Press, 1988), xii.

2   Flusser's position on these matters will be detailed elsewhere in this study. "Qumranites" refers to those who sponsored the Dead Sea Scrolls and were responsible for placing them in the caves near the Dead Sea. Not all manuscripts found in caves 1 through 11 were of Qumranite origin. There is enough unity among the manuscripts, however, to represent a "Qumran library" (i.e., "Qumran scrolls") and a Qumranite view of things. See James H. Charlesworth, ed., *Jesus and the Dead Sea Scrolls* (New York: Doubleday, 1992), for a list of common features of the scrolls that reflect international and critical scholarly consensus. This study will work from the position that Qumranites represent a group closely parallel to the Essenes described by Josephus, Philo and Pliny the Elder. I do not *equate* the sponsors of the Qumran scrolls with Essenes; the descriptions in Philo, Pliny and Josephus warrant caution in assuming they are the same group. Many others scholars (see Charlesworth, *Jesus and the Dead Sea Scrolls*, 2-3) judge that the Qumranites were one of the Essene groups; for example, see Hartmut Stegemann, "Qumran und das Judentum zur Zeit Jesu," *Theologie und Glaube* 84 (1994): 175-94, who bases his support of the Essene hypothesis on factors of hierarchy, initiation rites, community of goods, ritual baths, a common meal and views on marriage as well as calendar. Alternatively, Norman Golb estimates that the scrolls came from Jerusalem to a fortress at Qumran during the siege of Jerusalem around 70 CE; see Norman Golb, *Who Wrote the Dead Sea Scrolls? The Search for the Secret of Qumran* (New York: Scribner, 1995); "The Dead Sea Scrolls: A New Perspective," *The American Scholar* 58 (1989): 177-207. For comments on the value of comparative studies, see Flusser, *Origins*, xii-xvi, 75-87; "The Dead Sea Sect and Pre-Pauline Christianity," in his *Origins*, 23-74, reprinted from *Scripta Hierosolymitana IV: Aspects of the Dead Sea Scrolls* (Jerusalem: Magnes, 1958), 215-66; and "A New Sensitivity in Judaism and in the Christian Message," in *Origins*, 469-89, reprinted from *Harvard Theological Review* 61 (1968): 107-27. See also Ben F. Meyer, *The Early Christians: Their World Mission and Self-Discovery* (Wilmington: Michael Glazier, 1986); E. P. Sanders, A. I. Baumgarten and Alan Mendelson, eds., *Jewish and Christian*

This study outlines and summarizes research that has involved comparative analysis of the Dead Sea Scrolls and New Testament traditions about Jesus. Its objective is to consider the ground to be gained by scholarship if one works from the starting point that Jesus and his immediate followers were co-religionists with Qumranites whose origins predate Jesus by over a century. My comments will focus on researchers' proposals on this matter rather than analysis of primary sources. My working presupposition is that Jesus was not a Qumranite or Essene but likely was aware of Essenism in its widest definition, as well as the ideas and practices promoted in the Qumran scrolls.[3] I give minimal consideration to Pauline Christianity or the later developments of the emerging church in order to concentrate on questions relating to the historical Jesus.[4] This study works from the position that Jesus likely understood himself within an eschatological prophetic tradition.[5] This eschatological prophetic self-definition has parallels to views expressed in the Dead Sea Scrolls and this common factor ensures that using the scrolls to research the historical Jesus will be productive. Since the Qumran scrolls show no awareness of Jesus or his followers, a factor hardly surprising since most of the texts found in the caves near Qumran predate Jesus, the direction of the study will be on research that

---

Self-Definition; Volume Two: *Aspects of Judaism in the Greco-Roman Period* (Philadelphia: Fortress, 1980); Daniel J. Harrington, "The Jewishness of Jesus: Facing Some Problems," *Catholic Biblical Quarterly* 49 (1987): 1-13; and Frederick James Murphy, *The Religious World of Jesus: An Introduction to Second Temple Palestinian Judaism* (Nashville: Abingdon, 1991). See Geza Vermes, "Jewish Literature and New Testament Exegesis: Reflections on Methodology," *Journal of Jewish Studies* 33 (1982): 361-76, for comments on how New Testament sources should function as primary source material for researching contemporary Judaism.

3 Flusser, after 40-some years of comparative study of early Christian sources and the Qumran scrolls, holds the opinion that Jesus was not an Essene—indeed, that he consciously and deliberately rejected essential principles of Essenism (specifically their strict dualism, elitism as "sons of light" and separatism)—but that he was attracted to their views on poverty and sharing of wealth. See his *Origins*, xviii, 150-68. See also Charlesworth, *Jesus and the Dead Sea Scrolls*, 37-40, who details an international scholarly consensus rejecting the opinion that Jesus was an Essene or Qumranite and repudiating the view that early Christianity was a form of Essenism.

4 Early in his study of the Qumran scrolls, Flusser estimated that the scrolls had greater impact on the emerging church (on what Flusser refers to as the *kerygma* phase of developing Christianity; see "The Dead Sea Sect," 25), especially in regard to the influence of Qumranite dualism on Christian views of human nature and influence on Christian community organization. He has since modified this position. See Flusser, *Origins*, xviii.

5 See E. P. Sanders, *Jesus and Judaism* (Philadelphia: Fortress, 1985), and *The Historical Figure of Jesus* (London: Allen Lane, 1993). Another influence is Geza Vermes, *Jesus the Jew: A Historian's Reading of the Gospels* (London: Collins, 1973); *Jesus and the World of Judaism* (London: SCM, 1983); *The Religion of Jesus the Jew* (Minneapolis: Fortress, 1993). See also Martin Hengel, *The Charismatic Leader and his Followers* (New York: Crossroad, 1981); Ben F. Meyer, *The Aims of Jesus* (London: SCM, 1979); John P. Meier, *A Marginal Jew: Rethinking the Historical Jesus*, 2 vols. (New York: Doubleday, 1991-94).

investigates ground gained by Jesus and his followers on religious territory perhaps already staked out by the Qumranites, rather than the reverse.

The nature of research on Jesus and the Dead Sea Scrolls in the late-20th century means has led to heightened interest in the topic by the general public and especially by the news media. In an age when greater scholarly accountability is demanded by the public, such interest should be encouraged. Regrettably, a goodly amount of the interest feeds off those who make extreme claims about the scrolls and their relationship to the beginnings of Christianity. Academics who have argued for exaggerated intimacy between Jesus and Essenism or the Qumran scrolls have not convinced either researchers of the historical Jesus or Dead Sea Scrolls experts. Barbara Thiering and Robert Eisenman are examples of a small number of people who enthusiastically argue their case with mixed or negative reviews by a significant portion of their academic peers.[6] Thiering, in a curious use of scrolls material read in tandem with New Testament texts, suggests that the evangelists wrote in code and that their meaning can only be determined by a *pesher* reading of scrolls and gospels.[7] She concludes, for instance, that Jesus was part of the leadership of the Essenes and did not die on the cross. He married Mary Magdalene and they had children, then later he divorced her. Robert Eisenman estimates that the scrolls and the New Testament share a common messianic setting, and a portion of the scrolls reflect early Jewish Christianity. He estimates that the Teacher of Righteousness was James the brother of Jesus and that the Wicked Priest was Paul.[8] The overwhelming consensus of critical scholarship in every international

---

6   Robert Eisenman's proposals inspired Michael Baigent and Richard Leigh in *The Dead Sea Scrolls Deception* (New York: Simon & Schuster, 1991) to suggest that there is a Vatican-inspired conspiracy to limit access to scrolls material because they contain details that undermine traditional Christianity. The story line advanced by Baigent and Leigh has added fuel to public interest not only in the scrolls but in a possible interrelationship between Jesus and those who wrote the scrolls. This public interest has been exceptionally high in Germany, where *Dead Sea Scrolls Deception* enjoyed bestseller status for an extended period. For a counter to Eisenman, as well as to Baigent and Leigh, see Otto Betz and Rainer Riesner, *Jesus, Qumran, and the Vatican: Clarifications* (New York: Crossroad, 1994); Martin Hengel, "Die Qumranrollen und der Umgang mit der Wahrheit," *Theologische Beiträge* 23 (1992): 233-37; Hartmut Stegemann, "Qumran, Jesus und das Urchristentum: Bestseller und Anti-Bestseller," *Theologische Literaturzeitung* 19 (1994): 387-408; also see Joseph A. Fitzmyer, *Responses to 101 Questions on the Dead Sea Scrolls* (London: Geoffrey Chapman, 1992) and Hershel Shanks, "Is the Vatican Suppressing the Dead Sea Scrolls?" *Biblical Archaeology Review* 17 (1991): 66-71.

7   Barbara Thiering, *Jesus and the Riddle of the Dead Sea Scrolls: Unlocking the Secrets of his Life Story* (Toronto: Doubleday, 1992). The same book is published under the title *Jesus the Man* (Sydney: Doubleday, 1992).

8   Robert Eisenman, *Maccabees, Zadokites, Christians and Qumran* (Leiden: Brill, 1983) and *James the Just in the Habakkuk Pesher* (Leiden: Brill, 1986). Eisenman combined with Michael O. Wise to publish Qumran texts not easily available to scholarship and the general public, entitled *The Dead Sea Scrolls Uncovered: The First Complete Translation and*

context,[9] however, rejects the opinion that Jesus was a Qumranite, and the source material of early Christianity suggests that it rejected essential principles found in the Dead Sea Scrolls.

José O'Callaghan has proposed that Greek fragments in Cave 7 were from a number of New Testament texts, including Mark, Acts, Romans, 1 Timothy, James and a portion of 2 Peter.[10] He is most certain about fragments identified with 1 Timothy (7Q4) and Mark (7Q5). On the whole, O'Callaghan's thesis has met with scholarly skepticism since the fragments are extremely small, almost illegible, and his strongest case does not agree with known versions of Mark.[11]

Interpretation of 50 Key Documents Withheld for Over 35 Years (Rockport: Element, 1992). The primary flaw of this volume is that Eisenman's theory is forced onto the translations. This is done in spite of the fact that Eisenman's proposals have been rejected by an overwhelming consensus of scholarship since the mid-1980s.

9   For example, see Todd S. Beall, *Josephus' Description of the Essenes Illustrated by the Dead Sea Scrolls* (Cambridge: Cambridge University Press, 1988); Phillip R. Callaway, *The History of the Qumran Community* (Sheffield: JSOT, 1988); Philip R. Davies, *Behind the Essenes: History and Ideology in the Dead Sea Scrolls* (Atlanta: Scholars Press, 1987); Michael A. Knibb, *The Qumran Community* (Cambridge: Cambridge University Press, 1987); Lawrence H. Schiffman, ed., *Archaeology and History in the Dead Sea Scrolls* (Sheffield: JSOT, 1990); James C. VanderKam, *The Dead Sea Scrolls Today* (Grand Rapids: Eerdmans, 1994); and Geza Vermes, *The Dead Sea Scrolls: Qumran in Perspective* (London: Collins, 1977), *The Dead Sea Scrolls in English*, 3rd ed. (Sheffield: JSOT, 1987 [1968]).

10   José O'Callaghan, "Papiros neotestamentarios en la cueva 7 de Qumrān?" *Biblica* 53 (1972): 91-100 (trans. by W. L. Holladay, "New Testament Papyri in Qumran Cave 7?" *Supplement to the Journal of Biblical Literature* 91 [1972]: 1-14), and "Identifications of 7Q," *Aegyptus* 56 (1976): 287-94. Greek fragments of Jewish scripture (e.g., Lev, Num and Deut) were found in Cave 4, and in addition to Greek versions of Exodus and the Letter of Jeremiah (an appendix to Baruch) 17 unidentified Greek fragments were found in Cave 7.

11   Kurt Aland attempted to counter O'Callaghan's reading of the Greek fragments in "Neue neutestamentliche Papyri III," *New Testament Studies* 20 (1974): 357-81, and "Über die Möglichkeit der Identifikation kleiner Fragmente neutestamentlicher Handschriften mit Hilfe des Computers," in James Keith Elliott, ed., *Studies in the New Testament Language and Text* (Leiden: E. J. Brill, 1976), 14-38; see also M. Baillet, "Les manuscrits de la grotte 7 de Qumran et le Nouveau Testament," *Biblica* 53 (1972): 508-16; Pierre Benoit, "Note sur les fragments grecs de la grotte 7 de Qumran," *Revue Biblique* 79 (1972): 321-24, and "Nouvelle note sur les fragments grecs de la grotte 7 de Qumran," *Revue Biblique* 80 (1973): 5-12; Gordon D. Fee, "Some Dissenting Notes on 7Q5 = Mark 6:52-53," *Journal of Biblical Literature* 92 (1973): 109-12. Hartmut Stegemann, "Ein neues Bild des Judentums zur Zeit Jesu? Zum gegenwärtigen Stand der Qumran- und Essener-Forschung," *Herder Korrespondenz* 4 (1992): 175-80, has proposed that 7Q5 may be a genealogy. O'Callaghan's position has been endorsed by Carsten Peter Thiede, *The Earliest Gospel Manuscript? The Qumran Fragment 7Q5 and its Significance for New Testament Studies* (Exeter: Paternoster, 1992), originally written in German (three editions) and also translated into a number of other languages. For a succinct and thorough discussion of this topic see Betz and Riesner, *Clarifications*, 114-24.

O'Callaghan's proposal, despite these reservations, is a scholarly inquiry aiming to identify textual fragments, and thus differs substantially from the exaggerated proposals of Eisenman and Thiering. The final assessment of the Greek fragments of Cave 7 has yet to be made.

1.2 A Programmatic Caution

Philip Davies, in an article entitled "Redaction and Sectarianism in the Qumran Scrolls," identifies a number of challenges involved in using the scrolls to reconstruct historical information.[12] Davies makes a convincing case that important scrolls such as 1QS and 1QM[13] are products of a recensional process and that researchers cannot assume that the formation of a distinct historical and geographically-specific community was a necessary precondition for these texts.[14] He argues that literary analysis of the War and Rule materials from caves 1 and 4 suggests that the "Qumran community," or at least its ideal, was a product of a redactional process. Davies poses the question: Was a "Qumran community" fundamentally necessary for the War and Rule materials? He answers in the negative, based on literary analysis of 1QM, 4QM, 1QS and 4QS.[15] Further, in regard to the Rule material (1QS, 4QS, 5QS), Davies observes that references to sons of Zadok and community (יחד) are missing in rather crucial portions of fragments from caves 4 and 5. J. T. Milik previously noted these omissions and estimated that the material from Cave 4 was original and 1QS was an addition.[16] The point Davies makes is that researchers face a substantial challenge in reconstructing the practice and belief of Qumranites when they encounter the possibility of an "obsolete" text that was replaced by subsequent versions.[17] Davies' assessment is that 1QS was not written as a rule for a community, nor was it necessarily a rule coming from a community. Rather, it is a "repository of rules and other material relating perhaps to some community or communities whether past, present or future, and whether real

---

12 Davies' article is found in F. García Martínez, A. Hilhors and C. J. Labuschagne, eds., *The Scriptures and the Scrolls: Studies in Honour of A. S. van der Woude on the Occasion of his 65th Birthday* (Leiden: Brill, 1992): 152-63.

13 For an explanation of the system of abbreviations for Dead Sea Scrolls texts, see Joseph A. Fitzmeyer, *The Dead Sea Scrolls: Major Publications and Tools for Study* (Atlanta: Scholars Press, 1990), 1-93. [Eds.]

14 Davies, "Redaction and Sectarianism," 153.

15 See also Jean Duhaime, "Dualistic Reworking in the Scrolls from Qumran," *Catholic Biblical Quarterly* 49 (1987): 32-56; Geza Vermes, "Preliminary Remarks on Unpublished Fragments of the Community Rule from Qumran Cave 4," *Journal of Jewish Studies* 42 (1991): 250-55.

16 J. T. Milik, "Numérotation des feuilles des rouleaux dans le scriptorium de Qumrân," *Semiticia* 27 (1977): 75-81, esp. 78. Vermes, in "Preliminary Remarks," suggests that two traditions are reflected in the sources.

17 Davies, "Redaction and Sectarianism," 157.

or ideal. But the existence of variants to 1QS, simultaneously preserved and recopied, suggest that they almost certainly did not function as regulative texts within a community."[18] Davies cautions researchers that just because literature profiles a community or communities it does not necessary follow that the community is real or that a specific community produced the text. He observes that biblical scholarship is frequently driven by an agenda of translating realistic description into historical fact. Davies estimates that the scrolls and descriptions of Essenes from other ancient sources provide evidence for an historical community that might be equated with Qumranites, but he advocates a "programmatic caution, even a programmatic skepticism as the proper methodology for interpreting Qumran texts."[19] His advice that a delicate hand needs to be applied in arriving at assessments that pose a relationship between literary descriptions of community in the scrolls and any historical reality in Judaism at the turn of the Common Era is well taken, and highlights one of the primary challenges of using the Dead Sea Scrolls for historical-Jesus inquiry.

2. Factors of Dissimilarity between Jesus and Qumranites

Before describing scholarly work that identifies productive similarities between the Qumranites and the early Jesus movement, drawing attention to significant differences will discourage arriving at simple conclusions.[20]

2.1 Initiation Rites and Membership

Initiation requirements for new members seem to be minimal for the early Jesus movement. The requirement for individual repentance, willingness for the called

---

18   Davies, "Redaction and Sectarianism," 158.

19   Davies, "Redaction and Sectarianism," 160. A feature of Davies' assessment is that the *Sitz im Leben* of the Qumran scrolls can be located in scribal abilities to present what seems like a real community through "literary sectarianism" (161).

20   Some comparisons between the Dead Sea Scrolls and Jesus or the beginnings of Christianity—in addition to works cited at length in this study—include: Roland E. Murphy, "The Dead Sea Scrolls and New Testament Comparisons," *Catholic Biblical Quarterly* 18 (1956): 263-72; Krister Stendahl, ed., *The Scrolls and the New Testament* (New York: Harper, 1957); Matthew Black, *The Scrolls and Christian Origins: Studies in the Jewish Background of the New Testament* (New York: Scribner, 1961); Herbert Braun, *Qumran und das Neue Testament*, 2 vols. (Tübingen: J. C. B. Mohr, 1966); Jerome Murphy-O'Connor, ed., *Paul and Qumran* (London: Geoffrey Chapman, 1972); William Sanford La Sor, *The Dead Sea Scrolls and the New Testament* (Grand Rapids: Eerdmans, 1972); Joseph A. Fitzmyer, *Essays on the Semitic Background of the New Testament* (Missoula: Scholars Press, 1974), *A Wandering Aramean: Collected Aramaic Essays* (Missoula: Scholars Press, 1979), and "The Qumran Scrolls and the New Testament after Forty Years," *Revue de Qumran* 13 (1988): 609-20; Gerard J. Norton, "Qumran and Christian Origins," *Proceedings of the Irish Biblical Association* 16 (1993): 99-113.

to "follow" Jesus and perhaps to be baptized, although important for determining the full character of Jesus' public activity, do not compare to the intensity and prolonged initiation period of a novice who wished to be counted among the Qumranites.[21] The would-be Qumranite was expected to undergo a two-year probationary period that eventually involved giving over personal possessions to the community, initial and ongoing study as well as commitment to community rules, regular examination of belief and practice, willingness to adopt a calendar different from to the one used in the rest of society and commitment to special revelation that was the unique possession of Qumranites (see 1QS). This social structure ensured collective religious purity by creating a protective boundary between community members and the rest of society. Initiation into the Qumran community involved moving behind closed doors from the larger society and becoming a member of a group which placed a very high value on secrecy. These community features contrasted sharply with the open and accessible Jesus movement.[22] Jean Duhaime has pointed out that deprivation theories concerning modern new religious movements seem to work for understanding Qumranite conversion.[23] Strict boundaries were established to distinguish them from fellow Jews. This rigorous separation represents a significant difference between the Qumran group and Jesus.[24] Flusser has argued that Luke presents Jesus as speaking against the requirement of a Qumranite-type separation, and indeed warns his followers against such action.[25]

---

21 On who was expected to "follow" Jesus, see Hengel, *Charismatic Leader*, 16-88. For variant views on whether the historical Jesus in his public activity called for (national?) repentance, see Sanders, *Jesus and Judaism*, 223; James H. Charlesworth, "The Historical Jesus in Light of Writings Contemporaneous with Him," in Hildegard Temporini and Wolfgang Haase, eds., *Aufstieg und Niedergang der römischen Welt* (Berlin: Walter de Gruyter, 1982), part II, vol. 25.1, 458; Joachim Rohde, *Rediscovering the Teaching of the Evangelists* (Philadelphia: Fortress, 1968), 124.

22 See Howard Clark Kee, *Jesus in History*, 2nd ed. (New York: Harcourt Brace Jovanovich, 1977), 57; David Noel Freedman, "Early Christianity and the Scrolls: An Inquiry," in R. Joseph Hoffman and Gerald A. Larue, eds., *Jesus in History and Myth* (Buffalo: Prometheus, 1986), 97-102; John Riches, *Jesus and the Transformation of Judaism* (London: Darton, Longman & Todd, 1980), 130.

23 Jean Duhaime, "Relative Deprivation in New Religious Movements and the Qumran Community," *Revue de Qumran* 16 (1993): 265-76. Cf. Hans Mol, *Identity and the Sacred* (Oxford: Basil Blackwell, 1976).

24 This severe separation was based on extending the holiness of the Jerusalem Temple and cultic context to the Qumran community as a whole. See Shemaryahu Talmon, *The World of Qumran from Within* (Leiden: Brill, 1989); Elisha Qimron, "The Holiness of the Holy Land in the Light of a New Document from Qumran," in Moshe Sharon, ed., *The Holy Land in History and Thought* (Leiden: Brill, 1988), 9-13; and my article, "Sectarian Separation and Exclusion—The Temple Scroll: A Case for Wholistic Religious Claims," in Bradley H. McLean, ed., *Origins and Method: Towards a New Understanding of Judaism and Christianity: Essays in Honour of John C. Hurd* (Sheffield: JSOT, 1993), 362-81.

25 See David Flusser, "The Parable of the Unjust Steward: Jesus' Criticism of the Essenes," in Charlesworth, *Jesus and the Dead Sea Scrolls*, 176-97, who invokes a comparison

The early Jesus movement had only minimal community structure determining hierarchy and advancement of members;[26] a clear contrast to the Qumranites, who had well-defined plans for determining rank, order, advancement, demotion and punishment for those who disobeyed rules.[27] Indeed, the thrust of such texts as 1QS, CD, 1QpHab, 11QT and 4QMMT (texts with substantial content) suggests that Qumranites likely were unique in Second Temple Judaism with regard to the amount of formal training required of a novice. This feature stands in stark contrast to the apparent absence of formal training required to join the Jesus movement.

2.2 Inclusive and Exclusive Factors

It follows that if Qumranites had community boundaries that were difficult to cross and the Jesus movement had minimal initiation requirements, the two groups could be contrasted on the basis of the Jesus movement's inclusivism and the Qumranites' exclusivism.[28] While both groups had an eschatological vision for all of Israel,[29] the extreme elitism of Qumranites set rigorous conditions for

---

between Luke 16:1-9 (which refers to "sons of light") and 1QS 5.14-20, 10.17-20 and CD 6.14-15. Cf. Flusser, "Jesus' Opinion of the Essenes," in his *Origins*, 150-68.

26 Cf. Robert P. Meye, *Jesus and the Twelve: Discipleship and Revelation in Mark's Gospel* (Grand Rapids: Eerdmans, 1968); Lloyd Gaston, *No Stone on Another: Studies in the Significance of the Fall of Jerusalem in the Synoptic Gospels* (Leiden: Brill, 1970); Richard A. Horsley, *Jesus and the Spiral of Violence: Popular Jewish Resistance in Roman Palestine* (San Francisco: Harper & Row, 1987); Robert Hamerton-Kelly, *God the Father: Theology and Patriarchy in the Teachings of Jesus* (Philadelphia: Fortress, 1979).

27 See Devorah Dimant, "Qumran Sectarian Literature," in Michael E. Stone, ed., *Jewish Writings of the Second Temple Period* (Philadelphia: Fortress, 1984), 483-503; Hans G. Kippenberg, *Religion und Klassenbildung im antiken Judäa: Eine religionssoziologische Studie zum Verhältnis von Tradition und gesellschaftlicher Entwicklung* (Göttingen: Vandenhoeck & Ruprecht, 1982), 157-63. R. B. Y. Scott, in "The Meaning for Biblical Studies of the Qumran Scroll Discoveries," *Transactions of the Royal Society of Canada* 50 (1956): 39-48, suggested that Jesus warned against the impulse to rank his followers like the Qumranites.

28 See Joseph Coppens, "Où en est le problème des analogies qumrâniennes avec le Nouveau Testament?" in M. Delcor, ed., *Qumrân: Sa piété, sa théologie et son milieu* (Paris: Duculot, 1978), 373-83; G. Klinzing, *Die Umdeutung des Kultus in der Qumrangemeinde und im Neuen Testament* (Göttingen: Vandenhoek & Ruprecht, 1972). Also, see E. P. Sanders, *Judaism: Practice and Belief 63 BCE to 66 CE* (Philadelphia: Fortress, 1992)—esp. part III (352-63), which deals with "Groups and Parties" and includes important comments on Qumranite exclusivism.

29 See Herbert Braun, "The Significance of Qumran for the Problem of the Historical Jesus," in Carl E. Braaten and Roy A. Harrisville, eds., *The Historical Jesus and the Kerygmatic Christ: Essays on the New Quest for the Historical Jesus* (New York: Abingdon, 1964), 69-78; Sanders, *Jesus and Judaism*, 95-98, 116-19, 213-21; Meyer, *Aims of Jesus*, 222-40. See Hengel, *Charismatic Leader*, 61-63, on the matter of individual or "all of Israel" repentance in the claims of Jesus.

the salvation of Jews, and denied it for the rest of humanity. This elitism contrasts, on the whole, with the NT presentation of Jesus speaking to a broad spectrum of society.[30] For instance, Günther Bornkamm noted in his study on Jesus that the factor of inclusivism put substantial distance between Jesus and those who sponsored the scrolls, to the point that they represented very different segments of Second Temple Judaism—and likely appealed to very different sectors of the population.[31]

Geza Vermes likewise notes that a major point of contrast between Jesus and the Dead Sea Scrolls concerns Jesus' regular public contact with the disadvantaged and marginalized, an impossibility for Qumranites in light of the rigid life-style exhorted in the scrolls.[32] James Dunn cited this contrast in a study of Jesus and Qumranites on the topic of table-fellowship, where there are common affinities for expressing eschatological covenant ideals. Dunn, however, identifies an essential contrast in Jesus' promotion of inclusiveness through table-fellowship with a varied mix of meal companions.[33] To put it in blunt terms, Jesus liked to eat, drink and talk about his vision of religion. Qumranites extended the purity of Temple observance into their table-fellowship context; thus, only those who passed stringent initiation rites were able to share in the common meal, not only in this age but in the age to come.[34] In 1QSa 2.3-10 a list is provided excluding people with physical disabilities from both the common meal and from membership. The list is similar to Leviticus 21:17-21, which excluded physically-disadvantaged priests from functioning in cultic activities. Dunn rightly makes the point that Qumranite exclusivism was focused around intensifying purity norms and boundaries, and such severe community

30 See Jerome Murphy-O'Connor, "An Essene Missionary Document? CD II,14-VI,1," *Revue Biblique* 77 (1970): 201-29, and "The Damascus Document Revisited," *Revue Biblique* 92 (1985): 223-46; David Flusser, "The Social Message from Qumran," *Origins*, 193-201, esp. 194-95 (reprinted from *Journal of World History* 2 [1968]: 107-15); Martin Hengel, "Die Einladung Jesu," *Theologische Beiträge* 18 (1987): 113-19; Scot McKnight, *A Light Among the Gentiles: Missionary Activity in the Second Temple Period* (Minneapolis: Fortress, 1991).

31 Günther Bornkamm, *Jesus of Nazareth* (New York: Harper & Row, 1960), 60.

32 Vermes, *Qumran in Perspective*, 220.

33 James D. G. Dunn, "Jesus, Table-Fellowship and Qumran," in Charlesworth, *Jesus and The Dead Sea Scrolls*, 254-72. See Meyer, *Aims of Jesus*, 158-62, and Marcus J. Borg, *Conflict, Holiness and Politics in the Teachings of Jesus* (Lewiston: Edwin Mellen, 1984), 73-121; Karl Georg Kuhn, "The Lord's Supper and the Communal Meal at Qumran," in Krister Stendahl, ed., *The Scrolls and the New Testament* (New York: Harper, 1957), 67-70.

34 Dunn, "Table-Fellowship," 263-64. See also Bertil Gärtner, *The Temple and the Community in Qumran and the New Testament* (Cambridge: Cambridge University Press, 1965); A. R. C. Leaney, *The Rule of Qumran and its Meaning* (London: SCM, 1966); Michael Newton, *The Concept of Purity at Qumran and in the Letters of Paul* (Cambridge: Cambridge University Press, 1985).

exclusivism likely would be known in most quarters of ancient Palestine. He estimates that the episode detailed in Luke 14:12-24 (in which Jesus encouraged the maimed, lame, blind and poor[35] to be invited to dinners and banquets) was a counter position offered by Jesus to those excluded by the Qumranite lists from membership and participation in the messianic banquet.[36]

Qumranite exclusivism is most sharply presented in the pledge to hate opponents while loving fellow community members (see 1QS 1-2). Scholars frequently have cited Jesus' commandment to love one's enemies as at least an implicit counter to Qumranite theology, and perhaps a direct challenge to what Jesus saw as a severe limitation to the good that they might do.[37] Qumranite hatred of their opponents and the New Testament gospels' admonishment to love one's enemies represent an even more substantial point of contrast in the inclusive/exclusive antithesis. Jesus was prepared to be a minimalist in regard to observance of Torah in what Flusser has suggested was a new (perhaps renewed?) spiritual sensitivity of compassion for individuals in late-Second Temple Judaism, while the Qumranites were committed maximalists to Torah observance, which resulted in highly-developed rules subjugating the individual to an interpretative tradition on legal matters that distinguished them from their religious peers (see 4QMMT). He correctly estimates that Jesus represents a religious tradition (likely standing in a line initiated by such masters as Hillel) that refused to categorize humanity into divisions of "good" and "evil" on the basis of reward for the just and punishment of the sinner—and on that matter rejected an essential principle advanced in the Qumran scrolls. For the school of thought represented by the New Testament Jesus, "love was a precondition

---

35 The term "poor" was a Qumranite self-designation that did not refer to sociological and economic conditions, but was a reference to election. See Flusser, "Blessed are the Poor in Spirit," in his *Origins*, 102-14 (reprinted from *Israel Exploration Journal* 10 [1960]: 1-13), esp. 107.

36 See Dunn, "Table-Fellowship," 264-68. Similar lists excluding physically-disadvantaged people from the Qumranite community, as well as their vision of Jerusalem, are found in 1QM 7.4-6, 4QCDb and 11QT45.12-14.

37 See David Flusser, "Jesus, his Ancestry, and the Commandment of Love," in James H. Charlesworth, ed., *Jesus' Jewishness: Exploring the Place of Jesus within Early Judaism* (New York: Crossroad, 1991), 153-76; Otto Betz, "The Eschatological Interpretation of the Sinai Tradition in Qumran and in the New Testament," in his *Jesus: Der Herr der Kirche* (Tübingen: J. C. B. Mohr, 1990), 66-87; and Krister Stendahl, *Meanings: The Bible as Document and as Guide* (Philadelphia: Fortress, 1984), 137-49. See also Karl Schubert, "The Sermon on the Mount and the Qumran Texts," *Scrolls and the New Testament*, 120; and Yigael Yadin, *The Temple Scroll: The Hidden Law of the Dead Sea Sect* (New York: Random House, 1985), 241-42, for comments on sayings in the Sermon on the Mount as direct counters to Qumranite hatred of opponents. Cf. William Hugh Brownlee, "Jesus and Qumran," in F. Thomas Trotter, ed., *Jesus and the Historian* (Philadelphia: Fortress, 1968), 52-81; Akio Ito, "Matthew and the Community of the Dead Sea Scrolls," *Journal for the Study of the New Testament* 48 (1992): 23-42.

of reconciliation with God" and an appropriate summary of the law of Moses.[38] Qumranites were committed to an understanding of divine justice and membership in the age to come that was rewarded according to a maximalist pledge to Torah; they were encouraged to hate those who were not prepared to make a similar commitment (see 1QS). Jesus' commitment to the compassion commandment meant he naturally opposed the separatist principle of Qumranites because significant love expressed toward others would be minimal if one did not mix with the larger society.[39]

The scrolls are generally silent on the involvement of women in community matters, and the consensus is that if the Qumranites did not practice celibacy there was, at the very least, only limited contact with women and the wives of male members.[40] This factor stands in clear contrast to the regular presence of women in the public activity of Jesus as his followers and as participants in his mission.[41] While the Jesus movement was not quite as distinctive on this matter as some suggest, there is little question that the inclusion of women as active members of the Jesus movement was a factor that contrasted substantially with the apparent exclusion of women among Qumranites.

---

38 Flusser, "Commandment of Love," 166. See Flusser, "Social Message from Qumran," 198-201; Gustaf Aulén, *Jesus in Contemporary Historical Research*, trans. Ingalill H. Hjelm (Philadelphia: Fortress, 1976 [1974; 1973[1]]), 49, for comments on the scholarly consensus that Jesus' willingness to minimize observance of Sabbath and purity laws occurred when such observance came into conflict with the love/compassion commandment.

39 Flusser, "Social Message from Qumran," 197.

40 See Vermes, *Qumran in Perspective*, 106, 181-82; Hans Hübner, "Zölibat in Qumran?" *New Testament Studies* 17 (1970-71): 153-67; A. Marx, "Les racines du célibat essénien," *Revue de Qumran* 7 (1969-71): 323-41; Joseph Coppens, "Le célibat essénien," in his *Qumran*, 297-303; Joseph M. Baumgarten, "The Qumran-Essene Restraints on Marriage," in Lawrence H. Schiffman, ed., *Archaeology and History in the Dead Sea Scrolls: The New York University Conference in Memory of Yigael Yadin* (Sheffield: JSOT, 1990), 13-24; Davies, *Behind the Essenes*, 83-85; Meier, *Marginal Jew*, vol. 1, 335-45, 364 n. 57.

41 See Ben Witherington, *Women in the Ministry of Jesus* (Cambridge: Cambridge University Press, 1984); Elisabeth Schüssler Fiorenza, *In Memory of Her: A Feminist Theological Reconstruction of Christian Origins* (New York: Crossroad, 1987), and *Jesus, Miriam's Child, Sophia's Prophet: Critical Issues in Feminist Christology* (New York: Continuum, 1994); Annie Jaubert, *Les femmes dans l'Écriture* (Paris: Gabalda, 1992); Richard Atwood, *Mary Magdalene in the New Testament Gospels and Early Tradition* (Frankfurt: Peter Lang, 1993); Francis Martin, *The Feminist Question: Feminist Theology in the Light of Christian Tradition* (Grand Rapids: Eerdmans, 1994), esp. 75-115; Carla Ricci, *Mary Magdalene and Many Others: Women who Followed Jesus*, trans. Paul Burns (Minneapolis: Fortress, 1994). See also Winsome Munro, "Women Disciples: Light from Secret Mark," *Journal of Feminist Studies in Religion* 8 (1992): 47-64; Robert J. Karris, "Women and Discipleship in Luke," *Catholic Biblical Quarterly* 56 (1994): 1-20; Barbara E. Reid, "Luke: The Gospel for Women?" *Currents in Theology and Mission* 21 (1994): 405-14; M.-E. C. Fletcher, "The Role of Women in the Book of John," *Evangelical Quarterly* 12 (1994): 41-48. Cf. Jane Schaberg, "A Feminist Contribution to Experience of Historical Jesus Scholarship," *Continuum* 3 (1994): 266-85 (an earlier version of her paper in this volume).

2.3 Calendar

The topic of calendar has more to do with Dead Sea Scrolls research than the historical Jesus, as the gospels present Jesus observing the normative lunar calendar of Palestinian society—especially in his observance of sabbath and festivals.[42] Jesus debated with religious authorities on various issues but never on calendrical matters. Qumranites were a peculiar and obvious sectarian movement at the turn of the Common Era because of their adherence to a solar calendar, which put them at odds with the rest of society. Shemaryahu Talmon and Geza Vermes have demonstrated quite clearly that, by embracing a different calendar from the one advanced by Jerusalem authorities, Qumranites guaranteed that they would be a separate socio-religious entity with an entirely distinct religious rhythm.[43] Membership in the Qumran community demanded that one be willing to function outside of societal norms on this crucial feature of Jewish religious expression.[44] Although skilful efforts have been made by Annie Jaubert to link Jesus with the solar calendar of the Qumranites,[45] the overwhelming scholarly consensus is that Jesus was not observant of this essential sectarian practice.

2.4 Predestination

David Flusser, in his comparison of the Dead Sea Scrolls to "pre-Pauline Christianity," summarized the essence of Qumranite theology as a complete

---

42 See Meier, *Marginal Jew*, vol. 1, 372-433, esp. 392-95.

43 Shemaryahu Talmon, *Cult and Calendar in Ancient Israel: Collected Essays* (Jerusalem: Magnes Press, 1986), and *Qumran from Within*, esp. 147-85; Vermes, *Qumran in Perspective*, 175-79.

44 See Sanders, *Judaism*, part II on "Common Judaism"—especially the sections dealing with sacrifice, daily life and annual festivals (119-45).

45 See Annie Jaubert, *The Date of the Last Supper*, trans. Isaac Rafferty (Staten Island: Alba House, 1965) and Eugen Ruckstuhl, *Chronology of the Last Days of Jesus: A Critical Study* (New York: Desclée, 1965), for arguments that Jesus not only embraced the solar calendar of the Qumranites for observance of the last supper (Jaubert) but also held the supper in an "Essene" portion of Jerusalem where the cult was observed by the sectarians on different dates than in the Jerusalem Temple (Ruckstuhl). Jaubert estimates that the Qumranite cult would have been carried out in a private home (see her "Jésus et le calendrier de Qumrân," *New Testament Studies* 7 [1960-61]: 1-30). See also Annie Jaubert, "Le calendrier des Jubilés et de la secte de Qumrân: Ses origines bibliques," *Vetus Testamentum* 3 (1953): 250-64, "Les séances du sanhédrin et les récits de la passion," *Revue de l'histoire des religions* 166 (1964): 143-69, and "The Calendar of Qumran and the Passion Narrative in John," in James H. Charlesworth, ed., *John and the Dead Sea Scrolls* (New York: Crossroad, 1990), 62-75. These proposals have not met with much agreement in peer review. Cf. Raymond E. Brown, "The Problem of Historicity in John," in his *New Testament Essays* (Garden City: Doubleday, 1968), 187-217; Joachim Jeremias, *The Eucharistic Words of Jesus* (London: Scribner's, 1966), 15-88, esp. 24-25; and Josef Blinzler, *Der Prozess Jesu* (Regensburg: F. Pustet, 1969), 101-26, esp. 109-26.

religious system profoundly shaped by principles of predestination and divine determinism. Part of his summary on this matter is worth citing: "The world is divided into the realms of good and evil; [humankind] consists of the two camps: the Sons of Light—actually the community itself—and those who are of the Devil. The division is preordained by the sovereign will of God (double predestination). The Sons of Light are the Elect of Divine grace and were granted the Spirit which frees them from the sins of the flesh."[46] Although Jesus shared much of the Qumranites' eschatological orientation, especially in regard to the expectation of a forthcoming end of time,[47] the mixture of predestination and the division of humanity into two camps, represented by the designations "sons/children of light" (Qumranites only) and "sons/children of darkness" (all other Jews, and Gentiles) does not find a parallel in the New Testament Jesus—or, for that matter in any other Jewish group at the turn of the Common Era.[48] Lengthy texts such as the Manual of Discipline, the Damascus Document,

---

46 Flusser, "Dead Sea Sect," 72. See also David Flusser, "The Apocryphal Book of *Ascensio Isaiae* and the Dead Sea Scrolls," in his *Origins*, 3-22 (reprinted from *Israel Exploration Journal* 3 [1953]: 30-47); Jacob Licht, "An Analysis of the Treatise of the Two Spirits in DSD," *Scripta Hierosolymitana* 4 (1958): 88-100; Hermann Lichtenberger, *Studien zum Menschenbild in Texten der Qumrangemeinde* (Göttingen: Vandenhoek & Ruprecht, 1980); Carol A. Newsom, "Knowing as Doing: The Social Symbolics of Knowledge at Qumran," *Semeia* 59 (1992): 139-53, for comments on Qumran dualism. For studies on cosmic intermediaries in the scrolls see Marinus de Jonge, "The Role of Intermediaries in God's Final Intervention in the Future According to the Dead Sea Scrolls," in Otto Michel *et al.*, eds., *Studies on the Jewish Background to the New Testament* (Assen: Van Gorcum, 1969), 44-63; Yigael Yadin, *The Scroll of the War of the Sons of Light against the Sons of Darkness* (Oxford: Oxford University Press, 1962), esp. 229-42; Fred L. Horton, *The Melchizedek Tradition* (Cambridge: Cambridge University Press, 1976), 64-82; Otfried Hufius, "Gemeinschaft mit den Engeln im Gottesdienst der Kirche: Eine traditionsgeschichtliche Skizze," *Zeitschrift für Theologie und Kirche* 89 (1992): 172-96, dealing with the Christian liturgical background; Maxwell J. Davidson, *Angels at Qumran: A Comparative Study of 1 Enoch 1-36, 72-108 and Sectarian Writings from Qumran* (Sheffield: JSOT, 1992); Alan F. Segal, "The Risen Christ and the Angelic Mediator in Light of Qumran," in Charlesworth, *Jesus and the Dead Sea Scrolls*, 302-38. Cf. David Flusser, "The Hubris of the Antichrist in a Fragment from Qumran," in his *Origins*, 207-13 (reprinted from *Immanuel* 10 [1983]: 31-37).

47 See also Jean Carmignac, "Qu'est-ce que l'apocalyptique? Son emploi à Qumrân," *Revue de Qumran* 10 (1979): 3-33. Cf. John J. Collins, "Apocalypse: Towards the Morphology of a Genre," *Semeia* 14 (1979): 1-20; Hartmut Stegemann, "Some Aspects of Eschatology in Texts from the Qumran Community and in the Teachings of Jesus," in J. Amitai, ed., *Biblical Archaeology Today: Proceedings of the International Congress on Biblical Archaeology* (Jerusalem: Israel Academy of Sciences and Humanities, 1989), 408-26; Sanders, *Judaism*, 368-69; *Jesus and Judaism*, 77-119; Devorah Dimant, "The Apocalyptic Interpretation of Ezekiel at Qumran," in Ithmar Gruenwald, Shaul Shaked and Gedaliahu G. Stroumsa, eds., *Messiah and Christos: Studies in the Jewish Origins of Christianity* (Tübingen: J. C. B. Mohr, 1992), 31-51.

48 See Pierre Grelot, "L'Eschatologie des esséniens et le livre d'Hénoch," *Revue de Qumran* 1 (1958): 113-31; Jacob Licht, "Time and Eschatology in Apocalyptic Literature and

the War Scroll and especially the Thanksgiving Hymns depict the human condition as fully determined by a divine plan that is elitist and exclusionary. Qumranites were unequivocal in believing that only those destined to be "sons of light" would be counted among the saved. The separatist life-style intensified their perception that they were the elect. This view differs from the New Testament Jesus' inclusive, easily accessed and unconditional appeal.[49]

3. Similarities between Jesus and the Qumranites[50]

In recent comparative studies, Hartmut Stegemann suggests that Jesus and his immediate followers shared common ground with Qumranites on such matters as terminology, dualism, community organization, interest in the "kingdom of God" and their use of scripture for self-definition.[51] Klaus Berger proposes that productive comparisons can be made on topics such as community organization, terminology, messianism and the theme of justification,[52] while Hermann Lichtenberger estimates that common features between the scrolls and the Jesus movement include views on Temple, shared meals, messianic expectations and the linkage of John the Baptist to both groups.[53] Flusser, in his introduction to

---

Qumran," *Journal of Jewish Studies* 16 (1967): 177-82; Eugene H. Merrill, *Qumran and Predestination: A Theological Study of the Thanksgiving Hymns* (Leiden: Brill, 1975); Duhaime, "Dualistic Reworking in the Scrolls," 32-56.

49 See Flusser, "Dead Sea Sect," 28-30, 73-74, for comments that Pauline and Johannine forms of Christianity appear to incorporate features of Qumranite predestination into their religious formulations.

50 Charlesworth, in *Jesus and the Dead Sea Scrolls*, 9-74, esp. 9-20, lists some 24 points of major similarity between Jesus and the scrolls (contrasting with 27 points of major differences, 22-35).

51 Hartmut Stegemann, "Die Bedeutung der Qumranfunde für das Verständnis Jesu und des frühen Christentums," *Bibel und Kirche* 48 (1993): 10-19. Stegemann is of the opinion that productive comparisons do not materialize on topics such as baptism, last supper, community of goods and calendar; see also his *Die Essener, Qumran, Johannes der Täufer und Jesus* (Freiburg: Herder, 1993).

52 Klaus Berger, "Qumran und das Neue Testament," *Theologie und Glaube* 84 (1994): 159-74. See Paolo Sacchi, "Recovering Jesus' Formative Background," in Charlesworth, *Jesus and the Dead Sea Scrolls*, 123-39, for similarities between Jesus and Essenes on justification, calendar, impurity, messianism and divorce.

53 Hermann Lichtenberger, "Die Texte von Qumran und das Urchristentum," *Judaica* 50 (1994): 68-82. For studies on John the Baptist and Qumran, see Jean Daniélou, *The Dead Sea Scrolls and Primitive Christianity*, trans. Salvator Attanasio (Baltimore: Helicon, 1958), 16-24; Charlesworth, *John and the Dead Sea Scrolls*; and the extensive comments as well as bibliographical information by Meier in *Marginal Jew*, vol. 2, 19-99. See also William Hugh Brownlee, "John the Baptist in the New Light of Ancient Scrolls," *Scrolls and the New Testament*, 33-53; David Flusser, "The Magnificat, the Benedictus and the War Scroll," in his *Origins*, 126-49, and "Social Message from Qumran," 108-109; John A. T. Robinson, "The Baptism of John and the Qumran Community: Testing a Hypothesis," *Harvard Theological Review* 50 (1957): 175-91; Otto Betz, "Was John the Baptist an

Judaism and the Origins of Christianity,[54] affirms the position he took almost forty years ago that more parallels exist between Pauline and Johannine Christianity, as well as the later letters, than between the synoptic tradition about Jesus and the scrolls, but he remains convinced there are parallels of substance between Jesus and the Qumranites on ethical matters pertaining to poverty and wealth, as well as in their criticism of institutional religion.[55] The point of this brief survey is that, after nearly a half-century of comparative studies between sources on the historical Jesus and the scrolls, scholars continue to be convinced that there are helpful points of similarity between the two.

3.1 Charismatic Leadership in the Prophetic Mode

Most reconstructions of the history of the Qumranites identify the Teacher of Righteousness as an important force in the beginnings of this sectarian movement. Details on the place of this figure in Qumranite history need not be rehearsed here.[56] The point is that the Teacher of Righteousness was an important figure in the beginnings of the Qumranite community, in a manner similar to Jesus for early Christianity, through his capacity to provide charismatic leadership to a community of followers. Both men tap into a prophetic tradition that is defined to fit their vision of Israel's covenantal relationship with God. James Charlesworth, in a recent comparison of the Teacher and Jesus, proposes that the Teacher of Righteousness represented mystical and revelatory powers working within scriptural tradition toward a

---

Essene?" in Hershel Shanks, ed., *Understanding the Dead Sea Scrolls* (New York: Random House, 1992), 205-14.

54 Flusser, *Origins*, xviii. See also his "Dead Sea Sect," 23-25.

55 See David Flusser, "Some Notes to the Beatitudes," in his *Origins*, 115-25 (reprinted from *Immanuel* 6 [1978]: 37-47), and his "Social Message from Qumran," 195-201. Cf. F. M. Braun, "L'Arrière judaïque du Quatrième Évangile et la Communauté de l'Alliance," *Revue Biblique* 62 (1955): 5-44; Raymond E. Brown, "The Qumran Scrolls and the Johannine Gospel and Epistles," in Stendahl, *Scrolls and the New Testament*, 183-207; James H. Charlesworth, "A Critical Comparison of the Dualism in 1QS III,13-IV,26 and the 'Dualism' contained in the Fourth Gospel," *New Testament Studies* 15 (1969): 389-418, and "Reinterpreting John: How the Dead Sea Scrolls Have Revolutionized Our Understanding of the Gospel of John," *Bible Review* 9 (1993): 18-25.

56 See works cited in note 9. See also F. F. Bruce, *The Teacher of Righteousness in the Qumran Texts* (London: Tyndale, 1957); Jean Carmignac, *Le docteur de justice et Jésus-Christ* (Paris: Editions de l'Orante, 1957)—English translation (Katherine Greenleaf Pedley): *Christ and the Teacher of Righteousness: The Evidence of the Dead Sea Scrolls* (Baltimore: Helicon, 1962); H. H. Rowley, "The Teacher of Righteousness and the Dead Sea Scrolls," *Bulletin of the John Rylands Library* 40 (1957): 114-46; Jean Daniélou, "The Grandeur and Limits of the Teacher of Righteousness," in his *Dead Sea Scrolls and Primitive Christianity*, 80-85; Herbert Braun, "Jesus und der qumranische Lehrer," *Qumran und das Neue Testament*, vol. 2, 54-74; Sanders, *Judaism*, 343-45; Ben Zion Wacholder, *The Dawn of Qumran: The Sectarian Torah and the Teacher of Righteousness* (Cincinnati: Hebrew Union College Press, 1983), esp. 226-69.

better day for Israel.[57] A similar case might be made for characterizing Jesus. The Teacher of Righteousness consciously withdrew to the "safety" of the desert to give substance to his vision of a righteous Israel separate from the larger society, elect, exclusive.[58] The New Testament Jesus' vision, by contrast, is inclusive, intimately involved in all spheres of society. The factor to be emphasized is that the Teacher and Jesus provided essential directives for their respective communities that were formative for community self-definition. Both options taken by the Teacher and Jesus were drawn from biblical prophetic traditions. The Teacher withdrew into the desert in the tradition of Isaiah 40:3 in order to create a community that would bring about a new era for the people of God.[59] Charlesworth refers to the Teacher as "irrigator of the garden" in his capacity as leader of the Qumranites (cf. 1QH 8.4-11).[60] Jesus likely shared his religious self-understanding with John the Baptist,[61] and thus worked from a charismatic, eschatological, prophetic paradigm to give form and substance to his mission as an agent of God. Although both men came to tragic ends, the followers of Jesus were different from the Qumranites in their understanding that Jesus' death was redemptive and salvific—factors that Charlesworth proposes were anticipated by Jesus and informed by the prophetic tradition that had provided the context for Jesus' life and public activity.[62]

3.2 Eschatology and the Primacy of Future Expectations

Geza Vermes, in *The Dead Sea Scrolls: Qumran in Perspective*, identifies an essential point of commonality between the Qumranites and early Christianity:

---

57 James H. Charlesworth, "Jesus as 'Son' and the Righteous Teacher as 'Gardener,'" in his *Jesus and the Dead Sea Scrolls*, 140-75.

58 Charlesworth, "Jesus as 'Son,'" 160-61.

59 See Meier, *Marginal Jew*, vol. 2, 49-52.

60 Charlesworth, "Jesus as 'Son,'" 147. See Callaway, *Qumran Community*, 185-90, for comments on the Teacher of Righteousness as writer of all or part of 1QH. See David Flusser, *Die rabbinischen Gleichnisse und der Gleichniserzähler Jesus* (Bern: Peter Lang, 1981), esp. 265-81, where he suggests that Jesus was aware of the style and content of 1QH. Cf. Carol A. Newsom, "The Case of the Blinking I: Discourse of Self at Qumran," *Semeia* 57 (1992): 13-23.

61 See Sanders, *Jesus and Judaism*, 91-95, 117. Cf. Meier, *Marginal Jew*, vol. 2, 19-233—Part I, including "John Without Jesus: The Baptist in His Own Rite," and "Jesus With and Without John"; see esp. 116-30, which deals with whether Jesus was a disciple of John.

62 Charlesworth, "Jesus as 'Son,'" 159. See also Howard Clark Kee, "The Bearing of the Dead Sea Scrolls on Understanding Jesus," in his *Jesus in History*, 54-75. Cf. Joseph M. Baumgarten, "Does TLH in the Temple Scroll Refer to Crucifixion?" in his *Studies in Qumran Law* (Leiden: Brill, 1977), 172-82; Otto Betz, "Jesus and the Temple Scroll," in Charlesworth, *Jesus and the Dead Sea Scrolls*, 75-103; Joseph A. Fitzmyer, "Crucifixion in Ancient Palestine, Qumran and the New Testament," in his *To Advance the Gospel: New Testament Studies* (New York: Crossroad, 1981), 125-46; Martin Hengel, *Crucifixion in the Ancient World and the Folly of the Message of the Cross*, trans. John Bowden (London: SCM, 1977); J. Zias and James H. Charlesworth, "Crucifixion: Archaeology, Jesus, and the Dead Sea Scrolls," in Charlesworth, *Jesus and the Dead Sea Scrolls*, 273-89.

their confidence in being "sole beneficiaries of a New Covenant in the final age."[63] Further, Vermes states that, in regard to eschatology, both groups understood that their founder was involved in bringing about the last days. A solid case can be made for both Qumranites and the early Jesus movement that eschatological expectation was not only foundational for their view of the human condition but it was a first principle for ordering all other components into a complete practice and belief system. The scrolls consistently craft an expectation that involves fellow Jews joining their ranks or being destroyed along with Gentiles in a final war (1QM) which would result in two messiahs (priestly and secular; cf. 1QS 9.11; 1QSa 2; 4Q174 1.11-13; CD 6.11) ruling over better days.[64] The cultic system, as well as the entire city of Jerusalem, would be purified according to the stipulations of the priests at Qumran in a new (or renewed) Temple structure (11QT). The gospel traditions insist that Jesus' message in both word and deed concerned announcing the kingdom of God, not only already present in his public activities but also in the age to come, itself a result of an eschatological miracle of God. In John Meier's words, "It was this dynamic, multivalent, 'salvation-history-in-a-nutshell' quality of 'kingdom of God' that allowed Jesus to use it both of his pivotal ministry in the present and of the denouement of his ministry, soon to come."[65] It is worth noting that belief in God's rule in the past, present and future was standard fare for nearly

---

63 Vermes, *Qumran in Perspective*, 214. See Sanders, *Judaism*, 377, for comments on how the Qumran scrolls exhibit covenantal nomism involving grace, election, covenant, law, as well as obedience, reward, punishment and atonement; cf. his *Jesus and Judaism*, 334-40, for similar factors identified with the historical Jesus. See also Raymond F. Collins, "The Berith-Notion of the Cairo Damascus Covenant and its Comparison with the New Testament," *Ephemerides Theologicae Lovanienses* 39 (1963): 555-94; J. Gordon Harris, "The Covenant Concept among the Qumran Sectaries," *Evangelical Quarterly* 39 (1967): 86-92; J. A. Huntjens, "Contrasting Notions of Covenant and Law in the Texts from Qumran," *Revue de Qumran* 8 (1974): 361-80; Howard Clark Kee, "Membership in the Covenant People at Qumran and in the Teaching of Jesus," in Charlesworth, *Jesus and the Dead Sea Scrolls*, 104-22; Flusser, "Dead Sea Sect," 236-42. For the primacy of the Teacher of Righteousness for the Qumranite view of covenant, see N. Ilg, "Überlegungen zum Verständnis von *bryt* in den Qumrantexten," in Coppens, *Qumrân*, 257-63.

64 See Benedict Thomas Viviano, "The Kingdom of God in the Qumran Literature," in Wendell Willis, ed., *The Kingdom of God in 20th-Century Interpretation* (Peabody: Hendrickson, 1987), 97-107. For further comments on Qumranite eschatology, cf. Heinz-Wolfgang Kuhn, *Enderwartung und gegenwärtiges Heil:Untersuchungen zu den Gemeindeliedern von Qumran* (Göttingen: Vandenhoeck & Ruprecht, 1966); John J. Collins, "Patterns for Eschatology at Qumran," in Baruch Halpern and Jon D. Levenson, eds., *Traditions in Transformation: Turning Points in Biblical Faith* (Winona Lake: Eisenbrauns, 1981), 351-75; Moshe Weinfeld, "The Day of the Lord: Aspirations for the Kingdom of God in the Bible and Jewish Liturgy," *Scripta Hierosolymitana* 31 (1986): 341-72, for further comments on Qumranite eschatology.

65 Meier, *Marginal Jew*, vol. 2, 1042. See Meier's extensive treatment of "kingdom of God" in historical-Jesus research, 237-1038.

all religious viewpoints in Second Temple Judaism, and, "whatever his own message, Jesus was working within a religious tradition and with set religious symbols that had their own long history."[66] The challenge facing studies of the historical Jesus is to determine how he made his views of God's rule distinctive in light of competing views, such as those represented in the scrolls.[67]

3.3 Interpretation of Scripture

Two decades following the discovery of the Dead Sea Scrolls, Geza Vermes remarked that, although analysis of biblical interpretation in the scrolls at that time was not as advanced as it might be, it clearly was one of the more important aspects of scrolls research. Vermes' estimation was correct, and the issue of biblical interpretation and its impact on religious self-definition turns out to be a feature of significant commonality between the Qumranites and the early Jesus-movement. As Vermes noted, Qumranites and early Christians worked from a common first principle that the revelation contained in Jewish scripture had meaning for all generations including their own; that first principle dictated a second: practice and belief must somehow square with divine revelation.[68] While Qumranites were committed to a complex style of biblical interpretation that resulted in a formative legal system promoting community organization as well as a complex belief system,[69] Jesus was not a midrashist. The nature of the gospel tradition about Jesus, however, suggests that he regularly debated matters of scripture when it touched on his views about religious practice and belief.[70] Indeed, Jesus likely attracted as considerable a reaction to his views of scripture as the Qumranites did to their analysis of it. The point to be noted in this study is not what the Qumranites and Jesus did, or did not do, in their interpretation of scripture, but their common orientation

---

66 Meier, *Marginal Jew*, vol. 2, 270.

67 See A. E. Harvey, *Jesus and the Constraints of History* (Philadelphia: Fortress, 1982).

68 Geza Vermes, "Qumran Interpretation," in his *Post-Biblical Jewish Studies* (Leiden: Brill, 1975), 38.

69 See Lawrence H. Schiffman, *The Halakah at Qumran* (Leiden: Brill, 1975); "The New Halakic Letter (4QMMT) and the Origins of the Dead Sea Sect," *Biblical Archaeologist* 53 (1990): 64-73; Elisha Qimron and John Strugnell, *Qumran Cave 4*; Volume 5: *Miqsat Ma'a'se Ha-Torah* (Oxford: Oxford University Press, 1994). See also Johann Maier, "Die Bedeutung der Qumranfunde für das Verständnis des Judentums," *Bibel und Kirche* 48 (1993): 2-9, for a view that a particular priestly exegetical tradition was being promoted by Qumranites.

70 On the matter of Jesus being literate, see Meier, *Marginal Jew*, vol. 1, 268-78, 306 n. 124. Cf. Rainer Riesner, *Jesus als Lehrer: Ein Untersuchung zum Ursprung der Evangelien-Überlieferung* (Tübingen: J. C. B. Mohr, 1981), 225-39. See Sanders, *Jesus and Judaism*, 256-60, for his comments on Jesus as a midrashist when dealing with the matter of divorce; and Meier, *Marginal Jew*, vol. 1, 346-47, on Jesus' debate with Sadducees on the resurrection of the dead.

toward scripture as an affirmation of their views of religion, and their confidence that scripture, as divine revelation, was best mediated through them. The Qumranites worked from the principle that scripture had hidden meanings to be discovered and put into action now that the "last days" were realized by the formation of their community. They believed scripture preordained that the biblical prophets spoke directly to the Teacher of Righteousness and his followers in such texts as Habakkuk.[71] In *Jesus and Judaism*, Sanders has correctly estimated that it is "certain or virtually certain" that Jesus did not oppose the law on sabbath, purity laws and dietary observances, but there is strong evidence to suggest that Jesus did not consider the Mosaic law to be final or absolutely binding in light of his view of the last days.[72] Sanders also observed that, in regard to the story of the would-be follower of Jesus who first wished to bury his father (Matt 8:21-22; Luke 9:59-60), Jesus shares with the Qumranites confidence that he was "sovereign over the law" and thus able to decide which parts of the law should be obeyed.[73] Rather than contemplating disobedience of a commandment, the Qumranites asserted greater severity of obedience and absolute exclusiveness of access to the true meaning of scripture.[74] Qumranites might be characterized as promoting the intensification of the Mosaic law while Jesus advanced conditional adherence to it. While the Qumranites and Jesus share common ground in their orientation to scripture for self-definition, they differ sharply in the particular consequences of applying scripture to their religious claims.

3.4 Mixed Reviews of the Jerusalem Temple

The Dead Sea Scrolls and the gospel traditions about Jesus suggest that both the Qumranites and Jesus had mixed or negative views on the Jerusalem Temple,[75]

---

71 See F. F. Bruce, "The Dead Sea Scrolls and Early Christianity," *Bulletin of the John Rylands Library* 49 (1966): 69-90; S. Lowry, "Some Aspects of Normative and Sectarian Interpretation of the Scriptures (The Contribution of the Judaean Scrolls Towards Systematization)," in J. MacDonald, ed., *The Annual of Leeds University Oriental Society: Dead Sea Scrolls Studies 1969* (Leiden: Brill, 1969), 98-163; William Hugh Brownlee, "The Background of Biblical Interpretation at Qumran," in Coppens, *Qumrân*, 183-93, and his *The Midrash Pesher* (Missoula: Scholars Press, 1979); Michael Fishbane, "The Qumran Pesher and Traits of Ancient Hermeneutics," in Avigdor Shinan, ed., *Proceedings of the Sixth Congress of Jewish Studies* (Jerusalem: Magnes, 1977), 97-114; Maurya P. Horgan, *Pesharim: Qumran Interpretation of Biblical Books* (Washington: Catholic Biblical Association, 1979); George J. Brooke, *Exegesis at Qumran: 4QFlorilegium in its Jewish Context* (Sheffield: JSOT, 1985).

72 Sanders, *Jesus and Judaism*, 245-69, 326. Sanders makes the point that on the topic of divorce Jesus was prepared to declare a new law prohibiting it (267), a view similar to the Qumranite view on divorce.

73 Sanders, *Jesus and Judaism*, 249, 252-55.

74 See Vermes, "Qumran Interpretation," 40-41.

75 Cf. Craig A. Evans, "Opposition to the Temple: Jesus and the Dead Sea Scrolls," in Charlesworth, *Jesus and the Dead Sea Scrolls*, 235-53; "Predictions of the Destruction of

and for similar reasons: their views on eschatology and scripture had a serious impact on their reaction to the cultic system and the Jerusalem Temple.[76] For the Qumranites, their beliefs in Temple purity and adherence to a variant calendar indicate that they temporarily withdrew from sacrificial worship at the Jerusalem Temple in order to create a superior "house of holiness" in their community (following 1QS).[77] Jacob Milgrom correctly noted that maximum purity laws governing priests, Temple observance and rules for sacrificial portions of priestly meals were extended to laity among the Qumranites based on an ideal—if not "fundamentalist"—reading of the biblical Sinai traditions. Further, Qumranites understood that they atoned for the land not through sacrificial worship in the Temple but through community prayers as well as perfect obedience to God's revelation found in scripture, including their new revelation made known in this emerging eschatological era (cf. 1QS 9.4-5; 1QSa 1.3).[78] They looked forward to the day when they would control Jerusalem and its Temple (cf. 1QM and 11QT), reorganize or rebuild the Temple structure and impose their purity and calendar requirements on the holy site.[79]

Again we turn to Sanders' list of "certain or virtually certain" facts about the historical Jesus for insight into Jesus' view of the Jerusalem Temple.[80] He expected a new or renewed Temple. Jesus' challenge to the money-trade in the Jerusalem Temple precinct was intended to demonstrate that the cultic system had limited significance as an avenue for divine/human interaction. Meier comments on Jesus' challenge of the Temple with the following observation: "At least in Mark's theology, it functions as a prophecy in action, symbolizing

---

the Herodian Temple in the Pseudepigrapha, Qumran Scrolls, and Related Texts," *Journal for the Study of the Pseudepigrapha* 10 (1992): 89-147; Otto Betz, "Jesus and the Temple Scroll," in Charlesworth, *Jesus and the Dead Sea Scrolls*, 75-103.

76 See Sanders, *Judaism*, 47-54, 103-18, for comments on the primacy of sacrificial worship for Jews at the turn of the Common Era.

77 The Damascus Document seems to have a variant position allowing for partial participation in Jerusalem cultic worship. See Joseph M. Baumgarten, *Studies in Qumran Law* (Leiden: Brill, 1977); Philip R. Davies, "The Ideology of the Temple in the Damascus Document," *Journal of Jewish Studies* 33 (1982): 287-301; *The Damascus Covenant* (Sheffield: JSOT, 1982).

78 For comments on obedience to the law substituting for sacrifices see Klinzing, *Die Umdeutung des Kultus*, 80-87; Gaston, *No Stone on Another*, 127. Cf. Gärtner, *Temple and the Community in Qumran*; Newton, *Concept of Purity at Qumran*; Yigael Yadin, *The Temple Scroll*, 3 vols. (Jerusalem: Israel Exploration Society, 1977-83), esp. vol. 2, 125-30; and my "Sectarian Separation." See David Flusser, "Two Notes on the Midrash on 2 Sam. vii," in his *Origins*, 88-98 (reprinted from *Israel Exploration Journal* 9 [1959]: 99-109), esp. 91-92, where Mark 14:58 is compared to 4Q174 on the matter of the expectation of a new Temple based on a negative view of the existing Temple.

79 Cf. Yadin, *Scroll of the War*, 198-201.

80 Sanders, *Jesus and Judaism*, 61-90, 251-52, 267-69, 326. Cf. Meyer, *Aims of Jesus*, 170; Gaston, *No Stone on Another*, 86.

the rejection and destruction of the Temple, which Jesus will directly announce when he leaves the Temple for the last time in 13:2: 'Not one stone [of the Temple] shall be left upon another; it shall be completely pulled down.'"[81] In a tactic similar to the Qumranite withdrawal into the desert, Jesus anticipated that his challenge to the Temple trade not only symbolized the destruction of the Temple form of worship but demonstrated the coming to be of new things for individuals, as well as for all of Israel. The difference between Jesus and the Qumranites on the view of the Jerusalem Temple is similar to their approach to scripture (hardly surprising since Temple activities were based on scripture). Qumranites intensified their approach to Temple-related matters by extending Temple purity rites into their community context and expecting laypersons to act like priests. Jesus minimized Temple-related matters by speaking against it and symbolically indicating its destruction. The Qumranite position would have been well understood, as accusations against the purity of the Temple or its priests were standard fare for those not in positions of authority in the Temple. Jesus' view of the Temple, driven by his eschatological expectations, likely was confusing and potentially could be misunderstood by his contemporaries. Scholars are faced with determining how Jesus' negative views on the Temple would have been understood in his first-century setting in light of the competing views represented in the Dead Sea Scrolls.

3.5 The Historical Jesus

What can be said about the historical Jesus in light of characteristics shared with the Dead Sea Scrolls? The first point is that Jesus' profile as a charismatic, prophetic, public figure had a familiar ring for those acquainted with the history of the Qumranites—especially in regard to traditions surrounding the Teacher of Righteousness. The formation of a community based on ideals promoted by the Teacher of Righteousness would have served as a model for Jesus to consider when disciples began to follow his public activities. The sheer volume of future expectations detailed in the Dead Sea Scrolls confirms that Jesus would not have been viewed as dissimilar to the Qumranites on this matter—indeed, that he likely was faced with asserting how his expectation of last things and future developments were to be understood in light of competing views represented by groups such as those who sponsored the Dead Sea Scrolls. This study confirms the estimation that Jesus viewed scripture to be best mediated through him, but his conditional adherence to scripture likely distinguished him sharply from his contemporaries. As Sanders states, what is lacking "from ancient Judaism is a parallel to the attitude attributed to Jesus: that he saw himself as sovereign over the law and as being able to decide that parts of it

---

81   Meier, *Marginal Jew*, vol. 2, 886.

need not be obeyed."[82] A failure persistently to increase the obligation to obey scripture distinguished Jesus from the Qumranites (an exception is the "antitheses" section of Matthew's Sermon on the Mount). Research on Jesus' views of the cultic system and the Jerusalem Temple is assisted substantially by comparative analysis of the Dead Sea Scrolls. The scrolls indicate that some first-century Jews were willing actively and consciously to protest this dominant religious institution through programmatic challenge of Temple observance. While the Qumranites and Jesus differ on the course of action to be taken in regard to Temple worship, the scrolls help bring into focus the unusual nature of Jesus' claim about the destruction of the Temple and how his deeds and teachings offered an alternative. The scrolls also indicate that challenge to the Temple on purity matters had the potential to produce positive community self-definition (the ideals expressed in the scrolls) while Jesus' claims negating the Temple (based on something other than purity debates) had the potential to be misunderstood by Jerusalem authorities.

4. Conclusion

This study of similarities and differences identified by researchers comparing Jesus to the Dead Sea Scrolls suggests the following reconstruction of Jesus. He was a charismatic prophet-like leader promoting expectation of the last things and a better day in an open religious movement that mixed regularly with the larger society. Jesus showed particular interest in the disadvantaged and marginalized. One challenge in assessing Jesus in his first-century context concerns how he distinguished himself from his contemporaries in regard to eschatology and his apparent claims to be a sovereign mediator of scripture. The primary sources suggest that he was prepared to negate scripture for the sake of his eschatological mission. That would set him apart from his contemporaries—certainly from Qumranites. Moreover, Jesus' views on the Temple, although central to the gospel traditions, are at best confusing. The protest of the Qumranites against the Temple and cultic observances assists greatly in giving some context to this feature of the historical Jesus' public activity, but on this topic there are more differences than similarities. In the final analysis, we are left comparing Jesus' attitude toward the Temple to his attitude toward scripture. He was prepared, it would seem, to assume a negative stance against the Jerusalem Temple in order to give full force to his eschatological claims.

---

82 Sanders, *Jesus and Judaism*, 249.

17. Apocalypticism: Context

Dietmar Neufeld

Edith Humphrey's paper introduces the reader to the slippery concept of "apocalyptic" and the potential difficulties that it presents for authors of recent historical-Jesus studies. She insists on the centrality of "things apocalyptic" to the various contemporary discussions of the historical Jesus, and accordingly discusses three critical questions foundational to historical-Jesus research. First, given that the term apocalyptic is ambiguous enough conceptually to render it open to a plurality of meanings, how can its meaning be usefully fixed? Second, is it possible to understand Jesus in the context of apocalyptic thought, thus defined? Third, what difference does the definition adopted make for reconstructing the historical Jesus? Contrary to those who would argue that the Jesus of history is rendered incomprehensible by placing him in such a context, she avers that the category, rather than being an impenetrable veil, might well serve as a "beckoning vision in our understanding of Jesus."

The tensive potential and conceptually-ambiguous character of "apocalyptic" is readily seen in the nine representative scholars Humphrey surveys and with whom she debates. She shows that John Dominic Crossan, Burton Mack and Geza Vermes take apocalyptic in the traditional sense of the imminent cataclysmic judgment of this world, radically dualistic and apolitical, but one which ultimately does not belong to the authentic voice or stance of Jesus. Ed Sanders, Paula Fredriksen and Richard Horsley opt for a socio-political understanding of apocalyptic eschatology which speaks of the coming to an end of the present order in preparation for its renewal. Tom Wright, Elisabeth Schüssler Fiorenza and Marcus Borg argue for the flexible character of apocalyptic imagery which has a metaphorical component that points to transcendent realities, while not remaining insensitive to these realities' earthly ramifications or reflections.

There is no doubt that the understanding and evaluation of "apocalyptic" in relationship to Jesus and the gospels will have profound consequences on the picture of Jesus. Apocalyptic themes and images play an unquestionably important role in the writings of Paul and in the synoptic gospels, but not everyone is as confident that the apocalyptic thread can be tied to Jesus as securely as was once thought. Many new constructions of Jesus as a sapiential figure are dependent on a dichotomy between "apocalyptic" and "wisdom" perceived to be distinct and alternative Jewish cultural entities. Humphrey is of the opinion that a more appreciative understanding of apocalyptic will render irrelevant the stand-off between Jesus as a wisdom teacher and Jesus as an apocalyptic preacher.

The many attempts to reconstruct the historical Jesus during the 19th century focused primarily upon Jesus as a social reformer and teacher. In 1892 Johannes Weiss published a book which signalled a radical change from the usual liberal lives of Jesus by introducing the theme of "apocalyptic."[1] Albert Schweitzer gave force to this discovery by engaging in a thoroughgoing critique of German scholarship, showing, among other things, that the various scholarly reconstructions of Jesus were in large measure shaped by the horizons of a modern world-view.[2] He insisted that the first-century Jewish world-view was fundamentally alien to the modern. That first-century world-view, for Schweitzer, was essentially eschatological, and the teaching about the kingdom of God must be understood in eschatological terms. Jesus expected the coming of the kingdom of God, by which he meant that the end of the world was soon to come, perhaps even in his own lifetime.

Careful form- and redaction-critical studies of the synoptic gospels confirmed that the gospels were apocalyptic in outlook; but under the influence of Schweitzer's work, the word eschatology came to have a much broader range of meanings. Indeed, so broad-ranging were the connotations that in contemporary usage the term "eschatology" in particular risked being rendered almost meaningless. Taking note of the limited heuristic value of terms so broadly defined, many scholars argued for more narrow and precise meanings. Yet, despite disagreement over the meaning of the crucial terms, virtual unanimity remained about the eschatological core of Jesus' message.

Contemporary reconstruction of the historical Jesus witnesses to the weakening, and, in some circles, the total collapse of this consensus. In particular this collapse is reflected in studies of the sayings source Q. Initially posited to explain the relationship between the synoptics, Q contains brief narratives and sayings of Jesus, and appears to be heavily influenced by apocalyptic eschatology. Recently, however, John Kloppenborg has proposed a three-level stratigraphy for Q in which the apocalyptic element is attributed to a secondary redaction of a document originally construed as a non-apocalyptic wisdom writing.[3] The teaching of Jesus, one might then conclude, was "apocalypticized" by some elements in the early church. The developmental model of Q turned the tables on the older views of Jesus as an apocalyptic preacher and presented Jesus as engaging in a different style of speech altogether.

---

1   Johannes Weiss, *Die Predigt Jesu vom Reiche Gottes* (Göttingen: Vandenhoek & Ruprecht, 1964³ [1892¹])—English translation: *Jesus' Proclamation of the Kingdom of God*, trans. Richard Hyde Hiers and David Larrimore Holland (Philadelphia: Fortress, 1971).

2   Albert Schweitzer, *The Quest of the Historical Jesus: A Critical Study of its Progress from Reimarus to Wrede*, trans. W. Montgomery (New York: Macmillan, 1968 [1906]).

3   John S. Kloppenborg, *The Formation of Q: Trajectories in Ancient Wisdom Collections* (Philadelphia: Fortress, 1987).

A potentially serious challenge to these recent views comes in the form of new cross-disciplinary studies that not only undermine the notion of a Jesus insulated from concrete political-economic relations but also question the basis for the dichotomy between "apocalyptic" and "wisdom." Particularly important in this respect is some of Richard Horsley's work.[4] Recent scholarship of this nature points to the concrete socio-economic (and religious) relations in which both Jewish authors and the Jesus movement were embedded; it militates against the essentialism that is often the result of careful textual studies based on the historical-critical paradigm. "Apocalypticism" is one such synthetic, essentialist category which has been abstracted from apocalyptic literature. According to Horsley, these constructs "both generate and perpetuate false knowledge and block recognition of the historical forces and relationships in origins, social relations, and literary productions of ancient Jewish and early-Christian literature and movements."[5] Horsley criticizes Crossan, for instance, for insulating the cultural sphere from concrete political power-relations, and for being influenced by a false dichotomy between "apocalyptic" and "wisdom." He concludes that there is no basis in extant Jewish literature for such a distinction, let alone for viewing these constructs as dichotomous cultural movements. From the late-19th to the late-20th century our views on apocalypticism have changed. Humphrey's fine survey shows how the perspectives differ even within a single time period, and how they impact significantly on our visions of Jesus.

---

4   See especially Richard A. Horsley, "Innovation in Search of Reorientation: New Testament
     Studies Rediscovering its Subject Matter," *Journal of the American Academy of Religion*
     62 (1994): 1127-66.

5   Horsley, "Innovation in Search of Reorientation," 1142.

18. Will the Reader Understand? Apocalypse as Veil or Vision in Recent Historical-Jesus Studies

Edith M. Humphrey

> Jesus . . . because of a prophetic-visionary experience [was] . . . convinced
> . . . that Satan's power was broken.[1]
> He . . . sought [the] transformation [of his social world] in accord with an
> alternate vision.[2]
> So a social vision marks the difference between the Jesus people and the
> Cynics. . . . The Jesus people promoted a vision for social experimentation as
> an alternative to the status quo.[3]
> So now you're ready to live by my vision and join me in my program?[4]

1. Introduction

Prophetic-visionary experience, transformation, alternate vision, stance, social vision, program—the evocation of different scenarios in the samples above makes it clear that the word "vision" numbers among the ranks of theological "slippery words" such as "myth" and "eschatology."[5] Elisabeth Schüssler Fiorenza, Marcus Borg, Burton Mack and John Dominic Crossan, along with a host of other Jesus scholars, see in the figure of Jesus something distinct enough to warrant "visionary" language. But here the agreement ends. "Vision" runs the full gamut from outright mystical experience, the aspirations of a social dreamer, to a simple alternate stance in life. And, in the case of Crossan's famous last quotation, a social outlook is nourished imaginatively by drawing upon the evocative power of that elusive word "vision" in a quasi-evangelistic appeal.

The phenomenon of similar words used with subtly and sometimes radically different meanings is indicative of the general situation in historical-Jesus research. The research in our decade seems less a discussion or a dispute than a set of separate conversations which bypass each other. The typical lack of communication is parodied by Tom Wright[6] when Crossan's hypostatized tome,

---

1 Elisabeth Schüssler Fiorenza, *In Memory of Her: A Feminist Theological Reconstruction of Christian Origins* (New York: Crossroad, 1983), 114.

2 Marcus J. Borg, *Jesus, a New Vision: Spirit, Culture, and the Life of Discipleship* (San Francisco: Harper and Row, 1987), 16.

3 Burton L. Mack, "Q and a Cynic-Like Jesus," 35 (in this volume).

4 John Dominic Crossan, *Jesus: A Revolutionary Biography* (San Francisco: HarperSanFrancisco, 1994), xiv.

5 G. B. Caird, *The Language and Imagery of the Bible* (London: Duckworth, 1980), 241-44.

6 N. T. Wright, "Taking the Text with Her Pleasure: A Post-Post-Modernist Response to J. Dominic Crossan, *The Historical Jesus: The Life of a Mediterranean Jewish Peasant*," *Theology* 96 (1993): 303-309.

"Michelle" (i.e., *The Historical Jesus*), is approached by her admiring but critical reader (Wright himself). Part of the fun of this unorthodox response to Crossan is in the unlikely detente at the end of "Michelle's" inner turmoil: "They (Michelle, and Wright as reader) gazed at each other with unspoken questions and answers. . . . Ask me again, she said with her eyes. He asked her again, and now she found her voice. Yes, she said. Yes. Yes." As yet, however, there is no new covenant between differing approaches to the quest of the historical Jesus, and the vision of Wright's aged Alexandrian librarian has come to pass: "But I will tell you how it will be in the last days. There will be no agreement."[7] And for the most part, there is also little or no discussion between those who dissent.

The reasons for this "ships in the night" phenomenon are complex. A foundational issue, however, which obstinately refuses to provide common ground is the varied understanding and evaluation of "apocalyptic" in relationship to Jesus and the gospels. While there is common agreement with Käsemann that apocalyptic was the mother of Christian theology, there is little consensus as to whether that mother is a legitimate spouse or even descendant of the founder-figure. Do apocalyptic themes and ideas do violence to the original view, words or teachings of Jesus, or did Jesus share this imaginative world-view—and are such complexes in continuity with his aims? A further barrier to concord is less frequently acknowledged: this is the definition or undertanding of the term "apocalyptic" itself. At first blush, the statements of Paula Fredriksen ("Jesus was an apocalyptic preacher"[8]) and Burton Mack ("Jesus does not appear to have engaged in such fantasy"[9]) appear to be polar opposites. The actual denotation and attendant connotations of "apocalyptic" need to be explored, however, before such views can be assessed in relationship to each other. Finally, the amount of passion that has surrounded recent scholarly discussions about Jesus suggests that a third issue needs to be probed: the payoff or implications of the proposed sketch. What is at stake politically, ideologically or theologically in claiming that Jesus is or is not associated with things apocalyptic? So then, we have a set of three pointed questions to ask of representative scholars: What meaning is attached to "apocalyptic"? Is Jesus to be understood in terms of "apocalyptic," so defined? And, what are the implications of the assessment?

If "vision," "myth" and "eschatology" are slippery words, then "apocalyptic" is positively perilous.[10] One needs almost to trace the history of

---

7   Wright, "Taking the Text," 304.

8   Paula Fredriksen, *From Jesus to Christ: The Origins of New Testament Images of Jesus* (New Haven: Yale University Press, 1988), 124.

9   Burton L. Mack, *A Myth of Innocence: Mark and Christian Origins* (Philadelphia: Fortress, 1988), 74.

10 See also the discussion by Robert L. Webb, "'Apocalyptic': Observations on a Slippery Term," *Journal of Near Eastern Studies* 49 (1990): 115-26.

"apocalyptic" and apocalypse studies, both theological and literary, and to place a writer in the appropriate milieu, in order to determine how she or he is wont to use this word. Klaus Koch was *ratlos*[11] concerning "apocalyptic": how then can we escape? My own preference for the noun "apocalypse" and my hesitation over the use of the common adjective as a noun is indicated both by my title and by my use of inverted commas around "apocalyptic." Almost twenty-five years after Koch, and this side of two *Semeia* studies and several apocalypse colloquia, we know, I think, what an apocalypse is—we have paradigms, formal studies and various examples of the genre. I can discuss with others who share my interest the dangers of "reifying" genres, and the possibility of anachronistic classification; perhaps there will be a few works about which we disagree, on the fuzzy edges of the classification. Nevertheless, an apocalypse is understood at present, by almost everyone who studies the genre, as a visionary piece with a narrative framework and various formal distinctives, which discloses (often through a mediator) mysteries concerning past, present and future (temporal axis) and/or regions celestial and infernal (spatial axis).[12] There is enough agreement about the form and common content of the genre that the category serves as an adequate taxonomic device: I can hold an example of an apocalypse in my hand, read it, and analyze its peculiarities in light of others of its kind. Not so with "apocalyptic"—what is this grammatically and conceptually ambiguous term? Sometimes, of course, the term is simply used, even in the academy, in its popular sense, as a synonym for eschatology (however that is being defined by the particular author). Sometimes the term is used as a short form for "apocalyptic eschatology" on the assumption that apocalypses demonstrate a peculiar type of imminent eschatology which was or was not shared by Jesus. Increasingly, however, the term is taking on the colouring of the genre to which it is related, and that which is "apocalyptic" is so denoted because it bears some resemblance to an "apocalypse," in a certain convergence of characteristic formal features, motifs or ideas. This is, I think, sensible, if the term is not to become too narrow (and therefore redundant: do we need both "apocalyptic" and eschatological?) or too impossibly elastic. In this survey of representative scholars, I will search for explicit definitions of "apocalyptic," and in their absence, look for implicit understandings by reference to the entire contour of the genre "apocalypse." My method here is in conscious opposition to that of Richard Horsley, who is interested in finding the mood or orientation called "apocalypticism" (defined

---

11   Klaus Koch, *The Rediscovery of Apocalyptic: A Polemical Work on a Neglected Area of Biblical Studies and its Damaging Effects on Theology and Philosophy*, trans. M. Kohl (London: SCM, 1972 [1970]). *"Ratlos"* ("feeling helpless") was in the original German title.

12   The terms are from John J. Collins, "Apocalypse: Towards the Morphology of a Genre," *Semeia* 14 (1979): 1-20.

in a rather narrow sense) by using the literature as evidence for this.[13] That is, I prefer to move from the relatively straightforward examples of the genre to the more fragmentary expressions found in other types of texts, rather than beginning with the assumption of a world-view and measuring texts against this.

2. What is "Apocalyptic"?

2.1 Mack, Crossan, Vermes

We begin with an unlikely trio: Burton Mack, John Dominic Crossan and . . . Geza Vermes! Vermes, unlike the other two, does not espouse a Cynic-like view of Jesus, and insists on placing Jesus within a Jewish milieu. Moreover, he is certainly to be classed in terms of method as a member of the third quest, whereas Mack and Crossan have continued the quest for the authentic words of Jesus which was traditionally associated with the "new" (second) quest. Yet all three writers agree on their definition of "apocalyptic" and distinguish it sharply from "wisdom" material.

Although Mack does not give a precise definition of "apocalyptic," his understanding of the term is not difficult to glean. In his popularly-oriented *Lost Gospel*, Mack pronounces: "The languages of wisdom and apocalyptic assume different views of the world. . . . The theme of judgment is very closely related to an apocalyptic imagination."[14] Again, in his earlier, more sophisticated treatment of Mark, he describes the apocalyptic imagination as a scribal, sectarian and sometimes "pathetic" response to the gap between ideals and the actual state of affairs in Jerusalem: "apocalyptic visions were entertained as a way to imagine how the impossible ever could happen . . . [a] kind of fantasy born of sectarian desire."[15] A proper understanding of a particular apocalyptic writing, moreover, requires its social location in order to determine the "apocalyptic situation,"[16] that is, a probable point at which the strong social identities of an elite scribal group are challenged. In the apocalyptic imagination, things are so bad that only a divine act can overturn the evil *status quo*, and it is upon such a dramatic judgment, hopefully imminent, that apocalyptic writing focuses.

---

13 Richard A. Horsley, *Jesus and the Spiral of Violence: Popular Jewish Resistance in Roman Palestine* (Philadelphia: Fortress, 1987), 132. Horsley acknowledges the breadth of the genre, but retains the notion of "imminence" and "eager anticipation" in his own understanding of apocalyptic orientation, a popular mood which he tries to distil from the more elitist literature he cites as exemplary.

14 Burton L. Mack, *The Lost Gospel: The Book of Q and Christian Origins* (San Francisco: HarperSanFrancisco, 1993), 31.

15 Mack, *Myth of Innocence*, 38.

16 Mack, *Myth of Innocence*, 40 n. 10.

Similarly, Crossan understands apocalyptic as separate from wisdom and related to God's imminent cosmic action: "all apocalyptic is eschatological, but not all eschatology is apocalyptic."[17] John the Baptist, then, is the apocalyptic prophet par excellence, from whom Jesus makes an ideological divorce sometime after John's death: "John . . . [prepared] his followers for the imminent advent of God as the Coming One, but . . . Jesus, after having accepted that vision, eventually changed his response. . . . He then emphatically contrasted a follower of John and a member of the Kingdom."[18] Crossan's social and ideological quadrants, divided as they are by the separate categories of saptiential and apocalyptic thinking, assume the same definition of "apocalyptic" expressed by Mack. This separation is congenial to several scholars influential in both the Society of Biblical Literature Q Seminar and in the Jesus Seminar, who view the sapiential material as utterly different in tone from what is argued to be a later apocalyptic "patina."[19] So then, Crossan describes the dilemma of the scholar who finds strange "combinations and conflations of an apocalyptic and a sapiential vision of Jesus"[20] in the gospels.

Mack has also driven a wedge between the two world-views[21] when he suggests that the secondary Q community created a problem for itself when it atypically (and in his view unwisely) used the weapon of apocalyptic language, placing it in Jesus' mouth in order to censure those who were frustrating their mission: "The problem was how to merge the image of the teacher of wisdom . . . with the image of the apocalyptic prophet. . . . How to reconcile wisdom and apocalyptic teachings."[22] The question is, was this "the new challenge" confronting the second Q community, or is this a contemporary problem, based on certain fixed ideas of sapiential and apocalyptic incompatibility?

Geza Vermes also works on the hypothesis that "apocalyptic" is to be understood as "eschatological excitement" with "an increasing tendency towards the transcendental"[23] in the century and a half preceding Jesus. Vermes cites royal Messianism, apocalyptic eschatology "of a deluge of fire"[24] and the "coming of God's kingdom . . . as the sequel of the apocalyptic judgment of the Devil by God himself in the midst of . . . [cosmic] disturbances" as examples of typical "apocalyptic"; further, he notes the theme of transcendance in the Qumran literature, and its peculiar "mystic propensity."[25] For Vermes,

---

17 John Dominic Crossan, *The Historical Jesus: The Life of a Mediterranean Jewish Peasant* (San Francisco: HarperSanFrancisco, 1991), 238.
18 Crossan, *Historical Jesus*, 259.
19 The metaphor is Mack's, found in *Lost Gospel*, 41.
20 Crossan, *Historical Jesus*, 227.
21 Mack, *Lost Gospel*, 31.
22 Mack, *Lost Gospel*, 152.
23 Geza Vermes, *The Religion of Jesus the Jew* (Minneapolis: Fortress, 1993), 125.
24 Vermes, *Religion*, 126.
25 Vermes, *Religion*, 128.

"apocalyptic" means imminent judgment of evil by God, which tends to transmute the original "political" overtones of the kingdom idea into a transcendental, abstract idea of the "limitless power of the Deity"[26] enacted dramatically on earth at the "end of time."[27]

Crossan, Mack and Vermes, then, equate apocalyptic with imminent eschatology, highlight the idea of judgment and consider apocalyptic to be, in the technical sense, quietistic and "apolitical"—even though the actions of John the Baptist were seen by contemporary political powers as potentially dangerous.[28] John sent his newly baptized back to "wait for" the action of God (Crossan); apocalyptic eschatology led the sectarians into the world of "fantasy" (Mack); apocalyptic highlighted the limitless power of the Deity, had a propensity for the grand and the mystic and appealed to the transcendent for judgment of evil (Vermes). Differences between the three are to be found in their assessment of apocalypticism as a widespread phenomenon. Mack, for example, takes pains to minimize the apocalyptic response, arguing that its pervasiveness has been over-emphasized, whereas for Vermes and Crossan apocalypticism was one of several perspectives which shaped thinking in and around the time of Jesus.

2.2 Sanders, Fredriksen, Horsley

A second trio of writers defines apocalyptic differently. Ed Sanders, Paula Fredriksen and Richard Horsley stress the connection of apocalyptic language with social and historical events (hence apocalyptic is not apolitical). All three focus upon the central role of the Temple in this expected change of world order, although for Sanders and Fredriksen the practical and social implications of the climax are less important than they are for Horsley. That is, Horsley sees the apocalyptic texts as nourishing the hope for a this-worldly transformation, a social revolution from the bottom up, which would be completed by a divine act. Sanders and Fredriksen are less confident about the social implications of "restoration eschatology" (Sanders) or "apocalyptic eschatology" (Fredriksen), yet do not see such eschatological hopes as necessarily leading away from the concerns of this world. Fredriksen, in particular, asserts: "the nature of apocalyptic is political. . . . Its message of an impending new order at least implies a condemnation of the present one. . . . Apocalyptic theology . . . partakes of the broad Jewish consensus on what was religiously important: the people, the land, Jerusalem, the Temple and Torah."[29]

---

26 Vermes, *Religion*, 121.
27 Vermes, *Religion*, 106.
28 Crossan, *Revolutionary Biography*, 40-48.
29 Fredriksen, *From Jesus to Christ*, 124-25.

Sanders has been criticized, particularly by Marcus Borg, for an understanding of eschatology that leads inevitably to a "de-emphasis on human community and history."[30] This is, I think, to misconstrue Sanders' idea of the restoration. His earlier *Jesus and Judaism* remains ambiguous about the nature of the coming kingdom expected by those who held such hopes, but does not suggest that the present order was insignificant. His more recent article, "Jesus and the Kingdom," goes further to spell out the "distinct program"[31] of the earliest followers of Jesus, which he sees as being in continuity with the aims of Jesus, and which was not devoid of social implications. If Sanders is indefinite about the expected this-worldly or other-worldly nature of the kingdom, it is due to his unwillingness as a historian to push the evidence farther than it will go. At any rate, Borg's application of the "imminent-eschatology = no social interest" equation to Sanders is, I think, misplaced.[32]

For Sanders, Fredriksen and Horsley, then, the eschatological vision is imminent, yet it has political implications of one kind or another. The end of time is not in view; the focus is on the end of an old order, one challenged by apocalyptic language. Sanders and Fredriksen, for their part, are solely interested in eschatology, not in the larger scenario suggested by "apocalyptic."[33] Horsley goes somewhat beyond this to argue for a more sensitive understanding of apocalyptic writing and its imagery: "scholarly study

---

30 Marcus J. Borg, "Portraits of Jesus in Contemporary North American Scholarship," *Harvard Theological Review* 84 (1991): 22.

31 E. P. Sanders, "Jesus and the Kingdom: The Restoration of Israel and the New People of God," in his (ed.) *Jesus, the Gospels and the Church* (Macon: Mercer University Press, 1987), 225-39.

32 See also the clarifications of N. T. Wright, who attempts to draw out the meaning of "apolitical" by contrasting Sanders with Brandon. His suggestions, in *The Interpretation of the New Testament, 1861-1986*, 2nd ed. (Oxford University Press, 1988), 391-92, seem to have been borne out by Sanders' further clarifications in "Jesus and the Kingdom."

33 Sanders is well aware of the newer analyses of apocalypses, which he cites in *Jesus and Judaism* (Philadelphia: Fortress, 1985), 375-76 n. 3. His interests, however, lie within the narrower range of restoration eschatology, so he uses this term exclusively in his treatment of Jesus, avoiding "apocalyptic." Where Sanders has been concerned with the genre of apocalyptic literature, he has done so by reference to the "essentialist" approach—a definition of apocalyptic literature which combines revelation (as the essence) and restoration/reversal (as the content). His articulation of this definition is to be found in "The Genre of Palestinian Jewish Apocalypses," in David Hellholm, ed., *Apocalypticism in the Mediterranean World and the Near East: Proceedings of the International Colloquium on Apocalypticism, Uppsala, August 12-17, 1979* (Tübingen: J. C. B. Mohr, 1983), esp. 458. In my view, Sanders' definition, while well expressed, amounts to a reversion to the equation of apocalyptic with eschatology found in material prior to Klaus Koch—although it does give slightly more emphasis to the element of revelation. Many apocalypses (especially the non-canonical) are not adequately comprehended by his description, and the mystical element of apocalyptic literature is almost wholly suppressed. See the assessment of Sanders' approach by Webb in "Apocalyptic," 121.

has often fundamentally misunderstood apocalyptic texts and motivations because . . . out of a certain literalism and doctrinalism, it has failed to appreciate the distinctive apocalyptic mode of revelation and symbolization."[34] Over against Crossan and Mack, Horsley does not understand apocalyptic as an alienated yearning for the imminent end of things; rather, the dramatic language looks for a change to the present world order, a restoration or new age. Again, the cosmic perspective is not seen as pulling away from the real world, reducing the mundane to nothingness, but as a dramatic way of envisioning social and individual life. "The apocalyptic imagination had a creative envisioning function" which strengthened "the people's ability to endure . . . [even to the point of] resistance or revolt."[35] Horsley, then, is intent on discrediting the idea of apocalyptic as dissolute or decadent prophecy,[36] and wants to establish the apocalyptic imagination as a context for spirals of violence. Despite his sensitivity to the literature, however, he stresses mostly its temporal axis, pointing to its memorial impulse and its envisioning of a new order. It may be, also, that Horsley, under the heavy influence of such historical reviews as the Animal Apocalypse (*1 Enoch* 85-90), tames the apocalyptic imagery by connecting it too firmly with this-worldly events.[37] Apocalyptic symbolism becomes a cryptic way of speaking about the present world, a code to be cracked, rather than an imaginative construct which connects the mundane to the transcendent. Further engagement with the "demystifying" power of apocalyptic literature against the established order and a reintegration of theological with socio-political ideas would safeguard Horsley's discussion against this tendency to read the symbols in a static manner.

2.3 Wright, Schüssler Fiorenza, Borg

Horsley's concern for an appropriate understanding of apocalyptic language is shared by Tom Wright, Elisabeth Schüssler Fiorenza and Marcus Borg. These three, like Sanders, Fredriksen and Horsley, contend that apocalyptic hope did not look for the end of the world. In dealing with Jesus, in fact, Borg and Schüssler Fiorenza[38] stress the present in-breaking of the new age over and above imminent expectation; Wright seems to hold together both future and

---

34 Horsley, *Spiral of Violence*, 132.

35 Horsley, *Spiral of Violence*, 144.

36 An idea first made popular by Paul D. Hanson, "Old Testament Apocalyptic Re-examined," *Interpretation* 25 (1971): 454-79.

37 A surprising exception to this procedure is seen in the treatment of the Qumran material (specifically lQSb 5.23-29) where the imagery is understood as implying an "unreal, transcendent" war rather than actual earthly events. See Richard A. Horsley and John S. Hanson, *Bandits, Prophets and Messiahs: Popular Movements at the Time of Jesus* (Minneapolis: Winston, 1985), 130.

38 Schüssler Fiorenza, *In Memory*, 120: "Everydayness . . . can become revelatory."

present eschatology, considering that the most common stance among Jews around the time of Jesus was to yearn expectantly for God's dramatic action in history, while many believed that God was already decisively moving in the human arena.[39] Further, following G. B. Caird, Wright wants to see apocalyptic language "as a set of highly charged theological metaphors for talking about present realities,"[40] a way to "denote events within the space-time universe while investing those events with their full theological significance."[41] It is this latter assertion that divides Horsley, I think, from Wright, Borg and Caird: all three see the connection between this-worldly events with the apocalyptic symbolism, but Horsley is intent on the sociological reasons for revolution over against theological constructs. It is not accurate to reverse this characterization, saying that Borg and Wright privilege theology over sociology; rather, they see them as inextricably bound, especially in the climate of first-century Palestine.

A further point of agreement between Wright, Schüssler Fiorenza and Borg is their ease in joining together what is normally considered "apocalyptic" with sapiential motifs. Borg speaks of Jesus as both a "sage" and a charismatic prophet,[42] while Wright polemically addresses the dividers of Q: "Q looks more and more like a combination of wisdom-tradition and prophetic discourse; and there is every reason, within the actual known history of first-century Palestinian religion, as opposed to the mythical model constructed by some scholars, why such a combination should be perfectly natural."[43] Schüssler Fiorenza, too, as a specialist in the analysis of apocalypses, speaks of apocalyptic and wisdom with one breath: "apocalyptic scribes and wisdom leaders not only collected the prophetic oracles and the sayings of the fathers, but also wrote and collected whole new books of revelation and wisdom."[44] Wisdom, conceived in the mould of Job and Wisdom of Solomon (rather than quasi-Cynic rejoinders), breathes well in apocalyptic air. A consideration of such passages as *4 Ezra* 8-9 and *1 Enoch* 91-101 should be ample evidence that wisdom discourses co-exist peaceably with an apocalypse. As Seán Freyne notes, "the collection of Jewish apocalypses which now consitute *1 Enoch* shows how the circles in which this material was developed and transmitted could integrate this-worldly wisdom, Hellenistic cosmic speculation and varied

---

39 N. T. Wright, *The New Testament and the People of God* (Minneapolis: Fortress, 1992), 439. The evidence given for a combined realized/futurist eschatology is "The Community Rule" (1QS). Similarly, Bruce Chilton questions the distinction between eschatologies as a modern construct of NT scholarship, citing the dual nature of eschatology in the targumim, in "Kingdom Come, Kingdom Sung: Voices in the Gospels," *Forum* 3 (1987): 51-75.

40 Wright, *Interpretation*, 390.

41 Wright, *Interpretation*, 377-78.

42 Marcus J. Borg, *Conflict, Holiness and Politics in the Teachings of Jesus* (Lewiston: Edwin Mellen, 1984), 260-63.

43 Wright, *People of God*, 439.

44 Schüssler Fiorenza, *In Memory*, 113.

expressions of the divine-combat myth."[45] Why should it not be so, since apocalypses search out "all the secret things of heaven and future things" (*1 Enoch* 52:2), including the wisdom of God? Indeed, certain studies have highlighted the role of wisdom literature in the emergence of the macro-genre apocalypse.[46]

A final affinity between Schüssler Fiorenza, Borg and Wright is their appreciation of the flexibility of apocalyptic imagery. All three are aware of its "tensive" nature, and do not make rigid decisions regarding the metaphorical or metaphysical intent of apocalyptic language. That is, they are aware that apocalyptic language is often adopted as a literary device, but they do not close the door to the possibility of actual ecstatic or visionary activity. So Schüssler Fiorenza sees Jesus' break from John the Baptist as the result of an actual vision,[47] Wright argues that the mystical or literary quality of each apocalypse or quasi-apocalyptic passage needs to be considered individually,[48] and Borg's more recent book presents, in a rather popular form, "a new vision" of Jesus in which room is made for "a dimension of reality beyond the visible world of our ordinary experience, a dimension charged with power, whose ultimate quality is compassion."[49] Wright, Schüssler Fiorenza and Borg, then, represent writers who are concerned to hear the "polyphony"[50] of apocalyptic passages, with a sensitive ear to their symbolism or possible ecstatic impulse. Their main point is that apocalyptic language does not rely on a rigid dualism which plays off the celestial and the earthly, rendering social and political concerns irrelevant. Rather, apocalypses and related passages seek to view earthly events and issues from a transcendent perspective. They describe earthly matters in terms of heavenly, sometimes even daring to focus upon those mysteries beyond our realm which imbue human life with significance. We shall see that these authors, while agreeing in the main on the general role of apocalyptic literature, do part company at least to some degree in their understanding of how Jesus used such language. Such diversity is no surprise, since each of them argues for a complex and tensive potential for such visionary language.

3. Jesus and "Apocalyptic"

Of our nine representative scholars, three understand "apocalyptic" in the traditional Schweitzerian manner as having to do with the imminent judgment

---

45   Seán Freyne, "Galilean Questions to Crossan's Mediterranean Jesus" (in this volume).
46   Particularly Jonathan Z. Smith, "Wisdom and Apocalyptic," in Paul D. Hanson, ed., *Visionaries and Their Apocalypses* (Philadelphia: Fortress, 1983), 101-20.
47   Schüssler Fiorenza, *In Memory*, 114.
48   Wright, *People of God*, 290-92.
49   Borg, *New Vision*.
50   Wright, *People of God*, 282.

of the world (thus radically dualistic and apolitical), three argue that apocalyptic eschatology looks to the socio-political arena of a new (but somehow continuous) order, and three attempt to go beyond an understanding of apocalyptic as solely "eschatological."

3.1 Crossan, Mack, Vermes

It will come as no shock that the first trio which, like Schweitzer, views apocalyptic as foreign, also does not attribute this perspective to Jesus. Indeed, for Crossan, Mack and Vermes, the apocalyptic flavour (so defined) of the gospels and later Christianity represents a radical break from the authentic words and stance of Jesus. To be sure, the methods of Vermes differ, as does his insistence upon a Jewish context for Jesus' activities, but the bottom line is roughly the same: "more than once I have been rebuked by trans-Atlantic dogmatists for illegitimately arriving at the right conclusion, following a path not sanctioned by my critics' sacred rule book."[51] The picture that emerges from all three scholars is that of a Jesus cut down to size, a domestic Jesus with a certain approachability not considered possible if he had possessed, or been possessed by, an apocalyptic imagination.

Of the three sketches, Crossan's is the most radical. Although he takes issue with Schweitzer's application to Jesus of "apocalyptic eschatology"[52] (i.e., "the imminent ending of that evil world . . . [through] immediate divine intervention"[53]), he nevertheless depicts Jesus as "eschatological" in the sense of "world-negating." Hence, for Crossan Jesus is a voice for the brokerless kingdom, the model hippie in a yuppy Augustan age, possessed of a vision (to be sure) but not a vision of apocalyptic dimensions—rather, a program of open commensality, present healing and social change. "Apocalyptic" and titular "Son of Man" sayings were only later attached to Jesus, although Crossan finds it quite credible that Jesus should have used the expression generically as a term of solidarity with the poor and dispossessed (cf. Matt 8:19-20//Luke 9:57-58//*Gos. Thom.* 86).[54] In all his authentic teaching Jesus speaks of a kingdom that "is, was and always will be available to any who want it."

---

51 Vermes, *Religion*, 7.
52 In *Revolutionary Biography* (see 52-53), Crossan argues that Schweitzer's use of the term "eschatology" is too broad, and suggests that "apocalyptic eschatology" is a more precise term for Schweitzer's view of Jesus, erroneous though he considers this to be. It will be apparent by now that "apocalyptic eschatology" is by no means as simple a matter as Crossan suggests, and that the complex nature of this kind of language needs to be rethought in light of what we now know of the genre.
53 Crossan, *Revolutionary Biography*, 53.
54 Crossan, *Revolutionary Biography*, 30-31.

In contrast, Mack's sketch is rather less striking, described by himself as "the lackluster Jesus"[55] with a rather humble attraction, due to the typical Cynic virtue of "verve" in a "home-grown [Galilean] variety of Cynicism." There is even less of the "program" to Mack's Jesus, so that the non-apocalyptic stance is more consistent. Over against the announcer of a brokerless kingdom, Mack's Jesus simply adopts a challenging stance: "See how it's done? You can do it also."[56] If Jesus spoke about a kingdom, so too did the Cynics, and in patently non-apocalyptic terms. His challenge was to individuals, and not with regards to any specific social institution. Moreover, Mack does not target simply the apocalyptic language *per se*, but also the whole epic-apocalyptic sweep of the gospel story. Jesus is to be "credited for creativity and courage," but not "dramatized" as a charismatic. His method was always from below, the shrewd commentary of a peasant upon everyday matters, and devoid of even a new social program. The experimental, *ad hoc* nature of Jesus' wisdom stands in direct contrast to the programmatic mode of apocalyptic drama, although it may have been experienced by those who followed in his ways as "transformative." Nor did his earliest followers view his death from a cosmic or epic perspective: what mattered was the living, the counter-cultural stance.

Vermes's reconstruction merges elements found in Crossan and Mack, and in a sense is less rigorous than either; perhaps for that very reason his sketch will seem to some more compelling, more evocative of the messy state of reality. Apocalyptic writings are understood by Vermes as both envisaging the end, and as esoteric, but Jesus participates comfortably in neither mode. The "mystical propensity" of writings such as the Qumran documents and the book of Revelation are hardly "reconcilable with the mentality of Jesus."[57] Similarly, Jesus spoke from a "standpoint of immediacy" and was more concerned as an "existential teacher" with humanity's "attitude towards the Kingdom than with its essence or structure."[58] The parables are teachings concerning the mysterious nature of a kingdom which requires "human collaboration"[59] in order to be realized; then suggest a present growing phenomenon, with an existential appeal. The most important aspect of the earliest stories, but an element that continues throughout the traditional layers envisaged by Vermes, is the explicit demand "for a right moral response."[60] In particular, the stance of trust (אמונה) is urged by his teaching, and Jesus' domesticated view of God and the kingdom presented a figure like the "*paterfamilias* of rural Galilee,"[61] rendering

---

55   Mack, "Cynic-Like Jesus," 25 (in this volume).
56   Mack, *Myth of Innocence*, 73.
57   Vermes, *Religion*, 128.
58   Vermes, *Religion*, 137.
59   Vermes, *Religion*, 137.
60   Vermes, *Religion*, 139.
61   Vermes, *Religion*, 146.

the usual apocalyptic imagery more accessible. It is not a cosmic view that is presented in the piety of this charismatic teacher, but a more manageable, democratic view, similar to that of the tannaitic rabbis. His outlook (and that of his immediate followers), though, differed from others in that they considered that they had already entered the eschatological age; there was a break between their own experience and those preceding them. In concert with Crossan, Vermes sees all the titular uses of "Son of Man" as secondary; this view reiterates the same line of thought for which his earlier *Jesus the Jew* is well known—that "Son of Man" is an Aramaic periphrasis for the first person. Nevertheless, Vermes is unable to shake off entirely the Jewish apocalyptic context—perhaps because of his method and his predisposition to see Galilee in a particular Jewish context. In a summary which is rather at odds with his picture of Jesus' inaugurated eschatology, he says that the pious Jesus also looked for God to intervene at the appropriate time.[62] Meanwhile, individuals in need should be addressed, healed and taught, and Vermes considers, along with Crossan and Mack, that what is truly significant in Jesus' *modus operandi* was not fuelled by apocalyptic thought.

3.2 Sanders, Fredriksen, Horsley

We have noted already that Sanders, Fredriksen and Horsley define "apocalyptic" in terms of the imminent expectation of a new social order. For them, a careful delineation of apocalyptic thought is crucial, because Jesus is viewed within this context. Fredriksen is clear on this matter: "Jesus was an apocalyptic preacher, and the nature of apocalyptic is political." Fredriksen in particular is uneasy with a tensive or polysemous approach to apocalyptic actions or sayings, particularly sayings having to do with the kingdom or actions concerning the Temple. Thus, she considers Anthony Harvey's reading of the entry and Temple episode inadequate, due to the open nature of his constraints: "My sense is that an interpretative free-for-all ill conforms to the urgency of a public, apocalyptic ministry, especially at a moment of climax."[63]

---

62 In his oral response to my presentation of this paper at Calgary, Robert Webb emphasized this section and questioned the wisdom of classing Vermes with Crossan and Mack. What I sense again in re-reading Vermes is an enthusiasm for the Jesus of realized or inaugurated eschatology which renders this final picture of a futurist eschatological Jesus rather unconnected to Vermes's earlier arguments. Vermes finishes with a Jesus "always aware of the approach of the end of time"; he dwells, however, upon an "existential teacher" concerned with human attitudes and collaboration, and unconcerned about the actual essence of the kingdom, or its timing. In light of such ambiguity, the critic is forced to decide which to take as primary. In my opinion, it is the non-apocalyptic Jesus that Vermes himself puts in the foreground; the apocalyptic Jesus seems more a component of the broader Jewish environment, and less a part of what Vermes sees as significant.

63 Fredriksen, *From Jesus to Christ*, 113.

Harvey, however, finds apocalyptic polyvalence helpful in explaining how Jesus could have used thought-forms and symbolism familiar to his contemporaries (e.g., imminent eschatology), while moving beyond these to suggest a new, present way of approaching life, the "discovery" of "possibilities."[64] Such insinuation, such *finesse*, is foreign to the type of preacher envisaged by Fredriksen.[65] She instead sees Jesus' creative gestures as actions with the emotive volume of *fortissimo*, and fully explicable within the context of Jewish expectations: "[the act] would have been readily understood by any Jew watching as a statement that the Temple was about to be destroyed (by God, not human armies . . .) and accordingly that the present order was about to cede to the Kingdom of God."[66]

Sanders' understanding of Jesus and eschatology is similar, if less definite. Like Fredriksen, Sanders finds evidence for Jesus' own views within his actions as well as in his authentic words/teachings: indeed, he sets up this dual investigation as a self-conscious method. He begins his search for Jesus with the Temple action and sayings, and is well known for seeing these as indicative of national judgment—a judgment that forms an integral part of restoration eschatology. Jesus' speech about twelve followers and the consistent, although different, memories of his being attended by twelve is a second factor that points to "an otherworldly kingdom with analogies to the present order."[67] These two pieces of evidence lead Sanders to privilege those kingdom sayings which suggest a coming kingdom ordered socially (such as the sayings about the twelve disciples sitting on thrones and judging the twelve tribes of Israel). Nevertheless, for Sanders "'kingdom' does not always carry precisely the same meaning,"[68] even within the Jesus sayings. A certain tensive potential is allowed to accommodate sayings about a present kingdom alongside those with a "full eschatological sense": there is no inevitable disharmony here, since the kingdom, or God's rule, can be seen as extending to touch lives in the present, even if it is to be realized later. With regard to the thorny question of immortality and general resurrection, Sanders is unsure: "Possibly Jesus thought of 'the kingdom' in two ways and never brought the two into a systematic relationship."[69] Sanders' caution and ability to create a less-than-perfect portrait is here reminiscent of the style of Vermes.

Like Fredriksen and Sanders, Horsley states that "Jesus' proclamation and practice of the kingdom of God indeed belonged to the milieu of Jewish

---

64 A. E. Harvey, *Jesus and the Constraints of History* (London: Duckworth, 1982), 97.
65 Note, however, that Fredriksen does not fault Harvey here for the possible imposition of contemporary existential perspectives upon a Jewish rabbi.
66 Fredriksen, *From Jesus to Christ*, 122.
67 Sanders, *Jesus and Judaism*, 236.
68 Sanders, *Jesus and Judaism*, 126.
69 Sanders, *Jesus and Judaism*, 238.

apocalypticism."[70] Horsley's more complete conception of apocalypticism and his currency with the relevant literature lead him to consider many more elements than the eschatological focus seen in Sanders and Fredriksen. The apocalyptic "lore" of Beelzebul and angels, the symbolism of feasting, the demon-busting connotations of healing are all explored. Horsley is also bold in his reinterpretation of sayings usually considered to refer to the *parousia*, and therefore seen as secondary: for example, in their original form, references to the Son of Man are vivid pictures of judgment and/or vindication. They function as a proclamation and mediation or enactment of God's present and arriving kingdom, rather than evoking hope or fear of a future situation. It is the "certainty" and not the "suddenness" of God's action that is at issue. Horsley finds Dodd's term "inaugurated eschatology" congenial, and decodes Jesus' reference to the fall of Satan as a belief "that God had already begun, as it were, to implement the political revolution, even though it was hardly very far along." Hence, "his calling [was] to proceed with the social revolution . . . to begin the transformation of social relations in anticipation of the completion of the political revolution."[71] Jewish apocalypticism itself is redefined as the "eager hopes for an anti-imperial revolution to be effected by God."[72] Accordingly, the vision of Horsley's Jesus—an egalitarian society—is, in fact, very similar to that of Crossan, but he reaches this conclusion through the path of "apocalyptic" and not by way of detour.

3.3 Wright, Schüssler Fiorenza, Borg

Our final trio of writers, although beginning with similar views of "apocalyptic," actually move in quite different directions, ending with different sketches of Jesus. Wright has, unfortunately, not yet offered his second volume, in which his view of Jesus is to be carefully worked out. We can, however, glean his position from the hints to be found in articles and the general direction of his first volume. It seems that, despite his openness to the possibility of ecstasy within apocalypticism and his evident mastery of current studies on apocalypses, his major interest is in the temporal axis. Thus, although he is most comfortable with the idea of apocalyptic as a metaphorical system, it is unlikely that he would follow Caird in the latter's rigorous interpretation of Luke 10:18 as having only one possible meaning, the metaphorical. On the other hand, it is quite clearly the plight of Israel and Jesus' place in Israel's history that are crucial to Wright. Hence, Jesus' use of apocalyptic language, or his enactment of apocalyptic drama, invested historical events in Israel with theological significance: creational and covenantal monotheism, and the

---

70 Horsley, *Spiral of Violence*, 160.
71 Horsley, *Spiral of Violence*, 324.
72 Horsley, *Spiral of Violence*, 324.

eschatology which sprang from these, are the fixed points of Jesus' milieu. "It was to a people cherishing this hope . . . that another prophet came, announcing in the villages of Galilee that now at last Israel's God was becoming king."[73]

Paramount, then, in Wright's formulation of the quest are the difficult questions about Jesus' aims and self-consciousness within God's purposes for Israel. His popular *Who Was Jesus?* provides a picture of one who used apocalyptic language both to announce a fulfilment and accomplish a subversion of the "old hopes."[74] His reading of Matthew 11:12/Luke 16:16 is subtly different from that of Vermes: the latter sees the logion as an example of Jesus' "customary exaggeration in portraying his own success,"[75] whereas Wright sees this as a wry comment on the likelihood of bandits (λῃσταί) trying to crash the party of the kingdom.[76] There is something in Jesus' use of apocalyptic language to offend everyone! In the final analysis, Jesus' declaration of the kingdom "within you" (ἐντὸς ὑμῶν) is neither the proclamation of an internal or existential kingdom, nor simply the recognition of a new age about to dawn, but specifically, the implication "that this Kingdom was being redefined around himself."[77] Such an implication is seen as having serious political as well as theological consequences. So Wright fills in Sanders' important feature of the gathering of "the twelve" and wants to specify the nature of the kingdom, where Sanders will not dare, and Vermes considers it irrelevant.

Schüssler Fiorenza's interest in Jesus and "apocalyptic" is confessedly subordinated to her primary concern for feminist reconstruction in *In Memory of Her*. Nevertheless, neither Jesus nor apocalyptic is unimportant for her. In Schüssler Fiorenza's view, Jesus brings together apocalyptic and sapiential motifs in a way that rendered his activities "intrinsically sociopolitical."[78] Jesus' vision represented "an alternative prophetic renewal movement within Israel": for Schüssler Fiorenza present eschatology is the epitome of Jesus' teaching, and his aim was to subvert dominant structures, transforming his world. With Horsley, she sees the tensive power of apocalyptic imagery (such as the concept "kingdom," or βασιλεία) to be crucial: "the 'vision' of Jesus is expressed by [this] tensive symbol,"[79] "the key integrative symbol of the Jesus movement in Palestine."[80] Indeed, Jesus' apocalyptic world-view was the catalyst for his own mission as God-Sophia's mouthpiece and the watershed between him and John the Baptist. So important is one's "interpretation of the eschatological situation"

---

73 Wright, *People of God*, 338.
74 N. T. Wright, *Who Was Jesus?* (Grand Rapids: Eerdmans, 1993), 98.
75 Vermes, *Religion*, 140.
76 Wright, *Who was Jesus?* 98.
77 Wright, *Who was Jesus?* 100.
78 Schüssler Fiorenza, *In Memory*, 9.
79 Schüssler Fiorenza, *In Memory*, 111.
80 Schüssler Fiorenza, *In Memory*, 103.

that it issues in "different life-styles."[81] John looked for a future divine victory, whereas Jesus had beheld ecstatically the vanquishing of Satan. Whereas John's eschatology was steadfastly imminent, Jesus maintained a tension between present and future eschatology by focusing upon Israel as the locale for the kingdom—at least potentially. It is through this focus upon the people of Israel itself, in the announcement of a "prophetic possibility for Israel's wholeness,"[82] that Jesus and his movement integrated prophetic-apocalyptic and wisdom theology. In working out the implications of this integration, Schüssler Fiorenza herself moves quickly from "the community of Israel" to universal truth. In the final analysis, she leaves sacred history and Israel, and makes an overture toward universalism or existential living: "Everydayness . . . can become revelatory, and the presence and power of God's sacred wholeness can be experienced in every human being."[83]

The same kind of movement is to be found in Borg's presentation of Jesus and "apocalyptic." Appreciative of Schüssler Fiorenza's approach and sensitivity, Borg is most concerned to avoid imminent eschatology because of his perception that this leads to quietism. As aware as Mack of the transcendent view of reality implied in the gospels, Borg sees this as a challenge rather than as a threat, and does not suggest that Jesus moved "beyond" such a stance. Although he does not explicitly use the word "apocalyptic" in his presentation of Jesus in *A New Vision*, certainly the concepts found in fuller presentations of the apocalypse genre find a place in this book. It may be that Borg has avoided the term because of the difficulty of defining it adequately in a popular forum, and because of its common associations with imminent eschatology in the Schweitzerian sense. At any rate, reference to "transformation," "the experience of charismatic mediators,"[84] "alternate vision" and "a dimension charged with power . . . beyond the visible world"[85] move Borg's visionary Jesus onto a plane entirely different from that of Crossan's Jesus. Like Crossan, Borg's Jesus is a "transformative sage with a [social] vision"; as in Wright's view, Jesus uses the forms of wisdom to subvert conventional wisdom. Borg's aversion, however, to imminent apocalyptic, his suggestion that Jesus' prophetic warnings were merely "contingent,"[86] and perhaps his drive to make Jesus relevant, ultimately change the direction of his view of Jesus. All the authentic apocalyptic sayings are to find their referent in Jesus' own time, and the element of judgment is far less significant than the breaking in of the merciful kingdom upon Jesus' listeners. Hence, the ongoing import of Jesus' vision is reduced in

---

81   Schüssler Fiorenza, *In Memory*, 119.
82   Schüssler Fiorenza, *In Memory*, 120.
83   Schüssler Fiorenza, *In Memory*, 120.
84   Borg, *New Vision*, 34.
85   Borg, *New Vision*, 199.
86   Borg, *New Vision*, 202.

the end to an internal life, a vivid experience of the reality of the spirit which issues in meditation, compassion and religion of the heart[87]—albeit with an emphasis upon community.[88] Gone is the emphasis upon Israel, upon history, upon social change with concrete political dimensions. Questions such as why Jesus was crucified seem unimportant, and the historical particularities of Israel give way to a general ethic of mercy within a perspective which can grasp transcendence. Jesus, the founder of a movement to revitalize Israel, fades away. Borg leaves us rather with the picture of Jesus the holy and merciful person, the charismatic healer with a message of compassion. We move from the realm of historical investigation to the moral or spiritual.

4. What Difference Does it Make?

It is at this point that we move from reading the lines of the scholars' views of "apocalyptic" and "Jesus and apocalyptic" to read between the lines. What difference do these issues make, given the implicit or explicit concerns of the nine views we have considered? Of the first trio, Mack makes it most clear what is at stake for him. In both *A Myth of Innocence* and *The Lost Gospel*, Mack makes explicit reference to the phenomenon of apocalypticism today, and draws connections between his research and what he considers to be a problem area. To his mind, the apocalyptic imagination is both fantastic and dangerous, leading away from an engagement with the ordinary, privileging the spectacular and providing an epic scenario within which destructive political or social decisions can be justified. The focus upon glory, catastrophe and violence (especially against Jews) which is spawned by apocalyptic thinking has provided, in our time, the "gospel event" of the holocaust.[89] When political and social (or, in fact, individual) problems arise, those whose imaginations have been shaped by apocalypticism look to the patterns of vicarious crucifixion and apocalyptic destruction as paradigmatic—and such patterns can lead to "disastrous consequences."[90] For Mack the issues are not "simply academic." Rather, his deliberate eschewal of apocalyptic thinking, as he defines it, is borne out by the non-apocalyptic picture of Jesus which he has drawn from the earliest layers of Q. Thus Mack offers a challenge to apocalyptic and potentially destructive (American?) Christians to "join the human race."[91]

In the case of Crossan, the corrective emphasis is less obvious. Apocalyptic thinking is not an enemy; it is simply not representative of the historical Jesus. Apocalyptic is one approach to reality, perhaps a little more plebian than the

---

87 Borg, *New Vision*, 42-45.
88 Borg, *New Vision*, 199.
89 Mack, *Myth of Innocence*, 375.
90 Mack, *Lost Gospel*, 255.
91 Mack, *Lost Gospel*, 257.

sapiential. Where Mack is interested in discouraging apocalypticism, Crossan is intrigued by the *positive* aspect of Jesus' particular eschatological or world-negating radicalness. The open commensality of the egalitarian Jesus is the point at which Crossan's reconstruction issues the challenge to "conduct, religiously and theologically, ethically and morally, some basic cost accounting with Constantine."[92] If for Mack the danger is zealous and irresponsible apocalyptic thinking, for Crossan, the eternal enemy to humankind is hierarchy and paternalism. Against such an enemy, the apocalyptic prophet has no weapon, but the shrewd peasant radical, who eats and drinks with sinners, prevails. Christianity lost the vision of that Jesus, replacing it with the dream or nightmare of privilege and power. Despite the advertisements and dust jackets of the books of Crossan and Mack, which speak in old-fashioned accents of neutrality, and boast historical "discoveries,"[93] both Crossan and Mack make their presuppositions clear, and aim at alternative portraits. Answering the question, "So what?" or "Why is this important?" is therefore fairly straightforward in their cases.

Such transparency is not the case with Vermes, who still favours "a reading devoid of doctrinal preconceptions."[94] He is convinced "that historians have the right and duty to pursue their research independent of belief."[95] Moreover, he states his optimism that such historical work is valid and possible in working with the gospels, despite the fact that they are "non-historical works," because of the advances that have been made in our understanding of first-century Palestinian Judaism. Vermes, then, presents his findings from the perspective of a disinterested historian, and is one of the few writers who uses the work of critics in many different camps in pursuit of his object. To be sure, other members of the third quest are highlighted, but so too are the earlier new quest and parable studies, which he uses constructively rather than for rebuttal. In my opinion, Vermes's suggestion that Jesus pictured God as a *paterfamilias* or wealthy landowner, in domestic but not equalizing terms, is more in line with the gospel evidence, and certainly more probable than the radical egalitarianism detected by a zealous Crossan. On the other hand, there remains the problem of sorting out what difference it makes to Vermes that Jesus proclaimed a present, in some sense imminent, kingdom. It would seem that the future implications are not as central to Vermes's imagination as the points at which Jesus resembles the rabbis—demanding appropriate moral and ethical response, and submitting to the divinity through recitation of the *shema*. Where "Jesus seems to echo the same spiritual attitude,"[96] Vermes registers appreciation.

---

92 Borg, *New Vision*, 201.
93 See Wright, "Taking the Text," 304.
94 Vermes, *Religion*, 4.
95 Vermes, *Religion*, 4.
96 Vermes, *Religion*, 149.

Certainly he is aware of differences between tannaitic thinking and Jesus—and these are mostly eschatological! Nevertheless, his lack of integration at this point is apparent, especially in his reading of the parables. Vermes finds in the parables (reading some elements literally) evidence that Jesus' major message was that the kingdom required human co-operation, this in direct opposition to the majority of interpretations stressing that the kingdom appears suddenly, secretly, mysteriously and by the hand of God. For example, is the "Secretly Growing Seed" really about the concerted action of the farmer, field and seed—or about the mystery of the kingdom that arrives we know not how? Here it seems that Vermes's unspoken affinities for ethical and attitudinal teaching, coupled with a literalist understanding of apocalyptic language, prevents the apocalyptic passages from enriching his portrait. Apocalyptic is unavoidable, but not so very interesting, and so does not make its mark—this is a paler version, from a different perspective, and through a different method, of the portrait in Crossan's work.

Vermes finds a soul-mate in Sanders, whom he quotes approvingly for his lack of theological agenda. Sanders is perhaps the least penetrable of our selection in terms of what is at stake, and at more than one point calls attention to his own historical reserve, his refusal to go beyond the evidence where others who have such an agenda find the most interesting questions. With regard to the possible implications of his analysis of Jesus and eschatology (a sub-section of apocalyptic thought) he has a few cautionary remarks to make:

> I do not think that Jesus' positive position on Israel must govern thereafter every Christian stance towards every Jewish nation-state. We cannot easily leap from Jesus' view that in the coming kingdom God would restore Israel to, for example, the view that in the present the State of Israel must be unhesitatingly championed by Christians. Eschatological hope and practical politics are not necessarily the same. . . . On the other hand, however, Christians who are true to Jesus cannot say that their faith makes the nation of Israel a complete irrelevance—that we need think nothing at all about the national aspirations of Israel (as Bornkamm would have it). . . . Judaism has its own scandal of particularity: God chose Israel as his own.[97]

For Sanders, then, "apocalyptic" makes a difference in so far as it provides the greater context for restoration eschatology, an eschatology attributed to Jesus on the basis of actions as well as words; that implies (*contra* Borg) a positive stance toward the social reality known as Israel. Sanders gives us only one hint as to the ideological implications of his view: its implicit refusal to allow anti-Semitism.

Horsley's personal connection to his work is somewhat more patent, as has been already noted. He presents his sociological study as a concerted attempt

---

97   Sanders, "Jesus and the Kingdom," 239.

to read Jesus' preaching (where it displays apocalyptic elements) "less literally but with greater appreciation," "less doctrinally as a synthesis of theological ideas" but "without imposing the modern separation between religion and social-political life."[98] This endeavour, though, is no mean task, especially since Horsley begins by redefining Jewish apocalypticism as the "eager hopes for an anti-imperial revolution to be effected by God."[99] This predilection to see everything apocalyptic in terms of veiled social metaphor bears some weight in the light of studies pursued by Borg, Caird and Wright. On the other hand, Horsley's tendency to decode each element of the vision runs counter to his otherwise sensitive understanding of the apocalyptic imagination and seems unduly fuelled by his main drive to come to a sociological rather than a theological understanding of events and contexts. The anachronistic impulse of this divorce should be obvious.[100]

Our first trio considered "apocalyptic" only moderately important, or even irrelevant with regard to Jesus, after defining it in terms of dualism and a cataclysmic end to the world. Various ideological and religious concerns are to be found embedded in these portraits, and are not eschewed by Crossan and Mack, at least. The second trio approached "apocalyptic" insofar as it could shed light on the historical puzzles of Jesus' activities and words. Horsley's agenda is clearly spelled out, and propelled well by the manner in which he interprets apocalyptic language, whereas Sanders and Fredriksen have a narrower interest in eschatology, and, with a few notable exceptions, seldom take off the persona of historian.

Wright, Schüssler Fiorenza and Borg are more transparent about their concerns, but obviously approach the texts and issues from perspectives that are diammetrically opposed to their similarly-open colleagues, Mack and Crossan. Schüssler Fiorenza and Borg seemingly have very specific concerns that move alongside their historical inquiries: feminist reconstruction and an attack upon quietism. Despite the creativity of Schüssler Fiorenza's reconstruction and her subtle integration of apocalyptic and wisdom motifs, there remains a question (for me, at any rate) as to whether anything other than a feminist concern could have led to the adoption of Luke 7:35 as a foundational text. The combination of apocalyptic and sapiential ideas in Jesus' preaching may be convenient for Schüssler Fiorenza, but does not inevitably lead to "sophialogy." Again, with Borg, the concern for social engagement is accompanied by his observation that imminent eschatology leads to detachment. (Sanders is the exception that challenges this rule.) Nevertheless, the corporate implications of apocalyptic

---

98 Horsley, *Spiral of Violence*, 159.
99 Horsley, *Spiral of Violence*, 159.
100 See the timely comments of Seán Freyne regarding the inextricability of theology and socio-political realities in ancient cultures, in *Galilee, Jesus and the Gospels: Literary Approaches and Historical Investigations* (Philadelphia: Fortress, 1988), 200.

language serve Borg well, leaving a timely plea that Christianity not be dovetailed with individualism.

Of the last trio, Wright is especially *abordable* in terms of determining his orientation. His first volume sets out in unusual detail his presuppositions, his philosophical stance of critical realism and the painstakingly-developed views on how "apocalyptic" functions. For Wright, theology, history and literary analysis must go together in the study of the gospels, since these earliest lives of Jesus are both historical and theological texts.[101] Wright makes no apology for his personal engagement with the text and, like Freyne, pleads that theological concern need not in principle be any more distorting of historical judgments than are the claims to objectivity of those who show no such interest in the issue of Jesus. Freyne's concerns for a Jewish and an eschatological Jesus that makes sense of Christian "claims to ultimacy" and simultaneously forbids anti-Semitism is matched by Wright's own self-disclosure, and his questions as to who will own the vineyard. In his attempt to move beyond mere positivism and beyond the ghetto of pietistic subjectivism, Wright considers the possible implications of apocalyptic language in an analysis of Jesus that tries to cover as much of the evidence as possible. For some, his picture will appear too comprehensive, almost too confident; the messier sketches of Vermes, for example, might seem to ring more true. Again, his overarching narrative of God's dealings with Israel and the Israel reconstituted around her representative, Jesus, compels Wright to concentrate upon the temporal aspects of apocalyptic language. It may be that a more dynamic, and perhaps more problematic, picture of Jesus would emerge by allowing the spatial (vertical) axis of the apocalyptic language to have a stronger impact.

5. Conclusion

Schüssler Fiorenza has declared in her discussion of John the Baptist and Jesus that "different interpretations of the eschatological situation result in very different lifestyles."[102] This paper is an attempt to extend eschatology, the *sine qua non* detected by her and Borg, into the larger, more intriguing realm of things apocalyptic. It seems that there is still much scope for exploration of apocalyptic ideas and language in the New Testament that is not simply directed by popular and contemporary understandings of this world-view. Late-20th-century North American popular culture may well evince an apocalypticism that is world denying or escapist, but is this the only way such language is to be applied? Borg's vision of a world charged with meaning from beyond may be

---

101 Wright, *People of God*. See the lengthy introductory chapters, but especially 44-46, for his rationale.
102 Schüssler Fiorenza, *In Memory*, 119.

a corrective here—the mundane and everyday then takes on significance rather than being robbed by cataclysmic or dramatic visionary symbols. A wider and more appreciative understanding of apocalyptic might render the standoff between a sapiential and visionary Jesus irrelevant. Again, here is an opportunity to explore further the spatial axis of apocalyptic writing. While the historical and future perspectives are strong in the gospels, there are also telling glimpses in the New Testament of this other, cosmic, interest, an interest that we more generally associate with non-canonical apocalypses *per se*. Attention to such passages as Luke 10:17, "Lord, even the demons are subject to us in your name!" (surprisingly considered "probably authentic" by the Jesus Seminar), might produce problems for the scholar, but might also allow a more challenging picture of Jesus to emerge.

In full knowledge that there are some who are allergic to apocalypses, or to anything that bears similar spores, I must apologize for my enthusiasm. Nevertheless, it is clear that "apocalyptic" is not incidental to the various discussions about Jesus that are proceeding all about us. While the presentation of three trios is only representative,[103] I hope that it will have become apparent that each historian's decision as to whether and how Jesus shared in this language/perspective/experience of "unveiling" is often crucial to the picture that emerges. Does the reading of an apocalyptic passage render the Jesus of history incomprehensible because a veil or patina is over the eyes of the mythologically implicated? On the other hand, does response to the imagery, the vision, the imagination, lift the veil? Is apocalypse an impenetrable veil or a beckoning vision in our understanding of Jesus? It is certain that these questions will never be answered if those who see from different vantage points avoid conversation, difficult though this may be. It is also the case that those who are concerned about such matters may end up talking past each other without a careful choice and definition of terms, and an appropriate transparency regarding what, in their view, is at stake. "Let the reader understand" will be transmuted into the plaintive question, "Will the reader understand?"—either the New Testament text, or the varied readings which surround us.

---

103 Some will be concerned that none of the nine scholars considered here opt for a Jesus of futurist eschatology. While there are certainly some who have held out for this view (notably Ben Meyer, who is not treated here) and while there are some who will query my characterization of Sanders and Vermes, it is clear that this trend away from the Schweitzerian model is strong. On this see Marcus J. Borg, "An Orthodoxy Reconsidered: The 'End-of-the-World-Jesus,'" in L. D. Hurst and N. T. Wright, eds., *The Glory of Christ in the New Testament: Studies in Christology in Memory of George Bradford Caird* (Oxford: Oxford University Press, 1987), 207-17. It remains to be seen how much of this trend is reflective of our late 20th-century desire to reclaim eschatological language and how much of this reflects the actual ambiguity, polyvalence and potential of apocalyptic language itself.

19. The Christ of Faith: Context

Stephen Westerholm

One could almost wish that the quest for the historical Jesus were not an essential part of our job description. Sufficiently fascinating to provide scholars of Christian origins with an instant audience, it has, alas, also proved sufficiently baffling to puncture repeatedly any pretension that we might know much of what we speak. What pride can we take in belonging to an academic discipline that finds it agrees on virtually nothing? Can we even talk of a "discipline"? Yet how could we ignore the historical Jesus and feign competence in Christian beginnings?

In the paper that follows, Barry Henaut reminds us of a plague that continues to bedevil the quest. Let me put his point in a still wider context. While historians of any period must work with the data at their disposal, the mere collecting of data, or the arranging of source material into a more or less coherent story, does not yield history. History is the product of the minds of the historians who, on the basis of their own interests, frame their own questions, then—much as detectives find clues on which they base a reconstruction of what happened—bring their own intelligence to bear upon their sources until they arrive at answers to their own questions. Those answers, although prompted by the data, are inevitably the "constructs" of the minds of the historians. Alas, as Albert Schweitzer demonstrated in his lengthy and devastating review of historical-Jesus research up to his own day,[1] and as Henaut shows for more recent scholarship, supposed portraits of the historical Jesus, while inevitably the constructs of the historians' minds, have also all too frequently mirrored their creators' own ideals and convictions.

The pitfalls are real, and Henaut does well to remind us of them. His thesis can be supplemented with a few (largely methodological) observations.

First, Henaut has made it abundantly clear that historians' own predilections have often been imposed unnaturally upon the subjects of their histories. It is, however, worth adding that the biases of historians can also enable them to rediscover dimensions of the past to which the uninvolved are oblivious. The personal engagement of the historian *in itself* guarantees neither the accurate recovery nor the distortion of the past.

Second, while historians may well be tempted to find their own ideals and convictions in their subjects, it is only fair to add that not all historians all the time have succumbed to the temptation. The agenda for historical-Jesus research

---

1   Albert Schweitzer, *Von Reimarus zu Wrede: Eine Geschichte der Leben Jesu Forschung* (Tübingen: J. C. B. Mohr, 1906)—English translation: *The Quest of the Historical Jesus: A Critical Study of its Progress from Reimarus to Wrede*, trans. W. Montgomery (New York: Macmillan, 1968).

for the better part of the 20th century can be said to have been set by the insistence of Johannes Weiss, quite contrary to his own liberal Protestant preferences, that Jesus viewed his own career and times in apocalyptic terms. Henaut rightly points out that although theology has often exercised undue influence upon the work of historians, the latter has at times compelled the redirection of theology. Historical insights do occur—to those historians who refuse to ignore data that resist reduction to existing interpretations.

Third, whereas good methodology does not necessarily result in good history, bad methodology necessarily does not. An example is the naïve belief that a proper "objectivity" is brought to the quest for the historical Jesus when we confine our endeavours to isolating and paraphrasing the earliest possible sources. Historians are no mere regurgitators of data—even of the data they establish to be the most reliable. The delimiting and accurate control of data represents a precondition for historical work, not its culmination.

Fourth, the work of historians requires that they formulate their questions, put them to the available data and then use their insights to arrive at hypothetical answers. The insights that any historian is capable of reaching are undoubtedly limited by that historian's knowledge and experience. To that extent the answers proposed by historians are necessarily the subjective product of their (very individual) minds. Appropriate "objectivity" is achieved not by trying to eliminate the inevitably subjective involvement of the mind of the historian but by submitting its insights and hypotheses to rigorous and public counter-examination: Is this the only possible hypothesis that explains the data? Is it the simplest of the available hypotheses? What conditions would have to be met before we could judge the hypothesis to be true? If the bane of much historical-Jesus research has been the propensity of scholars to create a Jesus after their own likeness, the problem lies not so much with the subjectivity of their reconstructions as with their convenient neglect of the need to submit hypotheses with which they are enamoured to the demands of verification.

Fifth, disastrous for the progress of the "quest" has been the wont of many "questers" to eliminate from consideration all gospel material that does not meet the "criterion of dissimilarity": we can (it is supposed) only be sure that the material with which we are dealing is authentic if it demonstrably cannot have been derived from early Judaism or the early Christian church. Henaut draws attention to two weaknesses in the application of this principle. First, often implicit in its use is a conviction about Jesus' utter uniqueness. Even apart from that implication, the rigorous use of the criterion can only yield a Jesus completely isolated from his environment, since any tradition at home in that environment is effectively excluded from a role in the reconstruction of the historical Jesus. Second, in practice, the material excluded is commonly confined to that which could conceivably be derived from early Judaism or Christianity. *Not* excluded is material with, for example, a Cynic ring to it, although Cynicism too belonged to the environment of first-century Christianity.

Hence the application of the method may itself determine the outcome: in this case, a Cynic-like Jesus.

A further folly in the application of the criterion warrants mention. The data on which any reconstruction of the historical Jesus must be based are found almost exclusively in Christian sources. It is not surprising that a culling of such sources for Jesus material *in tension with* early Christian belief yields slim pickings indeed, and that, as Henaut indicates, scholars find themselves focusing on an ever-diminishing core of sayings. Again, the method has determined the outcome—and again the method is surely at fault. Can one plausibly exclude as evidence for the life and teaching of Jesus all that communities of his followers found worthy of belief and obedience? Only a method that allows for a measure of continuity as well as discontinuity has the potential to yield a persuasive account of Jesus and Christian beginnings.

Sixth, both the agenda that requires the maximal identification of Jesus of Nazareth with the Christ of faith and that which requires their maximal distinction are patently steered by dogma. The task of the historian is the subtler one of arriving at the portrait of Jesus of Nazareth and Christian beginnings that best accounts for *all* the relevant data by providing the most plausible explanation of how loyalty to the historical Jesus was developed and transformed into the christological faith of the early churches.

20. Is the "Historical Jesus" a Christological Construct?

Barry W. Henaut

> From now on, therefore, we regard no one from a human point of view; even
> though we once knew Christ from a human point of view, we know him no
> longer in that way. (Paul of Tarsus, 2 Cor 5:16)
> I regard the entire Life-of-Jesus movement as a blind alley. A blind alley
> usually has something alluring about it, or no one would enter it in the first
> place. It usually appears to be a section of the right road, or no one would hit
> upon it at all. In other words, we cannot reject this movement without
> understanding what is legitimate in it.[1]

1. Introduction: The Historical Jesus and the Christ of Faith

Is the "historical Jesus" merely another theological construct, like the "Christ
of faith"? To pose this question seemingly betrays over two centuries of usage
and threatens to undermine an essential philosophical and historical distinction
championed by David Friedrich Strauss. As a consequence of Strauss's famous
19th-century formulation, the "historical Jesus" is usually taken to refer to Jesus
"as he really was," the historical human being who lived in Galilee and was
crucified in Jerusalem (or at least what can be reconstructed of him using the
tools of academic history). The "Christ of faith," in contrast, is taken to refer
to the subsequent biblical proclamation of the risen Lord.[2] As Leander Keck
puts it, "'the historical Jesus' often has an anti-dogmatic, anti-theological, even
anti-Christian ring."[3]

The reasons for this distinction are as well known as they are obvious: with
the advent of the Enlightenment, scientific history could no longer make a
straightforward equation of these two entities (i.e., Jesus as he lived versus the
gospels' portrayal of this life). As will become clear, however, the
methodological problems implicit in the reconstruction of the "historical Jesus,"
combined with the inevitable unconscious forces at work in the process of such
analysis, ensure that every presentation of Jesus' life and thought creates a *de
facto* Christ of faith.

---

1   Martin Kähler, *The So-Called Historical Jesus and the Historic Biblical Christ*, trans. and
    ed. Carl E. Braaten (Philadelphia: Fortress, 1988 [1896]), 46.
2   David Friedrich Strauss, *Der Christus des Glaubens und der Jesus der Geschichte: Eine
    Kritik des Schleiermacherschen Lebens Jesu* (Berlin: Franz Duncker, 1865)—English
    translation: *The Christ of Faith and the Jesus of History: A Critique of Schleiermacher's Life
    of Jesus*, trans. Leander E. Keck (Philadelphia: Fortress, 1977).
3   Leander E. Keck, *A Future for the Historical Jesus: The Place of Jesus in Preaching and
    Theology* (Nashville: Abingdon, 1971), 18.

2. Martin Kähler: Against the Life-of-Jesus Movement

A major contribution to the "Jesus of history" and "Christ of faith" controversy came at the close of the 19th century with Martin Kähler's *The So-called Historical Jesus and the Historic Biblical Christ*. In conjunction with the work of Albert Schweitzer and Wilhelm Wrede, a major watershed can be marked in life-of-Jesus scholarship at the turn of the century. Kähler's analysis of the problem was to prove influential throughout mainstream biblical scholarship and neo-orthodox theology (especially upon Rudolf Bultmann and Paul Tillich). Indeed, in launching the so-called "new quest," Ernst Käsemann noted that, despite the (then) intervening 60 years, Kähler had never been refuted. Bultmann had really only "underpinned and rendered more precise the thesis of this [Kähler's] book."[4] An examination of Kähler, therefore, will be helpful not only in setting out the problem but also in revealing a number of tensions and contradictions which remain unresolved even today.

Regarding the entire life-of-Jesus movement as a "blind alley," Kähler sets out to understand the movement's strengths as well as its weaknesses. He argues that it is correct insofar as it sets the Bible (not the Jesus of History) against an abstract dogmatism. It becomes illegitimate, however, "as soon as it begins to rend and dissect the Bible without having acquired a clear understanding of the special nature of the problem and the peculiar significance of Scripture for such understanding."[5] The life-of-Jesus movement divorces Jesus artificially from his importance (as expressed in the biblical Christ of Faith): "In this whole discussion we are trying to explain how inadvisable and indeed impossible it is to reach a Christian understanding of Jesus when one deviates from the total biblical proclamation about him—his life as well as its significance."[6]

Kähler argues that we lack the sources for a life of Jesus which a historian can accept as reliable and adequate according to the canons of modern academic research.[7] The sources that we do possess cannot be traced to eyewitnesses. Furthermore, "these sources appear in two basic forms [synoptics and John] whose variations must—in view of the proximity of the alleged or probable time of origin of these forms—awaken serious doubts about the faithfulness of the recollections."[8]

Kähler also complains about the nature—and quality—of the current biographies of Jesus. Not heeding to problems of the sources, these biographers have not hesitated to compensate for a lack of historical evidence with

---

4   Ernst Käsemann, "The Problem of the Historical Jesus," in his *Essays on New Testament Themes*, trans. W. J. Montague (London: SCM, 1964), 16.
5   Kähler, *So-Called Historical Jesus*, 46.
6   Kähler, *So-Called Historical Jesus*, 68.
7   Kähler, *So-Called Historical Jesus*, 48.
8   Kähler, *So-Called Historical Jesus*, 49.

speculation and fantasy. They cannot, Kähler complains, refrain from discussions concerning irrelevant, but titillating, questions such as how handsome or homely Jesus was, his life at home and work, and even his temperament or individuality.[9] Historical research, Kähler insists, undoubtedly can explain and clarify features of Jesus' life and teaching, but this is insufficient for a biography in the modern sense of the word, and historians must recognize the limits placed upon them by the sources themselves. The New Testament accounts of Jesus were not written in order to describe Jesus' development, and this of necessity forecloses the possibility of a biography of Jesus.

In an anticipation of Herbert Butterfield's *The Whig Interpretation of History*,[10] Kähler complains that these biographies of Jesus actually have a propagandistic purpose:

> Today everyone is on his guard when a dogma is frankly presented as such. But when Christology appears in the form of a "Life of Jesus," there are not many who will perceive the stage manager behind the scenes, manipulating, according to his own dogmatic script, the fascinating spectacle of a colorful biography. Yet no one can detect the hidden dogmatician, whose job is to pursue consciously and intentionally the implications of basic ideas in all their specific nuances.[11]

These authors of "lives of Jesus" thus refract the image of Jesus through their own spirits—a criticism which Schweitzer was to amplify with devastating thoroughness. Kähler here has hit upon the central question we have set for ourselves in this discussion, and given it an affirmative answer. Not only are these so-called lives of Jesus distorted by subjectivism, they are in reality no less dogmatic than the gospels' portraits.

Kähler has a particular problem with these 19th-century "biographies": the use of the principle of analogy. In a telling passage, which sets forth his Christology, Kähler asks: "Is this method [the principle of analogy] justified in writing about Jesus? Will anyone who has had the impression of being encountered by that unique sinless person, that unique Son of Adam endowed with a vigorous consciousness of God, still venture to use the principle of analogy here once he has thoroughly assessed the situation? . . . The distinction between Jesus Christ and ourselves is not one of degree but of kind."[12] This sinlessness of Jesus is for Kähler nothing less than a facet of Jesus' status as

---

9   Kähler, *So-Called Historical Jesus*, 50.
10   Herbert Butterfield, *The Whig Interpretation of History* (Harmondsworth: Penguin, 1973 [1931]).
11   Kähler, *So-Called Historical Jesus*, 56-57.
12   Kähler, *So-Called Historical Jesus*, 53.

Christ and incarnate Son of God. We are confronted in the gospels with the question of "whether the historian will humble himself before the unique sinless Person—the only proper attitude in the presence of the norm of all morality."[13] But Kähler's solution to this "either/or" is to subordinate entirely the dictates of historical method to a christological *a priori*, thereby re-identifying the Jesus of history with the biblical Christ of faith. Indeed, Kähler insightfully asks for what the life-of-Jesus research is really searching. Is this not, in some measure, in fact a search for the biblical Christ of faith?

> Why do we seek to know the figure of Jesus? I rather think it is because we believe him when he says, "He who has seen me has seen the Father" (John 14:9), because we see in him the revelation of the invisible God. Now if the Word became flesh in Jesus, which is the revelation, the flesh or the Word? Which is the more important for us, that wherein Jesus is like us, or that wherein he was and is totally different from us? Is it not the latter, namely, that which he offers us, not from our own hearts, but from the heart of the living God?[14]

This re-unification of the historical Jesus with the Christ of faith is evident in Kähler's subsequent exposition of Jesus' nature. He was, Kähler tells us, like us, as scripture constantly emphasizes, "but hardly ever without adding expressions like 'without sin,' 'by grace,' 'in humility and perfect obedience,' etc. (Heb. 4:15; 7:26, 27; II Cor. 8:9; Phil. 2:6f.)."[15]

In the final analysis, then, Kähler insists that we commune with Jesus because in him we have redemption (Eph 1:7). Thus, do we really need to know more concerning him than what Paul delivered to the Corinthians (1 Cor 15)? This is the problem of the "embarrassment" of Pauline Christianity. If revelation and salvation—indeed, "authentic" Christianity—is dependent upon knowledge of the historical Jesus, then what of Paul's congregations? Not only did Paul not deliver them copies of the four canonical gospels, but even a cursory reading of his letters shows a considerable disregard for traditions of Jesus' teachings and deeds.

But Kähler's dilemma has another dimension. There is, in fact, a real call here for the "democratization" of the Christian faith. Kähler is concerned with what might be termed an elitist "scribal" form of Christianity, a form of Christianity which is so technical in its approach to Jesus that it all but excludes the tiniest minority and keeps the mass of Christians dependent upon this elite for access to the Christ. This is a particularly ironic "heresy"—one is tempted

---

13 Kähler, *So-Called Historical Jesus*, 55.
14 Kähler, *So-Called Historical Jesus*, 58.
15 Kähler, *So-Called Historical Jesus*, 59. It is noteworthy how Kähler here has turned to the letters of the New Testament and their theological exposition of the Christ of faith to establish the essence of Jesus' humanity.

to term it "histolatry" (the worship of history rather than the one true God)—to attach itself to the figure of the biblical Christ, given the gospels' polemic against the "scribes" and the apologetic insistence that Jesus was one who taught "with authority" (Mark 1:22), and given the long tradition within Christian exegesis of anti-Judaic polemic against the Pharisees and rabbis as those who built a fence around the Torah to keep the common people out.

Kähler's solution quickly returns to the biblical Christ, he who is proclaimed in the churches' preaching. As Kähler argues, whereas Christian dogmatics is a matter of judging data available to every Christian, historical research is highly technical and specialized: "In this field, no lay judgment is possible, except perhaps the kind made by inflated dilettantes."[16] Hence, for Kähler, either we must do without the revealed God, or the reality of Christ the saviour must be quite different from the inaccessible details of personal life and development which are essential to a modern biography.[17] The route out of this impasse is found in recognizing that a historic (in distinction to the merely historical) person is one who originates and bequeaths a permanent influence. This is the person who "lives on through his work, to which, in unforgettable words and personal characteristics, a direct impression of his dynamic essence often attaches itself."[18] With respect to the historic Jesus, his decisive influence is summed up in the phrase "Christ is Lord" (cf. 1 Cor 12:3; again echoing Paul's Christ of faith). For Kähler, this influence must be found in the proclamation of the entire New Testament, not in some remnant of historical reconstruction of authentic life-of-Jesus material from the gospels.[19]

There is one further aspect of Kähler's essay which warrants our attention. Owing to his insistence upon—and his desire to protect—"Christ's uniqueness," there is the problem of his negative assessment of Jewish and Hellenistic influences on Jesus. He argues that while it is "undeniable" that biblical thought-forms have conditioned Jesus' thought, such observations gain us little: "To assert anything more one must, in view of the silence in the sources, use as a means of research the principle of analogy with other human events—thus contradicting the whole tenor of the gospel portrayals of Jesus."[20] Kähler notes that long before Baur, Semler had discovered the "Judaistic tendencies" of the early Christian writers, yet Semler and his school "exempted Jesus from any such attachment to Judaism. Was this mere prejudice or was it the result of observation, of a correct insight?"[21] On the other hand, David Friedrich Strauss found Hellenistic influences in Jesus. Kähler then comments:

---

16 Kähler, *So-Called Historical Jesus*, 62.
17 Kähler, *So-Called Historical Jesus*, 63.
18 Kähler, *So-Called Historical Jesus*, 63.
19 Kähler, *So-Called Historical Jesus*, 65.
20 Kähler, *So-Called Historical Jesus*, 51-52.
21 Kähler, *So-Called Historical Jesus*, 54.

If we compare the Jesus of our Gospels with Saul of Tarsus, we do in fact see a great difference between the disciple of the Pharisees and the Master. On the one hand we see the true Jew, so profoundly and indelibly influenced by the cultural forces of his people and epoch; on the other we see the Son of Man, whose person and work convey the impression of one who lived, as it were, in the timeless age of the patriarchs. Thus a return to the first century does not appear to be very promising.[22]

Kähler is insisting that the historical principle of analogy, which situates Jesus firmly within his milieu of first-century Hellenistic Judaism, will not actually suffice for our understanding. Jesus' decisive influence on history ("Christ is Lord"), Kähler tells us, was unique and independent from mere historical trends: "Contemporary history contributed nothing to this affirmation, and Jewish theology still less."[23] He notes, for example, that Josephus mentions John the Baptist but not Jesus, and goes on to argue: "After he [Jesus] died as a sacrifice for the sake of the nation (John 11:49 f.), the Jews went raving and racing to their political destruction, without taking any notice of him. The small band of Nazarenes was of no importance to them."[24] Jewish theology, especially in its messianic expectations, actually constitutes (according to Kähler) a "stumbling block":

We surely know how vigorously the unpretentious Rabbi had to contend with the terrestrial hopes for a splendiferous Son of David who was to lay the kingdoms of this world, all in their glory, at the feet of his people. Those images and metaphors from Jewish eschatology which Christians drew upon in painting their vivid pictures of the Christian hope still constitute the stumbling block which is apt to betray the hope of faith into denial of itself.[25]

All of this is a very telling example of scholarly anti-Judaism, and it raises the question of the connection between anti-Judaism and an insistence on exclusivity and uniqueness for the historical Jesus.

Christ's enduring influence for Kähler, then, can be summed up in two characteristics: first, he evoked faith from his disciples (and the subsequent community), and second, this faith was confessed.

The real Christ, that is, the Christ who has exercised an influence in history . . . *this real Christ is the Christ who is preached.* The Christ who is preached, however, is precisely the Christ of faith. He is the Jesus whom the eyes of faith behold at every step he takes and through every syllable he utters—the Jesus

---

22 Kähler, *So-Called Historical Jesus*, 54.
23 Kähler, *So-Called Historical Jesus*, 64.
24 Kähler, *So-Called Historical Jesus*, 64.
25 Kähler, *So-Called Historical Jesus*, 64.

whose image we impress upon our minds because we both would and do commune with him, our risen, living Lord.[26]

"This is," Kähler insists, "no reassuring sermon. It is the result of a painstaking consideration of the data at hand."[27] This is also, as Freud would say, a telling instance of denial. For we can see throughout Kähler a deep desire to protect both the "Jesus of history" and the "Christ of faith" from the implications and dictates of the then-developing historical approach to the tradition. At all costs, Jesus' divine sonship, the uniqueness of his person and his exclusive office as bearer of salvation must be preserved and given some "objective" grounding, thus freeing Christianity from the necessity of viewing itself as only one among equals within the world's religions.

We may attribute this tendency to a number of sociological and historical factors current in the late-19th century. With the advent of scientific Darwinism and the increasing contact with other cultures due to colonialism and trade, European self-understanding was undergoing a crisis. Peter Berger's observations make a telling parallel to what we can detect in Kähler's response to the implications of life-of-Jesus research for Christianity:

> [Historicism] represents an attempt to deal philosophically with the overwhelming sense of the relativity of all values in history. This awareness of relativity was an almost necessary outcome of the immense accumulation of German historical scholarship in every conceivable field. Sociological thought was at least partly grounded in the need to bring order and intelligibility to the impression of chaos that this array of historical knowledge made on some observers. Needless to stress, however, the society of the German sociologist was changing all around him just as was that of his French colleague, as Germany rushed towards industrial power and nationhood in the second half of the nineteenth century.[28]

Kähler solves the problem by denying the possibility of a biography of Jesus, due to the nature of the sources, then retreating into a quick re-identification of the historical Jesus with the Christ of faith.

3. Ernst Käsemann and the New Quest

3.1 Käsemann and the Legacy of Bultmann

I now turn to Ernst Käsemann, whose 1953 lecture, "The Problem of the Historical Jesus," is credited with launching the so-called "new quest." The theological climate had changed somewhat since Kähler's essay, for, as

---

26 Kähler, *So-Called Historical Jesus*, 66.
27 Kähler, *So-Called Historical Jesus*, 67.
28 Peter L. Berger, *Invitation to Sociology: A Humanistic Perspective* (Garden City: Doubleday, 1963), 42.

Käsemann notes, the Jesus-of-history question had by now receded into the background of German scholarship. The era of form criticism had had its effect: the message of Jesus, it was now realized, was given in traditions overlaid by the preaching of the early churches, and this had led to the conclusion that the true bearer and moulder of the gospel had been the Easter faith. For most form critics, "Christian faith is . . . understood as faith in the exalted Lord for which the Jesus of history as such is no longer considered of decisive importance."[29] Käsemann's critique rests on three main points: the synoptic gospels contain more authentic material than Bultmann is prepared to admit; the most primitive elements at least within the Passion and Easter traditions are reliable, counteracting the antithesis of kerygma and tradition; and the systematic conception of a "salvation history" runs parallel to universal history (which is embedded within it yet separable from it).[30]

Following a lead from Kähler, Käsemann turns to the problem of the historical element in the gospels, observing that our knowledge of Jesus is derived from what has been narrated. Käsemann notes a difference between the gospels and the rest of the New Testament, for only in the gospels is the message of Christ presented within the framework of the earthly activity of Jesus. As for the other writings, only the cross and resurrection hold any real importance for them, with the result that the historical element of Jesus' story has shrunk almost to the vanishing point.[31] But the gospels also present us with Jesus' message in a theological form, for here we encounter Jesus who is Lord of the Community. It is only to the extent that from the very beginning Jesus was this Lord that his earthly life plays a role in the gospels. Since the importance for faith of Jesus' "lordship" from the very beginning almost entirely overshadowed his earthly activities, Käsemann argues: "In such circumstances we must question whether the formula 'the historical Jesus' can be called at all appropriate or legitimate, because it is almost bound to awaken and nourish the illusion of a possible and satisfying reproduction of his 'life story.'"[32] But a converse to the apparent impasse is soon found, for in spite of the difficulty in finding an answer to the question of the historical Jesus we are not justified in avoiding the problem. "No one," Käsemann warns, "may arbitrarily and with impunity exempt himself from tackling the problems which have come down to him from his fathers."[33] The question of the historical Jesus is raised by the New Testament itself, since the gospels ascribe the core preaching (κήρυγμα) to the earthly Jesus, thereby investing him with a pre-eminent authority. Furthermore, Käsemann argues, we must not allow the

---

29 Käsemann, "Problem of the Historical Jesus," 16.
30 Käsemann, "Problem of the Historical Jesus," 17.
31 Käsemann, "Problem of the Historical Jesus," 21.
32 Käsemann, "Problem of the Historical Jesus," 23.
33 Käsemann, "Problem of the Historical Jesus," 24.

exaggeration of insights, however correct in themselves, to "exempt us from the dialectic obtaining here or to drive us to one-sided solutions."[34]

Käsemann also displays a concern to exempt the Christian message from the allegation of "myth." Since the early churches identified the humiliated and exalted Lord, they not only admitted their inability to abstract their presentation of Jesus' story from their faith, but also demonstrated clearly that they would not allow myth to replace history nor a heavenly being to replace the human being from Nazareth.[35] This safeguarding of salvation from myth and relativity is to be found, according to Käsemann, in the particularity of the Christian revelation. Despite the fact that the gospels (with the slight exception of Luke) do not exhibit a desire to produce a comprehensive biography of Jesus nor to investigate the reliability of the reports concerning him, a primary concern throughout is the particularity of the eschatological event to be found in this person from Nazareth. In a passage reminiscent of Kähler, Käsemann tells us that "in revelation, I do not primarily experience some *thing* or other, but my ultimate Lord, his word to me and his claim upon me."[36] The existentialist element of Käsemann's dialectic is soon evident: "Briefly, that particularity of revelation which is manifested in its unbreakable link with a concrete history reflects the freedom of the God who acts and is the ground of our having a possibility of decision. In other words, revelation creates *kairos* which is a situation of grace or guilt, as the case may be."[37] Here again, as with Kähler, Käsemann has subordinated the demands of detached objectivity necessitated by the canons of academic history to the christological *a priori* of Jesus' presumed unique message. The blend of eschatological event, faith and history within the gospels combines for Käsemann to form a startling conclusion: "the Church" was not interested in the *bruta facta* but in eliciting from the past the essence of its faith. Hence, early churches agreed only in one judgment: "that the life history of Jesus was constitutive for faith, because *the earthly and exalted Lord are identical.* The Easter faith was the foundation of the Christian kerygma but was not the first or only source of its content."[38] This is a striking identification, one which cannot possibly be substantiated by the normal canons of historical research and one which can only predispose the gospel critic to treat "the historical Jesus" as a christological construct. Käsemann believes this bold (if dogmatic) assertion necessary to protect Christianity from the twin terrors of docetism and myth: "We also cannot do away with the identity between the exalted and the earthly Lord without falling into docetism and depriving ourselves of the possibility of drawing a line between the Easter faith of the

---

34 Käsemann, "Problem of the Historical Jesus," 25.
35 Käsemann, "Problem of the Historical Jesus," 25.
36 Käsemann, "Problem of the Historical Jesus," 31.
37 Käsemann, "Problem of the Historical Jesus," 31.
38 Käsemann, "Problem of the Historical Jesus," 33-34 (emphasis mine).

community and myth. Conversely, neither our sources nor the insights we have gained from what has gone before permit us to substitute the historical Jesus for the exalted Lord."[39]

It remains problematic whether Käsemann's beachhead of "history" within the earthly "ministry" of Jesus really does remove the eschatological event of salvation in Christ from the realm of myth. And given the disregard for historical biography in the Fourth Gospel's portrayal of Jesus, and Paul's profound indifference to Jesus' public activities, one might ask whether this insistence on the distinction between the historical Jesus and the Christ of faith in fact constitutes docetism or merely appears to be docetic to critics such as Käsemann.

3.2 Käsemann's Reconstruction of Jesus' Message

Käsemann returns at this point to the sources and a reconstruction of their authentic material. A genuine problem for Käsemann is that, apart from the parables, there are no formal criteria to identify authentic traditions. Further to this, it is precisely the earliest phase of the tradition that remains opaque to scholars, thus compounding the problem. The only solution to this impasse is to be found in Bultmann's criterion of distinctiveness, which still forms the single most important principle in life-of-Jesus research.

In his reconstruction of Jesus' message, Käsemann begins by noting that there is considerable agreement regarding the first, second and fourth antitheses in the Sermon on the Mount (i.e., Matt 5:21-22, 27-28, 33-34), for "these words are among the most astonishing to be found anywhere in the Gospels."[40] This distinctiveness is to be found in the unparalleled claim of authority surpassing even that of Moses to be found in the words "but I say . . ." (ἐγὼ δὲ λέγω). To this no Jewish parallels exist, nor could there be, since "the Jew who does what is done here has cut himself off from the community of Judaism—or else he brings the Messianic Torah and is therefore the Messiah."[41] It is thus precisely the unheard-of implication of this saying, he argues, which testifies to its genuineness, and proves that, while Jesus may have appeared as a prophet or rabbi, his claim to authority goes far beyond this: "Certainly he was a Jew and made the assumptions of Jewish piety, but at the same time he shatters this framework with his claim. The only category which does justice to his claim (quite independently of whether he used it himself and required it of others) is that in which his disciples themselves placed him—namely, that of the Messiah."[42] Without any apparent sense of anachronism, Käsemann can even

---

39 Käsemann, "Problem of the Historical Jesus," 34.
40 Käsemann, "Problem of the Historical Jesus," 37.
41 Käsemann, "Problem of the Historical Jesus," 37.
42 Käsemann, "Problem of the Historical Jesus," 38.

paint Jesus as a first-century anticipation of the dialectical theologian, for it is this "same dialectical relationship to the law, seeking the will of God and, in pursuit of it, shattering the letter of the law, [which] is reflected in the attitude to the Sabbath commandment and the prescriptions for ceremonial purity."[43]

It is instructive at this point to pause to examine more closely Käsemann's reconstruction of Jesus' message and his use of the criterion of distinctiveness. How has Käsemann's reconstruction borne up over the last forty years? His acceptance of the first, second and fourth antitheses from the Sermon on the Mount has not fared well. These verses are no longer accredited to Jesus precisely because of their sociological tie with the early churches' need to promulgate their own Torah and because of their implicit proclamation of Jesus as a new Moses (yet one beyond Moses in office and authority). They thus have clear ties with the Christian post-Easter proclamation, and their particular literary form seems heavily influenced by Matthean redaction. Similar is Käsemann's treatment of "the sabbath was made for humankind" (Mark 2:23-28) and the defilment sayings (Mark 7:1-23). Here Käsemann has again anachronistically attributed to Jesus the Pauline attitude to Torah. These sayings do not show a distinctiveness against the practice of the early churches (as required for attribution to Jesus on the grounds of this criterion); they agree entirely with Paul's theology as expressed in Galatians. Käsemann's reading of "the sabbath was made for humankind" logion also has to be strongly questioned, since the essence of this sentiment has clear rabbinic parallels. The rabbinic form of this sentiment is usually given as: "The sabbath was given to you, and not you to the sabbath."[44] Käsemann, one suspects, has seen in this saying a radical antithesis to Judaism because such an interpretation is particularly attractive to his Protestant sensitivities with its implicit distance from Jewish Torah and practice. The current scholarly evaluation of these sayings is well represented by E. P. Sanders:

> In a Jewish environment, observance of the Sabbath and the consumption of kosher food are largely matters of routine. That food and Sabbath were issues in the Gentile churches is shown by the letters of Paul, where they are the only two items other than circumcision which require special treatment (Gal. 2:11-14; 4:10; Rom. 14:1-6). Thus it is very probable that the issues of food and Sabbath are so prominent in the Gospels because of the importance which they assumed in the church. That is not to say, of course, that it can be proved that Jesus never debated such issues. This is another negative which cannot be proved. But that they *defined* his relationship to his contemporaries is most unlikely.[45]

---

43 Käsemann, "Problem of the Historical Jesus," 38.
44 Quoted in C. H. Dodd, *The Founder of Christianity* (New York: Macmillan, 1970), 71.
45 E. P. Sanders, *Jesus and Judaism* (London: SCM, 1985), 264.

Furthermore, there is the implication that it was a distinctive element of Jesus' "ministry" to share fellowship with the outcasts and sinners. This establishes a contrast of attitudes between Jesus and the Judaism of his day with the implication that the "outcasts" were religiously unclean and in need of a spiritual physician. This judgmental comparison is reminiscent particularly of Jeremias, who believed that it was the simple people of the land (עם הארץ) who figured predominantly among Jesus' followers. According to Jeremias, these people were "the uneducated, [and] the ignorant, whose religious ignorance and moral behaviour stood in the way of their access to salvation, according to the convictions of the time."[46] Implicit is a view of these people as "unwashed masses" held in disdain by the "morally smug" Pharisees and shown compassion by Jesus. Sanders, particularly, challenges this view. Surveying the appropriate rabbinic literature he states: "I maintain that there is absolutely no passage in the entirety of that literature . . . which in any way supports the assertion that the scrupulous and learned regarded the ordinary people as 'the wicked,' those who flagrantly and persistently disobeyed the law."[47]

Finally, there is the problem of Käsemann's reconstruction of Jesus as a dialectical theologian, and his portrait of Jesus as one who rejected outright the ancient notions of "the sacred and profane" and the existence of demonic powers. It is an ingenious bit of detective work, to say the least, to ascribe such modern (and progressive—to say nothing of congenial) attitudes to Jesus on the basis of only two or three "authentic" sayings. These reconstructions are almost entirely dependent upon Käsemann's own predispositions and assumptions, and amount to a christological portrait based on 20th-century assumptions. Schweitzer's warning has once again gone unheeded. In this regard, I must agree wholeheartedly with the following assessment of the exorcism accounts by Marcus Borg: "Whatever the modern explanation might be, and however much psychological or social factors might be involved, it must be stressed that Jesus and his contemporaries (along with people in most cultures) thought that people could be possessed or inhabited by a spirit or spirits from another plane. Their worldview took for granted the actual existence of such spirits."[48]

Käsemann finds another distinctive element in the teaching of Jesus, and here he sounds a note which was to echo prominently in subsequent reconstructions, most notably in the current Jesus Seminar. This is the reconstruction of Jesus as a teacher of wisdom. Bultmann before him had concluded that wisdom sayings were the least likely to be authentic and thus the

---

46   Joachim Jeremias, *New Testament Theology*; Volume 1: *The Proclamation of Jesus*, trans. John Bowden (London: SCM, 1971), 112.

47   Sanders, *Jesus and Judaism*, 180.

48   Marcus J. Borg, *Jesus, a New Vision: Spirit, Culture, and the Life of Discipleship* (San Francisco: Harper, 1987), 64.

least significant for historical interpretation.[49] Käsemann is aware of the difficulties but still believes that these sayings can meet the burden of proof required by distinctiveness. Käsemann gives two specific examples: Matthew 10:26-27 (Q 12:2-3), which is made up of two proverbs, the first of which enjoins caution because of the great difficulty in keeping secrets, and the second of which concerns why this warning is now converted into a demand (i.e., open proclamation). Käsemann sees the meaning as distinctively eschatological: in the last times caution must be thrown to the wind.[50] This logion would thus also accord well with the saying concerning anxiety in Matthew 6:25-27 (Q 12:22-25), which modifies the Jewish belief in providence "in a very odd fashion."[51] These sapiential sayings, Käsemann believes, are truly distinctive relative to first-century Judaism: "The portrayal of the teacher of wisdom [Jesus] accords but ill with that of the rabbi, because the former lives by immediacy of contemplation, such as is familiar to us from the parables of Jesus, while the latter's existence is determined by mediation and by the bond which keeps him tied to Scripture."[52]

Again, I must question Käsemann's procedure. The rabbinic ethos (supposedly so contrary to Jesus) of mediation and the bond to scripture is not attributed to Jesus because it is excluded in an *a priori* fashion due to the peculiar demands of distinctiveness. It is a frequent complaint against this methodology that it excludes those areas of religious practice and belief which Jesus and Judaism held in common. In particular, sayings which are based upon Hebrew scriptures cannot meet this criterion because of the strong possibility that the early Christians ascribed the sentiment to Jesus out of their own need to develop a holy law and practice. Many of these sayings, quite rightly, thus must be placed within the post-resurrectional history of early Christianity. The failure to authenticate such sayings, however, does not prove the opposite; this method cannot prove that Jesus did not share in these particular sentiments and take them over from his Jewish heritage. In fact, on general principles of historiography one can argue that Jesus, as a first-century Jew, must have shared in large measure the common cultural attitudes of his contemporaries toward Temple and Torah (although precisely what form these beliefs took is an open question, since Judaism was a diverse religion). One cannot escape influence from one's social ethos and culture. Hence, the methodology of distinctiveness in this regard only leaves a void where one can neither affirm nor deny Jesus' allegiance to any particular saying in question. Since Käsemann

---

49 Rudolf Bultmann, "The Study of the Synoptic Gospels," in Frederick C. Grant, ed. and trans., *Form Criticism: A New Method of New Testament Research* (New York: Harper, 1962 [1934]), 55. Cf. Barry W. Henaut, *Oral Tradition and the Gospels: The Problem of Mark 4* (Sheffield: JSOT, 1993), 37-38.

50 Käsemann, "Problem of the Historical Jesus," 41.

51 Käsemann, "Problem of the Historical Jesus," 41.

52 Käsemann, "Problem of the Historical Jesus," 41.

is obliged, due to his methodology, to assign virtually every synoptic saying which quotes or comments upon Hebrew scripture to the post-resurrectional churches, how can he possibly infer exactly Jesus' attitudes to scripture and Torah? And without this determination it is impossible to compare and contrast this attitude with that of the rabbis since a comparison, like the tango, takes two. Käsemann's identification of specific "indisputably" authentic sayings of Jesus has fared no better in subsequent scholarship than has his general contrast with rabbinic attitudes to Torah.

We see in Käsemann, like Kähler, too strong a desire to distance Jesus from the Judaism of his day and an assumption of Jesus' uniqueness in person and mission. These are theological assumptions which have, in large measure, predetermined the "historical" reconstruction. Admittedly, Käsemann made no pretence at indifference to theological concerns; indeed, he begins by noting the theological implications of his enterprise and maintains this theme throughout. But the key events of revelation and soteriology (associated with the Christ of faith) can hardly be viewed as recoverable by the tools of objective historical inquiry. That situation of grace or guilt (καιρός), and the necessity for decision occasioned by revelation which Käsemann sees as essential to the difference between myth and history,[53] cannot be held as something discernible or recoverable by the tools of academic history. Why then Käsemann's insistence on this point? One may only speculate, but the theme would seem to provide a strong apologetic for the Christian tradition in the face of the doubts caused by Bultmann's radical historiography and the results of form criticism. Käsemann avoids tying his version of Christianity too closely with what he perceives to be the subjective evils of myth and docetism. Revelation must be provided with some concrete, objective grounding in historical events themselves. If one cannot provide such a grounding for the "atonement" as such, then the next best alternative would appear to be the teachings of Jesus. At heart, Käsemann seems unwilling to embrace Paul's total reliance upon the Christ of faith as sufficient grounding for religious theology and experience, fearing in this the evils of subjectivism, relativism and myth.

4. Burton Mack and Jesus the Cynic

I turn now to a more recent, representative reconstruction of "the historical Jesus," that of Burton Mack and his "Cynic" hypothesis. His entire thesis is dependent upon two factors: the rhetoric of the *chreiai* at the core of the pronouncement stories, and the recurrent themes which guide the social critique and behavioural recommendations for the Jesus movement as seen in the earliest level of Q.[54]

---

53 Käsemann, "Problem of the Historical Jesus," 31.
54 Burton L. Mack, "Q and a Cynic-Like Jesus" (in this volume).

4.1 The Chreiai

Mack begins with the pronouncement stories. Many of these units can be reduced to a single exchange of challenge and response which produces the anecdote or maxim (χρεία) at the core. He provides ten such *chreia*-reconstructions from Mark.[55] Mack notes that these stories are similar to large numbers of stories told about Cynics. Although these Greek stories were not, admittedly, confined to Cynic circles, they were more frequent in the Socratic, Cyrenaic and Cynic traditions. Socially, these stories witness to a type of game played between Cynic and society, with the goal being to catch the Cynic in a compromise. In return, the Cynic took these encounters as the opportunity to expose the ridiculousness of normal expectations. The anecdote was the perfect medium for distilling the essence of such exchanges.

Mack then provides examples of such Cynic exchanges, of which the following are particularly significant:

> [A] When censured for keeping bad company, Antisthenes replied, "Well, physicians attend their patients without catching the fever." (Diogenes Laertius 6.6)
> [B] When someone said to Antisthenes, "Many praise you," he replied, "Why, what wrong have I done?" (Diogenes Laertius 6.8)
> [C] When someone reproached him for frequenting unclean places, Diogenes replied that the sun also enters the privies without becoming defiled. (Diogenes Laertius 6.63)
> [D] Crates declared that ignominy and poverty were his native land, a country that fortune could never take captive. (Diogenes Laertius 6.93)

When put on the spot, the Cynic first identified the issue underlying the challenge, then shifted the order of discourse to find an acceptable example of this behaviour or attitude. As Mack notes, the anecdotes attributed to Jesus operate by the same principle. Hence, Mark 2:17, which shifts the issue of contamination from meal codes to medical practices, is similar to the logic displayed in the response of Antisthenes concerning physicians and patients (above, example A). Mark 7:15 is particularly close to Diogenes' response regarding social contamination (above, example C). Mark 9:35 and 10:18 are a critique of common social values regarding class and display a similarity to the story concerning Antisthenes being praised by many (above, example B). We might also note that Crates' remarks concerning poverty and ignominy bear a striking resemblance to the saying of Jesus regarding prophet and native land (Mark 6:4).

---

55 For the text of these *chreiai*, see Mack's article above.

Mack sees in these sayings a challenge for traditional portraits of Jesus. Regarding the Cynic-like anecdotes, he observes: "Were we not accustomed to hearing Jesus' words as sharp ethical injunction coming from the imperious founder of Christianity who steps forth with divine authority in the narrative gospels, the cleverness of these retorts might yet cause a smile or two."[56] These sayings thus suggest for Mack that at an early phase within the Jesus tradition "playful rejoinder may have been enough to justify an unconventional practice in the face of . . . convention."[57]

But can these sayings be ascribed (as Mack implies) to the historical Jesus? There is the initial problem of form: Mack begins by reconstructing from the more elaborate pronouncement stories the essential challenge and rejoinder. This reconstruction relies, in part, upon the notion of an ideal pure form—that what is logically the core of the unit (particularly in regards to content) must of necessity have formed a separate unit historically. This implies that the remainder of these units are subsequent elaboration. This is a view of tradition as a process of unilinear growth, a notion challenged particularly by Werner Kelber.[58] Even if one keeps to this unilinear pattern, an even greater objection to Mack's reconstruction in the case of Mark 7:15 follows from the parallel with the *Thomas* 14c. Here we find a parallel only to the aphorism at Mark 7:15, suggesting that this alone (without question/playful rejoinder structure) is the earliest recoverable core to the unit.

A similar objection must be raised regarding Mack's reconstruction of the Rich Young Man episode (Mark 10:17-22), which removes entirely the discussion of Torah (vv. 19-21) in favour of the question whether Jesus might be called "good." Indeed, both this narrative and the preceding one may be said to reveal similarity in theological and social setting with the "Great Commandment" (Mark 12:28-34) and (to a lesser extent) with the question on the resurrection (Mark 12:18-27). All these units raise the issue of Torah and its place within the social ethos of the Christian community. Despite the Hellenistic background of the form of these pronouncement stories, their place within the context of Judaism is well attested.[59] Debate regarding Torah, as evident from Galatians (cf. Acts 15), was a prime concern of early Christians during the late 40s and on into the sixth decade of the first century. It is difficult, based on the particular demands of distinctiveness, to place these units much earlier than this phase of the tradition. Indeed, their post-resurrection

---

56 Mack, "Cynic-Like Jesus," 31 (in this volume).

57 Mack, "Cynic-Like Jesus," 31 (in this volume).

58 Werner H. Kelber, *The Oral and the Written Gospel: The Hermeneutics of Speaking and Writing in the Synoptic Tradition, Mark, Paul, and Q* (Philadelphia: Fortress, 1983), 2-8.

59 See, e.g., H. Polano, *The Talmud: Selections from the Contents of that Ancient Book, its Commentaries, Teachings, Poetry, and Legends* (London: Frederick Warne, 1978 [1876]), 230.

origin is implied in Mack's own reconstruction of Mark 7:15 as the original *chreia*: "When asked why *they* [the Christian community] ate with unclean hands." This emphasis upon the actions of the disciples, a narrative stand-in for the Christian community itself, is evident also in the introductions to Mack's examples of the fasting and wedding guests episode (Mark 2:19) and plucking grain on the sabbath (Mark 2:27). We have already noted the problem of Mark 2:27 and its rabbinic parallels, and Mack's exegesis does not provide a route around this central impasse. Regarding these three units as a set, their post-resurrection origins as formal compositions were recognized by Bultmann, and I see no reason to re-evaluate his conclusion. Bultmann argues:

> Clearly the typical character of a controversy dialogue is most marked when a single action like plucking corn or healing on the Sabbath constitutes the starting-point rather than when the opponent merely fastens on some general attitude of the person he criticizes. This fact also explains why an effort is made to describe some particular action, even when it is obvious that only a general attitude is under discussion; and when that is done the symbolic presentation in an imaginary scene is bound to appear artificial, as in Mk. 2:15f, 18, 7:1f. Just as these latter situations are thus imaginary, i.e. not reports of historical occasions, but constructions giving lively expression to some idea in a concrete event—even so does the same judgment apply to those situations in which the reported action is in itself more likely, that is to say to the plucking of corn and the miracles of healing.[60]

Furthermore, regarding the particular problem of the role of the disciples in these narratives, Bultmann notes:

> that it was the Church that gave form to these stories, and—even in cases of unitary conception—did not without further ado reproduce historical events, is shown very clearly by the fact that the conduct of the disciples is defended. They pluck corn on the Sabbath, they do not fast as John's disciples do, they eat with unwashed hands—but was Jesus himself so correctly behaved in all these things that he was not attacked? And how can we explain the free behaviour of the disciples if he were so conservative? Or did no-one dare to launch a direct attack on him? But if that were so, why should they venture to do so when he healed on the Sabbath? No! It is the disciples who are attacked, i.e. it is the Church, which defends itself by appealing to its Master.[61]

Finally, there is the question concerning dining with tax collectors (Mark 2:17). We still are faced with the problem of composition: the introductory question itself must be held to be a secondary and post-resurrection introduction

---

60 Rudolf Bultmann, *History of the Synoptic Tradition*, trans. John Marsh (New York: Harper & Row, 1963), 39.

61 Bultmann, *History*, 48.

to the saying. The particular issue and the implied critique, although this time directed toward Jesus himself rather than the disciples, again places us in a situation similar to the controversy over plucking grain on the sabbath. The entire unit seeks to defend (allegedly antinomian) Christian practice on the basis of Jesus' own words and deeds. The saying which forms the conclusion to the unit has an almost exact parallel in the aphorism attributed to Antisthenes above (Diogenes Laertius 6.6). How can this situation be deemed in any way different from that of the Golden Rule (with the sole exception that the proverb in question finds its parallel in Greek literature rather than the apocrypha)? There is nothing distinctive in the use of this sentiment within the Jesus tradition and thus no compelling reason to attribute it to Jesus.

One further problem with Mack's reconstruction may be noted. Mack defines the particular logic of these Cynic-style *chreiai* as that of "cunning intelligence" ($\mu\tilde{\eta}\tau\iota\varsigma$). Yet there is no compelling reason to limit the cultural background of such a hermeneutic to that of the Cynics. Bultmann's discussion of the rabbinic apophthegms is instructive at this point:

> To illustrate the spirit of this sort of argument I quote the well-known saying of R. Joshua ben Hananiah (Berachot, 8b): "They asked him: 'If the salt is bad, how shall it be salted?' And he answered, 'With the afterbirth of a mule!' 'But does a mule have an afterbirth?' 'Very well, can salt become unsalted?'" Here the counter-question itself is attributed to the opponent by the Rabbi's answer. Yet the basic form is quite clear: an argument by means of a counter-question leading the opponent *ad absurdum*.[62]

If, as I have tried to demonstrate, these units do not meet the burden of distinctiveness and cannot be attributed to Jesus, why have they mistakenly been "authenticated"? The answer appears to lie in a particular "literalness" regarding the usual definition of "distinctiveness" when applying this criterion. Distinctiveness is usually thought to authenticate only those sayings which can be said to be distinctive relative to the main emphases of both first-century Judaism and the early churches. Sayings which accord with either of these two streams of tradition are, of necessity, suspected of originating within the stream of tradition with which a parallel can be demonstrated. But in defining distinctiveness scholars do not normally think to include the main emphases of various Hellenistic religions and philosophies. Hence, *a priori* we are faced with a situation where the methodology makes it far more "reasonable" to reconstruct a "historical Jesus" who is much more at home within Cynic or Stoic Hellenism than within first-century Judaism. Where Jesus sayings overlap with the Hebrew Bible or rabbinic material the unit is suspected of having been borrowed from the pre-existing cultural heritage and ascribed to him by the

---

62 Bultmann, *History*, 45.

post-resurrectional churches; but where Jesus traditions show an equal degree of parallel with Cynic (or Stoic, etc.) philosophy, scholars seem far more willing to authenticate this material.

4.2 Aphorisms and Elaborations

Mack then turns to an examination of the aphorisms. Kloppenborg's argument that the wisdom traditions formed the earliest layer within the sayings document (Q^1)[63] is fundamental, and Mack notes that these sayings share common tenor, content and formal characteristics. These sapiential clusters are, in fact, examples of those rhetorical composition which the Greeks called elaboration. Within this stream of tradition Mack notes the following (Jesus Seminar polling result noted in square brackets):

> Blessed poor, Q 6:20 [red]
> Measure returned, Q 6:38 [grey]
> Blind leading blind, Q 6:39 [grey]
> Tree and its fruits, Q 6:43 [grey]
> Foxes have dens, Q 6:58 [pink]
> Ask and receive, Q 11:10 [pink]
> Hidden revealed, Q 12:2 [pink]
> Anxieties, Q 12:23-24 [pink]
> Treasure and heart, Q 12:34 [grey]
> Exalted humbled, Q 14:11 [grey]
> Saltless salt, Q 14:34 [pink]
> Serving two masters, Q 16:13 [pink].[64]

As Mack observes, these sayings have close ties with the proverbial literature of numerous eras and cultures; their distinctive character is found in their unnerving and humorous edge.

> These sayings are not unusually clever. Many are simply versions of age-old proverbial lore, and all need some life situation in which to score their point. But they are pungent observations, slightly unnerving, and mildly humorous in the sense that insights about human behaviour and desire have been pressed to the point of extremes, if not absurdity. They illustrate the aphoristic nature of the wisdom attributed to Jesus and bristle with the pointed style of Cynic maxims.[65]

---

63 See John S. Kloppenborg, *The Formation of Q: Trajectories in Ancient Wisdom Collections* (Philadelphia: Fortress, 1987).

64 Mack, "Cynic-Like Jesus" (oral form of the paper, 1993). For the results of Jesus Seminar votes, see Robert Funk and Roy Hoover, eds., *The Five Gospels: The Search for the Authentic Words of Jesus* (New York: Macmillan, 1993).

65 Mack, "Cynic-Like Jesus," 32 (in this volume).

The Cynic flavour of these sayings is enhanced, according to Mack, when we also consider hortatory Q^1 sayings. Among this class Mack notes the following (again with Jesus Seminar voting results added in square brackets):

Rejoice: reproach, Q 6:22 [grey]
Bless: curse, Q 6:28 [grey]
Offer other cheek, Q 6:29 [red]
Give to beggars, Q 6:30 [red]
Judge not, Q 6:37 [black]
Speck and timber, Q 6:42 [pink]
Leave the dead, Q 9:60 [pink]
Lamb and wolves, Q 10:3 [black]
Money, bag, sandals, Q 10:4 [grey]
At house: eating, Q 10:7 [grey]
Ask and receive, Q 11:9 [pink]
Fear not, Q 12:7 [pink]
Anxieties, Q 12:22 [black]
Heavenly riches, Q 12:33 [grey]
Judge yourselves, Luke 12:57 [black]
Hating family, Q 14:26 [pink].[66]

According to Mack, these sayings regard both house and public areas as places of encounter with those who (in distinction to the Jesus-tradition people) follow conventional codes. They thus witness to a conflict between counter culture and dominant culture: "The Jesus people were apparently taking up what we would call an alternative life-style. And their behaviour was causing a bit of friction. What they were doing was understood to be risky, but worth it. The advice was to be cautious, but also courageous. Take care, don't worry. Just make sure you do it."[67] Mack's analysis of these sayings indicates the following program: a critique of the rich (and their wealth), hypocrisy and pretension; fearlessness before the powerful; the renunciation of the usual necessary supports for life; voluntary poverty; fearlessness and the absence of anxiety; unashamed begging; an etiquette for responding to public reproach; nonretaliation; disentanglement from family ties; an independent vocation; personal integrity and authenticity; a natural life at any cost; reliance on the natural order; single-mindedness in the pursuit of God's reign; and confidence in God's care. This profile fits the pattern of the Cynics, and had this been the only distinguishing feature of the Jesus movement they would have been regarded as such. The major problem with the Cynic hypothesis, for Mack, is the way in which these sayings have been elaborated and taken up into expanded units (the expanded pronouncement

---

66 Mack, "Cynic-Like Jesus" (oral form of the paper, 1993). See also Funk and Hoover, *Five Gospels*.
67 Mack, "Cynic-Like Jesus," 32 (in this volume).

stories and the compositional clusters of Q). Here we in fact see a return to conventionality: "This feature of the Jesus traditions is odd, for it makes use of conventional logic to support a rhetoric intended to subvert that logic. Cynic-style rejoinders and aphorisms do not call for elaboration. They make their point by inviting insight. It is maxims, cases, codes and rules that need to be given firm foundation."[68] This indicates a subsequent stage within the Jesus traditions when the Cynic-like social stance was left behind, a process seen in the prophetic-eschatological redaction of Q, in the pronouncement stories with their attempted defence against various accusations brought against the community, and in the canonical gospels.

Two major developments explain this shift to a more serious and judgmental tone. First, the Cynic-like behaviour was soon turned into a code for authentic membership within the Jesus movement (e.g., the Cynic-like injunction to bless those who curse you became the command to love one's enemies, while the saying on the physician became expanded with the theme of calling sinners rather than the righteous). These kinds of elaborations demonstrate that the Jesus people were now taking themselves seriously as a movement and thus needed standards or codes of definition. This act of community boundary setting, for Mack, helps distinguish the movement from the Cynics.

Second, the Jesus people soon became preoccupied with the differences between their group and other such social systems which were governed by normal taboos against cross-cultural, cross-gender and cross-class association. "Especially prevalent," Mack tells us, "are the objections they took seriously that came from a Jewish point of view, objections that were grounded in a Pharisaic view of piety appropriate to Jewish identity."[69] This later stage, therefore, represents the group's defence in the face of opposition due to their inclusiveness despite traditional taboos. This very inclusiveness, in fact, described the group: "The Jesus people said, in effect, that, yes, they did have tax collectors and sinners among them (and Syrians and women, outcasts and other unlikely sorts) but that that was just the point of their movement. So the Cynic-style subversion of the dominant systems of purity and/or honour-shame was not all there was to the Jesus movement."[70]

Yet this aspect of Mack's reconstruction is also problematic. There is (as with Käsemann's use of wisdom sayings) the difficulty posed for the authenticity of this material by the sheer number of proverbial parallels. Mack is forced to admit that many of these sayings are simply "versions of age-old proverbial lore" which need a concrete life-situation for their point. Mack goes on to differentiate these sayings on the grounds of their "pungent" and "unnerving" character. But this "pungent" and "unnerving" aspect of these sayings is

---

68 Mack, "Cynic-Like Jesus," 33 (in this volume).
69 Mack, "Cynic-Like Jesus," 34 (in this volume).
70 Mack, "Cynic-Like Jesus," 34 (in this volume).

actually no different from the hermeneutics common to many oral traditions. As Kelber has shown, oral transmission is heavily influenced by audience and social circumstance. Sayings must therefore be memorable in order to survive the transmissional process; thus, such features as exaggeration, shock, reversal and antithetic parallelism are common to the oral medium. As Kelber states:

> Remembrance and transmission depended on the ability to articulate a message in such a way that it found an echo in people's hearts and minds. Primarily those sayings, miracle stories, parables, and apophthegmatic stories will have had a chance of survival that could become a focus of identification for speakers and hearers alike. This is not to dismiss the possibility that a group retained words precisely because they were alien or even offensive to its experience. The very oddness of the message could render it unforgettable. But a genuine incentive for transmission will have arisen from identification with words, not from a lack of it. In short, oral transmission is controlled by the law of *social identification* rather than by the technique of verbatim memorization.[71]

Kelber goes on to examine Gerd Theissen's thesis that wandering charismatics were responsible for the synoptic sayings which offend against the normal tendency to belong to family and kin and the respect for property and wealth (e.g., Luke 9:58, 60; 14:26; 18:25). This is a particularly significant discussion given Theissen's belief in a Cynic background to many of these sayings. Kelber sees this "antisocial" gospel as appealing most naturally to the economically and socially disenfranchised who lived on the periphery of society, especially the rebellious country folk. As Kelber argues:

> These were the people predisposed by their very experience as outsiders to perceive and accept the ethical radicalism of poverty, homelessness, rejection, and break with family ties. The social milieu for transmitting these antisocial sayings will therefore have been to a large degree the unsettled and—for established society—unsettling fringe, the margin of society. There the people lived who spoke and listened to the antisocial gospel, not because they studied and memorized it, but because it was true to their lives.[72]

He then notes that it is not possible to limit the transmission of these sayings to one social group, the charismatic itinerants.

> These prophets will have been the principal, but not necessarily the exclusive, carriers of the antisocial message. Experience teaches us that one can well remember and reproduce information without living out its content in one's personal life. By the same token, members of the more settled classes could

---

71 Kelber, *Oral and Written Gospel*, 24.
72 Kelber, *Oral and Written Gospel*, 25.

identify with these sayings as a matter of principle, and still not apply them in actuality. The concept of *social identification* allows characteristic speech forms to serve as focus of identification for more than one social group. The question is thereby raised about the form-critical thesis of *setting in life*, the notion that forms of speech are tied to specific social settings.[73]

These considerations raise serious problems for Mack's Cynic hypothesis, which ties these common proverbial sayings to such a specific cultural background. In point of fact, these sayings find a natural home within a number of social and cultural settings, and scholars must be careful about inferring a literal correspondence between saying and social setting.

It is also appropriate to reflect on the major shift in interpretation that has taken place from Käsemann to Mack regarding these wisdom sayings. Although Käsemann commented only briefly on a few of these traditions (as compared to Mack), the degree of difference between these two scholars regarding what these sayings tell of Jesus' teachings is striking. We see in Käsemann little hint of Mack's counter-cultural program of the marginalized people's critique of the powerful. Such discrepancies in interpretation elicit the question, what has changed so markedly to account for this: the sayings themselves or the social setting of the interpreters?

If we examine Mack's reconstruction more closely we see that, in fact, what is being offered is just as much a social program for Mack's contemporary audience as a reconstruction of the first-century Jesus tradition in its historical setting. Put another way, what is the appeal of Mack's reconstruction and what needs in his audience does it meet? Certain themes stand out: a counter-cultural critique of the rich and powerful (from the marginalized) and a radical questioning of the usual norms of society; inclusivity; nonconformism; an overthrow of status and privilege; equity; acceptance. These are the very goals of social action which have increasingly come to the fore since the 1960s and they thus speak well to the post-Käsemann era when both Christianity and the academy have become increasingly marginalized in Western society. Vietnam, Watergate, feminism and the decline of America's pre-eminence in the world all seem to have had their effect and are duly reflected in the exegesis. The distinction between the earliest ("authentic") stage and the later ("secondary") stage is particularly telling in this regard. Its appeal is simple: the advent of eschatology, for Mack, represents the group becoming more "judgmental" and "conventional" in its stance as it began to take itself more (too) seriously. What better way to inculcate a non-judgmental ("I'm OK, You're OK") attitude within his audience?

It should come as no surprise, therefore, that similar descriptions of the "true historical meaning" of the Jesus sayings are to be found throughout

---

73 Kelber, *Oral and Written Gospel*, 25-26.

scholarship covering a variety of presumed cultural backgrounds for the tradition. As noted above, following Theissen's lead Kelber (despite the fact that he accepts a core of eschatology within the earliest tradition) can speak in similar terms of the Jesus tradition as people predisposed by their outsider status to accept the "ethical radicalism of poverty, homelessness, rejection, and break with family ties."[74] For his part Richard Horsley, who also rejects the Cynic hypothesis and instead locates the Jesus traditions within a popular tradition of Moses and Elijah-Elisha,[75] can give the following reconstruction of the early Jesus tradition: "The different strands of the synoptic tradition share a conception of renewed community as familial, but with sharp criticism of the traditional patriarchal forms. . . . [T]he new communities are apparently those of siblings, with no authority figure prevailing among them . . . [;] clearly, relations were supposed to be egalitarian in the community, which was conceived of as an extended nonpatriarchal 'family' of 'siblings.' The movement rejected rank, power, and prestige, valuing instead service to the community."[76] Attentive readers will undoubtedly be able to expand the list of scholarly parallels. The point can be driven home more forcefully when we compare the exposition of Jeremias on the theme of "the Church" as the new family of God, noting particularly how the interpretation actually supports a social hierarchy of authority and status among early Christians: "In the eschatological family God is the father (Matt. 23:9), Jesus the master of the house, his followers the other occupants (Matt. 10:25). The older women who hear his word are his mothers, the men and youths his brothers (Mark 3:34 par.). And at the same time they are all the little ones, the children, indeed the *nēpioi* of the family (Matt. 11:25) whom Jesus addresses as children, although in age they are adults."[77]

5. Conclusion: Christological Functions of the "Historical Jesus"

Kähler, in an ironic sense, was prophetic in regarding the entire life-of-Jesus movement as a blind alley,[78] and one can only speculate what might have been had he followed through consistently on this essential insight. But he is also correct in his insistence that "we cannot reject this movement without understanding what is legitimate in it."[79]

---

74 Kelber, *Oral and Written Gospel*, 25.
75 Richard A. Horsley, *Sociology and the Jesus Movement* (New York: Crossroad, 1989), 112, 116-19.
76 Horsley, *Sociology*, 123.
77 Jeremias, *New Testament Theology*, 169.
78 Kähler, *So-Called Historical Jesus*, 46.
79 Kähler, *So-Called Historical Jesus*, 46.

What, then, is the positive contribution of the "historical-Jesus" movement? Its origins lie in the quest to distinguish the human being, Jesus of Nazareth, from the subsequent biblical portrait of the Christ of faith. The naïve identification of the two, which served Christendom well for almost 1700 years, suffered a severe shock in the Enlightenment, and Strauss was fundamentally correct in separating the two in order to allow the tradition to adapt to its modern setting. In this sense, the oft-observed tension between the two concepts, with the "historical Jesus" having (at times) an implicit anti-dogmatic character, has served as an essential source of renewal within the churches. This is true not only for Strauss and the 19th-century biographers but also for Kähler, Käsemann and more recent reconstructions. Undoubtedly, the view of biblical authority has changed and we do not find in Mack and most contemporary scholars the insistence upon exclusivity of revelation and mission so prevalent in Kähler and Käsemann. Yet we still have within virtually all reconstructions Kähler's fundamental dilemma: "*Why* do we seek to know the figure of Jesus? I rather think it is because we believe him when he says, 'He who has seen me has seen the Father' (John 14:9)."[80]

Further, every religion must adapt to its ever-changing social environment and thus reform itself and grow. One can see in many reconstructions of "the historical Jesus" an attempt to play off the "teachings of Jesus" against more traditional and dogmatic understandings of the tradition, and thereby ward off intolerance and fanaticism. Thus, to the extent that "the historical Jesus" allows for renewal and modification of the tradition it undoubtedly serves an essential function in defending against fanaticism and intolerance (both within the individual and within the tradition at large).

There is another aspect to the "historical Jesus" as an agent of renewal. A psychological dimension is at work here. When we recall the mythic dimensions of the narrative Christ within the gospels and the parallels between Jesus and the hero pattern of antiquity we have another clue to the enduring appeal of the "historical Jesus." In her examination of fairy tales, the Jungian analyst Marie-Louise von Franz found it difficult to avoid treating the central heroes as human beings. She concluded from this that these characters are psychological images which demonstrate the ego-building tendency. She goes on to identify these figures with the archetype of the Self, which has as its main function the supporting of ego consciousness.[81] Owing to the fact that human beings are able to deviate from their instincts (thereby causing a neurosis), it is important to have models or patterns which demonstrate the ego functioning in accordance with the instincts. This model is provided by the hero of myths and folktales,

---

80 Kähler, *So-Called Historical Jesus*, 58.
81 Marie-Louise von Franz, *The Psychological Meaning of Redemption Motifs in Fairytales* (Toronto: Inner City, 1980), 21.

thereby "reminding one of the right way of behaving in accordance with the totality of the human being."[82] The "historical Jesus" may be said to provide a similar model for modern Christians. No longer able to accept at face value the model provided by the narrative Christ of the gospels, with its mythic overtones, contemporary Christians have increasingly turned to the "historical Jesus." Yet this Jesus, reconstructed by the canons of academic history, does not emerge as a mere flesh and blood human being. Inevitably there is something within the reconstruction worthy of emulation and allegiance which provides a model for imitation and discipleship.

Another clue to the function of the "historical Jesus" is to be found in the very term "historical" itself. This aspect of the concept is particularly evident in Käsemann's passionate desire to protect Christianity from the suspicion of being a "myth." It is often said that Christianity is a historical religion; implicit in this statement is that it is a tradition grounded upon events which "really" happened in human history and which (by implication) can be recovered and verified via academic history. Frequently implicit here is a comparison of superiority to other religions which are not "historical" and which, by implication, are based only upon "myth." With the advent of the Enlightenment the "historicity" of the central elements of the Christ of faith (atoning death, resurrection and anticipated parousia) could no longer be maintained. Similarly, large portions of the gospel narratives came under suspicion: exorcisms, healings and nature miracles, to name but the most obvious cases. What then could be said to be the *historical* element of Christianity? Simply this: that the proclamation of the crucified and risen one pointed to a real human being in history. Hence the continuing desire to recover the "historical Jesus": the reconstruction of the human life behind the kerygma is intended, implicitly, to ground and thereby "authenticate" the power of the resurrected Christ of faith.

These benefits have been purchased at a cost. Increasingly, scholars must focus their attention upon an ever-diminishing core of sayings from the synoptic-*Thomas* tradition. What then of miracles, exorcisms, eschatological-apocalyptic sayings, the passion narrative and the resurrection? This tension and problem has only increased over the 20th century as ever more sayings and traditions have fallen by the wayside. In Kähler we see a brazen and clumsy attempt to protect the vast majority of the gospel traditions from the scalpel of historical criticism. In this case the tensions could be minimized. Jesus' uniqueness must, above all else, be a fundamental principle of the investigation and the use of "historical analogy" must be suspended. In Käsemann, we detect a similar desire to maintain the uniqueness of Jesus' mission and purpose: above all, Jesus' sublime freedom from Torah and his authority as one surpassing Moses must be upheld. Contemporary scholars are more modest in their claims

---

82   Von Franz, *Redemption Motifs*, 21.

at this point, yet the insistence on Jesus' radical egalitarianism and his thoroughgoing critique of status, power, privilege and patriarchy establish for modern audiences another form of uniqueness of mission and message no less "authoritarian" and "christological." Increasingly, however, scholarship has had to eliminate from its discussion of the "historical Jesus" the miracles, exorcisms, cross and resurrection traditions. These traditions can only be brought into the discussion of the "historical Jesus" via crude and ineffective apologetics for their authenticity which undermine the entire methodological procedure. Yet these traditions, as religious literature, had their proper place and meaning within early Christianity. In Pauline and Johannine Christianity they formed the central message of the Christian gospel and overshadowed completely the Jesus of the synoptic sayings tradition. Even in the canonical gospels, the sayings are given in a narrative of cross and resurrection which subordinates them to the logic of the mythological Christ of faith. If the "historical Jesus" actually serves christological functions, it must be admitted that it now does so divorced almost entirely from the Christ of faith and represents a narrowing of the tradition which has only emerged in the last forty or so years. Hence, we can now appreciate a central concern of both Kähler and Käsemann in a new light. Kähler complained that the life-of-Jesus movement divorced Jesus' teachings from his importance (as Christ of faith) and dissected the Bible.[83] Käsemann, similarly, noted the "impoverishment and distortion of the gospel which takes place wherever the question of the Jesus of history is treated as decisive for theology and preaching."[84] In a more contemporary setting, the rise of literary criticism undoubtedly serves as a compensating trend within the academy to preserve the mythic and narrative elements within the tradition.

Another effect of this apologetic desire to ground "revelation" in objective (and academically-recoverable) history is the treatment of other world religions, most notably Judaism. In this regard, the quest for the historical Jesus implicitly serves to establish a claim to superiority over other religions. These traditions must, in effect, be kept at bay and subordinated. Christianity must not be made to suffer their fate and be seen to be founded on such undesirable mechanisms as myth or subjectivity.

There is also Kähler's concern that subjecting faith to the dictates of academic history creates a social hierarchy within the churches and subordinates the vast majority of Christians to a professional elite. This impasse was not resolved by the so-called new quest, and we have here a deep irony. Despite the great frequency of the themes of "egalitarianism" and the "critique of status and privilege" within contemporary expositions of Jesus' message, the historical

---

83 Kähler, *So-Called Historical Jesus*, 46.
84 Käsemann, "Problem of the Historical Jesus," 15.

Jesus by necessity creates just such a hierarchical social division. Scholarship and the academy, by its very nature, is a hierarchy of learning which in turn creates a social hierarchy of power and status. In this sense, we might even regard expositions of the theme of "egalitarianism" and "status critique" as a compensation mechanism which allows scholars the best of both worlds: the social acceptability of consciously-stated striving toward inclusivity and equality, with, at the same time, a *de facto* social hierarchy of status.

Finally, there is the reverse side to the use of the historical Jesus as an agent of renewal and growth. Kähler saw clearly that many 19th-century lives were in fact social programs and little more than propagandizing tracts. There is in this a certain danger of not recognizing a christological construct for what it is: the claim to objectivity for the historical Jesus makes a christological construct more palatable to the general public. In this sense, I believe it best to reserve the term "the human Jesus" to refer to the actual human being who was born in Galilee and crucified in Jerusalem, and thereby regard "the historical Jesus" (with the implicit attempt to reconstruct the message of the human being) as a christological construct. Inevitably, such reconstructions must transgress the boundaries of historical reconstruction and supplement themselves with christological speculations. Furthermore, with the ever-changing "assured" results of higher criticism, Christianity became increasingly subject to the instability of faddism. Indeed, today it is only a slight exaggeration to say that with contemporary reconstructions of Jesus the peasant, and the trend toward viewing him as a proclaimer of social critique, we have now come full circle from the mid-19th century. While religions need a mechanism for adaptation and growth, Kähler correctly noted the opposite need for stability, thereby recognizing the problem of making faith dependent upon historical criticism. His insistence upon the "Biblical Christ" is but a recognition that even a "historical" religion such as Christianity must also have a grounding in a living spiritual tradition.

21. Continuing Historical-Jesus Studies: Context

Robert L. Webb

Larry Hurtado's essay surveys the work of eight scholars who have written monographs on the subject of the historical Jesus between 1984 and 1994: Ed Sanders (1985), Geza Vermes (1993), Ben Witherington (1990), John Meier (1991), Marcus Borg (1984, 1987), Richard Horsley (1987), Seán Freyne (1988) and John Dominic Crossan (1991). His examination of each work focuses on three areas: the methodology used, the picture of Jesus produced and the purpose or hermeneutical concern of the author. Hurtado concludes that in all three areas each scholar is significantly different from the others and that there is no consensus emerging among them. Hurtado does, however, demonstrate three unifying observations on the work of these eight scholars: the diverse character of the evidence, the importance of fully interacting with other scholars and viewpoints and the futility of claiming to approach historical-Jesus research without religious or existential commitments. He closes with the methodological observation that historical-Jesus research is like reconstructing an original reading in text criticism: all variants in the Jesus tradition need to be taken into consideration, and the reconstructed historical Jesus that best explains all the variants is the preferred picture of Jesus.

The essay is most helpful. Hurtado's comparison of eight scholars in these three areas provides a necessary matrix for evaluating where scholarship has come from and where it needs to go in historical-Jesus research, and he makes some constructive suggestions to guide this ongoing process.

I would like to interact with Hurtado's essay on two points in order to place it within a larger context. The first concerns the focus of the essay: it presents itself as a taxonomy, that is, a classification of individual items into groups based on similarities. Hurtado's taxonomy of these eight scholars consists of eight different categories: for Sanders, Jesus was the restorationist prophet; for Vermes, Jesus was the charismatic *hasid*; for Witherington, the messiah; for Meier, the charismatic eschatological prophet; for Borg, the social visionary; for Horsley, the social revolutionary; for Freyne, the Jewish universalist; and for Crossan, the Jewish Cynic. What Hurtado offers is a sound description of the individual items. But it is not, in fact, a taxonomy, for it does not seek deeper, underlying similarities among some of these scholars; rather, it stresses their differences. It is right and proper to observe differences between these scholars, but the existence of these differences does not mean that a taxonomy is impossible. In fact there are several possibilities for a taxonomy of recent Jesus research, of which I suggest only two.

First, one can perceive similarities among some scholars with respect to the overarching model used to portray Jesus. For example, among the eight scholars Hurtado surveys, three (Sanders, Meier, Horsley) explicitly use the prophetic model for portraying Jesus. We could, of course, add the names of other recent scholars who would concur with this overarching model, including as examples Maurice Casey and David Kaylor.[1] In addition, while among the eight scholars surveyed only Crossan argues for a Cynic model, other scholars could be included to form a group within a historical-Jesus taxonomy, such as Gerald Downing and Burton Mack.[2] Similarly, a group could be observed among those who stress the charismatic element in the life of Jesus, including Vermes, Meier and Borg.

A second possibility for a taxonomy of recent Jesus research is one which, rather than grouping scholars based on a similarity (as above), would place scholars along an axis which identifies a continuum with respect to a particular issue in historical-Jesus research. A number of such axes could be combined to form a more complex matrix. For example, one axis might be the extent to which eschatology (and which form of eschatology) played a role in the life and teaching of Jesus. Sanders and Meier would be placed toward one end of this axis while Borg and Crossan toward the other. The other scholars could be located somewhere in between. Examples of other axes one might use include the following questions: Does the concern or vision of Jesus have an individualistic focus or a corporate/national focus? Do Jesus' concerns concentrate primarily around religious or socio-political issues? To what extent does each scholar express hermeneutical concerns, and to what extent do these concerns shape his/her picture of Jesus?

This last suggestion leads to the second point with which I would like to interact, and that is the matter of a scholar's hermeneutical concerns. It is worthy of note that this observation has been made in other essays in this volume. It is long overdue for biblical scholars to admit and incorporate into scholarly endeavours the principle that we cannot do detached, "objective" history—there is no such thing! I would echo Hurtado's call to scholars that we become more self-conscious of our personal existential concerns, that we indicate candidly what these concerns are, and that we demonstrate in our work the ability to take these concerns into account and offset their effects in our work. A characteristic of some forms of postmodern thought is an appreciation

---

1   P. Maurice Casey, *From Jewish Prophet to Gentile God: The Origins and Development of New Testament Christology* (Louisville: Westminster/John Knox, 1991); R. David Kaylor, *Jesus the Prophet: His Vision of the Kingdom on Earth* (Louisville: Westminster/John Knox, 1994). By limiting himself to these eight scholars, Hurtado may have unnecessarily stressed differences between scholars; casting a wider net would have found other scholars with points of similarity in their portrayals of Jesus.

2   F. Gerald Downing, *Jesus and the Threat of Freedom* (London: SCM, 1987), and *Christ and the Cynics: Jesus and Other Radical Preachers in First Century Tradition* (Sheffield: JSOT, 1988); Burton L. Mack, *A Myth of Innocence: Mark and Christian Origins* (Philadelphia: Fortress, 1988).

that personal engagement with the object being studied can be a strength rather than a weakness.

Hurtado examines the hermeneutical concerns of each of the eight scholars surveyed. For some—especially Witherington and Borg,[3] to a lesser extent Vermes and Horsley—the hermeneutical concerns were obvious. But I found myself less convinced by Hurtado's observations about some of the other scholars, such as Meier and Freyne. Meier, for example, recognizes this issue and does essentially what Hurtado has called for scholars to do.[4] Yet Hurtado observes, concerning Meier: "it seems to me nevertheless that one can surmise some existential and hermeneutical concerns at work. . . . [T]he strong denial of the revolutionary and the social-reformer Jesus cohere with and likely serve a religious and social posture that rejects either option in the name of Jesus today." I would agree with Hurtado that this is a hermeneutical *implication* of Meier's work, but I am not convinced that it is Meier's own hermeneutical *concern*. Whatever stance Meier takes personally on this issue, what he argues about the teaching of Jesus would have hermeneutical significance. So I am left with the question of how to distinguish the hermeneutical *concern* of the scholar who writes the monograph about Jesus from the hermeneutical *implication* observed by another scholar who reads the same monograph.

---

3   For further insight into Marcus Borg's hermeneutical concerns see his "Me and Jesus: The Journey Home," *The Fourth R* 6/4 (July-August 1993): 3-9, and *Meeting Jesus Again for the First Time: The Historical Jesus and the Heart of Contemporary Faith* (San Francisco: HarperCollins, 1993).

4   John P. Meier, *A Marginal Jew: Rethinking the Historical Jesus*; Volume 1: *The Roots of the Problem and the Person* (New York: Doubleday, 1991), 4-6.

22. A Taxonomy of Recent Historical-Jesus Work

Larry W. Hurtado

1. Introduction

It is widely reported that we are in the midst of a revived and large-scale scholarly effort to investigate Jesus of Nazareth historically. The ample flow of major publications on Jesus has also prompted a number of other recent efforts to log and characterize the current enterprise.[1] The importance of the historical issues and the continuing pace of major scholarly work of which we must take account also prompt—indeed require—continuing attempts, such as the present essay, to assist in digesting and assessing what is being done.

In considering what has been called a recent "renaissance" (Borg) and "explosion" (Charlesworth) in Jesus research, three questions immediately come to mind. What historical factors have generated this phenomenon? Is there evidence that this renewed scholarly effort reflects, is producing, or is leading toward, a broad agreement on approach and results? If not, are there at least some partial gains to be derived from the current flurry of publications?

Several others have addressed the first question, and their thoughts are easily found.[2] The leading factors come readily to mind. Although it is increasingly common to find observers distinguishing Jesus research of the last decade or two, we probably have to set these works in the context of the larger post-World War II period. Early on, there was the theological course-modification regarding the importance of the historical Jesus among leading

---

1   Of these, note the following in particular: Craig A. Evans, *Life of Jesus Research: An Annotated Bibliography* (Leiden: Brill, 1989), covering work from 1768-1987; Stephen Neill and N. T. Wright, *The Interpretation of the New Testament 1861-1986*, 2nd ed. (Oxford: Oxford University Press, 1988), esp. Wright's analysis on 379-403; Daniel J. Harrington, "The Jewishness of Jesus: Facing Some Problems," *Catholic Biblical Quarterly* 49 (1987): 1-13; N. T. Wright, "Quest for the Historical Jesus," in David Noel Freedman et al., eds., *The Anchor Bible Dictionary* (New York: Doubleday, 1992), vol. 3, 796-802; Colin Brown, "Historical Jesus, Quest of," in J. Green and S. McKnight, eds., *Dictionary of Jesus and the Gospels* (Downers Grove: Inter-Varsity, 1992), 326-41; Marcus J. Borg, "A Renaissance in Jesus Studies," *Theology Today* 45 (1988): 280-92, and "Portraits of Jesus in Contemporary North American Scholarship," *Harvard Theological Review* 84 (1991): 1-22; James H. Charlesworth, "The Foreground of Christian Origins and the Commencement of Jesus Research," in his *Jesus' Jewishness: Exploring the Place of Jesus within Early Judaism* (New York: Crossroad, 1991), 63-83; Werner Georg Kümmel, "Jesusforschung seit 1981," *Theologische Rundschau* 53 (1988): 229-49; 54 (1989): 1-53; 55 (1990): 21-45; 56 (1991): 27-63, 391-420. See also the collection of essays edited by Bruce Chilton and Craig A. Evans, *Studying the Historical Jesus: Evaluations of the State of Current Research* (Leiden: Brill, 1994); and Marcus J. Borg, *Jesus in Contemporary Scholarship* (Valley Forge: Trinity Press International, 1994).

2   See, e.g., Wright's analysis in *Interpretation of the New Testament*, 379-403.

members of the Bultmann school, then taken up by North American Bultmannians such as James Robinson and Robert Funk. In addition, there were major archaeological finds, in particular the Nag Hammadi codex cache, the Qumran scrolls and the burgeoning of Israeli-sponsored archaeological work at various sites, all of which contributed to a renewed effort at setting Jesus in a more richly-informed historical context. The last forty years have also witnessed a changing demography of scholars in biblical criticism, once almost entirely a liberal Protestant enterprise, but since 1945 increasingly characterized by the participation of major Catholic and Jewish scholars—still more recently by others such as "Evangelicals," and even those who profess to live outside religiousness of any kind. Finally, with the eclipse of the biblical theology movement, we have seen a broad renewal of a historical investigation of the New Testament that resembles somewhat the history-of-religions endeavour of the early part of this century, and current historical-Jesus work is surely a reflection of this wider tidal change in the field.

This first question about the larger historical background of current Jesus research is relevant, to be sure, but for several reasons it is not my main concern. In this essay, I shall concern myself more with the present status and future prospects of historical-Jesus work. In the first section, I describe briefly the efforts of eight scholars who have made recent book-length contributions, focusing on the approach taken, the picture of Jesus produced, and the explicit or implicit purposes addressed in each study. To anticipate the results of this section, I shall demonstrate that these scholars exhibit significant differences in all three regards, and that no consensus is in sight. In the second section, I propose some points that we can learn from these works for the future pursuit of historical investigation of Jesus.

2. Jesus Research: 1984-93

As already indicated, one could justifiably refer to a post-World War II resurgence of scholarly work on the historical Jesus.[3] It is also increasingly common for recent observers to distinguish three major periods of Jesus research: the "old quest," documented famously by Schweitzer;[4] the "new quest," a movement among Bultmann's students and those influenced by them heralded by James Robinson;[5] and a subsequent approach often dated from the early 1970s, which Tom Wright has called the "third quest." Charlesworth

---

3   See, e.g., John P. Meier, "Reflections on Jesus-of-History Research Today," in Charlesworth, *Jesus' Jewishness*, 84-86.

4   Albert Schweitzer, *The Quest of the Historical Jesus: A Critical Study of its Progress from Reimarus to Wrede*, trans. W. Montgomery (New York: Macmillan, 1968 [1906]).

5   James M. Robinson, *A New Quest of the Historical Jesus* (London: SCM, 1966 [1959]).

labels work of the last couple of decades as "Jesus research" and means thereby
to distinguish it from the old and new "quests."[6]

Although one must be careful not to oversimplify, one can distinguish the
most current period of historical-Jesus research from the "new quest" of the
1950s and 1960s. In the last twenty years or so, historical-Jesus research has
taken a new turn in the road. Three characteristics of this newer stage of work
in particular can be cited. (1) Unlike the "new quest," the more recent
discussion is not simply an "in-house" Christian debate over the role of
historical-Jesus knowledge in Christian faith and theology, but is now a more
diverse enterprise involving scholars of various orientations and with broader
or more diverse hermeneutical agenda. (2) The newer Jesus research often
incorporates more programmatically a wider range of historical data and
questions, in particular archaeological data and questions about the social,
political, economic, geographical and religious settings of Jesus' life, often
drawing upon the data, insights and theories of other disciplines (especially the
social sciences). (3) The newer Jesus research reflects recently-(re)opened
debates about such important issues as what sources are to be used, what model
of first-century Palestinian Jewish life we are to employ, and what model(s) of
the development of early Christian groups we are to use in assessing the impact
of Jesus on his earliest followers.

Accepting, then, a distinguishable modern period of Jesus research, I wish
now to analyze some of its major and most recent contributors. To keep the
present discussion manageable, I have confined the coverage to book-length
works published between 1984-93. To be sure, this involves omitting other
notable works of a slightly earlier vintage,[7] but those dealt with here offer a
sufficient body of work on which to proceed. Also, limiting our coverage to this

---

6   Charlesworth, "Foreground," 78-83. "The singular most important difference between the
    quest and Jesus research, which began about 1980, is that during the former periods, both
    the old and the new quest, scholars were searching for Jesus. Now, scholars find themselves
    bumping into pre-70 Palestinian phenomena. . . . Jesus research is not a search for the
    historical Jesus. It is a response to many stimuli, some deriving from the intracanonical
    writings, including Paul's letters, others from the extracanonical documents, still others
    from amazingly unexpected archaeological discoveries, which are both literary and non-
    literary" (82-83).
7   I note in this category esp. Ben F. Meyer, *The Aims of Jesus* (London: SCM, 1979); John
    Kenneth Riches, *Jesus and the Transformation of Judaism* (London: Darton, Longman &
    Todd, 1980); Maria Trautmann, *Zeichenhafte Handlungen Jesu: Ein Beitrag zur Frage nach
    dem geschichtlichen Jesus* (Würzburg: Echter, 1980); Rainer Riesner, *Jesus als Lehrer:
    Eine Untersuchung zum Ursprung der Evangelien-Überlieferung* (Tübingen: J. C. B. Mohr,
    1984 [1981[1]]); Gaolyahu Cornfeld, *The Historical Jesus: A Scholarly View of the Man and
    his World* (New York: Macmillan, 1982); A. E. Harvey, *Jesus and the Constraints of
    History* (Philadelphia: Westminster, 1982); James Breech, *The Silence of Jesus: The
    Authentic Voice of the Historical Man* (Philadelphia: Fortress, 1983); Gerard Stephen
    Sloyan, *Jesus in Focus: A Life in its Setting* (Mystic: Twenty-Third, 1983).

decade is more appropriate if we wish to estimate where the discussion is currently and is likely to go in the immediate future.[8] I submit that even this latest vintage of recent Jesus research shows a significant diversity in approach and results. Moreover, one can also detect a diversity in the larger agenda being served, which include more than merely progress in scholarly knowledge. To make this diversity clear, I offer a sort of taxonomy of this recent work.[9]

2.1 E. P. Sanders: Jesus the Restorationist Prophet

E. P. Sanders' study, *Jesus and Judaism*, is a convenient place to begin.[10] Appearing early in 1985, this has been perhaps the most-discussed scholarly book on Jesus of the last ten years. Like Sanders' major book on Paul,[11] his Jesus book was both a detailed and highly critical interaction with previous scholarship as well as a notably fresh interpretation of the evidence.

As to approach, Sanders states that since "historical reconstruction requires that data be fitted into a context, the establishment of a secure context, or framework of interpretation, becomes crucial." Toward this aim, he submits three kinds of information as crucial: facts about Jesus' career, "the outcome of his life and teaching" and "knowledge of first-century Judaism."[12] On account of the difficulty of determining with sufficient confidence or sufficiently wide consent what is authentic to Jesus in the sayings material, Sanders eschews the previously typical focus on the sayings tradition characteristic of the new quest and much other Jesus scholarship. Instead, he prefers as "the evidence which is most secure . . . several facts about Jesus' career *and its aftermath* which can be known beyond doubt" and which must be accounted for in any

---

8   Limiting ourselves to those who have produced book-length contributions during the last ten years also means having to omit smaller but noteworthy contributions of this period such as Ben F. Meyer, "Master Builder and Copestone of the Portal: Images of the Mission of Jesus," *Toronto Journal of Theology* 9 (1993): 187-209, which contains both Meyer's seasoned reflections on some recent historical-Jesus work and a reformulation of his own view of Jesus' mission that builds upon his 1979 volume.

9   See also a recent contribution by N. T. Wright, *Jesus and the Victory of God* (Minneapolis: Fortress, 1993). In an earlier essay, Wright offers a summary of his thinking now developed more fully in this volume (N. T. Wright, "Jesus, Israel and the Cross," in Kent H. Richards, ed., *Society of Biblical Literature 1985 Seminar Papers* [Atlanta: Scholars Press, 1985], 75-95).

10 E. P. Sanders, *Jesus and Judaism* (London: SCM, 1985).

11 E. P. Sanders, *Paul and Palestinian Judaism* (London: SCM, 1977). Among the many discussions, see John Kenneth Riches, "Works and Words of Jesus the Jew," *Heythrop Journal* 17 (1986): 53-62; Bruce Chilton, "Jesus and the Repentance of E. P. Sanders," *Tyndale Bulletin* 39 (1988): 1-18; Dale C. Allison, "Jesus and the Covenant: A Response to E. P. Sanders," *Journal for the Study of the New Testament* 29 (1987): 57-78; and reviews in *Religious Studies Review* 6 (1986): 86-88.

12 Sanders, *Jesus and Judaism*, 17.

interpretation of Jesus.[13] These eight facts are: (1) Jesus' baptism by John the Baptist;[14] (2) Jesus' Galilean background, and healing and preaching activities; (3) his calling of disciples, in particular a group of twelve; (4) Jesus' confining of his activity to Israel; (5) a controversy about the Temple; (6) Jesus' crucifixion at Jerusalem by Roman authorities; (7) the continuation of an identifiable movement composed of Jesus' followers after his death; and (8) the persecution of at least parts of this movement by at least some Jews for at least a few decades.[15] Both in his emphasis on beginning with "facts" of Jesus' career, and in his readiness to use the character of the early post-crucifixion Jesus movement as an indication of Jesus' own views and intentions, Sanders has been innovative and bold. In addition to this approach to the Jesus tradition, Sanders emphasizes the importance of an accurate grasp of Jesus' Jewish religious matrix. Here Sanders brings to bear his impressive knowledge of the subject and his now famous biting critical style, pillorying many earlier Jesus scholars for their distorted representations of ancient Jewish religion.[16]

As to results, Sanders offers a prophet of restorationist eschatology, on the one hand part of a wider stream of Jewish tradition (especially John the Baptist) concerned with the renewal and salvation of Israel, but on the other hand innovative, even radical, in offering to sinners a full acceptance without the usual preconditions of penance and reformation of life. This radical readiness to admit sinners to full forgiveness brought Jesus criticism from other restorationist groups such as the Pharisees. But it was Jesus' prophetic announcement of doom for the Temple, symbolized in the Temple incident, that brought Jesus before the Jewish authorities and thence to his execution.[17]

---

13 Sanders, *Jesus and Judaism*, 10-11 (emphasis his).

14 In many current historical-Jesus studies Jesus' relationship with the Baptist is taken as important, sometimes crucial. That Jesus was linked with a prophet figure with a strong eschatological and restorationist agenda is thus offered as strong evidence of similar aims and orientations for Jesus. On the Baptist, see now the major study by Robert L. Webb, *John the Baptizer and Prophet: A Socio-Historical Study* (Sheffield: JSOT, 1991). See also Webb's essay, "John the Baptist and his Relationship to Jesus," in Chilton and Evans, *Studying the Historical Jesus*, 179-230. Note also the challenge to more common understandings of the Baptist as an eschatological prophet by Ron Cameron, who attempts to portray John as a Cynic figure: "'What Have You Come Out to See?' Characterizations of John and Jesus in the Gospels," *Semeia* 49 (1990): 35-69.

15 Sanders, *Jesus and Judaism*, 11.

16 Sanders has now produced a large study of ancient Jewish religion: *Judaism: Practice and Belief, 63 BCE-66 CE* (London: SCM, 1992).

17 This emphasis on Jesus' attitude and actions toward the Temple comes up in much recent historical-Jesus work, though with varying nuances. In light of the importance attached to the idea that Jesus was critical of, opposed to, and/or predicted the destruction of, the Temple, see the provocative essay by David Seeley, "Jesus' Temple Act," *Catholic Biblical Quarterly* 55 (1993): 263-83.

In short, Sanders' work can be characterized by a confidence in the ability to produce a historically-credible and testable picture of Jesus (a characteristic of all the most recent Jesus studies), an emphasis on "facts" about Jesus instead of a preoccupation with the sayings material, a readiness to consider the beliefs and practices of earliest Christianity as possible indicators of Jesus' own positions,[18] an emphasis on accurate and sympathetic knowledge of Jesus' Jewish religious setting, and a professed disinterest in the hermeneutical, theological question of the meaning or relevance of Jesus for today.

This last point is worth lingering over. Sanders is well aware of the perennial criticism of historical-Jesus work as being reflections of the particular religious/social/political preferences of the scholar. Consequently, he explicitly indicates that the Jesus he portrays is not the advocate or authority of Sanders' own "liberal, modern, secularized Protestant" religious orientation.[19] It is refreshing to have a scholarly portrait of Jesus conclude without lionizing Jesus as prefiguring some stance favoured or admired by the author.

But Sanders' work is not at all free from hermeneutical concern. In this Jesus book, as in his celebrated major study of Paul, Sanders was in fact concerned to correct the implicit and explicit anti-Judaism in much Christian representation of either figure, especially in the work of scholars who professed to be doing historical reconstruction. Sanders does not make Paul and Jesus into modern, liberal Protestants, but he does seek to deny Paul or Jesus to those who use them in support of an anti-Judaic Christian theology that claims historical foundations in these figures.[20] That there are such conscious or unconscious motivations for scholarly work does not in itself discredit the scholarship. But it is worth noting that this rigorous historical study does exhibit implicit and explicit purposes beyond "mere" historical reconstruction. The particular purposes I have identified help us to place Sanders in a taxonomy that includes both approach and motivational, or hermeneutical, concerns.

2.2 Geza Vermes: Jesus Rescued from Christianity

Geza Vermes has now produced three volumes devoted to Jesus since 1973, his most recent appearing within our time frame: *The Religion of Jesus the Jew*

---

18 Note esp. Sanders, *Jesus and Judaism*, 334-35, where he points to "a thread which connects Jesus' own intention, his death and the rise of the movement" as the "one vital point . . . at which the results of this study correspond to my own expectations." Indeed, Sanders finds the connecting links between the early post-crucifixion Jesus movement and Jesus "so obvious that it is hard to understand why so many have thought that there is no causal chain from Jesus' own view of his mission and the kingdom to his death and then to the church."

19 Sanders, *Jesus and Judaism*, 334.

20 This concern runs throughout Sanders' pitiless critique of many other Christian Jesus studies, and is explicitly reflected in his concluding pages, 335-40.

(1993).[21] In this book Vermes continues the approach and characterization of Jesus he developed in his 1973 study, filling out his picture of Jesus' religiosity and interacting with the work of other scholars that has appeared since his first Jesus book.

In some major respects, Vermes's approach and results are similar to those of Sanders. Both focus on Jesus' religious setting and aims. Both emphasize Jewish sources and traditions in interpreting Jesus. Both are concerned to correct misrepresentations of ancient Judaism in many treatments of Jesus by Christian scholars. There are also noteworthy differences—in approach, results and hermeneutical concerns—that require us to place Vermes in another taxonomic category. As to approach, Vermes seems even more concerned than Sanders to argue for the importance of rabbinic sources in defining first-century Judaism and in understanding Jesus.[22] Although a keen contributor himself to current Qumran investigations, Vermes emphatically prefers rabbinic materials for understanding Jesus' religious setting and orientation. Although the rabbinic sources are considerably later than Jesus (and later than Qumran and a good deal of Second Temple, extra-canonical, Jewish sources), Vermes posits that they often bear witness to the pre-Christian Judaism that nourished Jesus. Vermes finds valuable justification for his view in the similarities of themes and forms shared by the New Testament gospels and rabbinic sources.[23]

The Jesus Vermes portrays shares with Sanders' picture a strong eschatological orientation that conditions all that Jesus does, and, indeed, that distinguishes Jesus from the general category of *hasid* that Vermes otherwise urges as most appropriate for Jesus.[24] But for Vermes, Jesus is mainly a charismatic-type *hasid*, with a particular "elasticity" on some points of *halakhah*,[25] a distinctive non-exegetical style and a more single-minded focus to his parables,[26] and a strongly individualistic religiosity that together

---

21 Geza Vermes, *The Religion of Jesus the Jew* (Minneapolis: Fortress, 1993); Vermes, *Jesus the Jew: A Historian's Reading of the Gospel* (New York: Macmillan, 1973; 2nd ed., 1983); Vermes, *Jesus and the World of Judaism* (Philadelphia: Fortress, 1983), a collection of ten previously published essays. For fuller discussion of Vermes's approach and position, see Benjamin Jerome Hubbard, "Geza Vermes's Contribution to Historical Jesus Studies: An Assessment," in Richards, *Society of Biblical Literature 1985 Seminar Papers*, 29-44; and Humphrey, "Will the Reader Understand?" (in this volume).

22 See Vermes, *Religion*, esp. 7-10, for his latest views on the use of rabbinic materials in Jesus research.

23 Vermes uses rabbinic materials to illuminate the New Testament Jesus material, and often seems to do so effectively. He would not agree that a crucial critical step in his approach actually involves using the New Testament gospels to illuminate and accredit the rabbinic sources as often preserving traditions much earlier than the dates of the rabbinic works.

24 See, e.g., Vermes, *Religion*, 78-90, 117, 139, 147-50.

25 Vermes, *Religion*, e.g., 47, 70-75.

26 Vermes, *Religion*, 114-18.

emphasize "inward aspects and root causes of religious action."[27] As to the circumstances leading to Jesus' execution, Vermes says surprisingly little outside of a paragraph in his preface. Here he denies any direct basis in Jesus' own words and deeds, and posits "nervous authorities in charge of law and order" who became unduly alarmed at Jesus' ill-timed "affray in the Temple" and mistakenly executed him as a messianic claimant. But it was all a tragic mistake, for Jesus intended no such thing: "He died on the cross for having done the wrong thing (caused a commotion) in the wrong place (the Temple) at the wrong time (just before Passover). Here lies the real tragedy of Jesus the Jew."[28]

As with Sanders, so with Vermes it is possible to raise significant objections to major features of his Jesus work, among which I mention here a few by way of example. Is Vermes correct to attach so much importance to rabbinic sources and traditions? Is the Jesus of individual piety really borne out in the Jesus tradition, or is there not in the most assured material indication of a more collective vision of the divine purpose (as reflected, e.g., in the calling of the twelve)? Is the *hasid* model really adequate, given the several qualifications Vermes himself has to recognize? We could continue with other objections, but one must grant that Vermes has provided us with distinctive and sometimes valuable material for the current quest. With Sanders, he is especially salutary in insisting on the need for any portrait of Jesus to be credible within an informed picture of first-century Jewish religiosity. One final observation about Vermes's work is relevant, and this too must be stated, in part, as a criticism. From his earliest Jesus book onward, Vermes has presented himself as a "historian," who, because he is not a Christian theologian, is able to give a more objective portrait of Jesus. All along, however, the careful reader has been able to detect in Vermes his own hermeneutical aims and concerns, and in his most recent volume these come out quite explicitly, especially in the concluding chapter. Vermes is clearly concerned to deny to Jesus any role as "founder" of Christianity, and seeks "to re-instate him among the ancient Hasidim," toward fulfilment of Buber's "prophecy": "A great place belongs to him in Israel's history of faith."[29] In short, Vermes would rescue Jesus from Christianity, and make the hasidic Jesus a fixture in Jewish spiritual history. It is surely not too difficult to detect a hermeneutical and religio-political aim here.

---

27 Vermes, *Religion*, e.g., 189-95. The quote is from 195.

28 Vermes, *Religion*, ix-x. The quote is from x.

29 Vermes, *Religion*, 214-15. The whole of chapter 8 is a fascinating discussion, as revealing of Vermes as of any of the historical figures and subjects he addresses here. For example, in Paul, Vermes claims "a total shift in religious thought" from Jesus, "echoing the mystery cults of his age. . . . [O]ceans separate Paul's Christian Gospel from the religion of Jesus the Jew" (212). Vermes claims that "perhaps the greatest challenge" for "traditional Christianity" comes from "the chief challenger, Jesus the Jew" (215).

2.3 Ben Witherington: Jesus the Christian Messiah

If Vermes seeks to rescue Jesus from Christianity, Ben Witherington's 1990 study of Jesus seems intended to preserve Jesus as founder of Christianity, at least in the sense that Witherington argues for a direct connection between the Christian message about Jesus and his own self-understanding and purposes.[30] Witherington is explicit about his agenda and his theological concerns: "In this book, I intend to state as much as I think is plausible about how Jesus viewed himself, particularly with respect to christological matters, in an attempt to associate Christian faith with the life of the Jesus of history."[31] In a sense, then, although Witherington's study is clearly well informed by, and responds directly to, the (then) very latest developments in historical-Jesus work, his hermeneutical agenda reflects the new quest questions about the relevance of the historical Jesus for faith and about the extent of congruence between the Christology of the New Testament and the purposes, message and self-understanding of Jesus.[32] To be sure, these questions are fully understandable and legitimate, both for in-house Christian discussion, and, as Vermes's work shows, for wider circles who may wish to consider the religious and historical legitimacy of traditional Christology.

Witherington's historical approach to Jesus is designed to overcome what he perceives (rightly, I think) as the incomplete handling of relevant evidence by many others, and also quite deliberately to put forth a plausible case for Jesus' intentions and views of himself.[33] Witherington develops a three-pronged approach that addresses successively Jesus' relationships with significant figures and groups (John the Baptist, Pharisees, revolutionaries and Romans, the disciples), deeds (visionary experiences, miracles) and the sayings material. His sources remain canonical; in fact, in a book that is intended to be *au courant* with scholarship and wide-ranging in its approach, it is curious, to say the least, that there is no reference to the question of what to do with extra-canonical evidence, especially the *Gospel of Thomas*.[34]

---

30 Ben Witherington, *The Christology of Jesus* (Minneapolis: Fortress, 1990).

31 Witherington, *Christology*, 2. Very similar in intention and approach is the book by Ragnar Leivestad, *Jesus in his own Perspective: An Examination of his Sayings, Actions, and Eschatological Titles*, trans. David E. Aune (Minneapolis: Augsburg, 1987 [1982]).

32 Note that Witherington's preface begins with a reference to Käsemann and the new quest (ix), and that his first chapter setting forth the method and purposes of his study concludes with approving references to statements of Mussner, Kümmel and Keck (31), all of which have to do with the new quest issues.

33 See, e.g., Witherington, *Christology*, x: "Perhaps the most significant problem with some of the most recent studies on Jesus is the tendency to focus too much on one or another type of material to the exclusion of the rest of the evidence."

34 There is no reference, for example, to any extra-canonical Christian text in the reference and subject indices. Witherington (*Christology*, 234-43) draws upon Jewish extra-canonical

The Jesus that results from Witherington's study can be summarized as follows. In comparison with the Baptist, Jesus not only announced, but saw himself as bringing about, "the eschatological blessings promised in Isaianic prophecies."[35] His treatment of sabbath, sinners and issues of clean/unclean was likely perceived by the Pharisees as "a direct threat to Jewish survival and, in fact, a form of unfaithfulness to God."[36] In Jesus' mind, however, he was not a lawbreaker but felt commissioned to transcend "the old restrictions in light of the new situation created by the Kingdom breaking-in in his ministry."[37] In fact, Jesus saw himself as "the final eschatological agent [שליח] of God,"[38] God's anointed (משיח) "in the Danielic sense" (with Dan 7 and the "similitudes" of *1 Enoch* [37-71] as major background for Jesus' view of messianism).[39] In light of his picture of a Jesus with a strong "messianic, filial, or *bar enasha* [אנש בר, Son of Man/Human One] self-conception"[40]—indeed, "a transcendent self-image amounting to more than a unique awareness of the Divine"[41] —Witherington can argue that "the seeds of later christological development are found in the relationships, deeds and words of Jesus."[42]

2.4 John P. Meier: The Jesus of Scholarly Consensus

Although only the first volume of John Meier's planned trilogy on the historical Jesus appeared during our time frame, in light of his lengthy discussion in this first volume, and with the aid of a recent essay, Meier's views should and can be characterized.[43] In size and intended impact, Meier's work is probably to be compared with Crossan's book, which appeared in the same year.

---

texts to illuminate the Jewish background (e.g., *1 Enoch*), but I also find no discussion of the Christian extra-canonical Jesus-material in the body of the work.

35 Witherington, *Christology*, 54.
36 Witherington, *Christology*, 77.
37 Witherington, *Christology*, 78. Unlike the Pharisaic aim of "spreading the standards of priestly holiness," Jesus' "ministry [was] a rehabilitation and reclamation campaign, performing acts of compassion and breaking bread even with outcasts, toll collectors and sinners" (271).
38 Witherington, *Christology*, 55, 143.
39 Witherington, *Christology*, 261, 267-69.
40 Witherington, *Christology*, 274.
41 Witherington, *Christology*, 276.
42 Witherington, *Christology*, 277.
43 John P. Meier, *A Marginal Jew: Rethinking the Historical Jesus*; Volume One: *The Roots of the Problem and the Person* (New York: Doubleday, 1991), is a 484 page treatment of his approach to Jesus (theoretical concepts, sources, authenticity criteria) and Jesus' historical background (including language, education, socio-economic status and family). See my review in *Journal of Biblical Literature* 112 (1993): 532-34. In addition, for an overview see Meier's essay, "Reflections on Jesus-of-History Research Today," in Charlesworth, *Jesus' Jewishness*, 84-107. Volume 2 of Meier's work (*Mentor, Message, and Miracles* [New York: Doubleday, 1994]) gives his portrait of Jesus' activities and message.

Meier seeks to present "a limited consensus statement" on the historical Jesus, to which "all honest historians cognizant of first-century religious movements" could attend and whose arguments and conclusions they could engage, regardless of the religious or philosophical orientations of the historians.[44] This will be considerably less than what traditional Christian faith asserts about Jesus, and will also likely come far short of the "real Jesus" who actually lived. Meier explains that in reconstructing the "Jesus of history" or the "historical Jesus" one can only hope to discover "fragments of a mosaic, the faint outline of a faded fresco that allows of many interpretations"—in his view, still a worthwhile academic project.[45]

The commitment to detailed interaction with the work of others, to a consideration of all relevant evidence and issues, to a careful and explicit approach to the subject, is evident in the book throughout. One might well think that Meier's judgment on this or that issue is wrong, but it is hard to fault him for ducking many issues or for failing to indicate where there are major disagreements on the issues.[46] For example, Meier explicitly addresses the question of whether the *agrapha* and extra-canonical gospels give us valuable and authentic Jesus material, concluding in the negative.[47]

Between the extensive discussion of background material in Meier's 1991 volume and his essay published in the same year, it is possible to sketch the Jesus picture he produces. Jesus' baptism by John shows that Jesus subscribed to the Baptist's message of "the imminent disaster that was threatening Israel in the last days of its history, a disaster to be avoided only by national repentance."[48] This eschatological thrust remains crucial for Jesus, but his message underwent "a major shift" in comparison to John, with an emphasis on God "seeking out and gathering in the lost, the poor, the marginalized, yes, even the irreligious."[49] Thus, contra Vermes, Meier sees a strong corporate aim in Jesus to bring "the scattered people of God back into one, holy community."[50] Jesus certainly longed for a revolution in which "the poor will be exalted and the powerful dispossessed," but this would be God's doing alone, so Meier's Jesus was neither revolutionist nor world reformer.[51]

---

44 Meier, *Marginal Jew*, vol. 1, 1-2. Meier combines a commitment to common scholarly interchange and discussion across confessional, national and gender lines, with a recognition that scholars are human beings influenced by personal, cultural and religious/philosophical factors in their best scholarly efforts. See, e.g., 29-31 for his pointed comments.

45 Meier, *Marginal Jew*, 25.

46 The same commendation unfortunately cannot be given to Crossan. See examples in my review of his book in *Toronto Journal of Theology* 9 (1993): 256-57.

47 Meier, *Marginal Jew*, vol. 1, 112-66.

48 Meier, "Reflections," 89.

49 Meier, "Reflections," 90.

50 Meier, "Reflections," 90.

51 Meier, "Reflections," 92.

In Meier's view, Jesus' overtures to the sinful and societal outcasts amounted to "making acceptance of himself and his message the touchstone of true repentance," thus conveying a personal claim.[52] As to the Mosaic Law, Jesus behaved as a "true charismatic in the classic sense," affirming the Law as God's will, radicalizing it at times, but on some issues claiming to know better than "Jewish Law or custom." "In such cases, the Law had to give way to or be reinterpreted by the command of Jesus, simply because Jesus said so ('but *I* say to you')."[53] This "unheard-of claim to authority over the Mosaic Law and over people's lives" was the most disturbing feature of Jesus for pious Jews and Jewish authorities. This put Jesus "on a collision course not only with the Temple priests but also with sincere Jews in general."[54]

Although Jesus "gave no clear and detailed answer" as to who he thought himself to be, "he implicitly made himself the pivotal figure in the final drama he was announcing and inaugurating." The "monumental claims" reflected in Jesus' teachings were based at least in part on what Meier considers "his special [filial] relationship with God."[55] At a minimum, Jesus saw himself as "a prophet, indeed the final prophet sent to Israel in its last days." His disciples probably harboured messianic hopes of him, and such hopes are probably reflected in (and may have contributed to) Jesus' execution by the Roman authorities.[56]

Meier's explicit approach calls for the bracketing-out of religious belief and hermeneutical agenda; nevertheless, one can surmise some existential and hermeneutical concerns at work in this Catholic priest's scholarly "consensus" model of the historical Jesus. These concerns are perhaps more evident in what is denied rather than what is asserted by Meier. For example, I suggest that the strong denial of the revolutionary and the social-reformer Jesus cohere with and likely serve a religious and social posture that rejects either option in the name of Jesus today. Also, as with Witherington (although in a much more muted way), so in Meier's picture of a Jesus who makes strong personal claims and whose mission is a major critique of the then-dominant Jewish religious structure, authority and traditions, we have implicitly a Jesus more congenial to relatively traditional Christian christological affirmation. All this does not count against the academic validity of Meier's picture, to be sure, but it does illustrate how even in an effort at a rigorously historical, "neutral," statement the influence of modern concerns and agenda does not disappear.

---

52 Meier, "Reflections," 93.
53 Meier, "Reflections," 95.
54 Meier, "Reflections," 95.
55 Meier, "Reflections," 98.
56 Meier, "Reflections," 99-100. See also 105.

2.5 Marcus J. Borg: Jesus the Social Visionary

Marcus Borg has published two books on Jesus, the first a revision of his Oxford D.Phil. thesis in 1984, and in 1987 a second, more popularizing and broader-ranging treatment that builds on his earlier volume.[57] Borg is also an active member of the Jesus Seminar.

Borg's approach to Jesus involves positing a view of "the cultural dynamics of his social world" in which "the dominant ethos . . . its cultural paradigm or core value, was holiness, understood as purity." This concern for holiness generated sharp boundaries, especially between persons and social groups, producing "a politics of holiness."[58] Borg defines "politics" broadly to include social and religious values and arrangements, so he is able to describe Jesus' message and intentions as "political in the sense of being concerned with the shape and direction of the historical community of Israel."[59] In his second volume, Borg broadens his approach by drawing upon the phenomenological and anthropological categories of "holy man" and "revitalization movement founder" to analyze Jesus.

The picture of Jesus Borg offers in his works consists of the following major features: (1) Jesus as radically critical of holiness as the dominant social value and principle; (2) Jesus advocating "compassion" as the replacement value and principle to effect "transformation of Israel's life"; (3) Jesus as a "non-eschatological" (certainly a non-apocalyptic) prophet of a thoroughly this-worldly historical crisis for Israel;[60] (4) Jesus as "holy person" able to be "a mediator" and richly experienced in spiritual/mystical phenomena;[61] and (5) Jesus as "sage" or wisdom teacher proffering "a world-subverting wisdom" through his parables and aphorisms that "invited his hearers to an alternative path."[62] Although using both ancient Jewish evidence and modern social-science categories to place Jesus in the first-century Jewish world, Borg posits serious differences between Jesus and the Jewish religious leadership. In Borg's view, Jesus' message was heavily devoted to warning Israel of a dangerous

---

57 Marcus J. Borg, *Conflict, Holiness and Politics in the Teachings of Jesus* (Lewiston: Edwin Mellen, 1984). See summaries of this book by Wright, *Interpretation*, 387-91; and Borg, "Portraits of Jesus," 12-14. Borg's more recent book is *Jesus, a New Vision: Spirit, Culture, and the Life of Discipleship* (San Francisco: Harper & Row, 1987).

58 Quoted words from Borg, "Portraits of Jesus," 13. For discussion by Borg, see *Conflict, Holiness and Politics*, 27-72.

59 Borg, "Portraits of Jesus," 12.

60 Marcus J. Borg, "A Temperate Case for a Noneschatological Jesus," in Kent H. Richards, ed., *Society of Biblical Literature 1986 Seminar Papers* (Atlanta: Scholars Press, 1986), 521-35. The essay also appeared in *Foundations and Facets Forum* 2/3 (Sept, 1986): 81-102.

61 Borg, *New Vision*, esp. 39-75.

62 Borg, "Portraits of Jesus," 15.

nationalism and the divisive and misguided social value of "holiness." Although Jesus' execution indicates Roman perception of him as a rebel, Jesus was not a revolutionary. He was, however, a threat to the "established order" in advocating an alternative vision. Because he had a following, and because the religious authorities judged his vision to be wrong and false, Jewish leaders were probably involved in bringing Jesus to his death.[63]

Borg's hermeneutical or applicational concerns in Jesus research are clear. He wishes to pose his view of Jesus' message as meaningful for modern Christians and for the culture at large.[64] Borg's Jesus is "an epiphany of God" who "discloses that at the center of everything is a reality that is in love with us and wills our well-being." Jesus models a vision of life with three elements: a spirituality of freedom from self-preoccupation, compassion and a "dialectical *relationship to culture*" (emphasis his) in which one is "simultaneously less involved and more involved in culture" (by which Borg seems to mean an "alternative" approach to culture informed by the values he finds in Jesus).[65]

2.6 Richard A. Horsley: Jesus the Social Revolutionary

Richard Horsley's approach to Jesus emphasizes the political and socio-economic circumstances of first-century Palestine, and reflects what looks like a soft Marxian viewpoint on such matters.[66] Horsley established himself initially with studies of Jewish popular resistance to Roman rule, and he has consistently emphasized both the importance of the political and socio-economic setting and the negative effects of Roman rule on Palestinian Jews of the first century.[67]

In Horsley's view, Jesus' message and intentions had to do mainly with the creation of new, local social values and practices designed to overcome or sidestep the deleterious effects of Roman rule, such as heavy taxation, social conflict and oppressive institutional and class structures. Zeal for the Law was

---

63 Borg, *New Vision*, chapter 9, esp. 180-84.

64 See Borg, *New Vision*, chapter 10: "The New Vision of Jesus: His Significance for our Time."

65 Borg, *New Vision*, 192-96.

66 Richard A. Horsley, *Jesus and the Spiral of Violence* (San Francisco: Harper & Row, 1987). See also Horsley, *Sociology and the Jesus Movement* (New York: Crossroad, 1989), which both presents Horsley's own views about Jesus in briefer form and contains a detailed critique of the work of Gerd Theissen's *Sociology of Early Palestinian Christianity*, trans. John Bowden (Philadelphia: Fortress, 1978 [1977]); note also 116-19 for a critique of the Cynic-Jesus position.

67 In addition to numerous articles on Jewish response to Roman domination, see Richard A. Horsley and John S. Hanson, *Bandits, Prophets, and Messiahs: Popular Movements at the Time of Jesus* (San Francisco: Harper & Row, 1985). Among critical responses to this work, see Terence L. Donaldson, "Rural Bandits, City Mobs and the Zealots," *Journal for the Study of Judaism in the Persian, Hellenistic and Roman Period* 21 (1990): 19-40.

not a powerful collective force.[68] Jesus' apocalyptic language was symbolic and concerned with expressing reform of the existing society, not the supernatural appearance of a new world.[69] Jesus was not concerned with individual religiousness but with a reformed Jewish society freed from "oppressive historical enemies" and restored "in independence and righteousness under God's rule."[70] His teachings had specific social purposes encouraging "egalitarian social relations" in "local communities" that would overcome the social problems of Roman oppression,[71] and would promote "social-economic cooperation and autonomy."[72] Part of Jesus' message was the pronouncing of judgment against "the ruling institutions of Jewish Palestine," Temple and the high priesthood, and the call for a replacement of these institutions by the renewed society Jesus strove to effect.[73] All this amounts to a picture of Jesus as a non-violent social revolutionary. But Jesus' preaching and practice of God's rule in the here and now clearly implied that "imperial and high-priestly rule was excluded and was imminently to be judged by God," which is the major factor that led to Jesus' execution.[74]

Horsley does not explicitly make an applicational pitch or advocate a particular hermeneutical lesson from his Jesus. I suggest, however, that the implicit agenda served by this kind of Jesus is one of liberationist social and political aims. As teacher of "a social revolutionary principle" designed to "transform local social-economic relations," Jesus appears to be serviceable as paradigm and inspiration for similar social action today.

2.7 Seán Freyne: The Jesus of Galilee

Seán Freyne is perhaps known more for his studies of the historical characteristics of ancient Galilee than for historical-Jesus work.[75] A sizable section of his 1988 volume is devoted to Jesus and is a noteworthy historical statement to be considered among current historical-Jesus studies.[76] The

---

68 Horsley, *Spiral of Violence*, 121-29.

69 Horsley, *Spiral of Violence*, 129-45, 157-60.

70 Horsley, *Spiral of Violence*, e.g., 149-66 and chapter 7 (167-208); the words quoted are from 160.

71 Horsley, *Spiral of Violence*, chapter 8.

72 Horsley, *Spiral of Violence*, chapter 9. Cf. Douglas E. Oakman, *Jesus and the Economic Questions of his Day* (Lewiston: Edwin Mellen, 1986).

73 Horsley, *Spiral of Violence*, chapter 10.

74 Horsley, *Spiral of Violence*, 323.

75 Seán Freyne, *Galilee From Alexander the Great to Hadrian: A Study of Second Temple Judaism* (Wilmington: Michael Glazier, 1980).

76 Seán Freyne, *Galilee, Jesus and the Gospels: Literary Approaches and Historical Investigations* (Philadelphia: Fortress, 1988). Chapters 5-7 concentrate on historical matters, and 218-68 focus specifically on Jesus.

particular contribution Freyne makes and the major reason for including him here is his emphasis on Jesus' Galilean origin. Drawing upon historical sources and archaeological investigations, Freyne suggests how the social, geographical, religious and economic features of first-century Galilee should be taken into account in framing a historical picture of Jesus. In his emphasis upon the social and economic factors, Freyne can be compared with Horsley (as well as with Gerd Theissen).[77] But Freyne's approach and conclusions are noticeably different. In Freyne's view, the Galilee of Jesus' time was not nearly so oppressive and seething with discontent as Horsley thinks.[78] Moreover, Jesus' own artisan origins, together with the imagery of his sayings and the pattern of his associations, all are taken as amounting to a Jesus who cut across social classes, in place of a one-sided advocate for the downtrodden peasant.[79] Jesus' mobile nature may reflect his artisan background as well. Given the proximity of Graeco-Roman cities with Cynic-Stoic teachers, it is even possible that Jesus' style may reflect the influence of such traditions, but with strong Jewish adaptations and orientation.[80]

Freyne's Jesus offers a major re-interpretation of three traditional Jewish religious images: the Temple, the land and the Torah. In Freyne's view, Jesus did not oppose the Temple programmatically; thus, he dissents from Sanders' emphasis on explicit Temple-opposition as the cause of Jesus' arrest. Jesus was not "an oracular prophet of doom for Jerusalem and its Temple."[81] But the combination of authoritative teaching and miraculous deeds that crowds would have taken as authentication of this teaching made Jesus a potent threat to Temple and scribal authorities.[82] Jesus does not seem to have been a land-oriented reformer or revolutionary. Although some may have taken his message with more socially-revolutionary and apocalyptic overtones, this was probably not Jesus' own focus.[83] Jesus' vision of God's purposes seems to have been inspired by "prophetic re-interpretation" of Israel's nature and role from the Bible. Just as Jesus did not attack the Temple but "transformed its range and scope," so he also "translated" the basic meaning of the "land-symbol" into "a universal symbol that did not regard the confines of the land as important."[84] In

---

77 See, e.g., Theissen, *Sociology*. Theissen's novel about Jesus, *The Shadow of the Galilean: The Quest of the Historical Jesus in Narrative Form*, trans. John Bowden (London: SCM, 1987 [1986]), falls within our period but is not a scholarly reconstruction of Jesus intended for academic debate.
78 See, e.g., Freyne, *Galilee, Jesus and the Gospels*, 163-67, for interaction with Horsley on "social banditry" in Galilee.
79 See, e.g., Freyne, *Galilee, Jesus and the Gospels*, 245.
80 Freyne, *Galilee, Jesus and the Gospels*, 250.
81 Freyne, *Galilee, Jesus and the Gospels*, 238.
82 Freyne, *Galilee, Jesus and the Gospels*, 236.
83 Freyne, *Galilee, Jesus and the Gospels*, 244-46.
84 Freyne, *Galilee, Jesus and the Gospels*, 246.

his attitude toward Torah, Jesus highlighted "the universal dimensions of Israel's call," under the influence of "the wisdom and apocalyptic strands of thought current in his own day."[85] This universalizing tone makes Jesus resemble in certain ways features of the Hellenistic milieu.[86] But, although Jesus did not reflect the scribal approach to *halakhah* reflected in Mishnaic materials and probably already operative in some first-century Jewish circles, he remained thoroughly Jewish, maintaining Torah as God's will for Israel. Jesus' interpretation of Torah and the will of God, however, resembles that of a holy man, whose own charismatic experience and life setting are more influential and authoritative for him than a chain of scribal tradition.[87]

Freyne does not explicitly give his historical-Jesus portrait contemporary application, but, as with some others we have considered, it is possible to surmise hermeneutical relevance and possible coherence with contemporary religious/existential concerns.[88] Freyne's Jesus proclaims a radically re-interpreted Jewish religious world linked to the later church through "Hellenists" such as Stephen who "spoke openly against the Temple and the law," and the "Q-community" which conducted an unsuccessful mission in Galilee.[89] Moreover, Freyne posits a correspondence between Jesus' subversion of traditional Jewish religious images and the "comic kerygma of the folly of the cross confounding the wisdom of this world."[90]

2.8 John Dominic Crossan: Jesus the Jewish Cynic

Of the works considered in this essay, John Dominic Crossan's hefty 1991 volume is rivalled perhaps only by Sanders' 1985 study in the amount of attention it received at publication.[91] It is indeed a notable book: the first, full-scale portrait of Jesus as a Jewish Cynic sage.[92] Indeed, Crossan shows

---

85   Freyne, *Galilee, Jesus and the Gospels*, 248.

86   Freyne, *Galilee, Jesus and the Gospels*, 249-55.

87   Freyne, *Galilee, Jesus and the Gospels*, 259-61.

88   See esp. Freyne, *Galilee, Jesus and the Gospels*, 269-72.

89   Freyne, *Galilee, Jesus and the Gospels*, 271. But on the Hellenists see now Craig C. Hill, *Hellenists and Hebrews: Reappraising Division Within the Earliest Church* (Minneapolis: Fortress, 1992).

90   Freyne, *Galilee, Jesus and the Gospels*, 272.

91   John Dominic Crossan, *The Historical Jesus: The Life of a Mediterranean Jewish Peasant* (San Francisco: HarperSanFrancisco, 1991). See the amusing (and insightful) critique/sendup by N. T. Wright, "Taking the Text With Her Pleasure: A Post-Post-Modernist Response to J. Dominic Crossan, *The Historical Jesus: The Life of a Mediterranean Jewish Peasant*," *Theology* 96 (1993): 303-309.

92   To be sure, the view of Jesus as a Cynic sage has been around for some time. In particular, Mack has come down solidly for this view in his provocative book in which he attempts a programmatic recasting of the whole of Christian origins: Burton L. Mack, *A Myth of Innocence: Mark and Christian Origins* (Philadelphia: Fortress, 1988). For criticism of

elaborate concern to make an impact, both in style and substance, through his characteristic efforts at entertaining prose combined with an elaborate book-architecture that includes two hundred-plus pages of analysis of the Graeco-Roman cultural setting, seven appendices, and a rhetoric that reinforces the scholarly and scientific character of the work.[93]

Crossan seeks to be innovative in his approach to Jesus. He draws upon anthropological studies of peasants and class dynamics as a way of ascertaining the historical situation (his use of the "broker" metaphor is a prime example). He emphasizes the larger Graeco-Roman setting of Jesus, pointing out the penetration of Hellenistic culture in Jewish Palestine and urging wherever possible comparisons of features of Jesus' message and behaviour with Hellenistic, especially Cynic, traditions. Crossan also incorporates work of other scholars that is congruent with the social and anthropological nuancing of his discussion—for instance, Horsley on the economic and political situation of first-century Palestine, and Morton Smith on magic.

Crossan's choice of what to take as more authentic to Jesus frequently involves an adaptation of the criterion of multiple attestation, where the same or similar item seems to be attested in more than one early source. His application of this criterion will leave many others cold, for it depends upon a hypothetical (and dubious) reconstruction of early sources and their putative dates.[94] The connection to the Baptist which some would render crucial for understanding Jesus is minimized by alleging that Jesus made a major departure from John's apocalyptic and prophetic message and style, in the direction of a more universalizing and egalitarian program of "open commensality."[95] Crossan's Jesus operated with an "ecstatic vision and social program" that "sought to rebuild society upward from its grass roots but on principles of religious and economic egalitarianism."[96] Jesus did not attempt, however, a

---

Mack see my essay, "The Gospel of Mark: Evolutionary Or Revolutionary Document?" *Journal for the Study of the New Testament* 40 (1990): 15-32.

93 Note, e.g., the use of language of modern archaeological work in the "stratification" of early Jesus sources in Appendix 1, and in the Prologue (xxvii-xxxiv), where earlier work is likened to pre-scientific "pot hunting." Crossan's 224-page discussion of Graeco-Roman culture may be comparable in some ways to Meier's decision to give over the first volume of his study to the historical background of Jesus. Both show impressively-wide reading and an attempt to put the picture of Jesus on a broad scholarly base. Crossan can be faulted, however, for not connecting his discussion of Graeco-Roman culture more clearly and specifically to his portrait of Jesus.

94 E.g., Crossan dates to 30-60 CE "*Gospel of Thomas* I," the *Egerton Gospel*, Oxyrhynchus fragment 1224, Papyrus Vindobonensis Greek 2325, the *Gospel of the Hebrews*, the *Sayings Gospel Q*, his own "Cross Gospel" (now embedded in the *Gospel of Peter*), and a few other hypothetical sources, which he then treats in his discussion as firmly attested and acceptable for historical reconstruction.

95 Crossan, *Historical Jesus*, chapter 11.

96 Crossan, *Historical Jesus*, xii.

political revolution, but instead a social one that he sought to promote through addressing "the imagination's most dangerous depths," programmatically ignoring all social distinctions of "Gentile and Jew, female and male, slave and free, poor and rich."[97] Jesus both "symbolically destroyed" the "brokerage function" of the Temple and its priesthood, and other such religious structures, and also resolutely refused any particular significance for himself in the new kingdom he advocated, seeing himself merely as the announcer of an utterly unmediated relationship between God and humanity.[98] Jesus' healings and exorcisms demonstrated God's brokerless grace, and his meals were practical expressions of egalitarianism.

Given the strongly academic trappings of Crossan's book, is there a hermeneutical agenda or applicational spin-off?[99] If one accepts Crossan's emphasis that Jesus saw no special role for himself in God's kingdom, it would appear that the NT and practically every kind of early Christianity we know of got it very badly wrong. Whether one thinks of an early "Q-community" in which Jesus was the paradigmatic sage around whom the community gathered and through whose work it understood its own mission, or one invokes Christologies reflected in the Pauline letters and other NT documents, there does seem to have been rather massive misunderstanding among early Christians as to what to do with Jesus. Indeed, throughout Crossan's reconstruction of the historical Jesus he has to argue away Jesus tradition that reflects varying views of Jesus as the unique agent or "broker" of God's kingdom and purposes. But Crossan finds "no contradiction between the historical Jesus and the defined Christ [of early Christian proclamation], no betrayal whatsoever in the move from Jesus to Christ."[100] This profession is not explained: one may wonder if Crossan is being coy or is simply unwilling to follow through on the implications of his own work. Many of his readers may decide that, if Crossan's reconstruction of Jesus is accepted, there are profound questions to be faced about the relationship of Jesus and the Christian message about Jesus.

Accepting Crossan's self-professed disinterest in questioning traditional Christian proclamation, we may be able to surmise a more positive agenda served. His emphasis on a Jesus of egalitarianism whose aims made irrelevant all social distinctions, and whose intended audience was a universal "humanity," all fits comfortably with a particular (although widely-shared) modern, Western, sophisticated, intellectual outlook—just the sort of circles in which Crossan surely travels and whose values he surely affirms. Crossan's Jesus is no serious embarrassment to him or to like-minded others. The closest

---

97 Crossan, *Historical Jesus*, xii.
98 Crossan, *Historical Jesus*, 422.
99 Crossan, *Historical Jesus*, 422-26. Crossan's own explicit musings on this matter are concentrated in this epilogue.
100 Crossan, *Historical Jesus*, 424.

thing to a difficulty is Jesus' exorcistic and healing activities, but these are rendered meaningful and acceptable by interpreting them as tactics of social enfranchisement in service of Jesus' liberated social aims.[101]

3. General Assessment and Suggestions

The eight scholars considered here represent as many positions on the historical Jesus. One can see similarities linking some of them (e.g., Sanders-Vermes, Horsley-Freyne, Meier-Witherington, Borg-Crossan), but there are also sharp differences distinguishing individuals from those they most resemble, and one cannot really speak of clear schools of thought among them. One certainly cannot speak of an emerging consensus. There are differences in the evidence chosen for framing Jesus' historical background, differences in what one sees as more influential in Jesus' historical matrix, differences in whether to use religious concepts and categories or social-scientific ones to understand Jesus (and, if the latter are chosen, which ones to emphasize), differences over the dating and evaluation and identification of Christian sources (intra- and extra-canonical, extant and hypothetical), and certainly differences in the personal hermeneutical agendas and concerns that lie behind and help motivate the task. In that sense, therefore, if one hopes for some assured and representative results, the most current wave of historical-Jesus work can be judged collectively to have failed. But I suggest that not all the news is bad and that there are gains to be had from the work surveyed here. Some of these gains are the direct product of the work of these scholars. Other gains are potential lessons to be learned from their failings as well as from their intended contributions.

The first thing to emphasize is how these studies demonstrate collectively the breadth and diversity of evidence that must be considered, critically examined and analyzed, and then integrated in a persuasively balanced manner for a thoroughly satisfying historical reconstruction of "Jesus." The range of evidence is daunting: Second Temple Jewish texts (a galaxy of data and issues, even if one focuses on texts of Palestinian provenance and usage), archaeological data on first-century Palestine, larger historical, cultural and

---

101 In an earlier essay, Crossan refers to a modern "hermeneutical multiplicity" and accepts the point that historical-Jesus scholars should make explicit their individual commitments of this nature, indicating more candidly than in his book that his own theological preference "is certainly for a sapiential over an apocalyptic Jesus" ("Divine Immediacy and Human Immediacy: Towards a New First Principle in Historical Jesus Research," *Semeia* 44 [1988]: 121-40, esp. 124). He also states that "both interpretations were probably there from the very beginning" and that it is historically problematic to try to establish as earlier than all the others one interpretation of Jesus. This is especially curious since in his 1991 book Crossan seems concerned to do exactly that with his elaborate trappings of source "stratigraphy."

religious developments in and affecting first-century Palestine, economic and political data, evidence of the presence and influence of Hellenistic languages and cultures, appropriate models and theories to assist in interpreting and using all this data, and of course early Christian texts (the handling of which requires a thorough consideration of critical questions about the texts and putative sources of them, and reconstruction of early Christian groups and their beliefs). Given these demands, it is not at all difficult to see why some recent historical-Jesus studies are so large. But even among the lengthiest studies there are omissions of relevant issues and/or inadequate attention to relevant critical questions, or what look like arbitrary or ill-explained choices on what sources to privilege, what issues to omit and theories to accept.[102]

Points of focus vary. One scholar focuses on the Jewish religious ideas of Jesus' time and on Jesus' probable appropriation and modification of them. Another scholar emphasizes the political, social and economic dimensions of life in understanding Jesus. Still another scholar emphasizes the larger Graeco-Roman world and the intersection of Hellenistic and Jewish culture in Jesus' setting. Are the Qumran, pseudepigraphic and rabbinic texts to be weighed as to which is most to be used, or are they to be used in combination in some plausible manner? Is the Q material vestiges of a "Q Gospel" of a distinct Jesus movement (not to mention the hypothesis of strata of Q), and, if so, is it earlier and more directly relevant for historical-Jesus reconstruction? We could go on with other examples, but I think the point is clear.

These observations already lead into my second point. Sound historical work that is to be of broad and lasting use in the field must also interact fully with other scholars on all relevant issues. The oceanic amount of scholarly work germane to historical-Jesus research will make this difficult. It will require some clever authorial decisions to package the necessary scholarly debate so that it does not obscure but forms an integral part of the historical reconstruction of the historical Jesus. There are bound to be omissions, with the best will in the world. But, with few exceptions, even the most current and voluminous Jesus books show what must be judged either puzzling oversights or disappointing shortcuts and deliberate neglect of important work. If the aim is merely to get a splashy book off the press, or to get a personal brain-child or academic "beef" off one's chest, or if one imagines that one's personal opinion is so valuable and revered that one does not need to interact with others, then my plea can be

---

102 Charles W. Hedrick, "Introduction: The Tyranny of the Synoptic Jesus," *Semeia* 44 (1988): 1-8, puts the issue sharply about the need to establish a firm critical basis for the sources to use in historical-Jesus work. This issue of *Semeia* was devoted to the promotion of extra-canonical Christian materials for historical-Jesus work, with additional essays by John Dominic Crossan, James M. Robinson, M. Eugene Boring, Helmut Koester, Pheme Perkins and William D. Stroker. See also the essays in *Semeia* 49 (1990) on "The Apocryphal Jesus and Christian Origins."

ignored. But I suggest that it is at the very least a misjudgment to do so. There will certainly be the need for "general reader" books in which scholars are free to omit this direct interaction and elaborate justification for what is offered. I do think, however, that even in these the true scholar should indicate where issues are disputed and where his/her view is new, untested or a minority one, and should provide the reader with some further reading suggestions that reflect the diversity in the field. Otherwise, the general reader is in fact misled, and such publications represent mischief more than scholarship.

I turn to a third observation. Even the most recent and most scholarly works show how difficult (impossible?) it is to approach the historical Jesus free of the influence of one's own religious and existential preferences, commitments and concerns. I suggest two things. First, scholars should be expected to indicate as candidly as they can their own agenda and concerns of this nature, as they are relevant to historical-Jesus work. This will require as a preliminary step in historical-Jesus work that scholars do some self-examination and candid appraisal of themselves. Second, scholars should then be expected to demonstrate a bracketing or off-setting of the effects of their personal commitments in their historical-Jesus work. I do not ask that we try to escape who we are, only that we attempt to be self-critical. This should involve such things as a reluctance to use anachronistic and tendentious language in describing Jesus (e.g., as an advocate of "grace"), and particularly an effort to do justice to the factors in Jesus that do not mesh well with the scholar's concerns. A coherence or symmetry between a historical reconstruction of Jesus and one's own religious, political and social programs is not necessarily a mark against the reconstruction, but one at least ought to assess with double caution such agreements as perhaps suspiciously convenient and requiring extra-strong defence. Moreover, one should be expected to treat with special accuracy and care those features of the historical Jesus with which one is not comfortable. Dissonances or major differences between one's own preferences and one's reconstruction of Jesus are not necessarily evidence in favour of one's work, but they at least make it more difficult to be accused of fashioning Jesus after one's own image, and may indicate a proper scholarly rigour and self-critical ability.

In light of the many previous attempts to formulate criteria for historical-Jesus work, it may seem presumptuous to attempt yet another suggestion.[103] But I do so in light of the work surveyed here and on the basis of an analogy I propose between historical-Jesus research and another historical enterprise with which I am acquainted, New Testament textual criticism.[104]

---

103 See Dennis Polkow, "Method and Criteria for Historical Jesus Research," in Kent H. Richards, ed., *Society of Biblical Literature 1987 Seminar Papers* (Atlanta: Scholars Press, 1987), 336-56.

104 The basic point developed here had occurred to me when I happened across an essay by Crossan in which he makes a somewhat similar proposal ("Divine Immediacy," esp. 121-

The diversity in results in current historical-Jesus work sketched above arises in part from diversity in the evidence weighted or privileged as more important or more authentic. The fact is that there is a real diversity in evidence available and there are good reasons for taking more than one type of evidence in the Jesus tradition seriously, so it is not surprising that scholars come out differently in their reconstructions. There are, for example, Jesus traditions with a prophetic and eschatological emphasis, and other evidence of a sapiential and aphoristic nature, both in sources of early date and generally high value. We need to develop a procedure for dealing with the diversity in evidence and traditions about Jesus, especially where it is difficult to distinguish diverse traditions as to authenticity on the basis of the date of the sources, either because the sources are from the same approximate period or because we cannot agree upon the dates and provenance of the sources. We need a procedure involving something more than the preferences of the individual scholar. A certain analogy between historical-Jesus work and New Testament textual criticism permits a suggestion about how to proceed.[105] In both, it is a major objective to reconstruct a now lost "original," evidence of which is available only in the form of subsequent tradition. In both New Testament textual criticism and in historical-Jesus research, the extant evidence is less than uniform in its witness to the original, with variant readings or variant interpretations and traditions of Jesus respectively. In both endeavours, scholars seek to date and evaluate the extant sources as a means of assessing their witness to the "original" phenomenon, and in both lines of work there are difficulties and disagreements. Moreover, in both there appear to be variants in sources of approximately equal age, making the "external" factors concerning the quality of the source less than decisive.

In such cases in New Testament textual criticism, one takes account of "internal" factors in evaluating variants, and the particular matters considered are specific to the text-critical question (e.g., scribal habits). But in general terms the aim in weighing "internal evidence" is to reconstruct the reading that best explains all the variants. Here I suggest we may have a principle that can be adapted for historical-Jesus research. We should examine the variation in those sources for the Jesus tradition with strong "external" claims as to age and general value, preferring that reconstruction of the historical Jesus which best

---

27). Crossan proposes a "criterion of adequacy," but apparently without realizing that this amounts to adapting a key criterion from NT textual criticism in the search for the original NT textual reading (see, e.g., Eldon J. Epp and Gordon D. Fee, *Studies in the Theory and Method of New Testament Textual Criticism* [Grand Rapids: Eerdmans, 1993], 14).

105 In what follows, I sketch New Testament textual criticism as practised by what Epp and Fee describe as "reasoned" or "moderate" eclectics, as distinguished from the "thorough-going eclecticism" of Kilpatrick and his student Elliott, who disdain the step of trying to determine the age and general quality of the textual witnesses as a factor in deciding upon original readings (see Epp and Fee, *Studies*, 125-73). The "reasoned eclectic" approach advocated by Epp and Fee is shaped by Westcott and Hort, and Ernest Cadman Colwell, and has in turn shaped my own practice of textual criticism.

accounts for the variation in the sources of early provenance. In the Jesus traditions, the "variants" are not simply differences in words or phrases, but different factors in the tradition (e.g., Jesus' stance within his Jewish setting as well as innovations attributed to him in how to interpret and respond to God within that setting), different collections of material (e.g., miracles, sayings) and different "renditions" or interpretations of Jesus (e.g. synoptic, Johannine, Q, Pauline). Moreover, there are various other data to be accounted for and properly assessed, such as Jesus' relationships with the Baptist, the Pharisees and scribes, the Jerusalem Temple authorities and others.

Just as the text-critical assessment of readings on the basis of "internal" criteria involves taking account of historical factors affecting the textual transmission process, so in historical-Jesus reconstruction one should take into account historical factors that help to assess the variant traditions. These include such matters as Jesus' Galilean background and origins, his connection with (and continuing endorsement of) the activities of John the Baptist, his execution at Jerusalem by Roman authority, and, perhaps more important than is sometimes recognized, the fact and the nature of the enthusiastic religious movement that mushroomed in his name shortly after his execution and that quickly became trans-ethnic and trans-local in scope.[106] In short, I propose that, instead of merely playing off one "variant" in the Jesus tradition against another, we take all these variants as valuable evidence in the reconstruction effort, and attempt a reconstruction that can explain the variants in the light of what we know about the transmission process, thus producing a proposed reconstruction.

4. Conclusion

Perhaps the safest observation to make about the latest round of historical-Jesus research is that it shows no signs of diminishing. Millions of Christians, the general public (particularly in Western, educated circles) and the academy of scholars in New Testament and Christian origins, including related areas, will continue to give eager attention to the aim of a more accurate historical grasp of the Nazarene. Also, as this survey has illustrated, another reason why the current quest will probably continue unchecked is that there remain considerable disagreement and diversity in approach and results. In the light of this diversity, I have offered some observations and suggestions to consider in future attempts at Jesus research. If I am generally correct in pointing out the breadth and complexity of what is involved in seeking to produce more adequate historical-Jesus reconstructions, the impressive works surveyed here will have to be succeeded by even more demanding and carefully-considered analyses. Moreover, we will have to develop more satisfactory measures for treating the complexity of the earliest evidence of the Jesus traditions.

---

106 Sanders, *Jesus and Judaism*, 11, also draws explicit attention to these factors.

23. Enduring Concerns: Desiderata for Future Historical-Jesus Research[1]

Peter Richardson

The "third quest" of the historical Jesus is now in full swing, with new books appearing almost monthly. Methods of approach and concomitant theories are broad and varied, with some notable—even newsworthy attempts—being diametrically opposed to each other. There is no sign of the quest for Jesus abating; indeed, it can never be totally abandoned since it always needs to be tackled afresh in each generation. The current spate of studies promises some advance in the understanding of Jesus, but it is still questionable just how significant those advances will prove to be. The preceding surveys demonstrate many of the strengths and the weaknesses of the recent crop.

1. Surveys of Research: McCready, Humphrey, Henaut, Hurtado

McCready's excellent analysis of the state of historical-Jesus research on the Dead Sea Scrolls is well-balanced and based on intimate familiarity with the scrolls. He highlights important differences between the Jesus movement and the Dead Sea community in matters of initiation rites, membership, inclusiveness and exclusiveness, calendar and predestination; in the light of these differences he argues that Jesus actively "countered a Qumran-like separatist option for community self-definition," promoting inclusiveness of the marginalized and downplaying Torah if it conflicted with the love command. McCready also notes similarities between Jesus and Qumran: prophetic charismatic leadership, futurist eschatology, interpretation of scripture as the basis of the community's practices and beliefs, and mixed attitudes to the Temple. He argues for a Jesus somewhat like the Teacher of Righteousness, with conflicting views on Temple and scripture, but within a futurist and charismatic context.

Humphrey, in her review of nine scholars' views of Jesus' eschatology and apocalypticism, observes that the two who most defy characterization and resist analysis of their presuppositions are Sanders and Vermes, the two who try most clearly to write as historians and to emphasize Jesus' actions. Humphrey's analysis is sensitive to the presuppositions of each author she investigates; whether eschatology is peculiarly susceptible to veiled presuppositions is not certain, but it may well be, since our academic era is so widely suspicious of eschatological and apocalyptic notions, except on the fringes. Wright's and

---

1   It is with regret that I note that Ben Meyer died late in 1995. I should like to dedicate this chapter to him.

others' interest in an apocalyptic Jesus is for Humphrey part of a too-neat picture, theologically conceived in the service of specific theological purposes. Portraits with a few ends left untied are more convincing.

Is the historical Jesus merely another theological construct? Henaut sees the "historical Jesus" as an agent of renewal, constantly being adapted to new social realities, providing a model for modern Christians who face problems of myth and historicity. Those interested in the historical Jesus, however, find a diminishing core of sayings from the tradition to rely upon and a concomitant increasing dependence upon miracles, exorcisms and the like—i.e., actions—although even many of these traditions about actions have to be jettisoned. Henaut argues rather effectively that in such a situation the "historical Jesus" is just another Christology, serving as a social critique or social program, in much the same way as Kähler described many years ago. We have thus come full circle.

A taxonomy of recent interpretations of Jesus can be very useful, and Hurtado offers one excellent pattern to pigeon-hole contributions to the ongoing debate. The differences among his chosen examples defy simple analysis, but Hurtado finds some commonalities: the breadth of evidence used,[2] their interactions with the scholarly world and the continuing influence of one's own presuppositions on one's conclusions. Searching for a way to advance, Hurtado offers an important new, already-tested, suggestion drawn from textual criticism: "the reconstructed reading that best explains all the variants is to be preferred." These differences, he properly points out, are not minor variations but substantially different factors in the tradition, different collections of materials, different interpretations of Jesus. If we take into account the transmission process and attempt a reconstruction explaining the variants, Hurtado posits, we can avoid playing off one form of the tradition against others.

So where are we pointed? A historical Jesus who will explain subsequent christological traditions (Hurtado), who is just another christological construct (Henaut), who is susceptible—even at the level of eschatology—to scholarly presuppositions (Humphrey) and who is something like the Teacher of Righteousness (McCready).

2. Jesus and Herod: Must we Use Different Approaches to "Biography"?

My work has concentrated for many years on the "historical Herod"; I have sometimes reflected on the differences between the two tasks connected with Jesus and Herod.[3] The oddity of the phrase in quotation marks is immediately

---

2   I am much less impressed than he is on this score. See further below.
3   Peter Richardson, *Herod, King of the Jews and Friend of the Romans* (Columbia: University of South Carolina Press, 1996).

apparent. No one would think of tackling Herod in any other way, unless it were in some obviously non-historical fashion: Herod in the movies, in Renaissance art, in stained glass, in operas, in modern English literature. To undertake, as a historian, a study of Herod requires neither claim nor announcement that the project is on the "historical Herod." Why this difference from Jesus? One reason is obvious: Western society has given so much priority to the "Jesus of faith" that it is this scholarly tendency against which the various "quests of the historical Jesus" have had to tilt. The literary texts we use do not make it easy to win that jousting match, for they are themselves overlaid with material that, when it was written, aimed to portray the Jesus of faith. While the material on which we draw for a picture of Herod—mostly Josephus—also has its editorial biases and commitments, the (important) difference is that Herod is not now an object of veneration in the way that Jesus is. In Herod's case the editorial bias runs fairly obviously against him.[4] Although in both cases we might wish to approach the level of a biographical study, it is more nearly possible in the case of Herod than in the case of Jesus. We need, then, to be self-conscious of such differences in our work on Jesus, but we should beware of falling into the trap of thinking we are doing something unusual when we attempt an investigation of the "historical" Jesus.

A second aspect of this comparison between Herod and Jesus goes almost without saying: that Herod is better known than Jesus to secular Roman historians—not well-known, but better known.[5] Alongside this might be noted a related difference, that Herod apparently wrote his own *Memoirs*, which were consulted by Josephus in his lengthy treatment of Herod.[6] These ancient materials on Herod, together with records, decrees and other kinds of assessments of the man and his work, were available on the open market to anyone who might have wished to undertake a study of Herod, as Josephus did. The same is not true of Jesus. One of the fundamental differences and difficulties is that the materials about Jesus, almost without exception, went through a long oral phase before seeing ink and papyrus or parchment. As has long been recognized, literary studies have trouble penetrating this barrier and moving back to the person and personality of the exegete-teacher-healer-polemicist of the first century.

A third difference seems to me particularly instructive: historians have access to more and better evidence for a king (because of his prominence and activities) than for a messianic figure. One of the most useful kinds of evidence is numismatic—the coins Herod minted, set beside coins of his rival Antigonus

---

4   This is true of Josephus, but not one of his main sources, Nicolas of Damascus. So in fact the situation is just a little complicated.

5   Nicolas of Damascus's important study is regrettably lost.

6   Also, regrettably, lost.

and coins of his neighbours in Nabatea, Egypt, Syria and Chalcis. They constitute an impressively eloquent indication of programs and achievements, of propaganda for both internal and external consumption, a set of self-interpretive images and legends that indicate something of his view of himself. There is also an important group of inscriptions from a wide variety of places that show Herod's self-promotion on a wider stage; the language, although restrained, gives almost first-person insights. The remains of his buildings attest to certain features of his character and values, his skills and his interests, his religious convictions and his political-economic goals.[7] None of this type of first-hand evidence from *realia* is available to the scholar of Jesus; what is available does not apply directly to Jesus but to his society, although it is nonetheless useful and important data.

3. General Assessment

Reading between the lines of the various surveys on the historical Jesus—including those above, analyzing Qumran, apocalypticism, the third quest and current contributions—there seems a kind of pessimism about productive developments on the basis of purely literary reexaminations of the sources. What can be determined with most agreement are the biases and convictions of the *writers* (I mean the ancient authors, although it is equally true of modern scholarly writing), not the outlines of the *subject* himself. At the present, the most significant contributions to the current debate are those that draw on some other field of expertise to amplify the faint echoes heard in the literary sources. Thus, one might single out such contributors as Crossan with his interest in anthropology, Freyne with his interest in geography and economics, and Horsley with his interest in sociology as ways in which some modest advances are being made (to which might be added those who work with the evidence from the Dead Sea Scrolls). There is still too little social-scientific work on Jesus generally, and there are still some glaring gaps.

It is hardly appropriate to berate historical-Jesus scholars for not having the same kinds of evidence other scholars might have available. Evidence cannot be wished into existence, and we should be thankful for the rather rich literary remains bearing on Jesus that we do have, including the wider selection of literary evidence that scholars such as Mack, Crossan, Funk and Cameron have pressed into service when drawing a portrait of Jesus.

Nevertheless, it is possible to approximate more nearly the situation we have in Herod research (cf. also Antipas or Agrippa I or Bar Cochba) when tackling the figure of Jesus. We need more attention to the archaeological and artifactual data bearing on Jesus (Freyne refers to some recent advances); fuller

---

7   Details on all these issues in my *Herod*.

consideration of the social-historical setting for understanding Jesus (Crossan and Horsley go part way to filling this need); more detailed investigation of the substantial urban areas that surrounded Galilee in antiquity; deeper interest in trade and traffic and transportation; a more nuanced interpretation of Jewish religious life and life in Jewish towns and villages in the relevant regions. I will illustrate some of these desiderata.

4. Desiderata

4.1 Archaeological and Artifactual Data

There is more relevant data than is usually drawn upon for developing a picture of Jesus.[8] For example, in understanding Jesus' last week—one of the crucial periods of his life—there is impressive evidence for the Temple of Jesus' day, its courts, its architecture and its practices. The events of that last week are only rarely set in a clearly-understood and forcefully-presented concrete situation. Gaps remain: how sacrificial animals were bought and sold,[9] how larger animals were transported through the courts without disrupting the Temple's crowds, how the court of women worked, what prompted such a huge court of Gentiles, where the Sanhedrin met, are all important and unresolved issues.[10]

More important as an issue is the half-shekel tax, how it was paid and why it was important. The tax was paid annually by observant Jews in a silver shekel piece—a Tyrian shekel—that had Melqart (Herakles) on one side and a Tyrian eagle on the other. Jewish pilgrims had to exchange whatever coinage they had, in the case of Galilean and Judaean pilgrims their good aniconic coins, for a coin that honoured Melqart, in order to pay the tax. There are more plausible reasons for Jesus' action in turning over the tables in the Temple than, say, positing its role as a symbol of eschatological destruction.[11]

---

8   It is a good sign that a book has appeared that tries to gather up the relevant archaeological and artifactual materials for understanding Jesus. See John J. Rousseau and Rami Arav, *Jesus and his World: An Archaeological and Cultural Dictionary* (Minneapolis: Fortress, 1995). Hurtado's observation (above) that "newer Jesus research often incorporates . . . archaeological data" seems to me more prophetic than descriptive.

9   See E. P. Sanders, *Judaism: Practice and Belief, 63 BCE to 66 CE* (London: SCM, 1992).

10 On some of these, see Sanders, *Judaism*. A comparative example is instructive. The Temple of Bel at Palmyra had a below-grade gate from the outside, with an open-air but below-grade passage that led almost straight to the altar. This was presumably to allow animals to be brought into the precinct unobtrusively and without creating problems, ritual or otherwise. How was the same result accomplished in Jerusalem?

11 Further, Peter Richardson, "Why Turn the Tables? Jesus' Protest in the Temple Precincts," in Kent H. Richards, ed., *Society of Biblical Literature Seminar Papers 1992* (Atlanta: Scholars Press, 1992), 507-23. For the contrary position, see, *inter alia*, Sanders, *Jesus*.

4.2 Social-Historical Setting

A fragment from the Dead Sea Scrolls shows the importance of drawing on all the relevant data. 4Q159 shows that at Qumran the idea of an annual half-shekel tax for the Temple was strongly rejected, while it is equally clear that the Temple authorities expected all males over 18 years of age to pay annually. This social and religious controversy, which surfaces nowhere else in the literature, was likely to be of some significance. How did it shape Jesus' attitudes to the payment of the Temple tax? There is little indication of this controversy, which has come to our attention from the scroll fragments that have captured so much attention, entering into the discussions of Jesus scholars.

It is striking to see how little attention has been given, until very recently and then only by Israeli scholars, to analyses of Gaulanitis, Batanea, Auranitis and Trachonitis, the regions of Philip the Tetrarch to which Jesus went on numerous occasions and from whence a number of his closest disciples originated.[12] The same is true of Peraea, although to a slightly lesser extent. Fascination for Judaea and Galilee—together with more readily available literary evidence—has prompted scholars to constrain their sights rather significantly. What was the character of these regions, ethnically and economically and culturally? We simply do not yet know, even though these areas represent a substantial portion of Jesus' "sphere of influence."

There is no study whatsoever of Ituraeans, who occupied at various times much of the Huleh Valley, the northern Golan, Trachonitis, the slopes of Mount Hermon and the Beka'a Valley in Lebanon, including the ancient states of Chalcis and Abila—neither of which has been studied in any depth.[13] All of these are regions in which Jesus travelled, from which followers came, through which Christianity moved at relatively early stages.

Likewise, there is still no study of the character or the reign of Herod Philip in Gaulanitis and its adjacent regions, despite the fact that Jesus seems on more than one occasion to have gone into Philip's regions in order to avoid being in Antipas's areas. Until such a basic study is available, we cannot say with confidence why Jesus went there or what features of the area attracted him, and we thereby lose one important explanatory line of attack in understanding the outlines of Jesus' life. Scholars have fastened too much on the Roman political scene (crucially important for the final weeks of Jesus' life) and ignored the local political scenes in the north of the country, especially the rivalry between Antipas and Philip and the local conditions existing there. Each was a ruler in his own territories, free from direct Roman rule except in unusual cases such as tension with Nabatea

---

12 Dan Urman, "Public Structures and Jewish Communities in the Golan Heights," in Dan Urman and Paul V. M. Flesher, eds., *Ancient Synagogues* (Leiden: Brill, 1995), vol. 2, 375-617.

13 See especially the work of Shimon Dar and Z. Ma'oz, and the contrary views of Dan Urman, in "Public Structures."

4.3 Urbanism

Jesus is portrayed for the most part as a Mediterranean or Galilean peasant, or some variant thereof. That is helpful, of course. Galilee was essentially a rural area, with only two cities of any consequence, and one of those (Tiberias) was of very recent foundation and probably not much of an urban centre during Jesus' day;[14] the other (Sepphoris) was more significant, but not at this period a really large city. Despite the truth of this generalization, Galilee was ringed almost continuously by cities (πόλεις) or by other Hellenistic foundations, cities with rural areas attached to them that provided agricultural produce: Ptolemais on the west; Tyre on the northwest; Panias in the northeast; Hippos and Gadara and Pella on the east and southeast, all three on the other side of the Sea of Galilee-Jordan River; Beth Shean and Beth Yerah, also to the southeast; and Dor on the southwest. The only gap in this near-continuous ring was on the south, where Samaria bordered Galilee, although even there Sebaste was not far to the south in Samaritan territory. Every town in Galilee was less than a day's walk (32 km; 20 miles) from one or more Hellenistic cities.

The presence of these cities modulates quite significantly the rural and agrarian character of Galilee, for these cities influenced its patterns of trade and transportation, provided its currency, offered it outlets to the sea, acted as trading partners and so on. These cities also promoted cultural and religious activities that may well have been attractive to some: theatres, amphitheatres, odeia, baths, temples and the like. It is not clear how many Galileans may have availed themselves of these latter facilities, but it is certain that the economic connections were important, so it is not far-fetched to imagine that there was also some cultural and religious influence.

The Jesus traditions report such contacts, although they are often downgraded or overlooked entirely. Mark 7:24-9:30 is an obvious collection of this material that includes visits through the regions of Tyre and Sidon, a journey through the Decapolis, a visit to Panias-Caesarea Philippi—in short a long stay outside Galilee. Why? There is little discussion of this line of enquiry and even less attention to the relevance of the socio-religious character of these areas for interpreting Jesus.

4.4 Trade, Traffic and Transportation

Closely related to this last observation are the economic infrastructures of Galilee and Judaea.[15] Although these may influence the reconstruction of Jesus'

---

14 Founded in about 18 CE by Herod Antipas in honour of his patron, the Emperor Tiberius. Recent excavations have begun to develop a picture of some features of its early life, although not the first-century features.

15 See the debate between Richard A. Horsley and Eric M. Meyers on the upper Galilee in *ASOR Bulletin* 297 (1995): 5-28.

life somewhat less than other elements, they are nevertheless important since they affect his activities quite directly. What Jesus does, beginning with his own trade (carpenter? building worker?) and going on to include such matters as his itinerant activities, his movements back and forth across the Sea of Galilee, his preference at certain times for Galilee and at other times for Gaulanitis or other more remote regions—all these matters depend upon knowledge of how others in the general population did (or did not do) the same things.

Large assumptions are typically made about such matters, with too little sustained analysis of the real situation. That is changing through a number of studies of Galilee,[16] but even in these studies some of the unprepossessing features of ancient life do not get the treatment they need. There is no adequate full-scale study, for example, of nearby cities or any of the cities and towns in the land of Israel (even including Jerusalem) comparable in scope and approach to studies of Corinth, Ephesus and Rome.[17] This means that we are lacking crucial dimensions of the social-historical setting in which to situate an understanding of Jesus. There is still a need for informed studies of Nabatean trade and commerce, relations with Egypt and the influence of Syria on the northern parts of the region.[18]

4.5 Jewish Religious Life in Towns

Alongside application of insights from the study of the great Hellenistic cities that surrounded Galilee, applying information from typical first-century Jewish towns and villages to the study of Jesus is needed.[19] This has often been attempted, but usually predicated on inadequate understanding of the situation in the first century. Capernaum, for example, is often used as the "city of Jesus" without appreciating that much of Capernaum as it is known in the excavations is a Byzantine town; Sepphoris and Chorazin have been used more recently, with the same limitations.

Gradually a corpus of towns and villages is being built up that can be used to establish the character of life in small agrarian-based communities in the first

---

16 Most notably see: Seán Freyne, *Galilee, Jesus and the Gospels: Literary Approaches and Historical Investigations* (Philadelphia: Fortress, 1988), and *Galilee from Alexander the Great to Hadrian, 323 B.C.E. to 145 C.E.: A Study of Second Temple Judaism* (Wilmington: Michael Glazier, 1980); Lee I. Levine, ed., *The Galilee in Late Antiquity* (New York: Jewish Theological Seminary of America, 1992); Richard A. Horsley, *Galilee: History, Politics, People* (Valley Forge: Trinity Press International, 1995), and *Archaeology, History, and Society in Galilee* (Valley Forge: Trinity Press International, 1996).

17 For example, see Donald Engels, *Roman Corinth: An Alternative Model for the Classical City* (Chicago: University of Chicago Press, 1990).

18 For some elements of what is needed, see Fergus Millar, *The Roman Near East 31 BC to AD 337* (Cambridge: Harvard University Press, 1993).

19 Andrew Overman has begun to develop a clearly-reasoned understanding of these factors.

century. The first-century town with the most extensive archaeological excavations to date has been Gamla in the Golan.[20] It is not a city that Jesus is reported to have visited, but it remains extremely important, both for its associations with and evidence of the Great Revolt and for its pre-70 evidence of ordinary life in a Jewish town in a relatively remote location, not heavily influenced by Hellenization.[21] Even more important may be the excavations at Yodefat (Jotapata) for illuminating a medium-sized town almost in the centre of things in lower Galilee, only a few miles from Nazareth and Sepphoris.[22] Parts of the town are laid out on a Hippodamian plan, the whole is surrounded with a major fortification wall—the reason it played a part in the defence against the Romans in 67 CE under Josephus—and the upper part is surrounded with an earlier Hellenistic fortification wall. Perhaps eventually Bethsaida will become useful too, if in fact the current excavations are correctly identified.

In these sites there is a clear opportunity to study and to apply physical information from clearly datable contexts (Gamla and Yodefat both provide consistently pre-67 CE evidence) to an understanding of Jesus. These will show the features of semi-rural life in Galilee, almost exactly the correct context for Jesus' setting. Among the features that emerge strongly from such evidence is, at Gamla, the character of first-century synagogues: community-oriented, multi-purpose, relatively plain and unadorned structures, not fitting in many respects the later "rules" for synagogues.[23] It is, for example, not oriented properly to Jerusalem, has no provision for the Torah scroll, no public speaking platform (βῆμα); but it does have a closely adjacent ritual bath (מקוה), a study (מדרש בית, or similar structure), benches, and is near but not at the high point of the town. While no first-century Galilean synagogue has yet been found, Yodefat is the sort of place where one might find one.

In both cities several ritual baths have been uncovered, sometimes with olive oil installations, sometimes in private houses, once in conjunction with the synagogue. These indications of a concern for ritual purity correspond to other indications: the prevalence in multiple locations in each site of stoneware,

---

20 Shemarya Gutman, "Gamla," in Ephraim Stern, ed., *New Encyclopedia of Archaeological Excavations in the Holy Land* (Jerusalem: Israel Exploration Society, 1993), vol. 2, 459-63, and literature cited there.

21 Not heavily influenced, but affected to some extent by Hellenistic associations, are Tyrian coin hoards, an almost Hippodamian plan and some small iconic finds that show close associations with the dominant culture.

22 The current excavations there are sponsored by the University of Rochester, under the leadership of William Scott Green; the archaeological work is directed by Mordechai Aviam of the Israel Antiquities Authority.

23 I still believe, *pace* Howard Clark Kee and others, that it is appropriate to refer to these buildings as synagogues. See Rainer Riesner, "Synagogues in Jerusalem," in Richard Bauckham, ed., *The Book of Acts in its First Century Setting* (Grand Rapids: Eerdmans, 1995), vol. 4, 175-211. The dispute is largely definitional.

indicating that the mishnaic view that stoneware does not contract ritual impurity had already developed and that it was observed by a number of people in each location. There is strong evidence of local Galilean pottery, alongside evidence of some imported pottery.

Just as characters such as Herod need to be set firmly in their context, so Jesus must be set in the best available understanding of his context. Despite the great attention that has been given to Jesus, it is still rare to find him set solidly in the realities of first-century Galilee. And where that effort has been made, with some increased frequency recently, first-century Galilee is far too often pictured on the basis of literary evidence rather than artifactual, architectural and urban evidence.

How might this influence the resulting picture? Jesus will probably tend to become a more observant Jew, since the best evidence we have shows a reasonably high degree of observance of purity rules. He will have used ritual baths, bought stoneware in the market, used local and imported pottery at dinners with his acquaintances. While he may have eschewed the theatre at Sepphoris,[24] it seems reasonably likely that he knew it, knew other Hellenistic and Roman institutions such as the bath, had travelled in adjacent regions where he may have known a Temple of Apollo at Kedesh, temples to Pan and a Temple of Roma and Augustus at Panias, along with a wide variety of religious institutions in Decapolis cities. He probably knew a little about Tyrian, Nabatean and Iturean religion, together with their deities. If he travelled through Sebaste, he may well have known about Demeter and Kore, the quintessential Greek mystery. In his travels he might have happened upon Cynics at Gadara,[25] and no doubt other philosophical schools elsewhere. What is important is how Jesus might have behaved in the cross-cultural context that influenced Galilee and Galileans.

I do not suggest that research activities ought to be shaped by their potential for understanding Jesus and his world. It is noteworthy, however, that the research projects of scholars who are interested in the historical Jesus have tended to focus on obvious and well-trod paths, especially on the literary creations in the gospels, and have not ranged as broadly as they might have done.

4.6 Actions of Jesus

Considerable attention has been given to ways in which the social sciences might shape the research activities of Jesus scholars, from a variety of

---

24 For the claim he knew it well, see Richard Batey, *Jesus and the Forgotten City* (Grand Rapids: Baker, 1991), in an exaggerated fashion.

25 Why do so few who wish to make a case for a Cynic Jesus ignore the evidence for Cynicism just a few miles from the Sea of Galilee at Gadara? Although I am not an advocate of the Jesus-as-Cynic view, it seems to me the case could be strengthened by using some of the broader data available.

perspectives, but especially anthropology and sociology. The fresh insights into matters of honour and shame, patronage, kinship, protest movements, purity questions, roles of women associates, small group developments and related issues have helpfully opened up new ways of thinking about Jesus. Some of this has, almost as a spin-off, cast new light on some of Jesus' actions as he was influenced by Mediterranean customs and values.

Occasionally scholars have recognized the importance of giving preference to Jesus' actions in the quest for an adequate method of approach and for an adequate resultant understanding of him.[26] I have already referred to the "Temple-tantrum," which I believe is still badly interpreted and much misunderstood as a quasi-Christian action expressing anticipation of eschatological judgment on Judaism. This seems to me nonsense in the context. It is a protest against the defilement of the Temple's purity and holiness and a call to resistance to Temple authorities on the matter of the half-shekel tax. His action—or rather Peter's—in Capernaum in paying the tax is agreed to reluctantly and at no cost to himself, with the right coinage miraculously provided! His actions in remaining silent on messianic questions, in going to John for baptism, in entering Jerusalem, in travelling with women, in eating with sinners and prostitutes, become more important when looked at as deliberately chosen actions.

5. Conclusion

Beneath these comments lies a major methodological issue: what evidence should be heard and preferred? The evidence is of several kinds: literary (easily manipulated and adapted to new situations), especially Jesus' words (later church-related problems are read back into his utterances) but also his actions (requiring interpretation as much as words); archaeological (unspecific and general, and not pointing directly to Jesus); and social scientific (imposed from modern assessments, generally of modern cultures). Clearly no one kind of evidence will do and we will have to do the best job we can with the range of approaches and evidence that we have.

The stark reality, however, is that most scholars use primarily literary evidence to develop their pictures of Jesus. Within that literary evidence, most concentrate on Jesus' sayings. This set of scholarly convictions needs to change. Dependence upon literary evidence has virtually exhausted itself. More—much more—needs to be made of Jesus' actions and of the context in which he is to be understood, especially from what can be reconstructed from archaeological

---

26 I have in mind here particularly E. P. Sanders, *Jesus and Judaism* (Philadelphia: Fortress, 1985), although he did not consistently carry through with the program he laid out. In the current crop, John P. Meier, *A Marginal Jew: Rethinking the Historical Jesus*, 2 vols. (New York: Doubleday, 1991-94), is closer.

data. Just as we have begun to learn how to use social-scientific methods to raise new questions and to reshape the general outlines of the picture of Jesus, we should allow the investigations of first-century Jewish life, culture and relationships to reshape the picture, for Jesus was not so much "against culture" as "within culture," to use Niebuhr's categories. While we can only be grateful for the immense amount of work that has been done, however, especially in the last decade or so, on the historical Jesus, there is still a need for more work and in rather different directions from past studies.

CONCLUSION

24. Making and Re-Making the Jesus-Sign: Contemporary Markings on the Body of Christ

William E. Arnal

1. Recurring Themes: Significances & Undercurrents

If the collection of essays presented here is representative—and it appears to be—three issues seem to be broadly characteristic of scholarly "hot spots" in current work on the historical Jesus. They include the "Judaism" or broad cultural context of Jesus, apocalypticism and epistemic neutrality. All three topics are linked in terms of underlying world-views and all are intertwined in the essays collected in this volume.

1.1 The Judaism of Jesus

Several of the papers in this collection deal explicitly with that much-debated conundrum of contemporary Jesus scholarship, the Cynic hypothesis. John Dominic Crossan, Burton Mack and John Marshall all address this theme, as do three of the four surveys of scholarship in the second section (Wayne McCready's paper, focusing as it does exclusively on the Dead Sea Scrolls, is the exception). Leif Vaage, in his concluding remarks on the first section, also devotes considerable attention to this issue.

The basic point of the Cynic hypothesis—the essential commensurability of the social dynamics of Jesus' behaviour with that of the Cynics of his day—is not especially radical or shocking. What, then, drives people to excesses of judgment and choler (in one direction or another) about this question? Central to the debate are the implications of this assertion for Jesus' "Judaism" and the "Jewish context" in which he is assumed to have been firmly located. Surveys of the field tend to raise this truism as an objection to the Cynic Jesus; in fact, nearly all the papers in this collection which do not deal directly with the Cynic hypothesis nevertheless feel it necessary to comment on the extent to which Jesus was or was not an "observant Jew." This motif is a major theme of McCready's paper, Seán Freyne's (as much a critique of the Cynic hypothesis as it is a defence of a particular type of "Jewish Galilean" Jesus, the two most frequently serving as symbolic antitheses) and Peter Richardson's closing comments.

As Freyne makes clear, one of the driving forces behind the strong affirmation of the Judaism of Jesus is the spectre of anti-Semitism, particularly pronounced since the anti-Semitic horrors of Hitler's Germany. Yet advocates of the Cynic hypothesis are hardly open to charges of anti-Semitism. Mack, perhaps its most impassioned advocate, has contributed more to the exposure of anti-Semitism in Christian theology and mythology than many of his critics.[1]

Part of the phenomenon of talking past each other is a result of considering different types of evidence. Richardson's plea that *realia* be given more weight as evidence, especially in contrast to over-worked literary materials, serves a substantive, as well as a methodological, end: such an emphasis, he says, based on archaeological evidence (e.g., the possible remains of pre-70 CE synagogue buildings, purification sites or *mikvaoth*), will suggest reconstructions in which "Jesus will probably tend to become a more observant Jew." Freyne, also focusing on the immediate cultural context of first-century Galilee, arrives at a similar conclusion, placing the "Hellenization" of the Christian movement beyond Jesus both chronologically and geographically. At the other end of the spectrum, Crossan and Mack—and even Marshall, who directly criticizes them—rely on evidence of a primarily literary sort: Crossan on Q and the *Didache*, Mack mainly on Q, and Marshall on *Thomas*. There is little dialogue between factions, in spite of the fact that the "Cynic camp" and the "Jewish camp" are operating in direct and deliberate antithesis to one another. The literary evidence on its own simply cannot support the image of an observant Jesus, so must be supplemented with external interpretive devices by those who wish to construct Jesus as an observant Jew. On the other hand, the archaeological evidence does not really pertain, one way or another, to Jesus' comparability to Cynic philosophers, at least as the hypothesis has so far been articulated.

So we are left with a very peculiar phenomenon: no one denies Jesus' Judaism, yet it is bitterly contested; the parties do not debate the issue directly, only rarely addressing one another; and not all evidence is considered primary by everyone. Only time will provide the perspective necessary for a retrospective analysis, but a few observations are still worth making now.

No one denies that Jesus was a Jew. The issue cannot be whether Jesus was either "Jewish" or "Cynic/Hellenistic," in spite of it being framed this way far too frequently; it is instead *what kind of Jew* Jesus was, or, to put it differently, what the significance of his Jewishness might have been. Shylock's "What is a

---

1 Referring here most specifically to his *A Myth of Innocence: Mark and Christian Origins* (Philadelphia: Fortress, 1988). Note also Leif Vaage's *Galilean Upstarts: Jesus' First Followers According to Q* (Valley Forge: Trinity Press International, 1994), 66-86, in which he argues that the character of the critique behind the Q woes against the Pharisees is more sardonic than serious.

Jew?" requires an answer now at the historical and conceptual levels as much as it did in Portia's Venice at the philosophical level.

Those who advocate a Jewish Jesus imagine that Jesus' Judaism exercised a significant effect on his life, self-understanding and sense of purpose. And although everyone concedes that Judaism in the first century was diverse, and although even advocates of the Jewish Jesus vary somewhat in their understanding of what is *meant* by being observant, what the assertion boils down to is that in some way or another Jesus observed and had an explicit interest in sacrificial obligations, purity standards and notions of atonement (or *mitzvaoth* of some kind)—the *sine qua non* of religious Judaism.

The label "religious" is the crux of the matter. At its heart are the debates concerning categories, idealism and the meaning of "religion." That is, the very self-evident and uncontentious statement, "Jesus was a Jew," is taken to mean, by advocates of the observant Jewish Jesus, that Jesus was a religious person in the tradition of Judaism. Jesus, as a Jew, would have participated in his religion's essence. This view is by no means self-evidently false. It conceptualizes and hence manufactures "facts," however, on the basis of a fundamental preconceived outlook. In this instance, the preconceived outlook revolves around the reality of religion as *sui generis*: religion is an entity unto itself. "Jesus was a Jew" can *only* mean "Jesus was a religious Jew."

Advocates of the Cynic hypothesis assume that the claim to Jesus' Jewishness simply locates him ethnically and historically: one should not assume that Jesus' placement in first-century Galilee or his "racial" identity prevented him from being critical of or even unconcerned with certain aspects of his culture, including the religious ones. There is no reason, they argue, to isolate those elements we call "religious" from the politically and culturally-critical stance of Jesus toward his social matrix, and make them immune from the same range of choice as all other elements. In this view, there is no need to imagine that Jesus conceived himself as a religious figure or engaged in a "ministry": what we now call religion was so thoroughly a part of everyday life that it was indistinguishable from other aspects of culture, social life, politics and economics.[2] As a result, it is anachronistic to imagine a traditional and narrowly-defined "religious" Jesus, in much the same way that it is unrealistic to imagine that European peasants in the Middle Ages were particularly concerned with scholastic theology.

---

2   For one of the most interesting and successful recent attempts to provide a history of Galilee (as the context of Jesus and the location of earliest "Christian" developments) from this perspective, see Richard A. Horsley, *Galilee: History, Politics, People* (Valley Forge: Trinity Press International, 1995). See also his "Innovation in Search of Reorientation: New Testament Studies Rediscovering its Subject Matter," *Journal of the American Academy of Religion* 62 (1994): 1127-66.

The evidence does not allow us to pass judgment on these two options. Richardson can look at Galilee, find *mikvaoth* there and conclude that Jesus might well have been an observant Jew; Mack can find evidence that Galilee in the first century was cosmopolitan and open to various non-Jewish, Hellenistic influences, thereby making a case for Jesus as a Cynic. Richardson can cite the "Temple tantrum" as evidence for Jesus' orthodoxy, while Mack can point to the earliest aphorisms for signs that Jesus tended to ignore what we consider quintessentially Jewish religious issues,[3] and was more concerned with broad cultural critique: the everydayness of life, not its grand ontological significances.

One reason the evidence cannot decisively support one side or the other is that the dichotomy itself is one that pertains to our own time, not to antiquity. The issue of the place and significance of religion can only emerge and generate controversy once religion has been effectively separated from other socio-cultural phenomena. The debate represents a focal instance of one of the more significant intellectual issues of our time, the question of idealism and categories. Are products of the mind, its habitual classifications, real or not? Perhaps the greatest single impact of that discomfiting cultural process which we identify as "postmodernism" is its corrosion of categories. Its advent is inextricably bound with the conditions of living which alter the way in which we view the world.[4] In this regard, of particular importance is the experience of fragmentation which is increasingly affecting the apprehension of what it means to be a subject, and how we conceive of our subjectivity.[5]

For present purposes, the effects of this fragmentation are more directly relevant than its causes.[6] The main intellectual response has been an effort to

---

3   It is worth noting in passing that the standard "quintessential Jewish religious issues" are actually questions of Jewish-Christian relations and polemic. That is, the focus (regardless of the stance taken) tends to be on the cumbersomeness (or absence thereof) of Torah and related purity requirements, something that is assumed to be the major concern of first-century Jews simply because it has been, through the centuries, the major concern of Christians encountering Judaism.

4   This is a difficulty with N. T. Wright's criticism of Crossan ("Taking the Text with her Pleasure: A Post-Post-Modernist Response to J. Dominic Crossan, *The Historical Jesus: The Life of a Mediterranean Jewish Peasant*," *Theology* 96 [1993]: 303-309): it treats "postmodernism" as a theory to which one might posit reasonable alternatives, rather than an overarching world-view which affects all of us, regardless of theoretical or epistemic stance.

5   Hence, an example is Derrida's rejection of any ontological ground in the text, when it had tended to be taken for granted that either the subject reader or the subject author, as an irreducible whole, infused the act of communication with meaning; and again, Lacan, who undercut the unity of the subject at the psychological level; and Althusser, who argued simultaneously that the very constitution of the subject is imposed externally by ideological "interpellation," and is involved in the same sorts of struggles and contradictions that permeate the cultural organism as a whole. The list could go on. It is important to see these intellectual contributions as symptomatic, *not* as normative or "correct."

6   One of the best discussions of its causes is Fredric Jameson's *Postmodernism, Or, The Cultural Logic of Late Capitalism* (Durham: Duke University Press, 1991).

reconceptualize human affairs in ways that accord with our contemporary experience—to take our heritage, which includes not so much Jesus but the extent to which "Jesus" has been a meaningful part of our culture (including the various "quests"), and conceptualize and explain it in terms that make sense to us. As always, cultural development and change is not a neutral process; it requires a response. Typically, this response is one of resistance. It sometimes manifests itself in a reaffirmation of the validity of that which is lost, its proponents behaving with idealist assumptions and imagining that the struggle to retain our souls is being fought at the level of ideas. With such an assumption, the response involves the continual affirmation to the mind, with as much evidence as one can muster, that the concepts on which we base our world-view are still valid. The struggle for our souls, for our selves, our very identities, therefore takes place at the level of asserting and intellecually defending those very comfortable and threatened conceptions—or means of conceptualizing—which are losing their resonance, in an effort to rebuild them, revivify them and thus once again live in a (conceptually) stable universe.

The alternative, if one approaches the malaise from a materialistic perspective, is to recognize that conceptions are products of the actual construction of the world of social humanity itself, and that the failure of certain conceptions to persist in a meaningful way is due less to intellectual stagnation than it is to a world whose human relations suggest different and changing patterns to the mind. In a (North Atlantic) world in which religion for many has been reduced to a formal glaze upon the secular workings of an increasingly total culture, translation is required to turn "religion" into something that corresponds in some way to the social experience of the (post)modern mind. In a world (this is not limited to the North Atlantic) of multinational corporate holdings and interlocking boards of directors, it is difficult to imagine ownership, legal subjectivity or the self-boundedness of the autonomous subject. Since the subject or sense of personal/human groundedness cannot be created *ex nihilo*, it must be constructed within and upon the material culture in which we now subsist, a task which requires not only working *with* the conceptual framework dictated by those circumstances but also changing those actual circumstances in such a way that we are left with a world better suited to modern human needs. Such a perspective lends itself to ignoring and even opposing conceptual archaisms such as "religion," and reifications thereof, including "Judaism." From this stance comes the passion and interest invested by advocates of the Cynic hypothesis and other opponents of the "Jesus the Jew" reconstruction, which derive from the assumption that these ideal conceptions are not only archaic and meaningless, but counterproductive. Indeed, most advocates of the Cynic hypothesis (Crossan, Mack, Vaage) are patently interested in a world in which human interests and desires are given the prominence and respect due to them.

The debate about the Jewish Jesus, in other words, conceals and reflects a much larger stance toward the shifting faces of reality. The "Jewish Jesus" marks a cryptic appeal to an idealistic vision of reality in which loss of the subject in the face of postmodern fragmentation can be reclaimed with the purposeful reassertion of the basic conceptual contours of that subject. The Cynic Jesus and other reconstructions which reject the model of Jesus as observant and orthodox implicitly assert the irremediability of changes made to our world and call for the creation of meaning through practical changes rather than recourse to nostalgia.

1.2 The Issue of Apocalypticism

The apocalypticism of Jesus' original "message" is, if anything, even more hotly debated and current than that of Jesus' Judaism. One might imagine that the issue here is once again the question of a covert fight about ideal or ideological categories and their validity, a fight prompted by the postmodern dissolution of modernity's formerly unquestioned basic conceptions of reality. But the situation is more complicated than this. Those who defend the apocalypticism of Jesus do so, paradoxically, by calling into question the boundedness of that particular category itself. The validity of the label is promoted by denying the sufficiency of the label itself, which is quite the reverse of the process taken in the defence of Jesus' Judaism. Notably, those who defend the apocalypticism of Jesus tend also to tilt in favour of "Jewish Jesus" reconstructions.

Advocates of the apocalyptic Jesus have a long scholarly tradition behind them. The first scholarly effort to find the Jesus of history, undertaken by German academics in the 19th century, ran aground precisely in casting Jesus as a liberal ethicist with a moral message, ignoring completely the apocalyptic world-view deeply embedded in the gospels as simply too uncongenial to their own world-view. This collective effort to reconstruct an amiable and liberal Jesus was decisively stripped of its credibility, first by Johannes Weiss's work which presented a Jesus imbued with a sense of eschatological urgency,[7] and even more so by Albert Schweitzer, whose initial study[8] took a position similar to that of Weiss, and whose even more influential review of the field[9] sounded the death knell for the overly-subjective liberal Jesuses—and indeed, for several decades, for historical-Jesus research itself. Although by the late 1950s the quest for the historical Jesus had begun to recover from Schweitzer's onslaught, the apocalyptic Jesus was firmly entrenched in the scholarly imagination as a

---

7   Johannes Weiss, *Die Predigt Jesu vom Reiche Gottes*, 3rd ed. (Göttingen: Vandenhoeck & Ruprecht, 1964 [1892]).

8   Albert Schweitzer, *Das Messianitäts- und Leidensgeheimnis: Eine Skizze des Lebens Jesu*, 3rd ed. (Tübingen: J. C. B. Mohr, 1956 [1901]).

9   Albert Schweitzer, *The Quest of the Historical Jesus: A Critical Study of its Progress from Reimarus to Wrede*, trans. W. Montgomery (New York: Macmillan, 1968 [1906]).

dogmatic *sine qua non*. The effect of this has been to make any efforts to reconstruct a Jesus for whom an imminent future apocalyptic expectation is *not* a central part of his self-conception or agenda appear to be a self-serving "Jesus in one's own image" of the sort unmasked by Schweitzer. The proponents of the apocalyptic Jesus have made this very clear, and indeed have explicitly compared "Jesus the Cynic sage" to the liberal Jesuses of the 19th century.

Their basic position is this: to most academics, apocalypticism is an utterly alien world-view, whereas the image of Jesus the counter-cultural teacher (although this is not the only alternative to an apocalyptic Jesus) is decidedly congenial. Those who wish to deny that Jesus' message was apocalyptic in substance are therefore succumbing to the quite understandable (but unfortunate) desire to cast Jesus in their own image. Their resistance to an apocalyptic Jesus is simply a resistance to an alien or strange Jesus, a resistance to the uncongenial image of him which has in some measure secured the neutrality of scholarship for so many decades. The corollaries to this line of reasoning are that the non-apocalyptic Jesus, since congenial, is therefore *not* historical; meanwhile, those who advocate an apocalyptic Jesus have nothing to gain thereby, and thus their conclusions are more reliable, more likely to be based on the facts of the matter alone, than those of the tendentious liberals who wish to reduce Jesus scholarship to its state toward the end of the 19th century.

This position has its strengths and weaknesses. The first element of the critique certainly has considerable force, at least if it is limited to the observation that contemporary scholarship that denies Jesus' apocalypticism shows a strong tendency to use that denial as an opportunity to turn Jesus into a slightly disgruntled, liberal, university professor. But the corollaries are usually left unstated because they are not easily defensible. A view arrived at as a result of bias is not necessarily false. Advocates of a non-apocalyptic Jesus adduce a good deal of evidence to support their views; accusations of bias simply avoid having to deal directly with that evidence. To be sure, those who deny Jesus' apocalypticism may do so out of a desire to make Jesus appear less alien; at times also out of a desire to undercut contemporary brands of millenarian Christianity. But if their opponents have no corresponding impetus, no bias *toward* apocalypticism, what can be motivating their vehement denunciation of the "Jesus as sage" school?

One suggestion would be that, corresponding to some scholars' desire to make Jesus appear "like us," there is a desire to make him "different," a desire motivated by tendencies just as strong as those lending impetus to "Jesus the sage." This difference, one suspects, is not exclusively or even primarily a theological difference, a desire to assert Jesus' fundamental difference from others, although this may be a factor in some cases. Rather, apocalyptic eschatology—and this is said in spite of the definitional nuances revealed by Edith Humprey in her paper on the topic—appears in both the popular and scholarly imagination to be Other, in that it has no immediate temporal or terrestrial application. Marcus Borg, in his review of trends in North American Jesus scholarship, has already noted an inverse relation between Jesus the apocalypticist and Jesus the social reformer.[10] Thus the strength with which it is asserted that Jesus *must* have been apocalyptic in his world-view could, and in some instances doubtless does, stem from a conservative impulse to avoid (at all costs, even the cost of an alien Jesus) the characterization of Jesus as a radical with any social implications. More fundamentally, the assertion of Jesus' apocalypticism reveals a tendency to make Jesus a *religious* figure; to defend, in other words, our long-standing conception of him as a figure in the history of religions and as having what historical significance he possesses by virtue of this religious contribution. And that, in turn, not only plays into the covert debate about the category of religion, but allows a continuation of the assertion of Jesus' importance. For if Jesus is removed from the sphere of an exclusively religious history, his significance all but evaporates in the face of secular developments in politics, economics and culture, and the eventual success of his followers in establishing an important "religious" or social movement. It is clear that Jesus himself established a movement of no real immediate historical import, and equally clear that whatever social, political or economic program he might have had was a failure. In asserting that Jesus was an apocalyptic figure—even if his predictions did not come true—he is preserved for religion and escapes what scholars of any field fear most for their subject-matter: irrelevance.

Also notable is the theme of a wisdom-apocalyptic dichotomy as it occurs in several of the papers, especially in the second section of this collection. The most frequent statement made about this development is that "wisdom" (as a type of theology or world-view, or even genre) is not incompatible with apocalypticism, and that therefore the stratification of Q and/or the insulation of Jesus from matters apocalyptic is grounded on a fallacy.

Expressed in this manner, the critique is misguided. The stratification of Q may be far from certain and definitely requires further examination and critical peer review. So also there is no simple equivalence between the (alleged) secondary character of apocalypticism in Q from a literary perspective, and the secondary character of apocalypticism as an historical feature of earliest Christianity. But neither hypothesis requires the sharp dichotomy at times imputed to it. In the form in which it has been accepted by most historical-Jesus scholars,[11] the stratification of Q is argued on the basis of a coordination, across the document as a whole, of redaction-critically determined sequences of development within sub-units of individual units, as well as the agglomeration

---

10 Marcus J. Borg, "Portraits of Jesus in Contemporary North American Scholarship," *Harvard Theological Review* 84 (1991): 1-22.

11 John Kloppenborg's work remains central to this discussion. See his foundational study, *The Formation of Q: Trajectories in Ancient Wisdom Collections* (Philadelphia: Fortress, 1987).

of originally-independent complete pericopae. One finds material in Q which forms a distinctive and apparently self-suffcient block, and in which the prominent forms appear to be sapiential maxims and admonitions. Apocalyptic imagery and theology is absent. On the other hand, there is a mass of material in which apocalyptic imagery is marshalled in support of claims of judgment against (some of) the contemporaries of the people responsible for Q, alongside mythologized wisdom motifs, such as speeches of hypostatized Sophia. The second layer, as originally conceived, contains both sapiential motifs and apocalyptic motifs, even if one discounts the fact that the addition of the Q^2 material to Q^1 already involves a wisdom-apocalyptic admixture. The distinction between sapiential and apocalyptic stages in the history of Q is therefore in fact only a distinction between sapiential interests from which all trace of apocalyptic motifs are absent, and those (later) sapiential interests in which apocalypticism is a major motif among others. The two world-views (if that is what they are) need not be literarily or generically incompatible. What has happened is that the absence of apocalyptic motifs has been noted in Q material judged to be earlier on completely different grounds. This has raised the possibility that apocalypticism *may* have been a secondary development in Christian theologizing, a possibility which must be explored on the basis of the evidence.

1.3 The Issue of Epistemic Neutrality

A final common meta-concern of current historical-Jesus studies—well reflected in this volume—is the issue of bias. Normally this issue is treated entirely negatively, that is to say, as something to be avoided as much as possible. This is true despite the growing recognition that bias is ubiquitous and can never be eliminated. For decades the academic focus has been on identifying and "bracketing" bias in reconstructions. Most frequently (a function no doubt of the history of the discipline) bias is conceived as a theological predisposition to cast Jesus in certain doctrinally-acceptable ways. Larry Hurtado's paper demonstrates how "existential" biases persist—and can have a deleterious effect—even in the absence of any identifiable predisposition of a strictly *theological* variety. Halvor Moxnes makes a similar point.

The limitation of this strong concern in the field becomes apparent the instant one reads Jane Schaberg's and Grant LeMarquand's papers. It becomes even more apparent when one notes that, apart from these two papers, feminist and non-Western scholarship receives very little substantial attention in this collection (although more than usual), even in surveys of the field and analyses of the bias and motivation underlying current scholarship. This absence lends validity to claims that marginalized voices are in fact systematically excluded from the discipline. The assumption is often made that such scholarship is simply not a *serious* part of the discipline, that it neglects to shroud its work in the trappings of disinterest. As a result, it is relegated to the margins not so much because it is biased but because it is deliberately, self-consciously and openly biased.

One might ask what it is about feminist or African scholarship that leads to this refusal to adopt the cloak of disinterest. This question reveals what is ultimately at stake in the *desire* for objectivity: a desire to view the object of one's inquiry through the lens of things-as-they-are. The distinction between a fact and a value is itself not based on fact, but on a dichotomy between things as they are and things as one wishes them to be; the removal of so-called "value" from scholarship is really the removal of hope, something which is not central or necessary to the daily ideological work of the privileged. The ultimate value that undergirds the desire to avoid epistemic bias—hence the most basic and hidden epistemic bias of all—is the desire to conserve the world roughly as it is. Indeed, the drift in the direction of soteric, and away from cosmotrophic,[12] historiography in the work of "mainstream" scholars such as Mack and Crossan is, at least in part, an effect of the increasing loss of prestige of white, male scholarship. As the humanities lose their ideological supremacy to other cultural forces, the desire for change will become more openly a factor in the writing of history. The vehement response—silencing or castigation—that feminist and African efforts have called forth is reflective of the embattled identification of the professional intellectual with a bygone cultural hegemony.

This is not by any means to imply that older scholarship succeeded in eliminating all value from its assessment of the facts: it is just that it exhibited conservative values in its purported aim to treat only "the facts." This rhetoric has another purpose as well: the concealment of the ideological character and force of historical description. As Braun elegantly points out in his brief contextualization of the socio-rhetorical section of this collection, history is really about ourselves: it is a rhetorical game, played by certain rules, commenting elliptically on the world as it is by casting current categories and basic understandings into the past. This serves the universalizing function of ideology: to make particular and contingent world-views appear to be ubiquitous and absolute. So, for example, it is rhetorically more effective to do "objective" history—any history—in such a way that women are simply absent, than to come right out and say that, as far as "we" are concerned, women have no autonomous place in social life. The latter is just a male and patriarchal positional statement; the former is an assertion that this is "the way things are." Thus the value of the more-or-less postmodern insight that bias is inevitable—a value that so far has been capitalized on only by "unserious" biblical

---

12 The terms are applied respectively to "world-denying" and "world-affirming" rhetoric in Willi Braun's contribution to this collection, who has in turn drawn them from Gregory Alles, *The Iliad, the Ramayana, and the Work of Religion: Failed Persuasion and Religious Mystification* (University Park: Pennsylvania State University Press, 1994), 104-106.

scholarship—is the way it forces a recognition of the inevitable positionality of one's perspective. Scholarship, therefore, cannot avoid being affected by taking place in a patriarchal environment, making feminist scholarship arguably less biased than the supposedly neutral—and thus necessarily patriarchal— scholarship which routinely ignores it in the service of "objectivity." The same can be said, *mutatis mutandis*, for other types of liberationist discourses.

2. Contextualization and Neo-Luddism

It might finally be worth asking what is ultimately being communicated in the more current and creative studies on the historical Jesus. Most notable in these new reconstructions is their increasing emphasis on political and socio-economic contextualization. This emphasis has resulted in various portraits of Jesus which locate him in his socio-historical context while simultaneously pitting him against that context by presenting him as espousing values which run against the current of dehumanizing changes in the Mediterranean culture of the time—changes brought about, variously, by Antipas's intensification of the market (Freyne), Augustus's *pax romana* (read, global imperialism; Crossan, Mack) or the corrosive "politics of holiness" (Borg). Jesus is portrayed as reactive, and what he reacts to is the shifting economic and political organization of his culture, endeavouring to return to traditional patterns of social organization, or at least invoking them rhetorically in the face of, and as a foil to, configurations felt to be alienating. This may be most obvious in the case of Freyne's contribution to this volume: Jesus invokes the "traditional Jewish theocratic ideal" in order to defend antique patterns of patrimony against the encroachments of an emerging market economy in the agrarian sector. The same theme is also present elsewhere: Moxnes' focus on economic contextualization inclines the vision of Jesus in the same direction, as does Crossan's "open commensality" against the grain of the Augustan age's "yuppies." Even Mack's reconstruction, which consciously avoids attributing to Jesus any sort of social program, sees in Jesus an individualistic reactive rejoinder to "a soulless superimposition of law and order, a network of military surveillance and economic exploitation that was incapable of commanding the loyalty of the peoples they governed."[13] In all of these reconstructions, Jesus is counter-cultural in the sense of being anti-cultural, in the sense of reacting to and rejecting the imposition of artificial and anti-humane changes upon the ordinary aspects of daily life in Roman Galilee.

These otherwise quite different studies, in coming to such fundamentally similar conclusions, reflect a common feature of our own contemporary lives, one felt to be structurally commensurable with the backdrop against which Jesus

---

13 Mack, *Lost Gospel*, 65.

reacted. This feature is the shifting political and economic organization of postmodernity, the global village and the explosion of communications technology, the latter keenly felt by the academic. Greater forces than any single person can master or even conceptualize are changing the world, and it is consequently difficult to feel this force of change as anything but dehumanizing. Not only is this environment projected back onto the field of historical inquiry (in this case it is first-century Galilee), but also the desired, or at least imaginable, response to this situation, a return to the values of yore—more sympathetically, a rhetorical deployment of antiquated values against the dehumanizing application of new technology and evolving social systems.

The historical moment which illustrates this problematic most clearly is the Luddite response to the English industrial revolution. In this instance the appeal to old and disused apprenticeship regulations was used as a moral and sometimes even legal basis for challenging not so much the introduction of such technological innovations as the gig-mill, the shearing frame and the stocking-loom, but even more the corollary reduction of wages, the extension of the working day and especially the de-skilling of the entire textile industry. The Luddites looked back to the guild system and destroyed offending new implements—hence their characterization in the popular mind as anti-progressives or technophobes—but at the same time looked forward to the ten-hour day, minimum wage, legalization of unions and anti-child-labour legislation. It was through an appeal to the past that they were able to conceptualize and embody a progressive impulse toward the humane social organization of new technology.

The Jesus of recent scholarship emerges as a Luddite in his own time. The impulse to present him this way—or, one might say, the ability to recognize this dimension of his historical existence—arises from the Luddism and Luddite situation of the contemporary world, especially its scholastic dimension, a sphere as threatened with de-skilling as was the English textile industry at the beginning of the 19th century. We should see in this volume's eloquent and learned reconstructions a passionate appeal for a renovated, more humane world (which seems inevitable), an appeal effectively filtered through a persuasive and poetic reconstruction of our collective past.

CONTRIBUTORS

WILLIAM E. ARNAL
Centre for the Study of Religion,
University of Toronto, Toronto, ON

L. GREGORY BLOOMQUIST
Faculté de Théologie
Université St. Paul, Ottawa, ON

WILLI BRAUN
Department of Religion
Bishop's University, Lennoxville, PQ

WENDY COTTER
Department of Theology
Loyola University of Chicago, Chicago, IL

JOHN DOMINIC CROSSAN
Emeritus Professor
De Paul University, Chicago, IL

MICHEL DESJARDINS
Department of Religion and Culture
Wilfrid Laurier University, Waterloo, ON

TERENCE L. DONALDSON
College of Emmanuel and St. Chad
Saskatoon, SK

SEÁN FREYNE
Trinity College
University of Dublin, Dublin 2, Ireland

BARRY W. HENAUT
Centre for the Study of Religion
University of Toronto, Toronto, ON

EDITH M. HUMPHREY
Faculty of Religious Studies
McGill University, Montréal, PQ

LARRY W. HURTADO
Department of NT Literature and Theology
New College, Edinburgh, Scotland

WILLIAM KLASSEN
Emmanuel College
Toronto, ON

GRANT LEMARQUAND
Faculty of Theology
Wycliffe College, Toronto, ON

BURTON L. MACK
Claremont Graduate School
Claremont, CA

JOHN W. MARSHALL
Department of Religion
Princeton University, Princeton, NJ

WAYNE O. MCCREADY
Department of Religious Studies
University of Calgary, Calgary, AB

HALVOR MOXNES
Department of Biblical Studies
University of Oslo, N-0315 Oslo, Norway

DIETMAR NEUFELD
Department of Religious Studies
University of British Columbia, Vancouver

PETER RICHARDSON
Department for the Study of Religion
University of Toronto, Toronto, ON

JANE SCHABERG
Department of Religious Studies
University of Detroit Mercy, Detroit, MI

LEIF E. VAAGE
Emmanuel College
Toronto, ON

SANDRA WALKER-RAMISCH
Department of Religion
Carleton University, Ottawa, ON

ROBERT L. WEBB
Campion College
Regina, SK

STEPHEN WESTERHOLM
Department of Religious Studies
McMaster University, Hamilton, ON

INDICES

Subject Index

Modern Authors Index

Ancient Sources Index

Series Published by Wilfrid Laurier University Press for the Canadian Corporation for Studies in Religion / Corporation Canadienne des Sciences Religieuses

Editions SR

1. *La langue de Ya'udi: description et classement de l'ancien parler de Zencircli dans le cadre des langues sémitiques du nord-ouest*
   Paul-Eugène Dion, O.P.
   1974 / viii + 511 p. / OUT OF PRINT

2. *The Conception of Punishment in Early Indian Literature*
   Terence P. Day
   1982 / iv + 328 pp. / OUT OF PRINT

3. *Traditions in Contact and Change: Selected Proceedings of the XIVth Congress of the International Association for the History of Religions*
   Edited by Peter Slater and Donald Wiebe with Maurice Boutin and Harold Coward
   1983 / x + 758 pp. / OUT OF PRINT

4. *Le messianisme de Louis Riel*
   Gilles Martel
   1984 / xviii + 483 p.

5. *Mythologies and Philosophies of Salvation in the Theistic Traditions of India*
   Klaus K. Klostermaier
   1984 / xvi + 549 pp. / OUT OF PRINT

6. *Averroes' Doctrine of Immortality: A Matter of Controversy*
   Ovey N. Mohammed
   1984 / vi + 202 pp. / OUT OF PRINT

7. *L'étude des religions dans les écoles : l'expérience américaine, anglaise et canadienne*
   Fernand Ouellet
   1985 / xvi + 666 p.

8. *Of God and Maxim Guns: Presbyterianism in Nigeria, 1846-1966*
   Geoffrey Johnston
   1988 / iv + 322 pp.

9. *A Victorian Missionary and Canadian Indian Policy: Cultural Synthesis vs Cultural Replacement*
   David A. Nock
   1988 / x + 194 pp. / OUT OF PRINT

10. *Prometheus Rebound: The Irony of Atheism*
    Joseph C. McLelland
    1988 / xvi + 366 pp.

11. *Competition in Religious Life*
    Jay Newman
    1989 / viii + 237 pp.

12. *The Huguenots and French Opinion, 1685-1787: The Enlightenment Debate on Toleration*
    Geoffrey Adams
    1991 / xiv + 335 pp.

13. *Religion in History: The Word, the Idea, the Reality / La religion dans l'histoire : le mot, l'idée, la réalité*
    Edited by/Sous la direction de Michel Despland and/et Gérard Vallée
    1992 / x + 252 pp.

14. *Sharing Without Reckoning: Imperfect Right and the Norms of Reciprocity*
    Millard Schumaker
    1992 / xiv + 112 pp.

Comparative Ethics Series /
Collection d'Éthique Comparée

Dissertations SR

Studies in Christianity and Judaism /
Études sur le christianisme et le judaïsme

4. *Law in Religious Communities in the Roman Period: The Debate Over Torah and* Nomos *in Post-Biblical Judaism and Early Christianity*
Peter Richardson and Stephen Westerholm with A. I. Baumgarten, Michael Pettem and Cecilia Wassén
1991 / x + 164 pp.
5. *Dangerous Food: 1 Corinthians 8-10 in Its Context*
Peter D. Gooch
1993 / xviii + 178 pp.
6. *The Rhetoric of the Babylonian Talmud, Its Social Meaning and Context*
Jack N. Lightstone
1994 / xiv + 317 pp.
7. *Whose Historical Jesus?*
Edited by William E. Arnal and Michel Desjardins
1997 / vi + 337 pp.

The Study of Religion in Canada / Sciences Religieuses au Canada

1. *Religious Studies in Alberta: A State-of-the-Art Review*
Ronald W. Neufeldt
1983 / xiv + 145 pp.
2. *Les sciences religieuses au Québec depuis 1972*
Louis Rousseau et Michel Despland
1988 / 158 p.
3. *Religious Studies in Ontario: A State-of-the-Art Review*
Harold Remus, William Closson James and Daniel Fraikin
1992 / xviii + 422 pp.
4. *Religious Studies in Manitoba and Saskatchewan: A State-of-the-Art Review*
John M. Badertscher, Gordon Harland and Roland E. Miller
1993 / vi + 166 pp.
5. *The Study of Religion in British Columbia: A State-of-the-Art Review*
Brian J. Fraser
1995 / x + 127 pp.

Studies in Women and Religion / Études sur les femmes et la religion

1. *Femmes et religions**
Sous la direction de Denise Veillette
1995 / xviii + 466 p.
* Only available from Les Presses de l'Université Laval
2. *The Work of Their Hands: Mennonite Women's Societies in Canada*
Gloria Neufeld Redekop
1996 / xvi + 172 pp.
3. *Profiles of Anabaptist Women: Sixteenth-Century Reforming Pioneers*
Edited by C. Arnold Snyder and Linda A. Huebert Hecht
1996 / xxii + 438 pp.

SR Supplements

1. *Footnotes to a Theology: The Karl Barth Colloquium of 1972*
Edited and Introduced by Martin Rumscheidt
1974 / viii + 151 pp. / OUT OF PRINT
2. *Martin Heidegger's Philosophy of Religion*
John R. Williams
1977 / x + 190 pp. / OUT OF PRINT
3. *Mystics and Scholars: The Calgary Conference on Mysticism 1976*
Edited by Harold Coward and Terence Penelhum
1977 / viii + 121 pp. / OUT OF PRINT

Available from:

WILFRID LAURIER UNIVERSITY PRESS

Waterloo, Ontario, Canada   N2L 3C5